HANDBOOK

OF

HOUSE OF COMMONS PROCEDURE

VACHER DOD PUBLISHING

HANDBOOK
OF
HOUSE OF COMMONS PROCEDURE

by

Paul Evans

FOURTH EDITION
Fully revised and updated

Vacher Dod Publishing
1 Douglas Street, London SW1P 4PA

Telephone: 020 7828 7256 *Fax:* 020 7828 7269
E-mail: politics@vacherdod.co.uk
Website: www.Dod*on*Line.co.uk

ISBN: 0 905702 42 5

CONTENTS

CHAPTER 10 PUBLIC MONEY

CHAPTER 11 BILLS

CHAPTER 12 DELEGATED LEGISLATION

CHAPTER 13 EUROPEAN SCRUTINY

CHAPTER 14 THE GRAND COMMITTEES AND THE REGIONAL AFFAIRS COMMITTEE

CHAPTER 15 PUBLICATIONS AND PAPERS

CHAPTER 16 EARLY DAY MOTIONS

CHAPTER 17 SELECT COMMITTEES AND JOINT COMMITTEES

CHAPTER 18 HOUSEKEEPING

FIGURES

INTRODUCTION

The House of Commons both sustains and holds to account the government of the United Kingdom. Some knowledge of the rules, customs and conventions which underpin the work of the House, and its relationship with other parts of the constitution such as the House of Lords, the courts and the Crown, is essential for an understanding of what actually happens there and of the part it plays in reaching fundamental decisions about the governance of the nation and the freedom, security, wealth, welfare and well-being of those who live here. Like its predecessors, the fourth edition of this handbook is intended as a guide for those who need to understand the practice and procedures of the House: Members of Parliament and their staff; staff of the House, civil servants, journalists, lobbyists, pressure groups, charities and other professional and amateur observers of its proceedings.

While the standing orders of the House codify much of its procedure they do not describe it, and they have to be interpreted and applied to particular circumstances. Moreover, many of the ways in which the House does its work derive from precedent and custom, the sources of which often originate from long before any standing orders were formulated. Key precedents derive from rulings of the Chair over the centuries, but these too are subject to continual redefinition and reinterpretation. Parliamentary procedure is dynamic and organic, responding to changing circumstances and reflecting the changing composition and self-perceptions of the House. Like other such dynamic systems, its development tends to be made manifest by evidence not only of growth and innovation, but also of repetition and decay.

The period since the general election of May 1997, which produced one of the largest-ever turnovers of membership of the Commons, has been one of particularly rapid change in the procedures and internal culture of the House. Many of these changes have arisen from the deliberate choice of the House to "modernise" itself. The engine room of these reforms has been the Select Committee on the Modernisation of the House of Commons, first appointed in June 1997 and re-appointed in July 2001. Although many of these changes were taken into account in the third edition of this handbook, the process of change has continued in the last twelve months or so at a rapid pace, with some experimental changes becoming permanent, some being refined by further experience, and new experiments being tried. Few have been discarded, although some have proved not to work as well as first hoped.

The Modernisation Committee began its work with a report recommending the extensive revamping of the House's legislative procedures. The introduction of the reforms it proposed in that report and subsequently has mostly been done in a piecemeal and experimental fashion, rather than by a wholesale revision of the standing orders. However, the House has now adopted the practice of using "programme orders" to timetable the progress of government bills. It is now proposed to "carry-over" consideration of bills from one session to the next on a regular basis. A substantial number of draft bills have been issued by the government, and have been subject to pre-legislative scrutiny by ad hoc select committees, departmental select committees and joint committees of the Commons and Lords.

The sitting hours of the House have been radically revised, and "deferred divisions" have been introduced. There is a second chamber of the House in session three times a week in Westminster Hall on a permanent basis, now with extended procedural opportunities available to it, and Friday sittings have been all but abolished. The parliamentary calendar has been reformed, and the House now sits in September.

The period of notice for oral questions has been reduced, and "cross-cutting" question times with a panel of Ministers have been introduced to sittings in Westminster Hall. "Written statements" have been invented.

The House's Order Paper and the explanatory material published with bills have been modernised, and made more comprehensive and comprehensible. Other papers have been redesigned (including reports from select committees), and the publications of the House (including Hansard) are available on the web almost the instant they are published.

Generally, there has been a modest but significant growth in joint working between the two Houses. The Human Rights Act 1998, now a fundamental part of the constitutional machinery, has led to the establishment of the Joint Committee on Human Rights – a new departure in inter-House working. That Committee oversees the parliamentary implications for the legislative process of the Act. It also has responsibility for the scrutiny of "remedial orders" – a new form of delegated legislation. These, along with the regulatory reform procedures, patrolled in the Commons by the Regulatory Reform Committee, have brought a new dimension to the process of making the law. There are proposals in the air (as there have been for some time) for further reform of delegated legislation procedures.

Devolution has had its impact on the work of Westminster in a number of subtle ways, and will continue to do so. As the devolved institutions enter on their second generation of existence, following the 2003 elections, the existence of competing legislatures within the UK sharpens the case for modernisation at Westminster, and provides practical examples of different ways of doing things.

Though mostly outside the scope of this work, the resources available to select committees have been reinforced, their functions more explicitly defined, and their self-analysis and accountability improved. In a historical departure, the Prime Minister has begun to appear regularly before a select committee of the House to give evidence on the whole range of government activity. The provisions for select committees of the House to work together with each other, and with committees of the House of Lords and of the devolved legislatures, have been extended and simplified. The departmental select committees have been re-organised to reflect changes in the machinery of government, and a new select committee to oversee the work of the Constitutional Affairs Department has been established.

There have been other less obvious changes – the sub-judice rule has been updated, and the first tax tax law rewrite bill has passed through its joint committee procedures. The Code of Conduct for Members has been revised.

There remains the unfinished business of House of Lords reform. If it ever makes further progress, this is likely to require further changes in the Commons. Even while stuck at "Phase 1" of reform, the Lords have been making innovations in their own procedures, structure and approach to their role which resonate in the other House.

These, and other detailed changes, have been reflected in this edition. The process of change means that, once again, this handbook has been substantially updated from the previous edition. I owe thanks to those of my colleagues who responded readily to my requests for the benefit of their expert knowledge in my efforts to keep abreast of the rapidly changing detail of the House's procedures. In particular, I would like to thank Colin Lee and Carol Oxborough. I am once again grateful to the publisher, Edward Peck, and his production team at Vacher Dod Publishing Ltd, for all their help.

Paul Evans
July 2003

NOTE:

Where possible, the essential information in the chapters has been condensed into figures or diagrams. At the end of the book there is a glossary explaining certain key terms, and these are indicated in bold where they occur in the text. So far as possible I have tried to avoid repeating descriptions of certain procedures, but this has necessitated a very extensive use of cross references. There is a full index.

In the text the word Question, when capitalised, indicates a Question in the technical sense of a proposition before the House for decision, rather than an interrogative utterance. Member, when capitalised, means a Member of Parliament. Standing Orders of the House are indicated by the abbreviation 'S.O.' and their number thus: S.O. No. 1.

An up-to-date text of the House of Commons Standing Orders can be found on the web via www.parliament.uk (and is also published by The Stationery Office). However, a word of caution should be given about their use – almost all references to times of day in the text of the permanent standing orders have to be read in the light of the temporary standing orders (in effect to the next general election) relating to earlier sittings of the House on Tuesdays, Wednesdays and Thursdays. This makes it a complex exercise to understand the exact current terms of many of them.

The purpose of this handbook is to provide an answer to the question "How?" rather than "Why?", and historical or critical analysis of procedure and its outcomes has therefore in general been avoided; many other books have sought to address the question of whether Parliament works, and how its effectiveness might be judged or improved. The authoritative source for references to, and interpretation of, authorities and precedents is Erskine May's Treatise on the Law, Privileges, Proceedings and Usage of Parliament, edited and refined by successive Clerks of the House of Commons.

Chapter 1

THE HOUSE

1.1 THE CHAMBER AND THE LOBBIES

The Palace of Westminster

1.1.1 The House of Commons has met in the Palace of Westminster since it ceased to be the Sovereign's residence in the sixteenth century. When the Commons joined the House of Lords there the building became the Houses of Parliament. Parts of the building date back to the eleventh century, but the main parts of the present Palace date from the mid-nineteenth century when it was rebuilt after the fire of 1834. The Commons now occupy the northern end of the building and the Lords the southern. The present building was thus purpose-built to house the Commons and the Lords, though it has been much altered internally in the ensuing 150 years.

1.1.2 There are now several significant outbuildings which also form part of the parliamentary estate, in which are members of both Houses and their staff and the staff of the various departments of the Houses have their offices. In Portcullis House there are also now additional public rooms used by the committees of the House of Commons. A simplified plan of the surroundings of the Chamber of the House of Commons is at Figure 1 and of the parliamentary estate at Figure 2.

The Chamber of the House of Commons

1.1.3 The present Chamber of the House of Commons (see Figure 3) is modelled on the original home of the Commons at Westminster, St Stephen's Chapel (which now in reconstructed form forms the main entry route to the Palace). The dominant features are the ranks of terraced benches down each side of the Chamber on which the government and opposition parties sit facing each other. Between them is the **Table** of the House, which stands in front of the Speaker's Chair.

1.1.4 At the Table, immediately in front of the Speaker's Chair, are three seats for the **Clerks at the Table**, the seat to the Speaker's right being normally reserved for the **Clerk of the House**. At the far end of the Table is the rest on which the **Mace** is placed at the beginning of each sitting. It remains there throughout each sitting, to symbolise the constitutional participation of the Crown in the proceedings of the House. At either end of the Mace are **despatch boxes** at which Ministers and the official opposition **shadow** ministers stand when they address the House.

1.1.5 To the Speaker's right are the government benches. On the first of these, which reaches about half-way down the Chamber to where the benches are intersected by a lateral gangway, sit Ministers. On the first bench to the Speaker's left sit the front bench spokesmen and spokeswomen of the official opposition. Those who are leading in debate for their respective sides sit behind the despatch boxes. Behind the front benches sit the back bench Members of each party. "Below the gangway" (that is, in the half of the Chamber further away from the Speaker), certain benches on the opposition side are by custom reserved for members of the minority parties. Other than by custom, there are no reserved seats for individual Members or parties (see S.O. No. 7, but see also paragraph 7.2.1).

1.1.6 Above the floor of the House are galleries on all four sides of the Chamber (see Figure 4). Those on each side are reserved for Members (with a few seats for officers of the House) though they are rarely used, since the Speaker does not recognise Members in them to speak in debates. Above and behind the Speaker's Chair is the **Press Gallery**, which is reserved for representatives of the various news media. Immediately above the Speaker's Chair sit the **Hansard** Reporters. At the opposite end of the Chamber is the **Public Gallery**. Access to this is by permit. Members are able to obtain a limited number of such permits in advance for their guests. Otherwise permits are available on each sitting day on a first come, first served basis. In the front two rows of the Public Gallery are places reserved for members of the House of Lords and other distinguished guests. To each side of these benches are the Special Galleries (East and West) for which Members can obtain special permits for their guests from the **Serjeant at Arms**.

1.1.7 At floor level, behind the Speaker's Chair and to the right, is a boxed-in gallery in which sit civil servants who are advising Ministers in debate. At the diagonally opposite corner of the Chamber, facing the Speaker's Chair, is a small gallery known as the Under Gallery. On the other side at the same end is a glassed-in gallery from which the officials who operate the **annunciator** system observe proceedings. At this same end, the **Bar of the House** is marked by a white line across the floor. By this, on the opposition side, sits the **Serjeant at Arms** or one of his deputies, whenever the House is sitting. Just inside the Bar, on either side of the main gangway, are a few seats facing the Speaker's Chair. These are the "cross benches". Members cannot address the House from these places.

The Lobbies

1.1.8 Outside the Chamber, down either side, run the division lobbies (see section 9.6): the Aye lobby to the Speaker's right, behind the government benches; the No lobby to the Speaker's left, behind the opposition benches.

1.1.9 Leaving the Chamber by the door at the end opposite the Speaker's Chair, one enters the Members' Lobby. When the House is sitting, access to this area is generally restricted to Members and staff of the House, with the exception of certain accredited representatives of the media (known as **lobby correspondents**). When a **division** is taking place, only Members are permitted to enter this lobby.

1.1.10 Around the Members' Lobby are ranged the offices of the government, official opposition and third party **Whips**. There is an outlet of the **Vote Office** in the Lobby, and a Post Office for the use of Members is also off this lobby. The message boards, which provide an urgent mail/message service for Members (operated by the Serjeant at Arms' staff, known as the "doorkeepers" or "badge messengers") are also situated here.

1.1.11 Leading out from the Members' Lobby there are four corridors. To the left as one leaves the passage from the Chamber is a corridor (the old Ways and Means Corridor) leading to the **Library** and opposite are the stairs leading to **Westminster Hall** and the Members' Entrance in New Palace Yard. Opposite the entrance to the Chamber is the corridor leading to the **Central Lobby**.

1.1.12 The **Central Lobby** is the main public area of the Palace, to which access may be gained *via* St Stephen's Entrance, the public entrance to the Palace. From the Central Lobby passages lead off to the House of Lords and to the Lower Waiting Hall, through which the public may gain access to the committee rooms of the House on the first and second floors, where the House's select and standing committees meet.

1.2 THE COMMITTEE CORRIDORS

1.2.1 From the **Lower Waiting Hall**, entered from the **Central Lobby**, stairs lead to the **Upper Waiting Hall** on the first floor (which is often the site of temporary exhibitions of one kind or another). Off this is the **Main Committee Corridor** (see Figure 1), running almost the full length of the building. On this corridor are committee rooms of the two Houses. Rooms 1 to 4 are generally reserved to the House of Lords. Rooms 5, 6 and 7 are shared between the two Houses when demand is at a peak. Rooms 8, 13, 15 and 16 are select committee rooms (see paragraph 2.3.10 and Figure 8). Rooms 9 to 12 and 14 are standing committee rooms (see paragraphs 2.3.2 and 2.3.3 and Figure 7). On the floor immediately above the **Main Committee Corridor** is the **Upper Committee Corridor**, on which there are a further five select committee rooms (nos. 17 to 21).

1.2.2 In Portcullis House, which stands on the north side of Bridge Street opposite the clocktower ("Big Ben"), there are further select committee rooms. These are named rather than numbered, the main ones being the "Boothroyd", "Grimond", "Thatcher" and "Wilson" rooms (see Figure 5).

1.2.3 In the main Palace, off Westminster Hall, is the Grand Committee Room. It is here that sittings of the new parallel Chamber, known officially as the House sitting in Westminster Hall (see section 6.3) are held.

1.3 OFFICES, ETC.

Principal Offices

1.3.1 Above the Chamber is the Clerk of the House Floor. The **Journal Office**, the **Public Bill Office**, the Private Bill Office and the Upper **Table Office** are on this floor.

1.3.2 In the area outside the Chamber behind the Speaker's Chair is the Lower **Table Office** (see paragraphs 8.11 and 16.3). This is often the first point of call for those wishing to seek procedural advice, etc. from the Clerks of the House.

1.3.3 The corridor outside the Table Office leading directly away from the Chamber is known as the **Ministers' Corridor**. Off this is the office of the **Clerk of the House**. The corridor that goes to the left on leaving the Chamber leads to the offices of the **Chairman of Ways and Means** and his deputies (see paragraphs 3.2.1 to 3.2.5). In the other direction a corridor leads to the Speaker's Office. Along this are the offices of the Principal Clerk of the Table Office, the Clerk Assistant, the Clerk of Committees and the Librarian (see section 18.2). The **Hansard** reporters' room is on the floor above this corridor, and the offices of the **Editor** and his deputy are on the floor below. These are accessible *via* the staircase quaintly and now inaccurately signposted to the "Ladies Gallery" (see Figure 1).

1.3.4 The offices of the **Serjeant at Arms** and his deputies are off the **Central Lobby** (see Figure 1).

The Library

1.3.5 The Library runs along the river front of the House on the Principal Floor. Access to the Library is restricted. The research division of the Library is mostly located at the outbuilding at 1 Derby Gate, where there is also a branch library principally for the use of Members' staff. There is also an "E-Library" in Portcullis House.

The Outbuildings

1.3.6 The parliamentary estate extends to a number of buildings in the vicinity of the Palace of Westminster (see Figure 2). On the corner of Bridge Street and Embankment is Portcullis House, on the public floor of which are a number of committee rooms and other public meeting rooms. It is directly accessible to the public from the Embankment. There are also two other buildings on the Embankment (the old Scotland Yard headquarters of the Metropolitan Police), known as Norman Shaw North and South. These mainly house the offices of Members and their staff. The buildings on Parliament Street and at 1 Derby Gate house most of the research divisions of the Library, as well as the House of Commons **Information Office**. No. 7 Millbank currently accommodates the offices of most of the staff of the House's select committees and of its Finance and Administration Department.

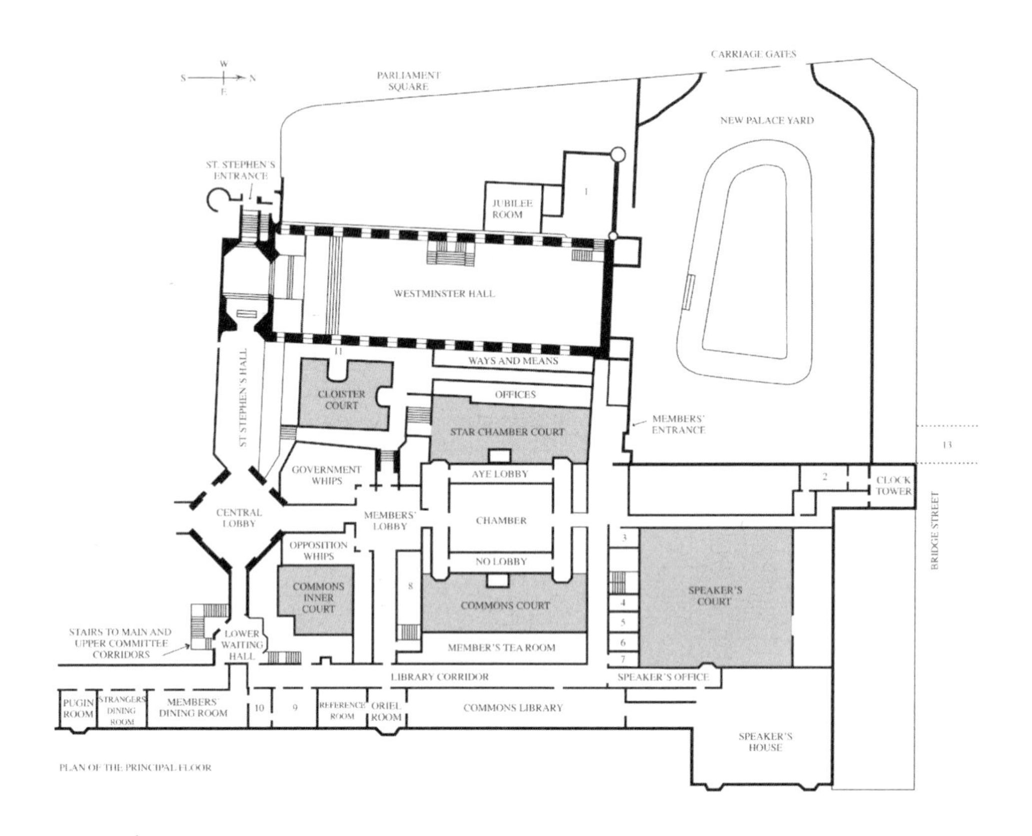

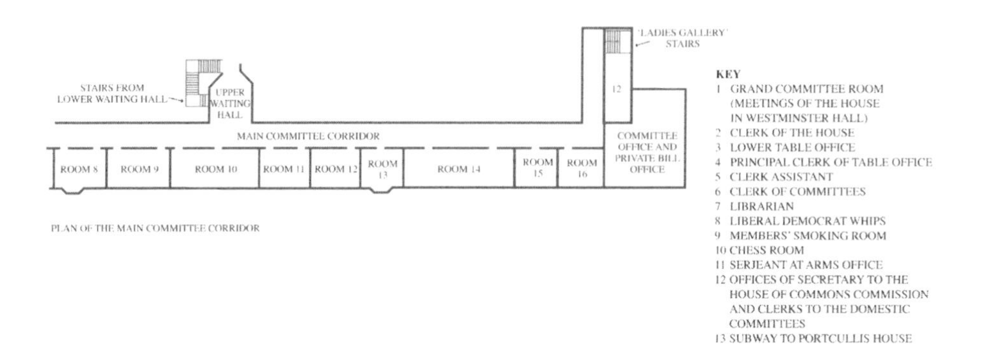

FIGURE 1
PLAN OF THE HOUSE OF COMMONS

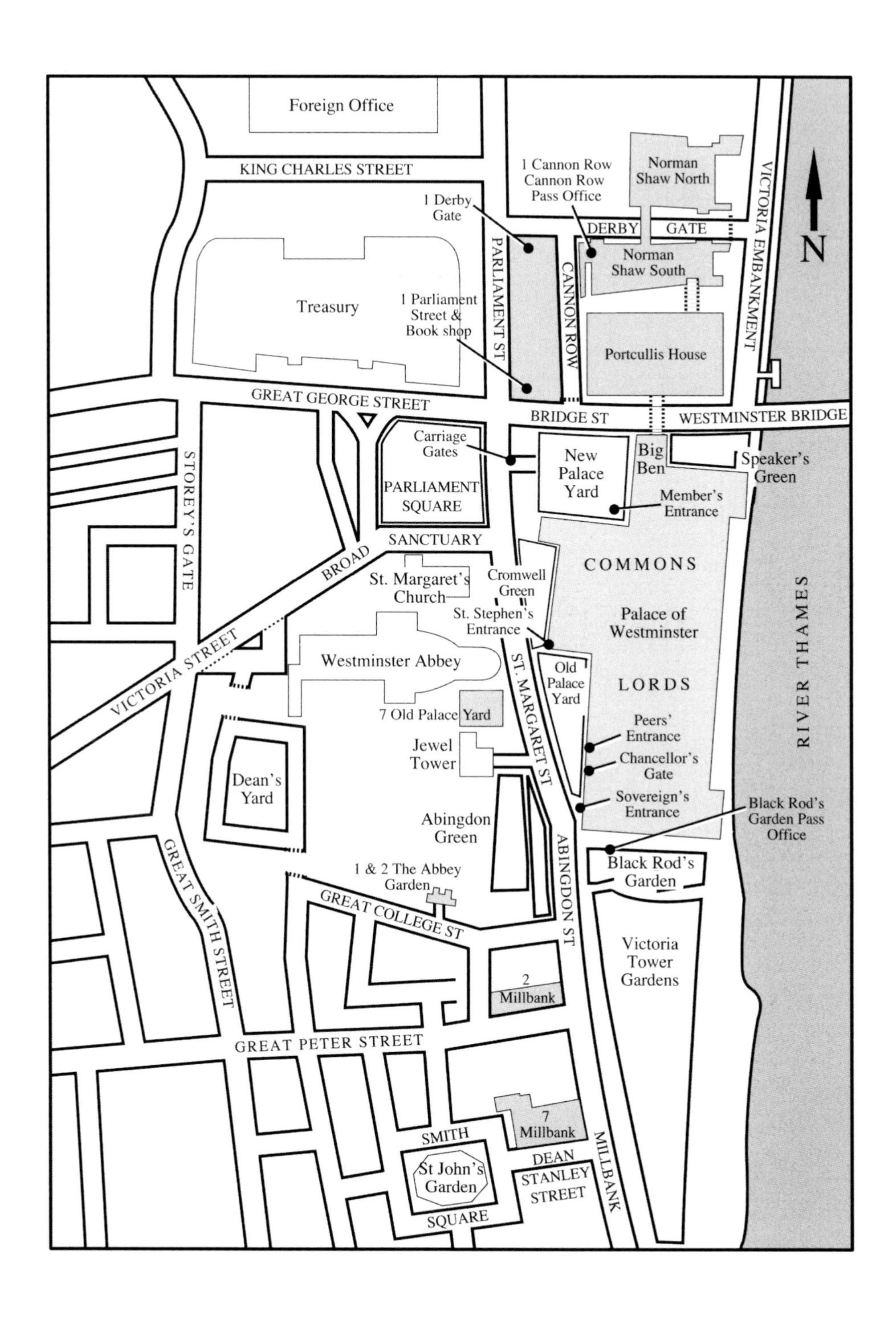

FIGURE 2
THE PARLIAMENTARY ESTATE

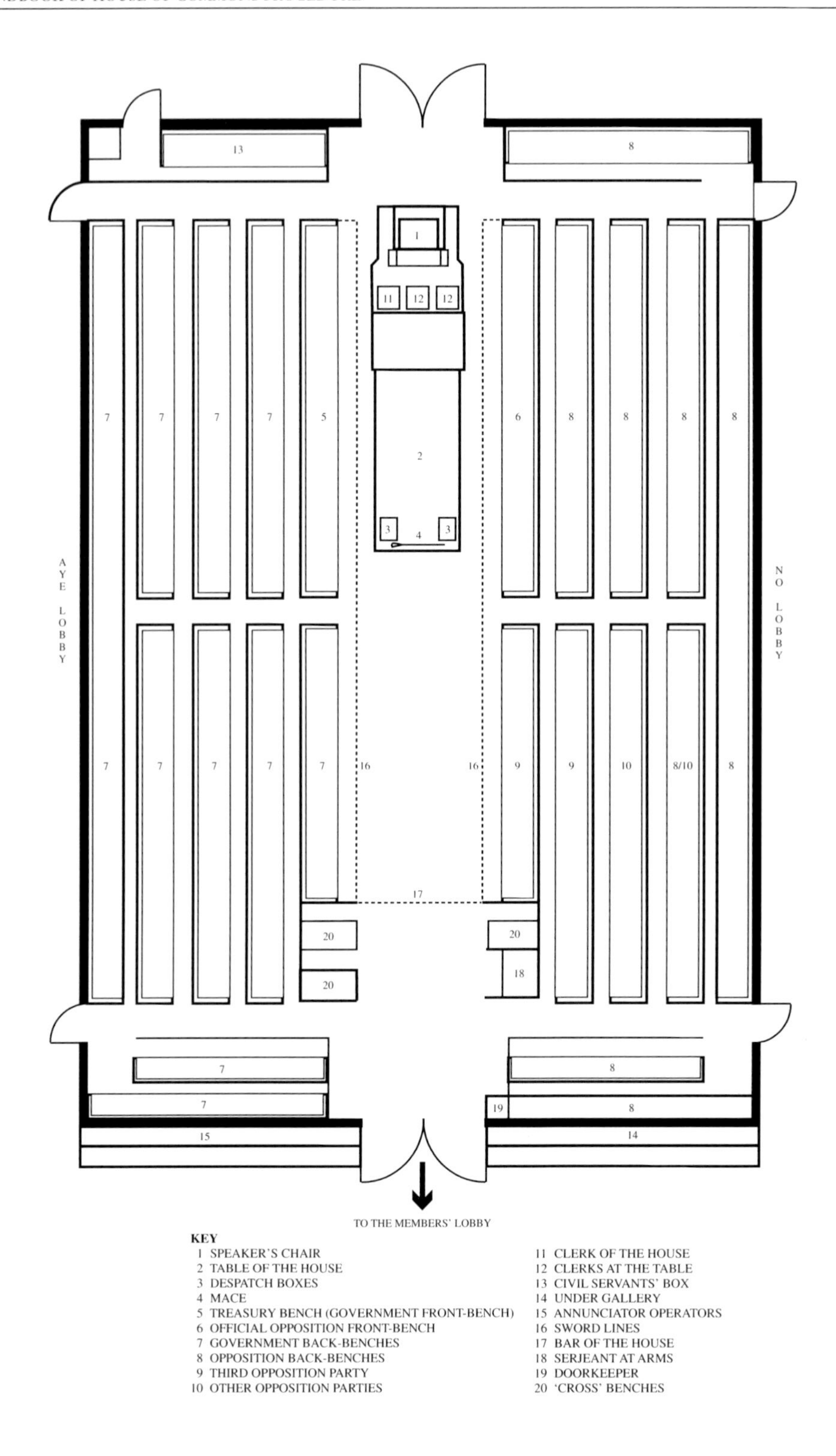

FIGURE 3

THE CHAMBER OF THE HOUSE (FLOOR LEVEL)

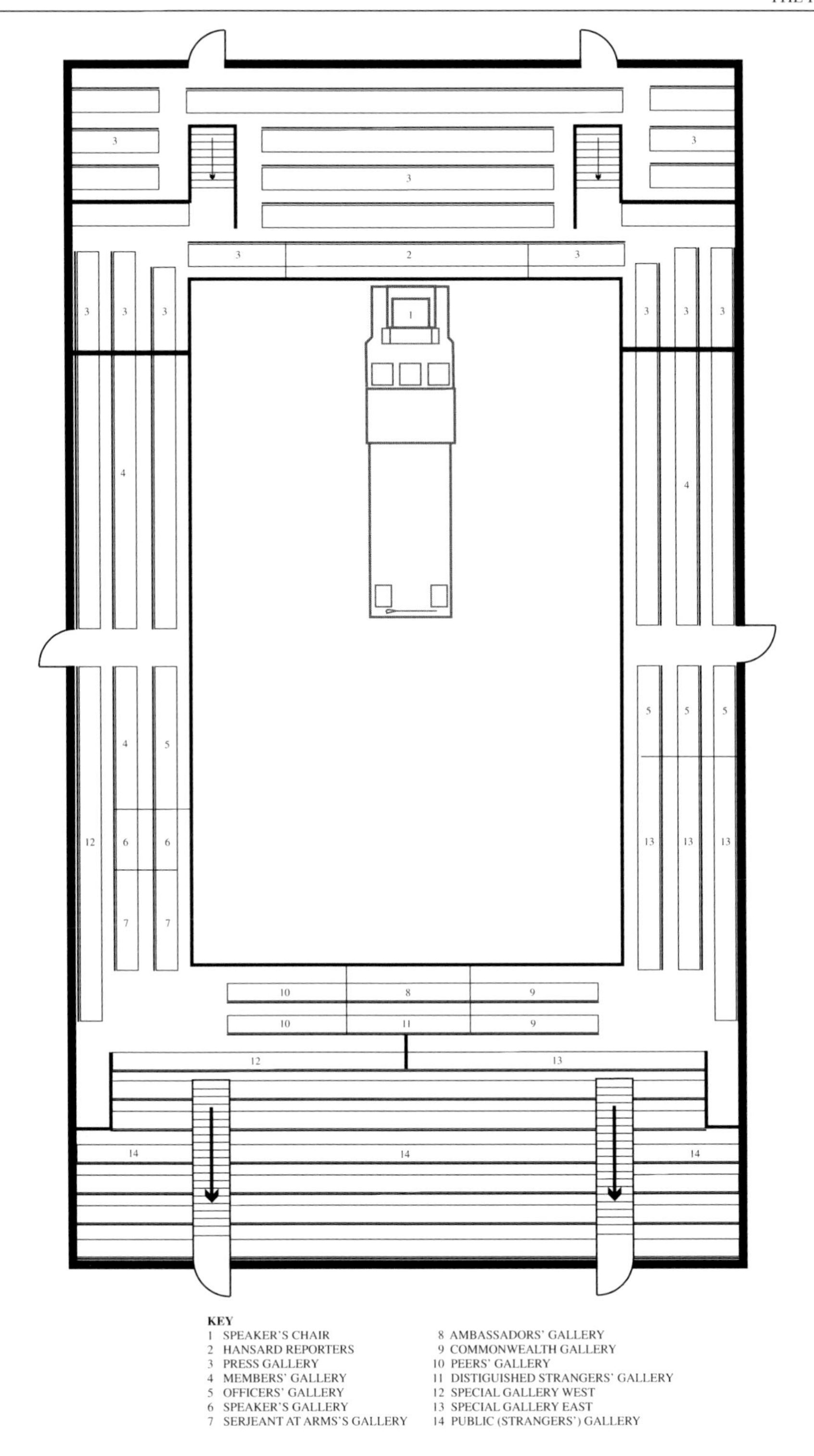

FIGURE 4
THE CHAMBER OF THE HOUSE (GALLERY LEVEL)

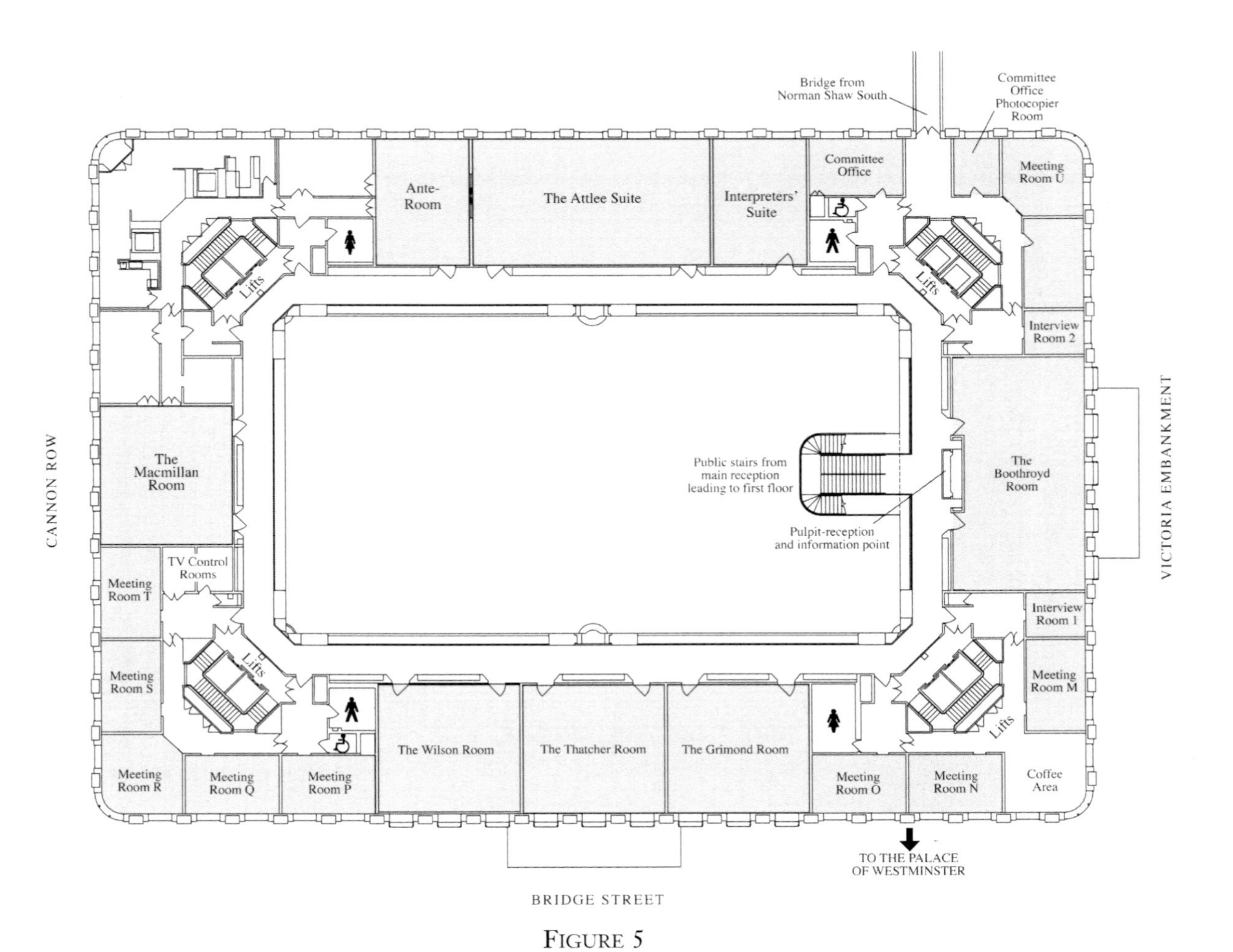

Figure 5
Public Floor of Portcullis House

Chapter 2

BUSINESS OF THE HOUSE

2.1 INTRODUCTION

2.1.1 The House of Commons is a debating chamber. A fundamental purpose of debate is to arrive at a decision. There are, however, times at which the House is sitting but not debating, such as the times set aside for prayers, parliamentary questions and ministerial or other statements. These types of activity are categorised under the general heading of **other business.** During the times set aside for government, opposition, private Members' and private business there must be at all times a Question before the House awaiting decision—though sometimes, where a substantive decision is not required, that Question is only to decide whether the debate should conclude.

2.1.2 The conduct of most of the business of the House is governed by its standing orders. These are largely designed to reinforce the ability of the party which can sustain a majority in the Commons to secure the passage of the legislation which the government formed from that party wishes to make. As the standing orders have developed over the last 150 years or so, the effect has been to cede to government (with the consent of the House) increasing control over the time available to the House and its agenda, while seeking to maintain essential protections for the minority against arbitrary power.

2.1.3 Additionally, over the last century the standing orders have been regularly revised so as to delegate an increasing proportion of the work of the House to its committees. The House has used select committees for the purposes of investigation and inquiry (rather than debate) since time immemorial; the use of committees for the holding of debates is a comparatively more recent development. Committees of this sort (still currently, if misleadingly, referred to by the generic term "standing committees") were first established in the latter part of the nineteenth century, and the range of business referred to them has been greatly extended. The use of standing committees to undertake the committee stages of bills has long been standard procedure. The default position in the standing orders is that delegated legislation (see chapter 12) and documents emanating from the institutions of the European Union, including proposals for legislation (see chapter 13), will also normally be debated in standing committees. The grand committees (see chapter 14) have terms of reference which enable them to proceed in effect as miniature versions of the Chamber, though their work has been much curtailed since devolution. The Standing Committee on Regional Affairs (see also chapter 14) has some similar characteristics. There has also been a trend in recent years to increase the number of committees (sometimes known collectively as "scrutiny committees") appointed to consider various types of legislation or proposals for legislation within narrowly drawn terms of reference. The latest development in this area is the establishment of a "parallel chamber" (Westminster Hall), which is something in the nature of a committee of the whole House (see section 6.3)

2.1.4 The section below describes the formal division of the time of the House between the various categories of business. However, it should be remembered that although the government determines what business is taken on most days on which the House sits, during those days much of the time available is taken by opposition front bench Members and back benchers from all parties. And although private Members' time is now formally restricted to private Members' bills on thirteen Fridays each session (see paragraph 2.2.4 below), back bench Members in fact have the right to initiate debate in what is technically "government time" on every day for the daily half-hour adjournment debate section 7.12) and at most of the sittings in Westminster Hall.

2.2 WORK OF THE CHAMBER

Government control of time

2.2.1 S.O. No. 14(1) states that, apart from the exceptions described below, government business shall have precedence at every sitting. S.O. No. 27 states that the order of business of each sitting will be determined by the government. Taken together, these give the government almost complete control of the agenda of the House. S.O. No. 14, however, makes two important exceptions to these rules. These are the provisions for opposition time and private Members' time.

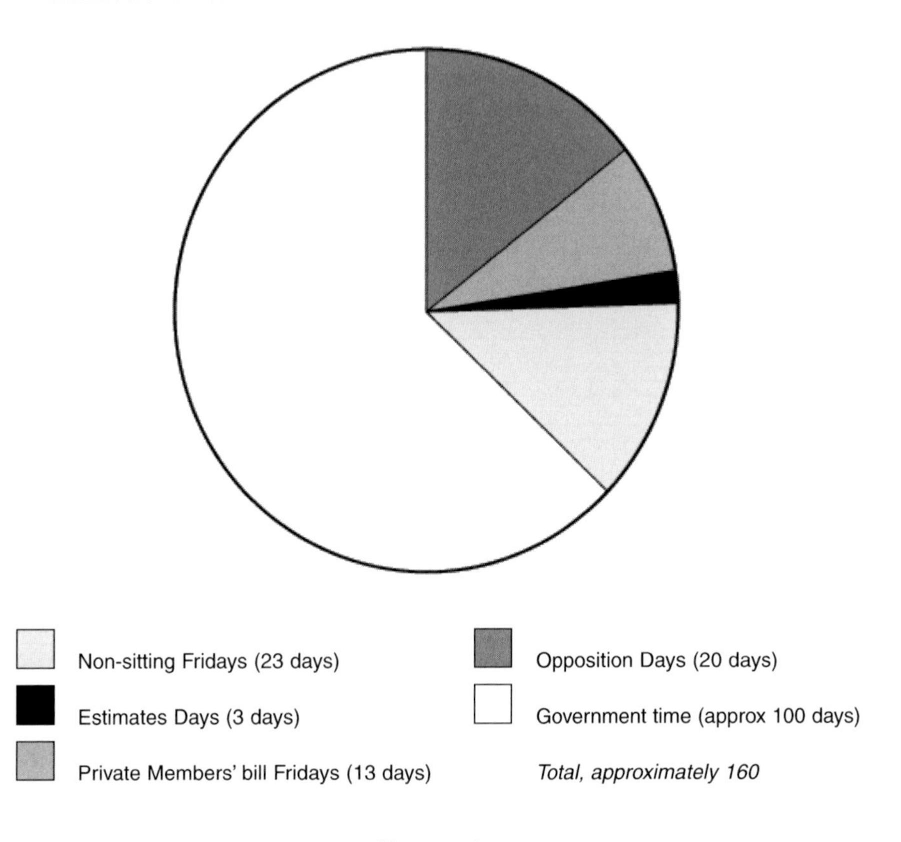

FIGURE 6
DISTRIBUTION OF DAYS DURING A TYPICAL SESSION

Opposition days

2.2.2 Under paragraph (2) of S.O. No. 14, on 20 **allotted days** in each **session** the choice of business to be debated by the House is made by the opposition parties. While the standing orders require there to be twenty such days in each session, their distribution still remains the gift of the government, although the choice of days is generally arrived at by agreement through the **usual channels** (see section 2.5 below). Seventeen of these days are at the disposal of the leader of the **official opposition** and the other three are at the disposal of the leader of the third largest party in the House. By the consent of the leader of that party, these three days are divided between the third largest party and other minor parties in the House. Two of the seventeen days allotted to the official opposition, and one of the three other days, may be taken in the form of half-days (see paragraph 7.9.3), though this is now a rare occurrence. The standing order also provides for two Friday sittings to count as one allotted day, but opposition time has never been taken on a Friday in recent years, and Fridays have anyway now become pretty much a *dies non* in the Commons.

2.2.3 On days on which opposition business has precedence, the leaders of the opposition parties invariably choose to have a debate on a substantive motion (usually critical of government policy). In recent sessions some of these days have been informally divided into two, with two subjects proposed for debate by way of two separate motions (see paragraph 7.9.6). (For the special procedure for calling government amendments on opposition days, see paragraph 9.5.3.) It may in theory be open to the opposition parties to choose another form of proceeding for these days such as debate on an adjournment motion, on a bill, on delegated legislation or any other type of business which the House may consider.

Private Members' Fridays

2.2.4 Under paragraph (4) of S.O. No. 14, on thirteen Fridays in each session **private Members' bills** have precedence over government business (see paragraphs 11.2.2 to 11.2.5). This may be varied by means of a sessional order (moved by the government). In sessions at the beginning or end of a Parliament which are expected to be unusually long or short, this allocation has sometimes been increased or decreased proportionately. A sessional order is passed towards the beginning of each session specifying the particular Fridays on which these bills will be considered (see paragraph 11.2.5).

Private Business

2.2.5 Standing Order No. 14 relates to public business. **Private business** which, with very few exceptions, means consideration of various stages of **private bills** (see section 11.19) is also sometimes taken during the time otherwise set aside for public business on sitting days. S.O. No. 20 provides for unopposed private business to be taken immediately after Prayers on Mondays to Thursdays. Where persistent objection (see paragraph 7.3.2) means that it is necessary to provide time for debate of private business on the floor of the House, the Chairman of Ways and Means may name 7 pm (or 4 pm) on a specified day other than a Friday for that business to be considered (see paragraph 7.9.2).

2.3 The Committee System of the House

Committees of the whole House

2.3.1 The House sometimes takes the committee stage of a bill or part of a bill on the floor of the House. In order to do so, it forms itself into a committee of the whole House (see paragraphs 11.11.1 to 11.11.6) where all Members of the House are automatically members of the committee.

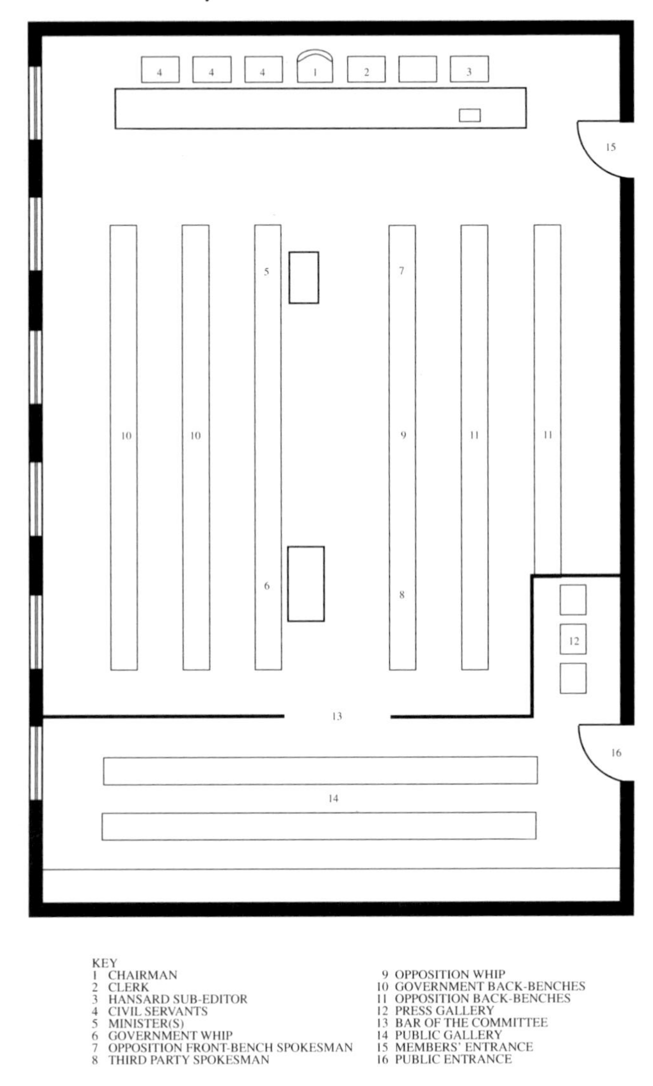

Figure 7

Layout of a Typical Standing Committee Room

Standing committees

2.3.2 The House uses standing committees to undertake the committee stages of bills (see section 11.10), to debate statutory instruments and other types of delegated legislation (see chapter 12) and to debate proposals for European legislation and other European Union documents (see chapter 13). Standing committees may also be used for second readings (see paragraphs 11.6.6 to 11.6.17) and (in theory though not in practice) for report stages of bills (see paragraph 11.13.14). There are also three standing committees known as grand committees, which are constituted to allow Members sitting for constituencies in Northern Ireland, Scotland and Wales to debate matters of particular interest to those countries (see chapter 14). The Standing Committee on Regional Affairs (see section 14.6) has analogous functions in relation to England, though it is differently constituted. The size of standing committees varies from a minimum of 13 members (for the European standing committees) to a maximum of 72 (for the Scottish Grand Committee). Standing committees on bills may have between 15 and 50 members, but are generally in the range of 16 to 30-odd.

2.3.3 Standing committees hold all their meetings in public (they could agree to sit in private, but there is no recent example of this). The style of debate is generally more relaxed in standing committee than on the floor of the House. However, the mode of proceeding in standing committee remains that of debate, rather than the select committees' mode of inquiry or deliberation. Since the basic rules of debate which apply in the House and in Committees of the whole House (see chapter 9) apply also in standing committee, the overall style is much the same in both contexts. This is reflected in the layout of standing committee rooms (see Figure 7) which are essentially scaled-down copies of the Chamber itself. No-one but a Member of the House (with a few exceptions for members of the House of Lords and in the exceptional case of Special Standing Committees, for which see paragraphs 11.11.7 and 11.11.8) can participate in the proceedings of a standing committee.

Select committees

2.3.4 The rather misleading title of "select committee" is a survival from a time when standing committees with a continuing existence were established to consider classes of bills and select committees were appointed by the House to consider a particular matter or bill, and once they had made their report they ceased to exist. In modern practice most select committees are established permanently in the standing orders and have a standing membership appointed for a whole Parliament, whereas most standing committees are appointed *ad hoc* to consider some particular item of legislation. Select committees are described in more detail in chapter 17.

2.3.5 The largest group of select committees is the so-called *departmentally-related select committees* appointed under S.O. No. 152 to monitor the activities of government departments. The standing order at present provides for 18 of these. They are described in section 17.2 below. The work of the Select Committee on Public Administration and the Environmental Audit Committee, which are both very similar in nature to the departmental select committees, is described in section 17.3. There are also the four *domestic committees* concerned with the internal workings of the House, appointed under S.O. No. 142. To these may be added the Broadcasting Committee appointed under S.O. No. 139 and the Finance and Services Committee appointed under S.O. No. 144, which are also concerned with domestic administrative matters.

Their work is described in chapter 18. The Procedure Committee, appointed under S.O. No. 147, is charged with considering proposals for reform of the House's procedures and related matters (see section 17.4) . Another distinct group of select committees (sometimes known collectively as the "scrutiny committees") includes the Joint/Select Committee on Statutory Instruments (see paragraphs 12.3.5 to 12.3.9), the Regulatory Reform Committee (see paragraphs 12.4.4 to 12.4.9), the European Scrutiny Committee (see paragraphs 13.2.2 to 13.2.5) and the Joint Committees on Consolidation, &c, bills (see paragraph 11.6.18) and on tax law rewrite bills (see paragraphs 11.6.20 to 11.6.22). These share the characteristic of being set the task under their standing orders of examining various types of legislation or proposals for legislation against fairly specific criteria. There is also the **Public Accounts Committee** (see section 10.5) which deals with public money and is considered the senior select committee. The work of the Committee on Standards and Privileges is described in section 4.1. The functions of the **Liaison Committee**, which brings together the chairmen of the select committees, is described in section 3.5.

2.3.6 The House continues from time to time to appoint select committees which are not specifically provided for in its standing orders to enquire into particular matters. In 1995 a select committee was appointed for the specific task of making recommendations on the implementation of the proposals of the Committee on Standards in Public Life (see section 4.3). In 1997 and again in 2001 a select committee was appointed to bring forward proposals for the modernisation of the House's procedures (see section 17.4). The quinquennial armed forces bills have by tradition been committed to a select committee appointed for the purpose (see paragraphs 11.11.9 and 11.11.10), as are hybrid bills (see paragraph 11.1.3). Public bills (and draft bills) are sometimes referred by the House to select committees or joint committees.

2.3.7 The Members of select committees are appointed on a motion made in the House. S.O. No. 121(1) requires that **notice** should be given of a motion to appoint or discharge Members to or from a select committee, and that the Members to be nominated should have given their consent. The nominations for membership of most of these committees are made by the **Committee of Selection** (see section 2.4).

2.3.8 Where the actual size of a committee is not laid down in a standing order, it will be specified in the order creating the committee. Though there is no explicit requirement in standing orders for the membership of select committees to be proportionate to the relative party strengths in the House, this convention is invariably observed. The balance of parties is calculated across the membership of all select committees – the smaller opposition parties will therefore be represented only on a proportion of select committees. The party which has a majority in the House can expect to have a majority on any select committee.

2.3.9 The public meetings of select committees (see paragraphs 17.1.4 to 17.1.6) are characterised by a degree of relative informality when compared to the Chamber or standing committees. Members address each other by name, rather than constituency. They are not called to speak by the chairman, though the chairman must exercise some degree of control. They remain seated throughout the proceedings, and should confine themselves to asking questions rather than making speeches of a debating nature.

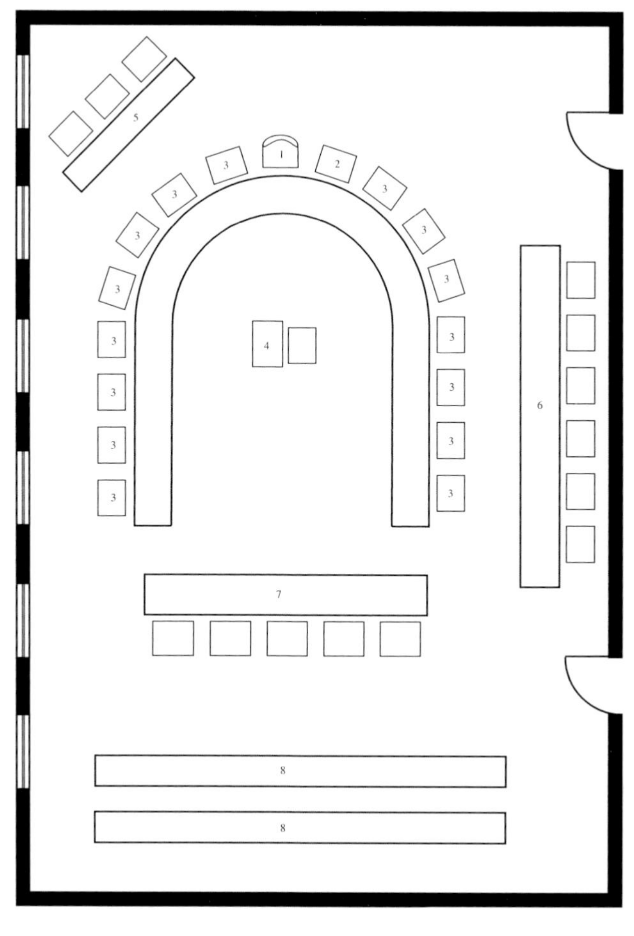

KEY
1 CHAIRMAN
2 CLERK
3 MEMBERS
4 VERBATIM REPORTER
5 ADVISERS/STAFF OF COMMITTEE
6 PRESS
7 WITNESSES
8 PUBLIC GALLERY

FIGURE 8

LAYOUT OF A TYPICAL SELECT COMMITTEE ROOM

2.3.10 The inquisitorial rather than adversarial nature of the select committees' public proceedings is reflected in the layout of the rooms in which they meet (see Figure 8). The Members are ranged round a horseshoe-shaped table, not in the government–opposite–opposition arrangement of the House or standing committees. The witnesses who are being examined in public session sit at a table at the open end of the horseshoe, and answer questions addressed to them by individual Members. Unlike standing committees, select committees often meet in private to discuss their work or consider draft reports. They are only allowed to admit the public to their evidence-taking sessions, but specialist advisers appointed by a committee may participate in deliberative meetings.

Joint committees

2.3.11 Joint committees are committees consisting of Members of both the Commons and the Lords. Four joint committees are established under standing orders. These are the Joint Committee on Human Rights (see paragraphs 17.5.10 to 17.5.17), the Joint Committee on Statutory Instruments (see paragraphs 12.3.5 to 12.3.9), the Joint Committee on Consolidation, &c. Bills (see paragraph 11.6.18) and the Joint Committee on Tax Law Rewrite Bills (see paragraph 11.6.20). S.O. No. 63(2) provides for joint committees on other public bills (see paragraphs 11.11.12 and 11.11.13) though there has been no example of such a committee in recent decades. However, in recent sessions the two Houses have appointed a number of joint committees to consider draft bills. The House might in theory propose a joint committee to the Lords on any matter. For example, in 1997 the two Houses appointed a joint committee to examine parliamentary privilege, and in 2002 another was appointed to consider reform of the House of Lords.

2.4 THE COMMITTEE OF SELECTION

2.4.1 The Committee of Selection does not directly appear in the public business standing orders because, by a quirk of history, it is established under the standing orders of the House relating to private business. It has nine members and a quorum of three. Its most active Members are the Pairing Whips from the government and official opposition (see paragraph 2.5.5) and the Whip of the third largest party in the House. Like select committees, the committee elects its own chairman and largely determines its own methods of proceeding.

2.4.2 The Committee's principal task is to appoint Members to standing committees (see paragraphs 2.3.4 to 2.3.10 above) and to private bill committees (see section 11.19) and to nominate Members for appointment to many select committees. Appointments to standing committees are made by way of a report to the House (see paragraph 15.1.24), and do not require the formal endorsement of the full House. Nominations to select committees have to be approved by resolution of the House on amendable motions.

2.4.3 Under paragraph (2) of S.O. No. 86, the Committee of Selection is required to have regard to the "composition of the House" in appointing standing committees. In effect this means that the proportions of government and opposition Members on a standing committee will reflect the relative strengths of the parties in the House. If the government has a majority (however small) in the House, it will have a majority of at least one on a standing committee. Additionally, the Committee of Selection is required to have regard to "the qualifications of those members nominated", and will as a matter of course put on a standing committee any Minister who wishes to be nominated and the recognised opposition front benchers who shadow those Ministers. There will also be a Whip from the government and opposition. The other parties will in general be entitled to a small number of places on a standing committee, and they will seek to allocate these amongst themselves by agreement. Once a standing committee has entered on its consideration of a bill, the Committee of Selection will only alter its membership in exceptional circumstances.

2.4.4 Under S.O. No. 121(2), the Committee of Selection also recommends to the House which Members should be appointed to the departmental select committees established under S.O. No. 152 (see section 17.2) or the domestic committees appointed under S.O. No. 142 (see paragraphs 18.1.6 to 18.1.9). A motion to appoint or discharge Members to or from committees established under either of those standing orders can be moved only by a member of the Committee of Selection. Amendments to such motions can, however, be proposed by any Member. At least two sitting days' notice must be given of such a motion; in other words the motions must appear on the remaining orders at least once before they can be placed on the effective orders.

2.4.5 The Committee of Selection does not enjoy any of the usual powers of select committees to take evidence, meet in public, travel or sit on days when the House does not.

2.5 The Usual Channels

Whips

2.5.1 Each party in the House has one or more of its Members designated as Whips. Their main task is to manage their party and negotiate with Whips of other parties about the management of the House's business. These discussions are often referred to as taking place through "the usual channels", a term which also includes the **Leader of the House** and his shadows. Although not part of the formal administrative machinery of the House, the Whips take a close interest in its administration, and representatives of the Whips' offices are likely to be found on the **domestic committees** and related committees.

2.5.2 The Whips' offices of the government and **official opposition** are each headed by a Chief Whip and a Deputy Chief Whip. The government Chief Whip may or may not formally be a member of the **Cabinet**, but will certainly attend Cabinet meetings. The other government Whips are Ministers, and some are members of the royal household with certain ceremonial duties attached to their posts. The official opposition Chief Whip and Deputy Chief Whip receive ministerial salaries.

2.5.3 A government and an opposition Whip are on duty in the Chamber at all times when the House is sitting. The government Whip in particular has a key responsibility for ensuring the smooth transaction of the government's business. Since all government Whips are Ministers, they will often take responsibility for moving items of government business on behalf of other colleagues where no debate is to take place (see paragraphs 7.8.2 and 9.7.11). Whips do not, as a rule, participate in debate either in the chamber or on standing committees. There will be a Whip from the government and official opposition as members of any standing committee on a government bill (see section 11.10) or on delegated legislation (see paragraphs 12.3.23 to 12.3.30). Their task is to ensure, so far as is practicable, the smooth running of the committee, and to negotiate on questions relating to the progress of business.

The "Whip" and whipped business

2.5.4 Each week, when the House is sitting, the Whips of each party send a bulletin to each of their Members in the House. This is known as the *Party Whip*. It advises their colleagues on the business which is anticipated to occur in the House over the forthcoming week or so. It also indicates on which items the "whip" is being applied: that is on which matters Members are being requested to vote in accordance with the party line. These requests are underlined once, twice or three times to indicate the importance attached to each item; hence the expressions "one line", "two line" or "three line" whip.

2.5.5 Members may make arrangements with Members in other parties to be "paired". This is an arrangement where they may both agree not to vote in certain divisions (see section 9.6), thereby cancelling out each other's absence and leaving the government's majority unaffected. These arrangements are not formally recognised in the procedures of the House, but some supervision of them is exercised by a Whip in each of the government and official opposition Whips' offices known as the Pairing Whip. They do not function when the government party has an overwhwlming majority.

The "All-Party" Whip

2.5.6 There is also a bulletin known as the "All-Party Whip", which announces events of a cross-party nature, in particular meetings of all kinds ranging from those of official "all-party" committees and groups (for example, say, on merchant shipping or Burma) through foreign language conversation groups to prayer meetings and bible study groups.

Committees of Debate		Scrutiny or Advisory Committees		
Primarily concerned with Legislation	**Other**	**Scrutiny Committees**	**Joint Committees**	**Other**
Committees of the whole House		Public Accounts	Joint Committee on Human Rights	Modernisation*
	European Standing Committees (A, B and C)			Procedure
Standing Committees on Bills (any number, called "A", "B", etc.)		European Scrutiny	Joint Committee on Statutory Instruments	Liaison
				Standards and Privileges
		Regulatory Reform	Joint Committee on Tax Law Rewrite Bills	Selection
Special Standing Committees on Bills	The Grand Committees (Scottish, Welsh and Northern Ireland)			Finance and Services
		Departmentally-related select committees (18)	Joint Committee on Consolidation, &c. Bills	Accommodation and Works
Delegated Legislation Standing Committees (any number, called "First", "Second", etc.)		Environmental Audit	*Ad hoc* Joint Committees on draft Bills*	Administration
				Broadcasting
Report Committees	The Standing Committee on Regional Affairs	Public Administration	Joint Committee on House of Lords Reform*	Catering
				Information

*Indicates a temporary committee

FIGURE 9
COMMITTEES OF THE HOUSE

Chapter 3

THE CHAIR

3.1 THE SPEAKER

Duties

3.1.1 The Speaker's primary duty as the presiding officer of the Commons is to maintain order in debate and to apply and interpret the rules, practices and traditions of the House. The Speaker's principal adviser on these matters is the **Clerk of the House**, who is the recognised authority on the law and practice of Parliament.

Powers

3.1.2 The Speaker exercises considerable control over the House's debates and other proceedings. Under the **standing orders** of the House the Speaker's main powers are:

- to decide which Members will be called to speak in debate or ask questions (see paragraph 9.3.2);
- to select which amendments will be put to the House for decision under S.O. No. 32 (see paragraphs 9.2.6 to 9.2.10);
- to refuse or accept certain types of Questions for debate or decision, principally those for the adjournment of debate under S.O. No. 35 (see paragraph 9.4.1) and for the closure of debate under S.O. No. 36 (see paragraph 9.7.4);
- to discipline Members who abuse the rules of order under S.O. Nos. 42 and 43 and to propose the suspension of a Member for defiance of the authority of the Chair under S.O. No. 44 (see paragraphs 9.3.23 to 9.3.31);
- to limit the length of speeches under S.O. No. 47 (see paragraph 9.7.3).

These powers are described more fully in chapter 9.

3.1.3 The Speaker also has the power to determine whether an application for an urgent debate under S.O. No. 24 may be allowed to be put to the House for decision (see paragraph 7.6.6); or whether to allow an **urgent question** to be asked under S.O. No. 21(2) (see paragraphs 7.5.5 and 8.26); and to rule that a division is unnecessarily claimed under S.O. No. 40 (see paragraph 9.6.8).

3.1.4 The Speaker has also been given by the House the responsibility to determine whether a complaint of **privilege** is one to which precedence ought to be given over other business of the House (see paragraphs 7.2.3 and 4.2.12).

3.1.5 The Speaker is also required to determine whether a bill is a money bill under the terms of the Parliament Acts 1911 and 1949 (see paragraph 10.2.15); under the same Acts to certify whether a bill is one to which the provisions of the Acts might apply (see section 11.17); and to certify under S.O. No. 97 whether a bill relates exclusively to Scotland (see paragraph 11.6.14).

3.1.6 The Speaker's authority is not circumscribed by the standing orders and statute. In practice, the Speaker makes decisions almost daily about the interpretation of the rules of the House and their application, and these decisions of the Chair in turn come to form part of the body of precedents from which those rules are derived. The Speaker also has a wide-ranging authority in determining what is acceptable parliamentary behaviour, extending to the general conduct of Members in discharging their parliamentary duties, and the maintenance of the principles of courtesy and moderation in all aspects of parliamentary life. The requirement that Members always address the Chair in debate (see paragraphs 9.3.9 and 9.3.10) is an important means whereby these principles are upheld. Due respect is shown to the Speaker by Members always bowing to the Chair when they enter or leave the Chamber (see paragraph 9.3.1), or when the Speaker passes in procession on the way to or from the Chamber.

Election

3.1.7 The Speaker is elected by the Commons from amongst the Members of the House at the beginning of each Parliament (see paragraphs 5.1.4 and 5.1.5), or when the office is vacated by reason of the death, disqualification or resignation of the holder or for some other reason.

3.1.8 Under S.O. No. 1, where the election takes place at the beginning of a Parliament (or on the death of the incumbent), it is presided over by the **Senior Member** or **Father of the House**. Where the Speaker has indicated an intention to resign, he or she may preside over the election of a successor unless unable or unwilling to do so, in which case the duty falls again to the Senior Member under S.O. No. 1. While presiding over such an election, the Senior Member enjoys all those powers normally exercisable by the Speaker. During these proceedings the Senior Member sits at the **Table**, in the place normally occupied by the **Clerk of the House**.

3.1.9 The procedure for electing a Speaker was extensively revised in 2000. In essence there are now two stages. If the Member who was Speaker at the time of a dissolution is returned to the House at a general election, when the House reassembles the Senior Member (under the provisions of S.O. No. 1A) must first ascertain whether the former Speaker is willing to be chosen as Speaker once again. If the candidate indicates willingness, the Senior Member immediately calls another Member who moves "That [the former Speaker] do take the Chair of this House as Speaker". The Senior Member must then put the Question without further debate, although the House may divide on it. If the motion is agreed, the proposer and another Member take the successful candidate from his or her place to the Chair, from the steps of which the Speaker Elect delivers a speech of thanks, after which Members may offer their congratulations and the House adjourns. However, if the motion were negatived, the standing order requires the Senior Member to adjourn the House to the next day, when the election proceeds under the same rules as if there were no returning incumbent Speaker.

3.1.10 Where the incumbent has been rejected by the House, or more probably where there is no incumbent, the House must, under the terms of S.O. No. 1B, conduct a secret ballot for the election of a new Speaker. (This procedure has not yet been used.) The **Clerk of the House** oversees the arrangements. Nominations must be submitted in writing to the Clerk between 9.30 am and 10.30 am on the day the election is to take place. To be valid, each nomination must be supported by the signatures of no fewer than twelve and no more than fifteen Members, and at least three of the signatories must be members of a party or parties other than that to which the nominee belongs. No Member may support the nomination of more than one candidate, and if a signature appears in support of two or more candidates it will be discounted in all cases. Nominations must be accompanied by a declaration from the nominee of their willingness to serve as Speaker. The list of nominations, together with the names of their supporters, should be published as soon as practicable after the closing time.

3.1.11 If only one nomination were submitted, when the House assembled at 2.30 pm, the election would proceed along the same lines as described in paragraph 3.1.9 above, except that the presiding Member would put the question without another Member having to propose it. If there are two or more candidates, the Senior Member invites each to address the House in turn, in an order determined by lot. The Senior Member then directs the House to conduct its secret ballot. Ballot boxes are placed in the lobbies, and each Member is issued with a ballot paper listing the candidates in alphabetical order. Each Member may vote for only one candidate, and the presiding Member may not vote.The ballot remains open for half an hour (or such other time as the presiding Member may determine). The votes are counted under the supervision of the Clerk, and the presiding Member announces the results to the House.

3.1.12 If any candidate has received more than 50 per cent of the votes cast, the Senior Member proceeds immediately to put the Question to the House that that Member be elected as Speaker. If no candidate has received more than 50 per cent, then the presiding Member must order another ballot. The name of the candidate who received the fewest votes is dropped from the ballot paper for the next round. So also are the names of any candidates who received less than 5 per cent of the votes cast. If two or more candidates tied for last place, their names can remain on the paper for the next ballot unless they received less than the 5 per cent minimum. Within ten minutes of the announcement of the result of an indecisive ballot, any other candidate can voluntarily withdraw their name from the next ballot.

3.1.13 The successive rounds of ballots may continue indefinitely until a candidate receives more than 50 per cent of the votes cast, though if the effect of the application of the rules described above is to reduce the number of candidates to one, then the presiding Member immediately puts to the House the Question for the election of that person as Speaker. In any event, the result of the process will finally be that the House must vote (in its usual way, rather than by secret ballot) on the Question whether the single candidate who finally emerges should be its Speaker. In the highly unlikely event that the House were then to negative the Question that that candidate should be Speaker, the Senior Member would have to adjourn the House to the next day, and the process would have to begin all over again.

3.1.14 When a Speaker has been elected, he or she is taken from their place to the Speaker's Chair. Standing on the steps of the Chair (as they are still Speaker Elect rather than Speaker), they may address the House and offer their thanks for the honour which has been conferred upon them. Other Members may offer their congratulations. The House then adjourns. On the following day the House reassembles and is summoned to the House of Lords to hear the Queen's approbation of the Speaker Elect expressed. The Speaker then lays claim, on behalf of the Commons, to "all their ancient and undoubted rights and privileges" (see section 4.2), and the Commons return to their House. There is a description of the ensuing proceedings in a new Parliament in paragraphs 5.1.5 to 5.1.7.

Status

3.1.15 The Speaker is not only the principal officer and highest authority in the House, but also the chief representative of the House in its relations with the other constituent parts of Parliament: the House of Lords and the Crown. The Speaker and his deputies often represent the House on formal occasions and in international gatherings of various kinds.

3.2 THE DEPUTY SPEAKERS AND CHAIRMEN'S PANEL

The Chairman of Ways and Means

3.2.1 The Chairman of Ways and Means is the principal Deputy Speaker, and in the absence of the Speaker may exercise all the authority of the Speaker, under the Deputy Speaker Act 1855. S.O. No. 3(2) also provides in these circumstances for the Deputy Speaker to exercise the authority of the Speaker in relation to the proceedings of the House; and S.O. No. 3(3) provides for the delegation of this authority to the first and second deputy chairmen (see paragraphs 3.2.4 and 3.2.5 below) when necessary.

3.2.2 The Chairman of Ways and Means is appointed at the beginning of a new Parliament on a motion made by the Prime Minister on the day on which the **Queen's Speech** is delivered, after the **sessional orders** have been disposed of (see section 5.1). No **notice** is required of the motion, and none could be given for the first day of a Session; but the **Procedure Committee** has recommended that consultations should take place before the names are published. Once elected, the Chairman remains in office for the remainder of the Parliament, unless he or she resigns or the office is vacated for some other reason.

3.2.3 The Chairman of Ways and Means has two particular responsibilities distinct from the Speaker. The first of these is the responsibility for general oversight of matters connected with **private bills** (see paragraphs 7.3.1, 7.3.2, 7.9.2, 11.1.2 and section 11.19). The second is his or her presiding role in relation to **sittings in Westminster Hall** (see section 6.3). The Chairman also chairs the **Chairmen's Panel** (see paragraph 3.2.6 below) and has (through the Panel) general responsibility for the oversight of standing committee procedure. He is also *ex-officio* chairman of any **committee of the whole House**.

The Deputy Chairmen

3.2.4 S.O. No. 2 provides for the House to elect two Deputy Chairmen of Ways and Means (the First and Second). This is normally done as part of the motion appointing the Chairman (see paragraph 3.2.1 above), and like the Chairman, the Deputy Chairmen normally remain in office for a Parliament.

3.2.5 The Deputy Chairmen share with the Speaker and Chairman of Way and Means the chairing of the House's sittings, and they exercise all those powers of the Speaker that are delegated to the Chairman of Ways and Means when he is chairing the House.

The Chairmen's Panel

3.2.6 Under S.O. No. 4, the Speaker appoints not fewer than ten Members to the Chairmen's Panel (currently nearer thirty in practice). Their principal task is to chair **standing committees** (see paragraph 2.3.2), but they may also act as temporary chairmen of the House when it is sitting as a **committee of the whole House**. For **sittings in Westminster Hall**, four senior members of the Panel are appointed by the House under S.O. No. 10(4) to act as Deputy Speakers at those sittings (see section 6.3).

Impartiality of Speaker and Deputy Speakers

3.2.7 Once appointed, the Speaker, the Chairman of Ways and Means and the Deputy Chairmen all withdraw from an active political role. They neither speak in debate nor make political speeches outside the House, nor do they take actions which might imply support for particular opinions. When some public action on behalf of their constituents is necessary they usually ask another Member to act on their behalf. They do not vote in **divisions** in the House, although in the event of a tied vote the Chair has a casting vote which is given in accordance with precedent (see paragraph 9.6.14). These restrictions do not apply to the four members of the Chairmen's Panel appointed as additional Deputy Speakers for **sittings in Westminster Hall** (see section 6.3).

3.3 STANDING COMMITTEE CHAIRMEN

Appointment and role

3.3.1 Under S.O. No. 85 the Speaker appoints a chairman or chairmen to chair each standing committee on a bill (see section 11.10) or on delegated legislation (see paragraphs 12.3.23 to 12.3.30) from among the members of the Chairmen's Panel (see paragraph 3.2.6). There may be additional chairmen appointed if necessary as the bill progresses. Seniority among joint chairmen is determined in accordance with their length of service on the Panel. A member of the Panel is also chosen by the Speaker to chair each sitting of one of the grand committees (see chapter 14) or of the European standing committees (see paragraphs 13.2.10 to 13.2.17).

3.3.2 Standing committee chairmen have a similar duty of impartiality as is imposed on the Speaker and Deputy Speakers in the House (see paragraph 3.2.7 above) within the context of standing committee proceedings which they chair.

However, they are not required to avoid political activity outside those committees except in relation to the particular bills over which they have presided. They do not vote in the House on stages of bills which they have chaired in standing committee.

Powers of chairmen

3.3.3 Under S.O. No. 89(3), the chairman of a standing committee has delegated to him or her the power:

- of selection of amendments under S.O. No. 32 (see paragraphs 9.2.6 to 9.2.10 and 11.10.10 and 11.10.11);
- to decide whether to accept a motion for proposal of the question (see paragraph 9.7.2) or for the closure (see paragraphs 9.7.4 and 9.7.5);
- to refuse to allow a dilatory motion to be moved (see paragraph 9.4.1);
- to order a Member who persists in irrelevance or tedious repetition to resume his or her seat (see paragraph 9.3.14); and
- in a standing committee on a bill, to put the question on clause stand part without debate (see paragraph 11.10.23).

3.3.4 The chairman of a standing committee also has a general responsibility to enforce the conventions and rules of debate set out in section 9.3. The means which the chairmen of standing committees must use to enforce discipline in cases of grave disorder in a committee are described in paragraphs 9.3.32 and 9.3.33.

3.3.5 The chairman of a standing committee fixes the time of its first meeting (except in the case of the grand committees), though he or she will usually allow the **Member in charge** to choose a convenient time. Where a standing committee adjourns before concluding its business, either pursuant to S.O. No. 89(1) or to its own decision, and no time has been fixed for its next meeting, the chairman may appoint a day and time for its next sitting.

3.3.6 A chairman has a general discretion to suspend the sitting of a committee as he considers expedient, subject to his duty to make progress with the bill or other matter before it (see also paragraphs 9.4.3 and 9.4.4). If a division is called in the House while a standing committee is sitting, the chairman *must*, under S.O. No. 89(4), suspend the sitting for long enough to enable Members of the committee to vote in the House.

3.3.7 A chairman may invite a Member of a standing committee to take the Chair in his place, if necessary, for a maximum of fifteen minutes. Such temporary chairmen do not enjoy any of the powers of a chairman described in paragraph 3.3.3 above.

3.4 SELECT COMMITTEE CHAIRMEN

Introduction

3.4.1 Although they share the nomenclature, the chairmen of select committees have a role quite different from that of the chair in the House or in standing committees. They are far more engaged in the "politics" of their committees, and although they generally seek to act as independent arbitrators they are not under the obligation of neutrality imposed on these other chairman. They have few formal powers.

Election

3.4.2 Each select committee (see paragraphs 2.3.4 to 2.3.10) elects its own chairman from among its members. It is agreed in advance through the **usual channels** (see section 2.6 but see also paragraph 3.4.5 below) whether the chairman is to come from among the government or opposition Members. By tradition the chairmen of the **Public Accounts Committee** (see section 10.5) and the Joint/Select Committee on Statutory Instruments (see paragraphs 12.3.5 to 12.3.9) are drawn from the opposition. Among the departmentally-related committees (see section 17.2), the chairmanships are generally divided between government and opposition by agreement, but these agreements may relate to different committees at different times, and will alter according to the balance of parties in the House.

3.4.3 When a select committee is first set up, or its membership is nominated for the first time in a new Parliament, the senior Member among those appointed (that is the Member with the longest service, whether interrupted or not, in the House) directs the Clerk of the committee as to the date and time of its first meeting. When the committee is convened, the details of any declarable interests of any Member in relation to the committee's responsibilities are circulated, and the members of the committee are given the opportunity to amend or add to them orally. In particular, they are encouraged to record interests which, although not requiring registration in accordance with the rules of the House (see section 4.3), have particular relevance to the remit of the committee concerned. The Clerk then calls a Member who moves "That . . . do take the Chair of the Committee". Other Members may be called and may move other motions nominating other candidates. These are moved as separate motions rather than as amendments to the first motion. After any debate, if there is more than one candidate, the motions are put to the vote in the order in which they were moved. The first name to obtain a majority of votes cast is elected chairman and immediately takes the Chair. The Member so elected remains chairman for the remainder of the Parliament (or the existence of the committee if shorter) unless he or she resigns from the post or is discharged from the committee, or is unseated by a motion to rescind the earlier decision of a committee. Occasionally, a Member may be elected to take the chair of a committee for a specified period, after which a chairman will again have to be elected. When a chairman is absent from a meeting, another Member is appointed (usually rather informally) by the committee to take the chair for that meeting.

Powers

3.4.4 There is normally very little formal procedure as such in the work of select committees, and their chairmen are not therefore required to apply and interpret rules in the way that the Chair in the House or standing committees is. By and large the committees regulate their own proceedings in accordance with their needs. Since their public work mostly involves the examination of witnesses, there is no requirement for the elaborate rules of debate which apply in the House and in standing committees. When meeting in private, select committees also generally proceed in an informal manner, though formal decisions are recorded in their published Minutes of Proceedings (see paragraph 17.1.19). The chairmen have no explicit powers under standing orders to regulate the proceedings of the committees and so must govern by consent. They do, however, take a much more active role in leading the committees, and are not under the strict obligations of neutrality that chairmen of standing committees are required to observe. For example, on the relatively rare occasions when divisions occur in select committees and there is a tied vote, the chairman may cast his or her vote on the basis of personal judgement, rather than in accordance with precedent (see paragraph 9.6.12).

3.4.5 Under a new standing order made in May 2002 (S.O. No. 122A), a select committee may not elect as its chairman a member who has served in that capacity for the two previous Parliaments, or for a continuous period of eight years, whichever is the longer.

3.4.6 On the same date, the House agreed in principle to giving extra payment to select committee chairmen. This has not yet been implemented.

3.5 The Liaison Committee

Membership

3.5.1 The Liaison Committee is appointed by the House under S.O. No. 145. It is a select committee (see section 17.1). No maximum number of Members is specified. Although it is not explicitly stated in the standing order, the membership of the committee is in fact comprised of the chairmen of all other select committees. At the beginning of the 2001 Parliament, a motion was passed specifying the committees of which the chairmen duly elected and reported to the House would automatically become members of the Liaison Committee. On that occasion, two named individual Members were also added to the Liaison Committee, one of whom was subsequently elected as its Chairman.

Functions

3.5.2 The Committee's terms of reference require it to consider general matters relating to the work of select committees. It has produced a number of reports on such matters, in recent sessions with increased frequency.

3.5.3 The Committee is also required to give such advice relating to the work of select committees as may be sought by the House of Commons Commission (see paragraph 18.1.1). In practice, this largely means advice on the distribution of the sum available for overseas travel and on other aspects of the financing of select committees' work. The Liaison Committee itself has no power to travel.

3.5.4 Under paragraph (2) of S.O. No. 145 the Committee makes recommendations to the House as to which **Estimates** should be debated on **Estimates Days** (see paragraph 10.3.10). The Committee also recommends select committee reports for debate at **sittings in Westminster Hall** (see section 6.3).

3.5.5 More generally, the Liaison Committee acts as a co-ordinator of the other select committees' work, and to an extent as a champion of their role in the House's proceedings. It has produced a number of reports on the work of select committees, and has committed itself to producing an annual report on this subject. The **Modernisation Committee** and **Procedure Committee** have, on occasions, sought the views of the Liaison Committee on proposals for reform of the select committees and related matters

3.5.6 Individual select committees are expected to consult the Liaison Committee before making a Special Report alleging a grave interference in their work (see paragraphs 4.2.13 and 17.1.14).

3.5.7 Under paragraph (5) of S.O. No. 145, the Committee has the power to appoint a sub-committee, with a quorum of three. This sub-committee has functioned as a "Bureau" or steering committee within the Liaison Committee, which is otherwise rather unwieldy in size. Under paragraph (4) of the standing order, the sub-committee has the power to make reports on its own behalf to the main Committee.

3.5.8 Under paragraph (1A) of S.O. No. 145, the Committee " . . . may also hear evidence from the Prime Minister on matters of public policy", a power which it has exercised. So far the Committee has indicated that it will hold such hearings twice a year.

Chapter 4
PRIVILEGES AND STANDARDS

4.1 The Committee on Standards and Privileges

4.1.1 The *Committee on Standards and Privileges* is guardian of the House's privileges and custodian of the standards of conduct of Members of the House. The Committee is a select committee (see paragraphs 2.3.4 to 2.3.10), and its powers and functions are set out in S.O. No. 149. It has eleven Members (with a quorum of five). The Committee has power to appoint two sub-committees of up to seven Members (with a quorum of three). The standing order implies that one of these sub-committees should have the principal task of examining complaints relating to Members' conduct, but in practice these inquiries have been conducted by the full Committee. Under paragraph (9) of the standing order, the Law Officers of the government who are Members of the House may attend meetings of the Committee and participate in its deliberations.

4.1.2 The Committee's role is to consider complaints relating to privilege and contempts (see section 4.2 below), to oversee the work of the **Commissioner for Standards** (see paragraphs 4.3.8 and 4.3.9), and to consider complaints (with the assistance of the Commissioner) relating to the Register of Members' Interests and breaches of the **Code of Conduct** (see paragraphs 4.3.5 and 4.3.6).

4.1.3 The Committee has the usual powers of a select committee (see section 17.1). However, in addition to these, the Committee has two unique powers under S.O. No. 149. Under paragraph (6) of the standing order it can *order* the attendance of a Member of the House to give oral evidence and can *require* a Member to submit documents in his or her possession (see also paragraph 17.1.10 in relation to witnesses taking oaths). And under paragraph (8) of the standing order it has power to refuse to allow the broadcast of its public meetings (see section 6.4). Under paragraph (7) it can also inspect the unreported evidence of its predecessor committees.

4.1.4 When a case relating either to a breach of privilege or contempt or to the standards of conduct of Members is referred to the Committee, it undertakes an inquiry and might in due course make a report to the House giving its findings and recommending some punishment, if the case were proved. Or the Committee might choose only to admonish the person (whether a Member of the House or an outsider) found to be at fault but recommend no further action. In any case, it is for the House to decide whether to accept the Committee's recommendation.

4.1.5 In November 2002 the Committee on Standards in Public Life published a report on standards of conduct in the House of Commons, which made a number of recommendations about the procedures of the Standards and Privileges Committee and the work of the Parliamentary Commissioner for Standards. These were considered by the Standards and Privileges Committee itself, which recommended their adoption with certain modifications. Among these was the recommendation that the Committee should have explicit power to appoint external legal advisers to assist in its work, and in June 2002 the standing order was accordingly amended.

4.2 Privilege and Contempts

4.2.1 **Erskine May** defines parliamentary privilege as "the sum of the peculiar rights enjoyed by each House collectively as a constituent part of the High Court of Parliament, and by the Members of each House individually, without which they could not discharge their functions, and which exceed those possessed by other bodies or individuals". In March 1999 the Joint Committee on Parliamentary Privilege published its report on the privileges of the two Houses. It made a number of recommendations for the codification, updating and amendment of the privileges of Parliament. Many of these will require legislation, and most have yet to be implemented.

4.2.2 The ancient privileges of the Commons which are claimed by the Speaker at the beginning of each Parliament (see paragraphs 3.1.14 and 5.1.5) are:

- freedom of speech;
- freedom from arrest;
- freedom of access to the sovereign; and
- that the most favourable construction should be placed upon all the House's proceedings.

Freedom of speech

4.2.3 Of these, the most significant nowadays (as the Joint Committee reaffirmed) is freedom of speech, which attaches both to the House collectively and to its individual Members when engaged in parliamentary proceedings. Any attempt to trammel this freedom by intimidation or inducements would be *prima facie* a breach of privilege. (The other privilege which attaches to Members individually, that of freedom from arrest, applies only to civil actions, not to criminal prosecutions and is largely irrelevant in times when Members are not threatened with arrest as a means of intimidation. The Joint Committee recommended its abolition.)

4.2.4 The privilege of freedom of speech is reinforced by Article IX of the Bill of Rights of 1688/9, which states that "the freedom of speech and debates or proceedings in Parliament ought not to be impeached or questioned in any court or place out of Parliament". In effect, this gives general protection to Members against any action for defamation or other civil action in respect of things said or done as part of the proceedings of Parliament. (This protective provision was modified by section 13 of the Defamation Act 1996, which allowed for individuals to waive their privilege under Article IX in certain circumstances in relation to proceedings for defamation. The Joint Committee has recommended the repeal of this provision, and its replacement by a provision for the House as a whole to waive privilege in particular cases.)

4.2.5 Any document published by the House or one of its committees is equally protected from any action for defamation or other legal challenge. This protection extends to words spoken or written by witnesses giving evidence to the House or one of its committees (though that privilege may not be absolute). The broadcasting or publication of proceedings of the House is also privileged, though again such privilege may be qualified (for example, if it is shown that a publication had a deliberately malicious intent). Papers published by order of the House (see paragraph 15.3.2) are also privileged under the provisions of the Parliamentary Papers Act of 1840. The Joint Committee has recommended that this Act be repealed and replaced by a new statute giving more qualified protection.

Other privileges

4.2.6 The other significant privileges held by the House collectively are the right to:

- provide for its own proper constitution (that is to determine who may be its Members);
- regulate its own proceedings (otherwise known as its "exclusive cognisance");
- compel witnesses to attend and give evidence; and
- exercise penal jurisdiction (that is to punish those who attack or disregard its privileges or who commit contempts against it).

4.2.7 The limits of privilege and its application to particular cases are not clear cut. The investigation of particular allegations of breaches of privilege or contempts is the function of the **Committee on Standards and Privileges** (see section 4.1 above). Privilege is, however, a complex area, and any reader seeking a full discussion of the development and modern state of parliamentary privilege should consult **Erskine May** or the March 1999 report of the Joint Committee on Parliamentary Privilege.

Contempts and breaches of privilege

4.2.8 Contempts are often conflated with breaches of privilege. Any breach of the privileges of the House is a contempt. However, a contempt may be an action which, while not in breach of one of the privileges of the House, is an act of disobedience to its commands, is a libel against one of its Members or officers, is an attempt to obstruct or impede it in the performance of its functions, or is an attack on its authority and dignity.

4.2.9 It is a contempt of the House to attempt to interfere with or seek to influence a witness before the House or one of its committees. This protection afforded to witnesses is reaffirmed by the House at the beginning of each session in one of the sessional orders passed on the first day (see paragraph 5.2.6).

4.2.10 The House has also declared that it is a contempt to attempt to suborn or bribe any of its Members to influence them in the exercise of their parliamentary duties. A resolution of the House of 1965 described the offering of bribes to Members as "a high crime and misdemeanour". The Joint Committee has recommended that these matters should be brought within the general law on bribery and corruption.

Ministerial accountability

4.2.11 On 19 March 1997 the House passed the following resolution:

(1) Ministers have a duty to Parliament to account, and be held to account, for the policies, decisions and actions of their Departments and Next Steps Agencies;

(2) *It is of paramount importance that Ministers give accurate and truthful information to Parliament, correcting any inadvertent error at the earliest opportunity; Ministers who knowingly mislead Parliament will be expected to offer their resignation to the Prime Minister;*

(3) *Ministers should be as open as possible with Parliament, refusing to provide information only when disclosure would not be in the public interest, which should be decided in accordance with relevant statute and the Government's Code of Practice on Access to Government Information;*

(4) *Similarly, Ministers should require civil servants who give evidence before parliamentary committees on their behalf and under their directions to be as helpful as possible in providing accurate, truthful and full information in accordance with the duties and responsibilities of civil servants as set out in the Civil Service Code.*

Though this is largely a restatement of what was considered to be the pre-existing position, its status as a resolution of the House would suggest that failure to comply with its terms could be more readily construed as constituting *prima facie* a contempt of the House. The terms of the resolution are, however, undoubtedly open to interpretation.

Investigation of contempts

4.2.12 A Member who believes that a breach of privilege or contempt of the House has occurred should raise the matter at the earliest opportunity. He or she should write to the Speaker setting out the grounds of complaint. The Speaker will promptly reply in writing, indicating whether he proposes to give the matter the precedence allowed to matters of privilege (see paragraph 7.2.3). If he does decide to grant it precedence, he will announce that decision in the House; the Member seeking to raise the matter would then table a motion in appropriate terms which would appear on the following day's **Order Paper** at the head of all other business. The motion would normally be to refer the alleged breach or contempt to the **Committee on Standards and Privileges** (see section 4.1 above) for investigation and report.

4.2.13 If a select committee makes a special report to the House that its work has been significantly interfered with by the premature disclosure of its deliberations (see paragraph 17.1.14), such a report stands automatically referred to the **Committee on Standards and Privileges** (see section 4.1 above).

4.3 Interests and Standards

Introduction

4.3.1 The House has for many years sought to bring a degree of transparency to the relationship between Members and persons outside the House, particularly if these relationships involve monetary or other material advantage to a Member, in order to ensure that there can be no suspicion of bad faith attaching to Members in the discharge of their parliamentary duties.

4.3.2 In 1858, the House resolved that "It is contrary to the usage and derogatory to the dignity of this House, that any of its Members should bring forward, promote or advocate any proceeding or measure in which he may have acted or been concerned for or in consideration of any pecuniary fee or reward". This rule is interpreted to mean that any Member who is likely to receive *direct* pecuniary benefit from any decision of the House should not participate in any relevant debate or vote on any relevant Question. But this restriction applies only to direct and personal benefits, not to any which might come to a Member as one of a general class of persons.

4.3.3 In 1947 the House resolved "that it is inconsistent with the dignity of the House . . . for any Member . . . to enter into any contractual agreement with an outside body, controlling or limiting the Member's complete independence and freedom of action in Parliament . . ." This resolution was reaffirmed on 6 November 1995 and reinforced to state that "no Member . . . shall, in consideration of any remuneration, fee, payment, reward or benefit in kind, direct or indirect, which the Member or any member of his or her family has received, is receiving or expects to receive – (a) advocate or initiate any cause or matter on behalf of any outside body or individual, or (b) urge any other Member of either House of Parliament, including Ministers, to do so, by means of any speech, Question, Motion, introduction of a Bill or amendment to a Motion or Bill." On 14 May 2002 the words, "or any approach, whether oral or in writing, to Ministers or servants of the Crown" were added. This is generally described as the rule against "paid advocacy". Its interpretation is elucidated in the code of conduct (see below).

The Code of Conduct

4.3.4 It has long been the practice of the House that a Member should make an appropriate public declaration of any interest they might have which might be regarded as potentially influencing their opinion, before participating in any debate to which that interest might be relevant. Since 1974 the House has required Members to register any relevant "interests" in the form of payments, financial relationships, paid employment, gifts or benefits in kind in a register (known as the Register of Members' Interests) which is made publicly available.

4.3.5 A code of conduct for Members, to assist them in applying the rules of the House in respect of these matters, was first adopted in 1996. In May 2002 the House agreed to a revised code of conduct (see Figure 10) in the terms set out in the ninth report from the Committee on Standards and Privileges (House of Commons Paper 763 of Session 2001–02), and also to a guide to the rules relating to the conduct of Members included in that report. A copy of the code and guide is sent to every Member when elected.

4.3.6 The rules and the guide are complex, and any attempt to paraphrase them risks misrepresentation. In particular, the guide sets out details of the kinds of interests which must be registered, the manner in which these interests must be declared in debates and in other kinds of proceedings, the interpretation of the resolution of the House against paid advocacy, and the procedure for making complaints that an alleged breach of these rules has occurred.

The Code of Conduct for Members of Parliament

I. Purpose of the Code

The purpose of the Code of Conduct is to assist Members in the discharge of their obligations to the House, their constituents and the public at large. The Code applies to Members in all aspects of their public life. It does not seek to regulate what Members do in their purely private and personal lives.

II. Public duty

By virtue of the oath, or affirmation, of allegiance taken by all Members when they are elected to the House, Members have a duty to be faithful and bear true allegiance to Her Majesty the Queen, her heirs and successors, according to law.

Members have a duty to uphold the law and to act on all occasions in accordance with the public trust place in them.

Members have a general duty to act in the interests of the nation as a whole; and a special duty to their constituents.

Personal conduct

Members shall observe the general principles of conduct identified by the Committee on Standards in Public Life as applying to holders of public office:–

"Selflessness

Holders of public office should take decisions solely in terms of the public interest. They should not do so in order to gain financial or other material benefits for themselves, their family, or their friends.

Integrity

Holders of public office should not place themselves under any financial or other obligation to outside individuals or organisations that might influence them in the performance of their official duties.

Objectivity

In carrying out public business, including making public appointments, awarding contracts, or recommending individuals for rewards and benefits, holders of public office should make choices on merit.

Accountability

Holders of public office are accountable for their decisions and actions to the public and must submit themselves to whatever scrutiny is appropriate to their office.

Openness

Holders of public office should be as open as possible about all the decisions and actions that they take. They should give reasons for their decisions and restrict information only when the wider public interest clearly demands.

Honesty

Holders of public office have a duty to declare any private interests relating to their public duties and to take steps to resolve any conflicts arising in a way that protects the public interest.

Leadership

Holders of public office should promote and support these principles by leadership and example."

Members shall base their conduct on a consideration of the public interest, avoid conflict between personal interest and the public interest and resolve any conflict between the two, at once, and in favour of the public interest.

Members shall at all times conduct themselves in a manner which will tend to maintain and strengthen the public's trust and confidence in the integrity of Parliament and never undertake any action which would bring the House of Commons, or its Members generally, into disrepute.

The acceptance by a Member of a bribe to influence his or her conduct as a Member, including any fee, compensation or reward in connection with the promotion of, or opposition to, any Bill, Motion, or other matter submitted, or intended to be submitted to the House, or to any Committee of the House, is contrary to the law of Parliament.

Members shall fulfil conscientiously the requirements of the House in respect of the registration of interests in the Register of Members' Interests and shall always draw attention to any relevant interest in any proceeding of the House or its Committees, or in any communications with Ministers, Government Departments or Executive Agencies.

In any activities with, or on behalf of, an organisation with which a Member has a financial relationship, including activities which may not be a matter of public record such as informal meetings and functions, he or she must always bear in mind the need to be open and frank with Ministers, Members and officials.

No Member shall act as a paid advocate in any proceeding of the House.

No improper use shall be made of any payment or allowance made to Members for public purposes and the administrative rules which apply to such payments and allowances must be strictly observed.

Members must bear in mind that information which they receive in confidence in the course of their parliamentary duties should be used only in connection with those duties, and that such information must never be used for the purpose of financial gain.

FIGURE 10
CODE OF CONDUCT FOR MEMBERS OF PARLIAMENT

Written declaration of interests

4.3.7 While the rule on declaring interests has long applied to debates, since 1996 this rule has also applied to what might be termed written proceedings. A Member with a declarable interest is required to indicate this when giving: notices of questions, whether for oral or written answer (see chapter 8); notices of early day motions or of a name added in support of such a motion (see chapter 16); notices of motions for leave to bring in a bill under the ten minute rule or notice of presentation of bills (see section 11.3); notices of amendments to bills or of names added in support of these (see section 11.9); and any other notices of motions, amendments or names added in support of such. Where a Member has made such a declaration, this is indicated on the printed notice by an [R] after his or her name. Anyone who wishes to ascertain what the relevant interest is should normally be able to deduce it from the Member's entry in the **Register of Members' Interests**.

The Parliamentary Commissioner for Standards

4.3.8 To assist Members in complying with the rules of conduct and to maintain the register of interests, S.O. No. 150 provides for an officer of the House to be appointed to be known as the Parliamentary Commissioner for Standards. He is assisted in the task of the maintenance of the register of interests by another officer of the House known as the Registrar of Members' Interests. This term of appointment is fixed by a resolution of the House of 26 June 2003 at five years, and is non-renewable. (The present Commissioner's term of office expires on 25 June 2008.) Paragraph (9) of S.O. No. 150 provides that he can be dismissed only if unfit or unable to carry out his duties.

4.3.9 The standing order also provides for the Commissioner to monitor the operation of the rules and of the register and to make recommendations to the Committee on Standards and Privileges (see section 4.1 above). He is also empowered to receive, and conduct preliminary investigations into, complaints concerning the declarations made in the register or other allegations that Members have broken the rules of House, and to report his findings to the Committee. As a rule, the Committee will subsequently publish these findings as an appendix to any report they make on the matter of the complaint.

4.3.10 The standing order was amended in June 2003 to give the Commissioner discretion to use a "rectification procedure" in cases of minor breaches of the Code of Conduct, without his being required to report the case in full to the Committee on Standards and Privileges. He is, however, required to report to the Committee that he has used the procedure.

4.3.11 The standing order was also amended to provide for the appointment of investigatory panels to assist the Commissioner to help him establish the facts in serious cases of alleged breaches of the Code of Conduct, when asked by the Committee to do so, or exceptionally on his own initiative. These panels comprise the Commissioner as chairman, a "legally qualified person", and a Member of the House who is not a member of the Committee appointed by the Speaker. The standing order provides for the Panel to appoint counsel, and requires it to give an opportunity to the Member being investigated to appear before the Panel and to cross-examine witnesses. The Commissioner determines the procedure of the Panel, and the lay assessor is required to report at the conclusion of the investigation on whether its proceedings have been consistent with the "principles of natural justice". The Member on the Panel has the discretion to make a report about the conduct of the Panel (in respect of the customs and traditions of the House) as well.

4.3.12 The amendments made to the standing order in June 2003 also include a requirement on the Commissioner to make an annual report to the House on his work.

Chapter 5

PARLIAMENTS AND SESSIONS

5.1 PARLIAMENTS

Dissolution

5.1.1 A general election is initiated by the issuing of a **proclamation** dissolving a Parliament and summoning a new one. This power is a prerogative of the Crown. In other words, its exercise is a decision of the Prime Minister. The decision to seek a dissolution before the end of the period defined in the Septennial Act (see next paragraph) is, therefore, at the sole discretion of the government of the day. However, constitutional convention requires that where a government fails to obtain the endorsement of a majority of the House of Commons on a vote of confidence, the Prime Minister must tender the resignation of his or her government to the sovereign promptly thereafter and, other than in very exceptional circumstances, would advise the Crown to dissolve parliament and thereby initiate a **general election**.

5.1.2 Under the Septennial Act (so called because, until amended by the Parliament Act 1911, it fixed the maximum length of a Parliament at seven years), five years is the maximum period that may elapse between the date at which a Parliament was summoned to assemble after a general election and its dissolution to allow the next general election to take place. (The duration of Parliament was extended by Act of Parliament beyond this limit during the First and Second World Wars, but see paragraph 11.17.5).

5.1.3 A dissolution may be announced when the House is adjourned for a period. On other occasions, Parliament has been prorogued, and the proclamation effecting the dissolution issued while the prorogation was in effect. Sometimes, when an intention to seek a dissolution has been announced by the Prime Minister, a negotiated period follows during which necessary legislative business may be completed with the consent of the opposition parties.

The New Parliament

5.1.4 The main features distinguishing the opening of a new Parliament from the opening of a normal annual session are the election of the Speaker and the swearing of new Members.

5.1.5 After a **general election**, on the day specified in the proclamation which dissolved the previous parliament and summoned the new one, the House assembles and goes up to the Lords, where they are directed on behalf of the Queen to return and elect a Speaker, which they then do in accordance with the procedure set out in paragraphs 3.1.7 to 3.1.14. On the following day, when the House returns from the Lords where the Queen's approbation of the Speaker Elect has been signified, the Speaker takes the **Oath**, followed by other Members (see next paragraph). Each Member takes the oath or affirms at the government **despatch box** (see S.O. No. 5), then signs the **Test Roll** and is introduced to the Speaker by the **Clerk of the House**.

Swearing-in days

5.1.6 After the Speaker, other Members take the oath or affirm. Members are invited to swear or affirm in the order: Cabinet Ministers, official opposition **front benchers**, other **Privy Counsellors**, then other Members in order of seniority of continuous service in the House. When the Speaker and other Members who wish to take the oath on the day after the Speaker's election have done so, the Speaker adjourns the House to the next sitting day at which further Members may attend to take the oath or affirm. Usually, some three or four sitting days in all are set aside for swearing in, although Members may take the oath or affirm on any subsequent normal sitting day (see S.O. No. 6). Except during the election of the Speaker, no Member who has not taken the oath or affirmed may sit or speak in the Chamber, or vote in any division. Nor will he or she be paid any salary. However, since a resolution of the House of January 2002, Members who have been duly elected, but have not taken the oath, may have use of the facilities of Westminster, and may receive the **office costs allowance** (though not their salary).

5.1.7 At the end of the last day set aside for swearing of Members, the House adjourns to the day which has been fixed for the **Queen's Speech** (see paragraph 5.2.5). On that day, the motion appointing the **Chairman of Ways and Means** and the **Deputy Chairmen** (see paragraphs 3.2.1 to 3.2.5) is passed, as well as the usual sessional orders (see paragraph 5.2.6). From then on the session proceeds as for a normal session, as described in the next section.

5.2 SESSIONS

Prorogation

5.2.1 Each Parliament (the period between two general elections) is divided into a number of sessions. The end of a session is marked by a prorogation (or a dissolution if it is the last session of a Parliament). The beginning of a new session is marked by the **State Opening** and the **Queen's Speech**. The prorogation of Parliament (like its dissolution) is a prerogative act of the Crown. In other words, the length of a parliamentary session is determined by the government of the day, although this freedom is to an extent circumscribed by constitutional convention. A normal session runs from early November of one year to late October of the next. The pattern of a normal session is shown in Figure 8. Following a general election, the first session of a Parliament will usually continue to the October/November of the year following, and may thus be substantially longer than a year.

5.2.2 Because during a prorogation all parliamentary business is suspended, (so no questions or motions can be tabled and no committees may sit) its duration is generally kept to a minimum. In a normal year, after its return for a short period in October, Parliament will be prorogued, and the **State Opening** will take place in the following week.

5.2.3 On a day on which Parliament is to be prorogued, the Commons usually arranges to meet in the morning. When the House has assembled, it is summoned to the House of Lords, and Members process there behind the

Speaker. The Members of the Commons stand at the Bar of the Lords and listen to the **Lords Commissioners** read out the Queen's Speech and the proclamation proroguing Parliament and naming the day for its reassembly. This is usually preceded by the signifying of the **royal assent** by the Commissioners to the last few Acts of that session agreed to by the two Houses. The Commons then return to their House where the Speaker (sitting at the **Table**) reports the royal assents and the terms of the prorogation, and directs the Queen's Speech to be printed in the **Votes and Proceedings**. Parliament then stands prorogued to the day named.

5.2.4 The effect of prorogation is (as it is usually described) to "clear the decks". Motions (including **early day motions**) lapse, questions which have not been answered fall, and any sessional order of the House (for example altering standing orders, appointing certain committees, naming certain days for various types of business to be transacted, etc.) ceases to have effect. In current practice, and most significantly for the way in which Parliament operates, any bill which has failed to obtain the royal assent by the end of the session in which it is introduced "dies", and has to start again from scratch if it is reintroduced in the next session. The House agreed, however, on 29 October 2002, to a temporary standing order (in force to the end of the current Parliament) providing for a mechanism for Bills to be "carried over" from one session to the next. A fuller description is given in section 11.18.

Opening of a Session: the Queen's Speech

5.2.5 A few days after prorogation, on the day named in the proclamation, the Commons reassembles, usually at 11.30 am. Shortly thereafter, the House is summoned by **Black Rod** to the House of Lords to hear the **Queen's Speech**. Members process behind the Speaker to the Lords, starting with the front benches on either side. The Members stand in the area below the Bar of the House of Lords and listen to the Queen deliver her speech (which is immediately published and made available in the **Vote Office**). The Commons then return to their Chamber where the **Mace** is placed on the **Table** to indicate the House is in session. The sitting is then suspended till 2.30 pm.

Opening of a Session: the Sessional Orders

5.2.6 On its return at 2.30 pm, the House's first business is to pass a series of orders known as the sessional orders. These are of traditional form and relate to such matters as the protection of witnesses, the publication of the **Votes and Proceedings** and **Journals** of the House, and the placing on the Commissioner of the Metropolitan Police of a duty to maintain unimpeded access to Westminster for Members. Before the sessional orders are disposed of, a bill (by long standing tradition the **Outlawries Bill**) is presented *proforma*, to symbolise the House's assertion of its right to legislate on matters not included in the Queen's Speech.

Opening of a Session: Debate on the Queen's Speech

5.2.7 Because of the minimum two-day period of notice for oral questions specified in S.O. No. 22, no question time takes place on the first three sitting days of a new Session. After the **sessional orders** (see above) have been made, the

Speaker reports (but does not read) the Queen's Speech to the House. The **Loyal Address** in response to the Queen's Speech, which takes a set form thanking the Sovereign for her speech, is then moved. By tradition, this motion is moved and seconded (the only occasion when the notion of a **seconder** applies in the House) by two **back benchers** on the government side. The **leader of the opposition** then makes a response, followed by the Prime Minister and the leader of the third party.

5.2.8 The debate on the Queen's Speech (more formally known as the debate on the Loyal Address) continues for a further four or five days. The subject matter for the debate on each of these days is indicated informally, eg "foreign affairs", "trade and industry", "the economy", etc. The Ministers and front benchers who open and close debate on these days will be those with responsibilities relating to the declared theme for that day. However, virtually any subject within the competence of government is in order in the debate on the Queen's Speech, except on the final two days of the debate, when the scope of debate may, at least in theory, be limited by the terms of the opposition amendments customarily moved on those days (see next paragraph).

5.2.9 On the penultimate day of the debate on the Queen's Speech, an amendment to the Loyal Address in the name of the **leader of the opposition** is usually debated, and voted upon at the end of that day's sitting. On the final day, a further amendment in the name of the leader of the opposition will usually be called and voted on at the end of the debate. S.O. No. 33 provides that when that amendment has been disposed of, a further amendment may be moved and voted upon **forthwith**. This is always used to give an opportunity for the leader of the third largest party to move an amendment. After the amendments have been disposed of, the Loyal Address itself will be voted on. (Convention has in the past suggested that it is inappropriate to vote against this formal motion of thanks to the Sovereign, but this convention seems to have decayed.)

Pattern of a Session: terms and vacations

5.2.10 The House generally follows a regular pattern of sittings over the course of a session. On 29 October 2002, it agreed in principle to the introduction of a "fixed" parliamentary calendar, and to the introduction of sittings in September. The calendar for the 2002-03 session was accordingly announced in advance, though it was subsequently adjusted in the light of a delay in the introduction of the Budget. In procedural terms, the House fixes its vacation periods by agreeing to a motion that on its rising on a named day, it will adjourn till a day other than that which would normally be fixed by the standing or sessional orders. Under S.O. No. 25 these motions are not debatable. They are generally agreed about a fortnight in advance of the proposed break.

5.2.11 In a normal session the House rises in the week before Christmas until the week after New Year. It adjourns for a "constituency week" around the time of school half-term in mid-February. The House rises again for between one and two weeks around the Easter weekend and again for a similar period around the weekend of the Spring Bank Holiday in late May (and it does not sit on the Bank Holiday Monday in early May). In current practice, at some date in mid-

July it rises until mid-September, when it resumes sitting for a further two weeks or so. It then adjourns again until mid-October for the "conference recess" (during which the main party conferences are scheduled), when it resumes for a period (colloquially known as the "spill-over") of around one to three weeks, before being prorogued (see paragraph 5.2.1 above).

5.2.12 These periods when the House is not sitting are properly known as "holiday" or "periodic adjournments", though nowadays they are generally referred to as a **recess**, a term which strictly speaking applies only to a period when the House is prorogued.

5.2.13 **Select committees** are almost all given the power, either under standing orders or their order of appointment, to meet "notwithstanding any adjournment of the House". This means that they may meet on days when the House is not sitting. Under S.O. No. 88(3), **standing committees** may also now meet on days when the House is not sitting. No committees may meet during a prorogation or, of course, a dissolution.

Urgent recall of the House

5.2.14 When the House is in recess and the government wants it to be recalled for some urgent purpose, or when an emergency occurs which demands a meeting at a weekend or some other non-sitting day, S.O. No. 13 gives the Speaker (or, in his absence, one of the Deputy Speakers) power to summon a meeting of the House if requested to do so by a Minister.

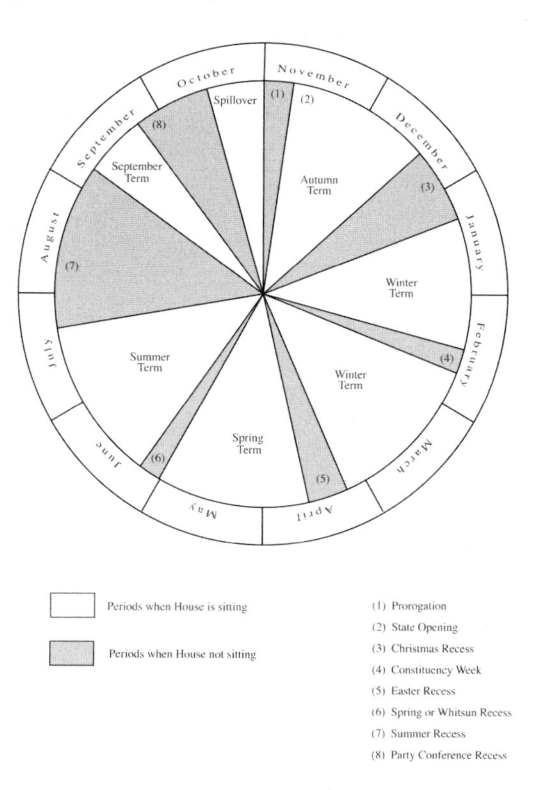

FIGURE 11
PATTERN OF SESSIONS

Chapter 6

SITTINGS OF THE HOUSE AND ITS COMMITTEES

6.1 SITTINGS OF THE HOUSE

Introduction

6.1.1 The government determines the length of Parliaments and sessions and the House decides its own vacations (see chapter 5). The pattern of the sitting week and the length of each sitting day is largely determined by the standing orders, although the government can, and often does, temporarily vary these to make additional time available for its business. Each sitting begins with prayers, and ends with a half-hour adjournment debate. The normal time at which the main business of the day ends and the daily adjournment debate begins (which is frequently overridden by one device or another) is fixed by the standing orders, and is known as the "moment of interruption".

The sitting week

6.1.2 Taken together, S.O. Nos. 9, 10 and 11 fix the pattern of the sitting week. Although S.O. No. 9 still states that "on Mondays, Tuesdays and Wednesdays the House will meet at half-past two o'clock . . .", on 29 October 2002 the House agreed to temporary amendments to the standing orders (to have effect until the end of the current Parliament) which vary these and other provisions relating to the timing of events which occur during a sitting.

6.1.3 These temporary provisions have effect to set the regular meeting times of the House at 11.30 am on Tuesdays and Wednesdays with the moment of interruption at 7 pm, and at 11.30 am on Thursdays with the moment of interruption at 6 pm. On occasions when the House returns from one of its periodic adjournments (see paragraphs 5.2.10 to 5.2.12) on a Tuesday or a Wednesday, the timings for that day are nonetheless as if it were a Monday.

Friday sittings

6.1.4 Fridays have always had a distinct flavour, which distinguishes them from other days of the week. The House not only meets earlier (at 9.30 am), but also rises sooner (around 3 pm). There is no question time on Fridays, and no provision for taking most of the miscellaneous items of business that occur at the commencement of public business on other days. Urgent questions (see paragraph 7.5.6) and statements (see paragraph 7.6.4) take place at 11 am on a Friday. On 29 October 2002 the House agreed that, until the end of the current Parliament, it would sit only on Fridays on which private Members' bills were to have precedence – which is fixed by paragraph (4) of S.O. No. 14 at thirteen in each session (see paragraph 7.2.4).

Non-sitting Fridays

6.1.5 Despite this, S.O. No. 12 still provides that the House should not sit only on ten Fridays in each session. Under the current arrangements, the provisions of this standing order apply to all Fridays in sitting weeks except those thirteen on which private Members' bills are debated. In any week other than one in which such a Friday has been fixed, the House automatically adjourns on Thursday to the following Monday (unless that falls during a holiday adjournment). The standing order provides for parliamentary questions and amendments to bills to be tabled on these days (between 11 am and 3 pm). It does not provide for the tabling of motions (including early day motions) or amendments to motions, except (under the temporary provisions) notices of motions relating to bills which have been committed to a standing committee.

The sitting day: the moment of interruption

6.1.6 S.O. No. 9(3) provides that debate shall be automatically interrupted at a fixed time if it has not previously been concluded. This is the so-called **moment of interruption**. On Mondays this is 10 pm. Under the current provisions this is now amended to 7 pm on Tuesdays and Wednesdays, and on Thursdays to 6 pm. On Fridays, under S.O. No. 11(2), the moment of interruption is at 2.30 pm.

6.1.7 The operation of the moment of interruption automatically ends debate and so prevents a sitting being indefinitely prolonged. It thus enables opponents of a proposal before the House to "talk out" a debate and prevent a decision being taken. After the moment of interruption, any business which is *opposed* (that is if there is any attempt to continue the debate or there is a call of "object" when a Member attempts to move a Question) cannot be proceeded with. Only the government may move a motion under S.O. No. 15(2) to suspend, either indefinitely or for a specified period, the effect of the moment of interruption. Exceptions to the rule against opposed business being taken after the moment of interruption are described below in sections 7.10 to 7.12. By limiting the length of any one sitting, and by allowing only the government to lift that limitation, the standing orders restrict the time available to private Members and the opposition parties and reinforce the government's control over the time available to debate business and reach decisions on the floor of the House.

6.1.8 There may be occasions when the Chair suspends a sitting until a specified time, even though a debate has come to its natural conclusion. This may occur for example on **Estimates days**, when the standing orders prevent a decision being taken on the Estimates before the House the moment of interruption (see paragraph 10.3.11) or when opposed private business (see paragraphs 2.2.5 and 7.9.2) has been set down by the Chairman of Ways & Means for 7 pm, 4 pm or 3 pm, and often occurs at sittings in **Westminster Hall** when one of the timetabled debates has ended before the next one is due to begin.

6.1.9 After the moment of interruption on each day, S.O. No. 9(7) provides for the half-hour **daily adjournment** debate (see section 7.12). At its rising each day the House automatically stands adjourned to the next weekday, unless that is a non-sitting Friday (see paragraph 6.1.5 above) or it falls during one of its holiday adjournments (see paragraph 5.2.10).

6.2 SITTINGS OF COMMITTEES

Sittings of standing committees

6.2.1 Since the beginning of the 2002-03 session, standing committees (see paragraphs 2.3.2 and 2.3.3) may, under S.O. No. 88(3), meet on any day, whether or not it is one on which the House is due to meet. However, no standing committee has yet taken advantage of this new freedom. Nowadays, the proceedings in standing committees on government bills will almost always be governed by a programme order and resolution of a Programming Committee (see section 11.18). Otherwise, under S.O. No. 88(1), the first meeting of a standing committee to consider a bill or some other matter is on a day and at a time fixed by the chairman (except in the case of the grand committees, for which see paragraph 14.2.3). In practice, the chairman will summon the committee at the time requested by the **Member in charge** (who for all government bills will be a Minister), so long as his or her proposal is not grossly unconventional or impracticable. In the case of a bill committee, the first sitting will normally be about a week after a bill has received its second reading. A standing committee may only sit once on its first day of meeting to consider a particular bill, unless a previous order has been made by the House lifting this restriction (which, in the case of a government bill, is likely to have been done as part of a programming order).

6.2.2 Standing committees on government bills (see section 11.10) generally meet on Tuesdays and Thursdays, while Standing Committee C (see paragraph 11.10.8) generally meets on Wednesdays to consider private Members' bills. In current practice, under which the vast majority of government bills are subject to a **programme order** (see section 11.18), the pattern of sittings, both morning and afternoon, will have been fixed by a resolution of the programming committee. In the currently rare cases where their proceedings are not governed by a programming order, standing committees on bills which expect to require more than one sitting for their work fix their timetable by agreeing a "sittings motion" (see paragraphs 11.10.13 to 11.10.15). The European standing committees (see paragraphs 13.2.10 to 13.2.17) also generally meet on Wednesday mornings. These are not, however, hard and fast conventions, and are varied. Delegated legislation committees (see paragraphs 12.3.23 to 12.3.30) meet at various times of the week.

6.2.3 Standing committees do not meet on Monday mornings or on Fridays except in very rare circumstances. On other days, the committees generally meet in the mornings at either 8.55 am (for bill committees and European Standing Committees) or occasionally 9.55 am (for delegated legislation committees). Under S.O. No. 88(1), on days when the House is to meet at 2.30 pm the standing order provides that the chairman must adjourn the committee at 1 pm. Under the standing order as altered by the temporary standing orders until the end of the current Parliament, on days when the House is to meet at 11.30 am, the equivalent time is 11.25 am. The standing order forbids standing committees from sitting between 1 pm and 3.30 pm on days when the House meets at 2.30 pm or (under the temporary provisions) between 11.25 am and 2 pm on days when it meets at 11.30 am. Afternoon sittings can begin at various times, but 2.30 is the normal time.

Adjournments of standing committees

6.2.4 Under S.O. No. 88, as altered by the temporary standing orders until the end of the current Parliament, the chairman interrupts debate at 11.25 am (or 1 pm) and adjourns the committee without putting any Question. The committee then stands adjourned until the day and time fixed by any sittings motion or resolution of the programming committee or sub-committee (which may be that afternoon or a subsequent day). In exceptional circumstances the standing order allows the chairman to extend the sitting for fifteen minutes if, at that time, he believes that the committee is likely to conclude its consideration of the *whole* bill before it within that time, or if, in the case of the standing committees on delegated legislation (see paragraphs 12.3.23 to 12.3.30) or European standing committees (see paragraphs 13.2.10 to 13.2.17), the time limit set for debate would expire within that fifteen minutes. If the **Member in charge** of a bill wishes a committee to adjourn before 1 pm (or 11.25 am), he or she must move the appropriate motion to enable it to do so.

6.2.5 Under S.O. No. 88, a committee meeting in the afternoon could in theory continue to sit until 1 pm (or 11.25 am) the following day unless it agreed to adjourn before then. However, in current practice, the termination of the sitting will generally have been fixed by the programming committee or sub-committee. In other circumstances, the chairman will generally only accept a motion to adjourn from the **Member in charge** (which in the case of a government bill means the Minister or the government **Whip**, or the Member in charge of a private Member's bill). This can be moved at any time when the Member in charge is called by the Chair. If it is moved immediately after some Question has just been disposed of, it takes the form "That further consideration of the bill be now adjourned"; if moved during debate on a Question it takes the form "That the debate be now adjourned". Although debatable, such motions are usually agreed without debate. After it has been agreed, the Whip or Member in charge may, if it is necessary for the convenience of the committee, move a second motion to fix a time to resume consideration of the bill which may differ from that specified in a sittings motion previously agreed. Otherwise, after the motion to adjourn has been agreed, the committee stands adjourned to the day and time fixed by a sittings motion or determined by the chairman.

6.2.6 Afternoon sittings which begin at 2.30 pm are often scheduled to end without the need for an adjournment motion at 5 pm, under the programme order. In the nowadays rare circumstances of the Member in charge not having moved the adjournment of an afternoon sitting by about 7 to 7.30 pm, the Chairman would normally suspend the committee for a period of around an hour and a half for a dinner break. If, after the committee resumes around 8.30 to 9 pm, it continues to sit beyond about 10.30 pm, the Chairman will periodically suspend the sitting for a break of perhaps half an hour to allow Members to refresh themselves. While, in theory, the sitting may continue throughout the night, even after the House itself has adjourned, late sittings of standing committees are much rarer in these days of programming than they once were.

Sittings of standing committees away from Westminster

6.2.7 With the exceptions of the grand committees (see sections 14.3, 14.4 and 14.5) and Special Standing Committees on Scottish bills (see paragraph 11.11.8, but which are unlikely in post-devolution circumstances), standing committees may meet only at Westminster, unless given permission or required to do otherwise by a specific order or instruction of the House.

Meetings of select committees

6.2.8 Most **select committees** (see paragraphs 2.3.4 to 2.3.10 and chapter 17) are given the power under their order of appointment or the standing order under which they are established to "sit notwithstanding any adjournment of the House". This exempts them from the restrictions of S.O. No. 123 which would otherwise prevent them from meeting on days when the House is not sitting. Select committees generally exercise this freedom sparingly.

6.2.9 Select committees decide their own times of meeting but there is none of the paraphernalia of time limits, sittings motions, programmes and adjournment motions that apply to sittings of standing committees. As with their other proceedings, they generally agree their timetable informally, or leave it to the discretion of their chairman. The most popular days of the week for meetings of select committees are Tuesdays and Wednesdays.

6.2.10 Most select committees are also given the power to "adjourn from place to place". This permits them to hold their meetings in any place of their choosing, including away from Westminster. It also permits them to travel in an official capacity, even if they do not hold formal meetings. In a few cases this freedom is restricted to travel within the UK. Most select committees with this power exercise it from time to time (see paragraph 17.2.10).

6.3 Sittings in Westminster Hall

6.3.1 Following an experimental period from the beginning of the 1999–2000 session to the end of the 2001–02 session, the House has now agreed to a permanent standing order (S.O. No. 10) providing for sittings of a "parallel Chamber", known as "the House sitting in Westminster Hall". These sittings, which can only commence in each session after the debate on the **Queen's Speech** has concluded (see paragraphs 5.2.7 to 5.2.9), are held in the Grand Committee Room off Westminster Hall (see Figure 1). An essential element of the character of this parallel Chamber is that it debates relatively uncontentious business which might otherwise not be found time for on the floor of the House. No divisions can be take place at sittings in Westminster Hall. The consensual nature of the business to be taken in the parallel Chamber is emphasised by its layout – which is a version of the hemicycle arrangement favoured by many other parliaments (see Figure 13).

6.3.2 Under S.O. No. 10, the sittings in Westminster Hall take place on three fixed periods each sitting week (see Figure 12). While the current arrangements for the House to meet in the mornings on Tuesdays and Wednesdays continue, these are: on Tuesdays and Wednesdays between 9.30 am and 11.30 am and (following a suspension of the sitting) for a further two and a half hours from 2 pm; and on Thursdays for three hours starting at 2.30 pm. The afternoon sittings on Tuesdays and Wednesdays, and the Thursday sittings, must be extended to allow for time taken out of the allocation by suspensions to allow Members to vote in divisions in the House.

First day back after Recess	Tuesday and Wednesday	Thursday
Private Members' Adjournment Debates	Private Members' Adjournment Debates	
9.30 am to 11 am	9.30 am to 11 am	
11 am to 12.30 pm	11 am to 11.30 am	
12.30 pm to 1 pm	*Sitting suspended from 11.30 am to 2 pm*	
1 pm to 1.30 pm		
1.30 pm to 2 pm		
	2 pm to 3.30 pm*	2.30 pm to 5.30 pm*
	3.30 pm to 4 pm*	Once a month: oral questions for first hour*
	4 pm to 4.30 pm*	Single adjournment debate on either a topic chosen by the Government or on a select committee report chosen by the Liaison Committee

*Finishing time may be extended to take account of time taken for divisions in the House

FIGURE 12

PATTERN OF SITTINGS IN WESTMINSTER HALL

6.3.3 The Tuesday and Wednesday sittings are currently allocated to private Members' debates on an adjournment motion, divided up into timed slots. These are currently a one-and-a half hour debate at the start of the morning and afternoon sittings followed by one (in the morning) or two (in the afternoon) half-hour debates. The slots are awarded to Members by ballot, which is organised by the Speaker's Office and held each preceding Wednesday. For the half-hour debates, the same rules apply broadly as apply to the daily adjournment in the House (see paragraph 7.12.1). In the longer debates, other Members than the one who has initiated the debate may participate, in addition to the Minister who responds. All these "slots" are, as it were, the property of the Member selected by the ballot to have the right to initiate debate and choose the subject. If they are not present to open a debate, another Member cannot do so on their behalf. If a debate comes to a natural conclusion before the time fixed for the next one to begin, the Chair suspends the sitting to that time. There is a rota for the government departments which will respond to debates on these days, so that each Department is "on duty" only on alternate weeks. This rota is published in the Order Paper. Members must therefore enter a subject in each week's ballot which is relevant to one of the duty departments for the following week.

6.3.4 The Thursday afternoon sittings normally consist of single debates, and these are divided between those at which select committee reports chosen by the Liaison Committee (see section 3.5) are debated and those at which debates take place on other matters proposed by the government (for example Green

Papers) for which time is not normally found in the House. Paragraph (13) of the standing order provides that the Speaker shall appoint no more than six Thursday sittings in each session for debates on select committee reports. In practice, so far, the **usual channels** have volunteered far more than this minimum amount, and so the Speaker has not had to formally exercise this power.

6.3.5 Paragraph (3) of the standing order allows for the Chairman of Ways and Means to make arrangements for oral question times to be held in Westminster Hall. Currently, about once a month this provision is used to hold a "cross-cutting" question time for the first hour of a Thursday sitting. A subject which engages the responsibilities of a number of government departments is announced, and junior Ministers from the relevant departments will all be present at the sitting in Westminster Hall to respond to questions. (Examples of such topics might be "children and young people" or "illegal drugs".) The Chairman of Ways and Means makes arrangements for the tabling of questions in advance by Members, which is done in much the same way as for normal oral questions (see chapter 8). The difference is that the questions are not (unlike in the main Chamber) addressed to a specific Minister. They are printed on the Order Paper for the appropriate sitting in Westminster Hall, and the proceedings follow a similar pattern as question time in the main Chamber, except that different Ministers from different departments may offer replies to questions and supplementaries. After the time fixed by the Chairman of Ways and means has passed, the question time is terminated and a debate (which will probably be on an entirely unrelated topic) takes place for the remaining two hours of the sitting.

6.3.6 Paragraph (7) of the standing order provides a mechanism whereby a Minister may move a motion in the House for an order of the day to be taken at a sitting in Westminster Hall. The Question on such a motion is put **forthwith**, but it may only be moved with the **leave** of the House. In effect, this means it can only be passed with unanimous consent. Such a motion cannot be moved on a Friday. This would enable the main Chamber to agree that, for example, a stage of a bill, or proceedings on delegated legislation, could be debated in Westminster Hall. So far this provision has not been used.

6.3.7 No formal decisions can be taken at sittings in Westminster Hall unless by unanimous consent. Paragraph (6) of the standing order provides that were a substantive decision on any matter agreed at a sitting in Westminster Hall, this would become a decision of the whole House immediately on its being reported by the Chair of that sitting. Paragraph (9) of the standing order provides that, where there was any objection to the decision, rather than a decision being taken there and then, the matter would be reported to the House, where a Question could be put for decision on the same Question without further debate. Paragraph (10) of the standing order provides that if six Members were to rise in their places to object to any further proceedings on any Question (except an adjournment motion) at a sitting in Westminster Hall, the debate would be automatically adjourned and the Question referred back to the House. Taken together, these provisions would essentially allow sittings in Westminster Hall to debate and decide on any kind of business, so long as that business was in effect wholly unopposed. So far, however, no substantive business on which a decision could be taken has been referred to a sitting in Westminster Hall.

6.3.8 The principal presiding officer in Westminster Hall is the **Chairman of Ways and Means**. He is assisted by the **Deputy Chairmen** and four senior members of the Chairmen's Panel who are appointed on a sessional basis as additional Deputy Speakers for sittings in Westminster Hall (see section 3.2). These Members are addressed at such sittings as Mr/Madam Deputy Speaker. Any member of the Chairmen's Panel may be asked by the Chairman of Ways and Means to take the chair at sittings in Westminster Hall, and on such occasions are addressed by name. The power of selection under S.O. No. 32 (see paragraphs 9.2.6 to 9.2.10) would apply, if any business other than adjournment debates were to be taken at a sitting in Westminster Hall. The disciplinary powers of the Chair, described in paragraphs 9.3.23 to 9.3.33, do not apply to sittings in Westminster Hall, though the power to order a Member to discontinue his or her speech if guilty of irrelevance or tedious repetition does (see paragraph 9.3.14), as do the provisions of S.O. No. 47 on short speeches (see paragraph 9.7.3), though a decision to set time limits would have to be made by the Chairman of Ways and Means before the start of a sitting, if it was to be enforced by the Deputy Speakers. The general conventions of debate (described in paragraphs 9.3.1 to 9.3.22) also apply, including the general prohibition on speaking more than once to a Question (see paragraph 9.3.4). Since these are sittings of the House, though taking place in another place than the Chamber, all Members of the House are of course able to participate in these proceedings. The quorum necessary for a sitting in Westminster Hall to continue is three.

6.3.9 The business set down for future sittings in Westminster Hall is listed in section B of the future business section of the **Order Paper** each day (see paragraph 15.1.16). It indicates the topics to be raised, and the Members initiating debate, for each of the timed adjournment debate slots on Tuesdays and Wednesdays, as well as the business for Thursdays. The proceedings in Westminster Hall are reported in the appropriate daily edition of **Hansard** (including written answers to unreached oral questions), and a formal minute of any proceedings are appended to the daily **Votes and Proceedings**.

6.4 Broadcasting

6.4.1 There is continuous recording and a live feed of the proceedings of the Chamber, and broadcasting companies are allowed to make live transmissions or use recorded extracts largely at their own discretion. Sittings in Westminster Hall (see section 6.3 above) are also recorded, at the discretion of the broadcasters.

6.4.2 Sittings of standing committees, and select committees when meeting in public, may also be recorded and transmitted either for video or audio transmission, but there are only limited facilities to do so. It is, by and large, for the company appointed to provide such services to decide whether and which committees to record for television or sound broadcasting. The Committee on Standards and Privileges, however, uniquely has the power to refuse to allow its public meetings to be broadcast (see paragraph 4.1.3).

6.4.3 The ground rules covering use of broadcast proceedings are framed and monitored by the Broadcasting Committee (see paragraph 18.1.8), with the day to day supervision of the service under the **Supervisor of Broadcasting** (see paragraph 18.2.8).

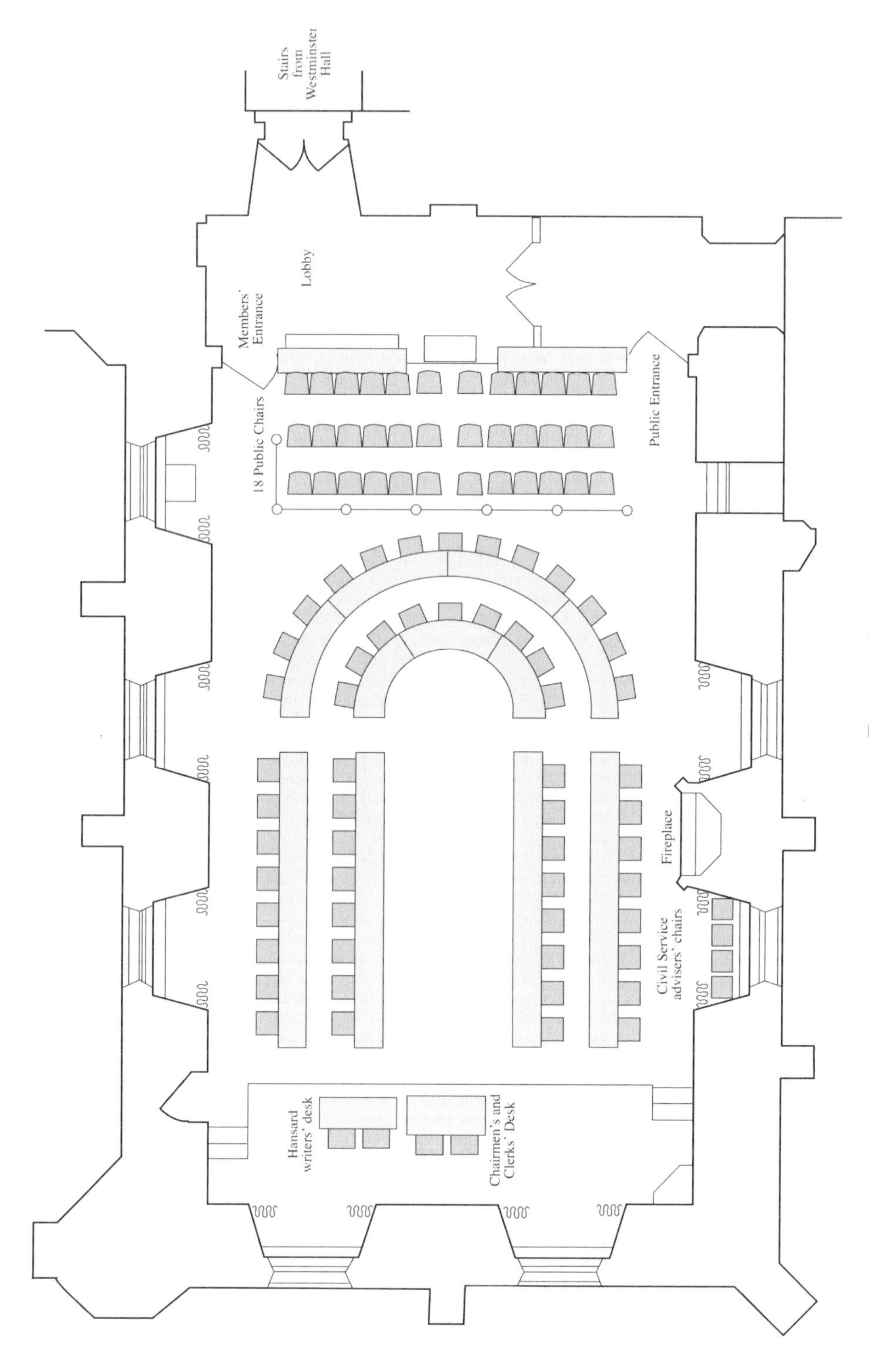

FIGURE 13
"WESTMINSTER HALL"

Chapter 7

THE SITTING DAY

INTRODUCTION

7.1.1 This chapter describes the types of business that the House may consider at each of its sittings, and the order in which they are taken. The arrangements for sittings in Westminster Hall are described in section 6.3. Figure 14 shows the general pattern of sittings on each day of the week. Figure 15 details the order of all the items of business which may occur in a sitting day. Most of the types of business listed in Figure 15 will occur only irregularly and some very infrequently. Some require **notice** (that is will appear in terms on the Order Paper). Other items may occur apparently unannounced, though in most cases the House will be expecting them (urgent questions and statements are, for example, advertised on the **annunciator**). An explanation of the **Order Paper** as a guide to the day's sitting is given in paragraphs 15.1.6 to 15.1.14. The descriptions below apply to the proceedings of the House on Mondays to Thursdays except where indicated. The particular arrangements for Friday sittings (see paragraph 6.1.4) are described where relevant.

7.2 PRELIMINARY PROCEEDINGS

Prayers, etc.

7.2.1 The Speaker leaves his office about five minutes before each sitting is due to begin and processes via the **Central Lobby** to the Chamber, preceded by the **Serjeant at Arms** carrying the **Mace**, which he installs in its place on the **Table**, between the **despatch boxes**, to show that the House is in session. The division bells are rung once when the Speaker is in the Chair to indicate the start of the sitting. **Prayers** begin each sitting. During prayers, only Members of the House, the Serjeant at Arms and the **Speaker's Chaplain** are admitted to the Chamber. Under S.O. No. 8, a Member present for prayers may reserve his or her seat for the remainder of the sitting (which is done by placing a card in the slot on the bench provided for this purpose). At the end of prayers, the division bells are rung again, and the Clerks and others are admitted to those parts of the Chamber where they are allowed, and the general public, officials, the press and others are admitted to the public and other galleries (see paragraphs 1.1.6 and 1.1.7). Immediately after prayers there may occasionally be the ceremonial presentation (by one of the **Whips**) of the Queen's answer to an Address.This could be followed by formal communications from the Speaker, but these are rare events. It is also at this time that the Speaker may make the formal announcement of the death of a Member.

Motions for new Writs

7.2.2 When a seat has been vacated because of the death or **disqualification** of a Member, the process of initiating a by-election to fill the vacancy is done by a motion requiring the Speaker to issue a **writ** for the election of a new Member. The motion is traditionally moved by the **Chief Whip** of the party of the Member who held the seat, although any Member may move it. The mover must inform the Speaker's Office in advance of his or her intention. These motions are generally carried without debate, but if a Member does rise to oppose such a motion, the Speaker will order the debate to be held over until after question time and any urgent questions or statements. Under S.O. No. 19, if such a motion is proposed on a Friday on which private Members' bills have precedence and is opposed, the proceedings on it immediately lapse, and it has to be moved again on another day.

7.2.3 Motions for new writs are moved at this time because the filling of a vacancy in the House's membership is considered to be a matter of **privilege**. The usual time for taking other matters of **privilege** is after questions and statements, etc.

7.2.4 There is no rule requiring a vacancy to be filled in a specified time, but the agreed convention is that the writ should be moved within three months of the vacancy arising. Broadly speaking, a **by-election** takes place on the third Thursday after the motion to issue the writ has been agreed.

7.3 PRIVATE BUSINESS

Unopposed Private Business

7.3.1 On Mondays to Thursdays, after any of the above types of business have been concluded, the House may consider any private business which has been put on the Order Paper by the **Chairman of Ways and Means** (see paragraph 15.1.7). As well as private bills at various stages of their consideration, there may be motions contingent upon such bills (for example, to carry over a bill from one session to the next). A brief description of the process of private legislation is given at section 11.19. Although unopposed private business can in theory be taken on Fridays, in practice the **Chairman of Ways and Means** never sets it down for a Friday.

7.3.2 No items of business in this category can be proceeded with at this time if they are opposed. Such opposition is indicated either by a call of "object" from a Member when the item is reached or, in certain cases, by the presence on the Order Paper of certain types of notices of motion in respect of whatever stage a bill is at (see paragraph 7.9.2 below).

Committee of Selection

7.3.3 Because they are technically private business, motions relating to the membership of the **Committee of Selection** (see section 2.4) are also taken at this time.

7.4 MOTIONS FOR UNOPPOSED RETURNS

7.4.1 At this point (or, on Fridays, after presentation of public petitions) a motion for an unopposed **Return** may be made. Notice of such a motion will appear on the **Order Paper**. It is an instruction by the House to the government to lay before the House a document which the government is willing to produce (indeed, the motion will normally stand in the name of the Minister in charge of the relevant department). The modern purpose of ordering a Return is often to provide the full protection of parliamentary privilege (see paragraph 4.2.4) to the document so ordered (for example, the report of some board or tribunal of inquiry set up by the government). As their name suggests, such motions are not debatable.

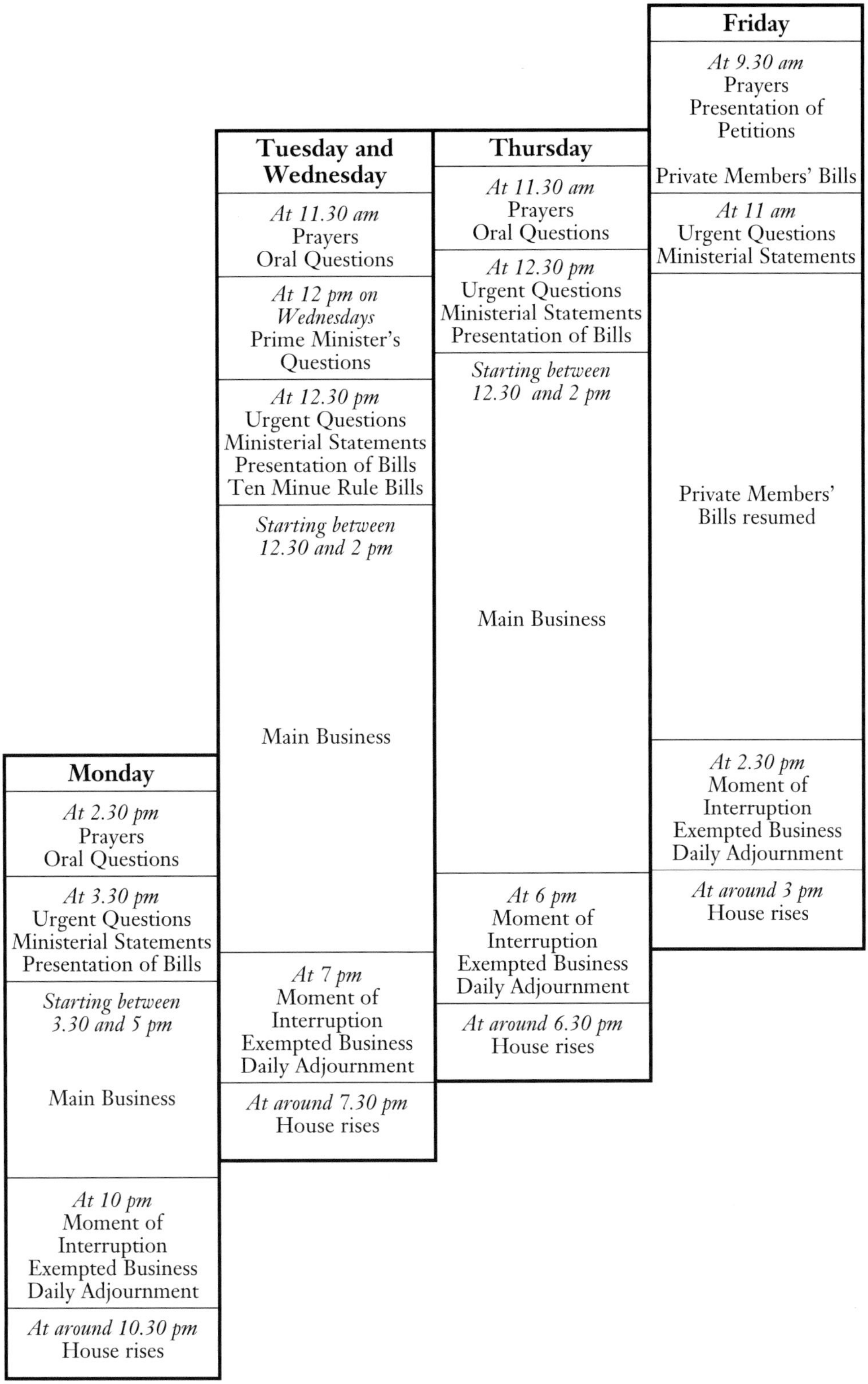

Monday

At 2.30 pm
Prayers
Oral Questions

At 3.30 pm
Urgent Questions
Ministerial Statements
Presentation of Bills

Starting between 3.30 and 5 pm

Main Business

At 10 pm
Moment of Interruption
Exempted Business
Daily Adjournment

At around 10.30 pm
House rises

Tuesday and Wednesday

At 11.30 am
Prayers
Oral Questions

At 12 pm on Wednesdays
Prime Minister's Questions

At 12.30 pm
Urgent Questions
Ministerial Statements
Presentation of Bills
Ten Minue Rule Bills

Starting between 12.30 and 2 pm

Main Business

At 7 pm
Moment of Interruption
Exempted Business
Daily Adjournment

At around 7.30 pm
House rises

Thursday

At 11.30 am
Prayers
Oral Questions

At 12.30 pm
Urgent Questions
Ministerial Statements
Presentation of Bills

Starting between 12.30 and 2 pm

Main Business

At 6 pm
Moment of Interruption
Exempted Business
Daily Adjournment

At around 6.30 pm
House rises

Friday

At 9.30 am
Prayers
Presentation of Petitions

Private Members' Bills

At 11 am
Urgent Questions
Ministerial Statements

Private Members' Bills resumed

At 2.30 pm
Moment of Interruption
Exempted Business
Daily Adjournment

At around 3 pm
House rises

FIGURE 14
THE SITTING WEEK

7.5 Question Time

General procedure

7.5.1 Under S.O. No. 21(1), on Mondays to Thursdays, after the disposal of any or all of the above business, question time begins, (for the general arrangements relating to oral questions see paragraphs 8.12 to 8.18). The terms of the questions are printed in the **Order Paper** (see paragraphs 15.1.6 to 15.1.14) and when called by the Speaker, the Member whose question is next will rise in his or her place and simply say "No. 1", "No. 2", etc and the Minister will then give his or her reply from the **despatch box**. The Member asking the question then has the opportunity to ask a **supplementary question** (which must relate to the subject of his main question as printed on the Order Paper), and after the Minister's reply to that, the Chair may call a number of other Members to ask supplementaries (which must likewise be relevant to the main question), before proceeding to call the Member whose question comes next on the Order Paper. It is extremely rare for the whole list of printed questions to be answered in the time available. Ministers are at liberty to group together questions on the same subject for answer, and a Member whose question has been so grouped will have priority in asking a supplementary following the answer to the first question. Details of such groupings are shown on the **annunciator** before the sitting begins. Although the questions as printed are always addressed to the senior Commons Minister in the department (usually the Secretary of State) they are usually answered by the Minister who has direct responsibility for the matter in question, who may be one of the junior Ministers.

7.5.2 The rota setting out which Departments or Ministers will answer oral questions at which times on which days is drawn up in accordance with the government's instructions (see paragraph 8.12) and published shortly before the end of each parliamentary term.

Prime Minister's Questions

7.5.3 On Wednesdays, questions to the first Department answering are interrupted and questions to the Prime Minister are taken for the second half of the hour. These are also printed on the Order Paper, but generally take the identical form of asking the Prime Minister to list his official engagements for the day. This device (known as the "open question") enables supplementaries to range over the whole field of government activity (see paragraph 8.10). Members listed to ask an engagements question do not (after the first one) bother to say "No. 2" etc, but proceed directly to their supplementary when called by the Speaker. Occasionally, however, a Member may have a substantive question to the Prime Minister listed on the Order Paper. By convention, the **leader of the opposition** may be called by the Speaker to ask more than one supplementary question on these occasions (currently up to six supplementary questions in total).

At the end of oral questions

7.5.4 A Minister may defer answering any question for oral answer that stands on the **Order Paper** to the end of question time. A Minister may also elect to give an oral answer at that time to any question for written answer which stands on the

Order Paper for that day. This is done in cases where a question requires, or provides an opportunity for, a more extended answer which might otherwise have taken the form of a ministerial statement (see paragraph 7.6.3 below).

Monday to Thursday	Friday
The House meets for Prayers at 2.30 pm on Mondays and at 11.30 am on Tuesdays, Wednesdays and Thursdays *After Prayers:* Reports of Queen's Answers to Addresses. Formal Communications by the Speaker. Motions for New Writs. *Private Business. *Motions for unopposed Returns. *After Questions:* Urgent Questions. Ministerial Statements. Introduction of New Members. Proposals to move the Adjournment under S.O. No. 24. *Motions for leave of absence. Ceremonial speeches. Personal Statements. *Preliminary Business:* *Presentation of Public Bills. *Business Motions (except under S.O. No. 152(2)). *Motions put forthwith for the referral (or de-referral) of Bills, statutory instruments and 'matters' to or from various standing committees (see separate Table). *Ten Minute Rule Motions (S.O. No. 23) (Private members may move these on Tuesdays and Wednesdays only. *Main Business:* *Orders of the Day and Notices and Motions in the order in which they appear on the Order Paper. *At 7 pm on Mondays or at 3 pm on Tuesdays to Thursdays:* *Private Business set down under S.O. No. 20. Motions for the Adjournment under S.O. No. 24. *At 10 pm on Mondays or 7 pm on Tuesdays and Wednesdays or 6 pm on Thursdays:* *Business motions under S.O. No. 15(2). Business which may be taken after the moment of interruption: Proceedings on a bill under a programme order. Divisions (which started at or before the moment of interruption). Questions consequential on a Closure. Bills founded on Ways & Means Resolutions (eg the Finance Bill). Public Business exempted by a business motion. Unopposed Public Business (taken "on the nod"). Exempted Business (see separate Table). *At the conclusion of Main Business:* Presentation of Public Petitions. *Adjournment Debate under S.O. No. 9 (30 minutes). **indicates business of which notice is required*	The House meets for Prayers at 9.30 am *After Prayers:* Reports of Queen's Answers to Addresses. Formal communications by the Speaker. Motions for New Writs (which if opposed lapse). Private Business. Petitions (but at 10 am, any further Petitions are postponed). *Motions for Unopposed Returns. *Preliminary Business:* *Presentation of Bills. *Business Motions (except under S.O. No. 15(2)). *Main Business:* *Private Members' Bills. *At 11 am:* The debate may be interrupted for an urgent Question or a Ministerial Statement. *At the conclusion of Public Business:* (Any Petitions postponed from 10 am). *Adjournment debate under S.O. No. 9.

FIGURE 15

DAILY ORDER OF BUSINESS

Urgent Questions

7.5.5 Under the provisions of S.O. No. 21(2), at the end of question time an **urgent question** may, with the Speaker's leave, be asked. A description of the procedures for seeking the Speaker's leave is given in paragraph 8.26. Since an urgent question by its nature cannot be printed on the Order Paper, the Member asking it must state its terms orally. Supplementaries to an urgent question may continue for as long as the Chair permits, though rarely for more than around thirty minutes.

7.5.6 On Fridays, if an urgent question is allowed by the Speaker, debate is interrupted at 11 am for the question to be asked and answered, and resumed afterwards.

The Business Question

7.5.7 S.O. No. 21(2) also allows for urgent questions to be asked which do not meet the usual criteria of urgency and importance but which relate to the arrangement of the House's business. This provision allows for the so-called **business question.** Each Thursday when the House is sitting, a Member from the opposition front bench, at the conclusion of question time, asks the **Leader of the House** what the forthcoming business of the House will be. In reply, the Leader of the House announces the main items of business to be taken on each day for the following two sitting weeks (though the details of the second week's business may not be fully fleshed-out). He or she may also take the opportunity to indicate other future events such as debates due to take place in the European standing committees (see paragraphs 13.2.10 to 13.2.17 below), the subject of Thursday debates in Westminster Hall (see paragraph 6.3.6), any changes to the dates of a holiday adjournment, and an anticipated prorogation or the opening of the next session. As soon as the answer is given, photocopies of it are made available from the **Vote Office**. Supplementary questions following this answer tend to range widely over the many topics of debate or items of business that might have been, but were not, included in the programme announced and provide a weekly opportunity for Members to raise topics of particular concern to them. These supplementaries are generally allowed by the Chair to continue for a period of around thirty minutes.

7.5.8 A full description of the rules and procedures relating to parliamentary questions for both oral and written answer is given in chapter 8.

7.6 After Questions

Business Statements

7.6.1 When other Ministers propose to make statements (see paragraph 7.6.3 below) on a Thursday, and it is thought convenient that these should have precedence over the Business Question, the House's future business is instead announced after any statements as a ministerial statement by the Leader of the House. This does not much affect its format. Not infrequently the Government will decide to change the arrangement of business previously announced. The **Leader of the House** will normally inform the House of such changes, if necessary, by means of a supplementary business statement on a day other than a Thursday. Generally speaking, the Chair restricts questioning following such a statement.

Ministerial Statements

7.6.2 After questions, including any urgent question, the House may hear ministerial statements. There is no explicit provision in standing orders for such a procedure, although it is a very common feature of the parliamentary day. This may account for the traditional introductory words "with permission" being used by Ministers at the beginning of a statement to suggest that the Chair has discretion whether to allow the statement to be made, even though the right to make a statement at this time is treated as a prerogative of Ministers. Statements may relate to any area of a Minister's responsibilities. At the conclusion of the statement the Chair allows a period in which other Members may respond to the statement or question the Minister on its contents. The duration of this period is dependent on the significance of the statement, the number of Members indicating a wish to intervene and the pressure of time on subsequent business.

Statements on Fridays

7.6.3 On Fridays, under S.O. No. 11(4), statements are made at 11 am, when the debate taking place is interrupted to allow for the statement and resumed on its conclusion.

Written Statements

7.6.4 Under a procedure introduced from the beginning of the 2002–03 session, Ministers may also make "written statements" (see paragraph 8.3.9). These cover the kinds of announcements that previously were often made as a response to a "planted" question tabled by a friendly backbencher. The written ministerial statements to be made on any sitting day are listed on the **Order Paper** at the end of all the other material relating to the day's business.

Introduction of new Members

7.6.5 Where a Member has been newly elected at a **by-election**, he or she must be introduced to the House and swear the oath or make the affirmation (see S.O. No. 5) before taking his or her seat. Traditionally, this happens on the Tuesday following the Thursday of the by-election (if the House is sitting). The new Member must wait below the **Bar of the House** until the conclusion of questions and any urgent question or ministerial statements (see S.O. No. 6). The Speaker then says "Members desirous of taking their seats will be pleased to come to the Table" and, flanked by two Members acting as sponsors, the new Member approaches the Table, bows, and is greeted by a Clerk at the government **despatch box** where the oath or affirmation is made. The Member then signs the **Test Roll**, and is announced to the Speaker and the House by the Clerk (see also paragraphs 5.1.6 and 5.1.7).

Proposals to move the adjournment under S.O. No. 24

7.6.6 S.O. No. 24 provides that on Mondays to Thursdays a Member may make an application in a speech lasting no more than three minutes to move a motion for the adjournment of the House for the purpose of discussing a specific and important matter that should have urgent consideration. Under paragraph (3) of the standing order, the Member must notify the Speaker of his or her intention to make such an application by 12 noon on a day when the House meets at 2.30 pm or 10.30 am on a day when the house meets at 11.30 am if it is known about by then. Under paragraph (4), the Speaker must test the urgency and importance of the subject against certain criteria, and after hearing the application in the House he will indicate publicly to the Member whether he is satisfied that it meets those criteria. Paragraph (5) prevents the Speaker giving reasons for his decision. He may defer giving a decision till later in the sitting. If the Speaker's consent for the application to proceed is given, the Member seeking the urgent debate must either obtain the unanimous leave of the House, the support of at least forty Members rising in their places or, with the support of at least ten Members rising in their places, may press the matter to a **division**. Applications for such leave are relatively infrequent since the Speaker discourages Members from making hopeless applications. Even where applications are made, the Speaker's consent to their proceeding is extremely rare. Where the Speaker's consent is given, therefore, there is rarely any objection made to the leave being granted for the debate to take place. A description of the procedures for a debate under S.O. No. 24, if leave is obtained, is given at paragraphs 7.9.4 and 9.8.2.

Ceremonial Speeches

7.6.7 At this point the House may, very occasionally, permit ceremonial speeches, for example to mark the death of a former Speaker or other distinguished figure. Such events are rare.

Motions for leave of absence

7.6.8 In former times, any Member who wished to absent himself from parliamentary duties required leave of absence. Nowadays, only if the Speaker desires to absent himself for some reason (a Speakers' conference overseas or some ceremonial occasion for example), will the **Leader of the House** need to move a motion at this point to grant such leave. Under S.O. No. 3(3), the Speaker has a general leave of absence on Fridays on which the House sits.

Personal statements

7.6.9 Members other than Ministers (or Ministers themselves) may very occasionally make personal statements at this point. The opportunity to make a personal statement is in the gift of the Speaker. The most common reason is to allow a Member to give an explanation of conduct which might appear to have offended against the dignity, privileges or traditions of the House and perhaps to offer an apology, but the privilege has been granted in less opprobious circumstances. The **Committee on Standards and Privileges** sometimes recommends that a Member should be required to apologise to the House in this way if they have been found to have breached the **Code of Conduct**. Traditionally, Cabinet Ministers who resign are granted such an opportunity, if sought, to explain the reasons for their resignation. Personal statements are heard by the House without interruption, and no questioning or debate may follow such a statement.

7.7 PRELIMINARY BUSINESS

The commencement of public business

7.7.1 Having disposed of any of these other types of business, the House moves on to the public business of the day. The standing orders provide for certain kinds of public business to be taken immediately before the House enters upon the main business of the day. These are described below.

Presentation of Bills

7.7.2 On any day on which the House sits, a Member may present a bill under S.O. No. 57. To do so, he or she must have given notice of the short and long titles of the bill to the **Public Bill Office** no later than the rising of the House on the previous day. The terms of the notice will be printed on the Order Paper.

7.7.3 On the day on which the notice of presentation appears on the **Order Paper**, the Member waits behind the Speaker's Chair until called. A **dummy** copy of the bill is provided by the Public Bill Office on which the long and short titles of the bill, the name of the Member presenting it and of any supporters and other details are written. When called, the Member simply hands this to the Clerk at the Table who reads out the short title. The Speaker then asks "Second Reading what day?", and the Member names a day, usually one of the Fridays designated for private Members bills to have precedence (see paragraph 2.2.4).

7.7.4 Ministers also usually present their bills under this standing order or under S.O. No. 50 (see paragraph 11.3.2 to paragraph 11.3.4), and the procedure is the same, except that the Clerk will already have been provided with the "dummy" bill and a Minister merely nods when called by the Chair. When the Speaker asks for the day for second reading, a **Whip** will reply "tomorrow". This does not mean that the second reading *will* be tomorrow, it merely has the effect of placing the bill on the **remaining orders** (see paragraphs 15.1.17 to 15.1.19) until the day which the government appoints for its second reading.

7.7.5 A full explanation of the procedures relating to legislation is given in chapter 11.

Business motions

7.7.6 A motion may be moved at this point by a Minister to regulate the subsequent business of the sitting (for example, providing for certain business to conclude at a given time). Such motions are debatable and can be amended. However, they are nowadays rare. It is currently more common for this kind of motion to be passed on an earlier day, making provisions for fine-tuning the timetable of the House.

Motions put forthwith

7.7.7 Standing orders provide for a variety of types of motion to be moved and decided without debate at the commencement of public business. These mainly relate to the referral (or de-referral) of bills, statutory instruments and so called "matters" to or from various standing committees. These are listed in Figure 16. If such motions are put down for the end of the sitting, they are not exempted business (see section 7.10).

S.O. No.	Type of Motion
59(2)	To de-refer a Law Commission Bill from a second reading committee
60(2)	To provide for a bill to be proceeded with as a tax simplification bill
60(4)	To de-refer a tax simplification bill from a second reading committee
90(1) and (2)	To refer a Bill to a second reading committee
92(1)	To refer a Bill considered before second reading by a Second Reading Committee or the Scottish Grand Committee to a report committee
106(2)	To refer a Bill to the Welsh Grand Committee before a second reading
107(5)	To refer a "matter" to the Welsh Grand Committee
114(1)	To refer a "legislative proposal" or a "matter" to the Northern Ireland Grand Committee
118(4)	To refer a statutory instrument or Measure or other item to a standing committee on delegated legislation
119(2)	To de-refer a Document from a European standing committee

FIGURE 16

QUESTIONS PUT FORTHWITH AT THE COMMENCEMENT OF PUBLIC BUSINESS

The Ten Minute Rule

7.7.8 S.O. No. 23 provides for one private Member to move a motion on each Tuesday and Wednesday for leave to bring in a bill. The Member must have given notice of this motion. Further details are given in paragraphs 11.3.5 to 11.3.10.

7.7.9 The informal title **Ten Minute Rule Bill** derives from the provision in S.O. No. 23(1) for a Member moving such a motion to make a brief explanatory speech in support of his proposal, this having been fixed by tradition at ten minutes maximum. The Member begins the speech by saying "I beg leave to bring in a bill to . . . [the terms set out on the Order Paper are recited]". When the first Member has concluded his or her speech, it is open to another Member to speak against the motion (having indicated beforehand his or her intention to the Speaker's Office and to the proposer of the motion). At the end of the speech (or speeches) the Chair puts the motion to the House. The Speaker has deprecated Members speaking against a motion and then failing to give voice to their vote against it (by calling "No" when the Question is put). It is not considered necessary, however, for the Member to press the matter to a division.

7.7.10 If leave is granted, the Speaker asks "Who will prepare and bring in the bill?" The Member who moved the motion, standing in his or her place, then reads out the list of supporters ending with the words "and myself". The Member then goes down to the Bar of the House, bows, advances five paces, bows again, advances to the **Table**, bows once more, and takes the **dummy bill** to the Clerk at the Table, who reads out the short title (see paragraph 11.4.1). The Speaker asks "Second reading what day?" and the Member names a day, usually one of the Fridays designated for private Members bills to have precedence (see paragraph 2.2.4).

7.7.11 The standing order also makes provision for Ministers to use this procedure on any day except a Friday. There is, however, no discernible reason why a Minister should nowadays choose to do so.

7.7.12 The standing order also provides for this procedure to be used for the nomination of select committees, but it has been used only once for this purpose since the 1970s.

7.7.13 Paragraph (3) of S.O. No. 23 provides that where notice of such a motion has been given for the day of a **Budget Statement** that notice shall be automatically deferred to the same time on the following Monday.

7.8 MAIN BUSINESS

Orders of the day and notices of motions

7.8.1 When any of these types of preliminary business which can be taken at the commencement of public business have been disposed of, the House proceeds to the main business of the day. The orders of the day and notices of motions are set out on the **Order Paper** in a numbered sequence. Proceedings on an order of the day are initiated by the Clerk reading its title, and on a notice of motion by the Speaker calling a signatory of the motion to move it.

Orders and Motions

7.8.2 The distinction between orders of the day and notices of motions is now more of technical than of practical significance. In essence, orders of the day are items which the House has previously ordered to be placed on its agenda and normally relate to the stages of bills. Notices of motions are placed on the Order Paper by a Member (more often than not a Minister) at his or her own initiative. The theory that Ministers act collectively on behalf of the Crown means that any Minister may move a *government* motion, whether or not his or her name is attached, and many such motions are moved by whichever government **Whip** happens to be on duty. Other motions may only be moved by a Member who has added his or her name to the notice of motion. The name of the **leader of the opposition** will frequently appear at the head of the list of supporters of a notice of motion to indicate that it is an official opposition motion, but the motion itself will usually be moved by another signatory from his front bench. An order of the day on the other hand, being as it were the property of the House rather than any individual, may, in theory, be moved by any Member.

7.8.3 The process by which debate is initiated, conducted and concluded, and the rules of debate are described in detail in chapter 9. The particular characteristics of debates on stages of public bills are described in chapter 11.

7.9 At the half-way Point

7.9.1 7 pm on a day when the House meets at 2.30 pm (or 4 pm on Tuesdays and Wednesdays or 3pm or 4 pm on Thursdays depending on the nature of the business under debate) marks the half-way point of the main debating period, both formally and informally.

Opposed Private Business

7.9.2 Under S.O. No. 20(5), the Chairman of Ways and Means may have set down opposed private business for debate at one of these times (see paragraph 7.3.2 above). This is now a relatively infrequent occurrence. Such business will normally be a stage of a **private bill** (see section 11.19), but it may be some other motion relating to private business. Debate may continue to the moment of interruption, but if concluded earlier the House may return to any debate that was interrupted.

Opposition half-days

7.9.3 Under S.O. No. 14(2), two of the days allotted to the official opposition and one of the days allotted to the minor parties (see paragraphs 2.2.2 and 2.2.3) may be taken in the form of half-days. These either conclude at 7 pm or 4 pm or commence at 7 pm or 3 pm. A Friday counts as a half day. This provision is nowadays only infrequently invoked.

S.O. No. 24 debates

7.9.4 If the leave of the House is obtained for an urgent debate under S.O. No. 24 (see paragraph 7.6.6 and 9.8.2), in cases where the urgency is sufficient, the Speaker may direct that the debate takes place at 7 pm or 3 pm on the same day that leave is granted. Various standing orders provide, in relation to various types of business, that in such an eventuality the moment of interruption will be deferred at that sitting for a period after the normal **moment of interruption** equivalent to the period spent on the S.O. No. 24 debate. That urgent debate itself must terminate at the normal **moment of interruption**.

Estimates days

7.9.5 S.O. No. 54 provides that one of the three **Estimates days** (see paragraphs 10.3.9 to 10.3.11) may be taken in the form of two half-days. Paragraph (3) of the standing order provides for these half-days to end at 7 pm or 4 pm or begin at 7 pm or 3 pm. Additionally, when the **Liaison Committee** recommends the **Estimates** for debate on a full Estimates day (see paragraph 3.5.4), it may also recommend a time limit of two or three hours on the first debate, thereby bringing that debate to a conclusion around the half-way point. In either case, the standing order prevents any vote on any Estimate being taken before the **moment of interruption** on such days (see paragraph 10.3.11).

Informal half-days

7.9.6 It has become common practice for the **Leader of the House** to announce in the business question/statement (see paragraphs 7.5.7 and 7.6.1 above) that an item of business on a certain day will continue "until about seven (or four) o'clock". This may apply to an opposition day on which two separate motions are set down for debate (see paragraph 2.2.3) or to an item of government business. Such a time limit depends on the willingness of Members to abide by it, rather than on any enforceable rule.

7.9.7 Not infrequently, the House will pass a business motion (see paragraph 7.7.6 above) which fixes the termination of debate on an item or group of items of business at the half-way point (though any other hour may be chosen), or three hours after its commencement. Such a motion may include provision for the Chair to call and put for decision a series of questions at that hour, in addition to the one that is formally before the House.

7.10 THE MOMENT OF INTERRUPTION

7.10.1 At the times specified in S.O. No. 9(3) (as amended by the temporary standing orders until the end of the current Parliament), and at 2.30 pm on Fridays (under S.O. No. 11(2)), the moment of interruption occurs (see paragraphs 6.1.6 and 6.1.7). Any debate still in progress at this time is interrupted by the Chair and stands adjourned (or if it is an adjournment motion, lapses). This marks the normal termination of the main business of the sitting, but a wide variety of devices are available to override this cut-off. The main examples of these are discussed below.

Opposed and Unopposed business

7.10.2 The moment of interruption arrests the progress of business which is *opposed*. Unless the business is exempted from the effect of the rule by one of the devices described below, it has the effect of preventing any further progress if a single Member signifies his or her opposition by rising to continue debate or by calling out "object" when another Member attempts to move an order of the day or notice of motion. Any business which is so opposed can make no progress. If it is an order of the day (see paragraph 7.8.2 above) a Member may name another day for it to be set down (if no such day is named, it becomes a **dropped order**). If it is a notice of motion (see *ibid*), it lapses unless the notice is renewed for another day.

7.10.3 However, *unopposed* business may continue after the moment of interruption. Although it is clear what constitutes opposed business, there is not a precise definition of what constitutes unopposed business. If no Member rises to speak or objects to an order or motion being moved, and if, when the Chair puts the Question on it, there are no calls of "No", the business is self-evidently unopposed and may proceed (see paragraph 9.7.11). The appearance on the **Order Paper** of a notice of amendment to a motion or the existence of a notice of an amendment to a bill would normally be taken to indicate that that business must be opposed and therefore incapable of making progress after the moment of interruption. On rare occasions, however (especially in respect of private Members' bills), the Chair has prolonged a sitting to allow amendments to be moved and made after the moment of interruption if there is no evidence of opposition to them. Generally speaking, it is not possible to have any debate at all on business after the moment of interruption unless it is somehow exempted from the rule. In theory, however, debate might be allowed so long as Members were expressing only their unqualified support for the proposal before the House and again, on rare occasions, Members have been allowed, with the indulgence of the Chair, to speak to business after the moment of interruption on those terms.

Motions to suspend the moment of interruption

7.10.4 Under S.O. No. 15(2), a Minister may move a motion (often still known, despite the many different times of the moment of interruption at present, as a '**ten o'clock motion**') at the moment of interruption to exempt specified items of business on the **Order Paper** for that sitting from the operation of the moment of interruption. The exemption can be for a specified period after debate on the item of business has begun, until a specified time, or indefinitely. Notice of the motion must appear on the Order Paper. The Question on such a motion is put **forthwith**, without debate.

Divisions and deferred Divisions

7.10.5 If a division (see section 9.6) begins or is in progress at the moment of interruption, it may be concluded. If there are any further Questions dependent on the Question which was the subject of the division, these may also be put (and may be divided upon) after the moment of interruption. The most obvious example of this is when the House is dividing on an amendment to a motion at 10 pm, 6 pm, 7 pm or at 2.30 pm – the main Question (amended or not as the case may be) may also be settled after the decision on the amendment. The other obvious case is where a division on the closure (see paragraphs 9.7.4 and 9.7.5) is taking place at the moment of interruption. If the closure is successful, clearly the Question which has been closured (and any Questions contingent on it) must also be settled **forthwith**. There cannot, however, be any further debate on these Questions after the moment of interruption – they must be moved and put forthwith.

7.10.6 For the application of the new arrangements for taking deferred divisions on Questions put after the moment of interruption, see paragraphs 9.6.10 to 9.6.12.

Exempted business

7.10.7 A large number of categories of items of business are exempted by standing orders from the operation of the moment of interruption. The main varieties of these are listed in Figure 17.

7.10.8 Any bill brought in upon a Ways and Means resolution is exempt under S.O. No. 15(1)(a). In practice this applies almost exclusively to Finance Bills (see paragraphs 10.2.19 to 10.2.24). Debate on any stage of these bills may continue after the moment of interruption.

7.10.9 Under S.O. No. 15(1)(c), a motion under S.O. No. 121(2) to appoint a Member or Members to a departmental select committees (see paragraph 2.4.4 and section 17.2) may, if it has previously been objected to at an earlier sitting, continue until one hour after the moment of interruption would normally have intervened or for one hour after debate commenced, when the Question must be put.

S.O. No.	Type of Motion
9(4)	Closure and consequentials
15(1)(a)	Bill brought in upon Ways and Means resolutions
15(1)(c)	Motion for nomination to a departmental select committee which has previously been opposed (1 hour)
16	Motions to approve statutory instruments or take note of European Community Documents (1½ hours)
17	Motions relating to statutory instruments subject to negative resolution (prayers) (until 1½ hours after the moment of interruption)
18	Motions to approve regulatory reform orders where the Regulatory Reform Committee has recommended approval on division (1½ hours) or has recommended against approval (3 hours)
24	Postponed proceedings following emergency adjournment debate
52(1)(a)	Money resolution on day other than day on which Bill to which it relates has second reading (45 minutes)
63(3)	Committal motions involving the splitting of a bill between two types of committee (two ten minute speeches)
91(4)	To extend 28 day limit within which a special standing committee must hold its evidence sessions
155	On a petition of present personal grievance
–	Business under a programme order

FIGURE 17

BUSINESS EXEMPTED FROM THE EFFECT OF THE MOMENT OF INTERRUPTION

7.10.10 The other major category of business exempted from the moment of interruption is proceedings on various types of delegated legislation (see below).

Affirmative instruments

7.10.11 Under S.O. No. 16, a motion to approve a statutory instrument subject to the affirmative resolution procedure which has not previously been considered by a standing committee (see paragraphs 12.3.10 to 12.3.14), which covers the overwhelming majority of business embraced in the phrase "proceedings under any Act of Parliament", may continue for an hour and a half, regardless of the moment of interruption. The Chair must put the Question on such a motion at the end of this period. In current practice, this provision is usually overridden by an earlier business motion.

European Community Documents

7.10.12 Debate on a motion relating to any European Community Documents which have not previously been considered by a standing committee (see chapter 13) is also permitted to continue under S.O. No. 16 for an hour and a half, regardless of the moment of interruption. The Chair must put the Question on such a motion at the end of this period. Again, in current practice, this provision is usually overridden by an earlier business motion.

Negative instruments

7.10.13 Under S.O. No. 17, debate on a motion relating to a statutory instrument subject to the negative resolution procedure which has not previously been considered by a standing committee (see paragraphs 12.3.15 to 12.3.22) may continue until an hour and a half after the normal time of the moment of interruption. Such a debate cannot commence later than one hour after the normal moment of interruption but may start before the moment of interruption. An hour and a half after the normal moment of interruption the Chair is required to put the Question on the motion unless of the opinion that there has been insufficient time for debate. This standing order also applies to cognate motions relating to instruments not statutorily subject to the negative resolution procedure, or those in respect of which the "praying time" (see paragraph 12.3.16) has expired.

Regulatory Reform orders

7.10.14 Under S.O. No. 18, the Question to approve a draft regulatory reform order may be put forthwith if the Regulatory Reform Committee (see section 12.4) has unanimously recommended its approval, or after an hour and a half if the recommendation from the committee to approve the order was not unanimous. If the Committee has recommended against approving the order the House must first resolve to disagree with the Committee in a debate which can last no longer than three hours, after which, if the House has resolved to disagree with the Committee, the motion to approve the order may be put **forthwith**. These Questions may be decided after, and the time limits may run over, the moment of interruption.

Questions put forthwith after the moment of interruption

7.10.15 Standing orders provide for a wide variety of Questions to be decided **forthwith** after the moment of interruption, even though opposed. There can be no debate on such Questions, but they may be moved and are immediately put to the House, whereupon a decision may be taken, including a division (which may be deferred). There are two main categories of such motions. The first is motions relating to statutory instruments or European Community Documents which have been previously debated in, and reported from, standing committees (see paragraphs 12.3.23 to 12.3.30 and 13.2.10 to 13.2.17 and paragraphs 7.10.10 to 7.10.13 above). The second is various types of motion contingent on stages of consideration of bills (see paragraphs 11.6.15, 11.7.3, 11.7.5 and 11.18.4). There are a number of other types of Question

S.O. No.	Type of Motion
25	Motion to fix dates of holiday adjournment
33	Additional amendment on last day of Queen's Speech
44(1)	Naming of a Member
51(3)	Budget Resolutions after first one
52(1)(a)	Money and Ways and Means resolutions on same day as bill to which they relate has second reading
54(5)	Estimates
55	Second and third readings of Consolidated Fund Bills
58(4)	That a Consolidation Bill be not committed
60(8)	To discharge a commitee of the whole House from considering a tax law rewrite bill
63(2)	Committal of a bill immediately after second reading
82	To agree with the report of a Business Committee
97(2)	To refer a bill to the Scottish Grand Committee before second reading
97(5)	To commit a bill referred under 97(2)
97(7)	To refer a bill to the Scottish Grand Committee before third reading
97(10)	Third reading of a bill reported from the Scottish Grand Committee
98(1)	To refer a statutory instrument to the Scottish Grand Committee
98(3)	Motion relating to a statutory instrument reported from the Scottish Grand Committee
100(1)	To fix meetings of the Scottish Grand Committee and business to be transacted
106(1)	To refer a bill to the Welsh Grand Committee before second reading
107(1)	To refer a "matter" to the Welsh Grand Committee
108(1)	To fix meetings of the Welsh Grand Committee and business to be transacted
113(2)	To refer a bill to the Northern Ireland Grand Committee before second reading
113(4)	On second reading of a bill reported from the Northern Ireland Grand Committee
113(5)	To refer a bill to the Northern Ireland Grand Committee before third reading
113(8)	On third reading of a bill reported from the Northern Ireland Grand Committee
115(1)	To refer a statutory instrument to the Northern Ireland Grand Committee
115(3)	Motion on a statutory instrument reported from the Northern Ireland Grand Committee
116(1)	To fix meetings of the Northern Ireland Grand Committe and business to be transacted
117(6)	To fix meetings of the Regional Affairs Committee and business to be transacted
118(6)	Motion on a statutory instrument reported from a delegated legislation standing committee
119(9)	Motion (or amendment) on a document reported from a European standing committee
145(2)	To agree a report from the Liaison Committee relating to Estimates Days
163	To sit in private

FIGURE 18

QUESTIONS PUT FORTHWITH WHICH MAY BE DECIDED AFTER THE MOMENT OF INTERRUPTION which may be despatched in this way after the moment of interruption under various standing orders. These are listed in Figure 18. There will be an italicised rubric on the **Order Paper** under such motions indicating that they are to be decided without debate.

Business exempted by a business motion

7.10.16 A business of the House motion (see paragraph 7.7.6 above) may provide for specified items of business to be exempt from the moment of interruption for specified periods, and require the Chair to put certain specified Questions at the end of these periods. Where such a motion has been agreed on a previous day, there will be an italicised rubric under the relevant item of business on the **Order Paper**, indicating its effect.

Business taken under a Programme Order or Guillotine

7.10.17 Where a programme order or guillotine (see section 11.18) has been applied to a bill, it will almost always provide for various types of questions to be taken after the moment of interruption, usually without debate. The currently still temporary standing orders relating to programmes apply such provisions to classes of questions which may be moved at various stages of a bill's progress. Certain types of question relating to the programme motion or supplementary programme motions are likewise exempted.

7.11 PUBLIC PETITIONS

7.11.1 On Mondays to Thursdays, at the end of business, and immediately before a **Whip** moves the adjournment under S.O. No. 9 (see paragraph 7.12.1 below), Members may present public petitions under S.O. No. 154(1)(a). A Member who has indicated an intention to present a petition rises in his or her place when called by the Speaker, gives a brief description of the nature of the petition and may read out its final paragraph. The Member then takes the petition and, without further ceremony, deposits it in the large green bag hanging behind the Speaker's Chair. A full description of the procedures relating to public petitions is given in chapter 19.

7.11.2 On Fridays, under S.O. No. 154(1)(b), public petitions are presented immediately after Prayers (see paragraph 7.2.1 above). If, however, it is a day on which private Members' bills have precedence, which in current practice covers all sitting Fridays (see paragraph 2.2.4), and petitions are still being presented at 10 am, the petition then being presented and any further petitions stand over to the adjournment.

7.12 THE DAILY ADJOURNMENT

7.12.1 The last business of each sitting day is the so-called "half-hour" or "daily" adjournment. When all the other business listed on the **Order Paper** has been disposed of, a **Whip** moves the motion to adjourn the House. Under S.O. No. 9(7), debate on this motion may last half-an-hour. In theory the House is debating whether or not it should adjourn but, by long-standing tradition, this has become an opportunity for a back bench Member to raise a topic of his or her choice with a Minister. The subjects chosen are often matters of local constituency interest, but may range more widely. The subject matter should not entail legislation, though under S.O. No. 30, the Chair may choose not to apply this rule strictly. The right to raise a topic on each day is determined by a ballot held by the Speaker's Office each Thursday morning for the days of the week following, except that the choice of the Member for each Thursday slot is made by the Speaker from amongst those applications which were unsuccessful in the ballot for the other days of the week. The half-hour available should be divided roughly equally between the backbencher and the Minister responding, unless the proportions are varied by agreement. The Chair will not allow any other Members to participate unless satisfied that both the Minister and the Member initiating the debate have agreed to this.

7.12.2 If the adjournment is moved before the **moment of interruption**, because all the previous business has already been disposed of, the adjournment debate may continue up to the moment of interruption and may then be renewed for a further half an hour. In these circumstances, the Chair may sometimes call other Members who indicate that they wish to participate. If the adjournment concludes before the half-hour is over, or even before the moment of interruption, the Chair will not recognise further Members who may seek to raise other subjects, but will put the question and adjourn the House.

7.12.3 If the full half-hour after the moving of an adjournment motion has passed, under the standing order the Chair adjourns the House automatically, and the House stands adjourned either to the next weekday or to a later day if the House has previously so ordered (see paragraph 5.2.10).

7.12.4 The name of the Member chosen to initiate debate on the adjournment and the subject he or she proposes to raise is indicated on the Order Paper at the end of the Main Business of the Day (see paragraph 15.1.12).

7.13 Broken Sittings

7.13.1 It is possible (though very unlikely in the era of programme orders) that business exempted from the moment of interruption may continue for so long that the sitting lasts beyond the time at which the next day's sitting should, in accordance with the standing orders, start. If this happens, the next day's sitting is lost entirely, even if the House then concludes the extended sitting before the normal time for the conclusion of the sitting on the following day.

Chapter 8

ASKING QUESTIONS

8.1 INTRODUCTION

8.1.1 There are two basic forms of parliamentary question (PQ): questions for oral answer and questions for written answer. Questions for oral answer are answered orally by Ministers on the floor of the House during question time (see section 7.5), and have become probably the best known aspect of the House's proceedings since the introduction of broadcasting. Questions for written answer are answered by Ministers in writing. The written answers appear as a supplement to each day's **Hansard** (see paragraph 15.4.3).

8.1.2 Until recently, PQs were known only as a proceeding in the House itself. For about a decade, the Scottish, Welsh and Northern Ireland Grand Committees have been able to have a question time at certain sittings (see paragraph 14.2.5). In 2003 a version of oral questions was introduced at some of the sittings in Westminster Hall (see section 6.3). The same rules apply in most essentials to these other versions of questions as apply to oral PQs on the floor of the House.

8.2 RULES FOR PQS

8.2.1 The purpose of a PQ, as stated in its classical form by **Erskine May**, is either to seek information or to press for action. Around these two basic principles a body of practice has been elaborated by successive decisions of the House and of the Chair about what is and what is not in order to ask in a question. None of these rules is contained in standing orders.

8.2.2 The fundamental rule is that a PQ must be a question, not a disguised statement or debating point. Expressions of opinion within PQs are therefore disorderly. By the same token, PQs which are highly tendentious in the supposition on which they appear to be based, or are apparently without basis, are not in order. Similarly, PQs which are clearly tendered in a spirit of mockery or with ironic intent, or are designed merely to annoy, are also out of order. A PQ which appears incapable of answer is clearly not a question, and by extension one which is so vague as to be unanswerable, or one which is so wide as to require an answer of improbable length, is not in order.

8.2.3 The other most fundamental tenet by which a PQ is judged to be orderly is that it should engage the responsibilities of the government. The government is not, in general, responsible for matters of history, though it is in order to ask questions seeking statistical information from up to thirty years in the past. There are areas of public life, as well as most areas of the private life of individuals, for which no Minister is answerable to Parliament. These exclusions extend, in most cases, to the affairs of private businesses or public limited companies. Nor can Ministers be asked about matters which are the direct responsibility of other duly constituted statutory bodies such as local authorities or devolved executives. Ministers are not generally responsible for the actions or decisions of either House of Parliament nor, by and large, those of the courts. Questions must not breach the sub judice rule (see paragraph 9.3.16). Nor are

Ministers responsible for the actions of other governments except where these are taken in concert with the UK or through the medium of some international organisation of which the UK is a member; although they may be asked about matters "which might be expected to be the subject of a report from an ambassador", an exception which is open to fairly liberal interpretation. Ministers cannot be held responsible for confirming or denying rumours in the press or other media, or for the content of statements made by persons not representing the government in any official capacity.

8.2.4 Questions raising points which would be disorderly in debate (see paragraphs 9.3.13 to 9.3.22) are in general out of order, since in most cases such matters are required to be raised by way of a substantive motion. This includes questions reflecting on the conduct of the sovereign or the royal family, or inquiring into advice given to the sovereign about awards and honours. Questions about actions notionally taken by the sovereign under the royal prerogative but in fact taken only on the advice of Ministers are, however, in order.

8.2.5 Questions must in general be directed to the government. With the exceptions described below, it is not possible to table PQs to Members of the House who are not Ministers. *Written* questions to the chairmen of the select committees concerned with the administration of the House (see chapter 18) are permitted. There is special provision for the Second Church Estates Commissioner, a back bench Member, to answer written and oral PQs about certain aspects of Church of England administration. The Chairman of the **Public Accounts Commission** (see paragraph 10.5.9) answers written and oral PQs on its work, as does the Chairman of the Finance and Services Committee (see paragraph 18.1.3) and a **back bench** Member on behalf of the **House of Commons Commission** (see paragraph 18.1.1). A Member of the Speaker's Committee on the Electoral Commission also answers oral and written questions on behalf of that statutory committee.

8.2.6 It is not in order to seek to question one Minister on matters for which another is more properly responsible, or to attempt to set one Minister against another by way of a PQ. Following the creation of the Scottish Parliament, the National Assembly for Wales and the Northern Ireland Assembly, it is not in order to question Ministers about matters which by statute are the exclusive preserve of those bodies or the executives which they sustain in office (unless, in the case of Northern Ireland, the devolved institutions have been suspended and direct rule reimposed). However, there are wide exceptions to this rule for questions which, for example, seek information which the UK government is entitled to request from a devolved body, matters covered by UK legislation, matters relating to the concordats between devolved and UK bodies for which a Minister is responsible, matters concerning which UK Ministers retain administrative powers and, most permissively of all, "matters which UK Ministers have taken an official interest in". Between them, these exceptions do not demand much ingenuity in devising orderly questions to the Secretaries of State for Northern Ireland, Scotland and Wales.

8.2.7 Where a question has already been answered once in a session, it cannot be asked again in the same session, unless there are grounds for supposing the situation has altered. Where a Minister has refused to answer a question, for example on grounds that the information is not held centrally or that the cost of compiling an answer would be disproportionate, it cannot be asked again for three months. In some circumstances, for example where a Minister has refused to answer on grounds of commercial confidentiality or national security, the same question or other questions on the same subject may be "blocked" for the remainder of that session.

8.2.8 It is not, generally speaking, in order to table an *open question* for *oral* answer, that is one which does not indicate a subject which might reasonably limit the scope of supplementaries. However, the practice of the House is to allow oral questions to the Prime Minister to be tabled (usually asking him to list his official engagements) which are in effect open questions.

8.3 TABLING OF QUESTIONS

8.3.1 Under paragraph (1) of S.O. No. 22, PQs must be tabled by being delivered to the **Table Office**. Notice of questions must be given in writing (which includes, under certain conditions, texts sent in electronic form), and may be sent by post or handed in to the **Table Office** by anyone authorised to act on the Member's behalf. If they are not handed in by a Member in person, each notice of a question must be signed either by the Member in whose name it is given or by another Member acting on his behalf. Each question, under paragraph (3) of the standing order, must indicate the Minister to whom it is addressed and whether it is for oral or written answer, and if the latter, whether it is for written answer on a "named day". Where a Member has a relevant declarable interest relating to the question (see section 4.3), he or she must indicate this when tabling a question, and an [R] appears beside the question when it is printed.

Oral questions

8.3.2 There is no question time on Fridays. On each of the other days of the week there is a rota of four main departments to take their turn to be first for questions. A major department will therefore be first for questions approximately once a month when the House is sitting. Following the questions to the lead department, on certain days there are questions to other Ministers such as the Solicitor General and the Commons Minister representing the Department for Constitutional Affairs or to those Members answering for the **Public Accounts Commission** or the Church Commissioners. There may also be questions to the **Leader of the House**, with which are included questions to the Member answering for the **House of Commons Commission** and to the Chairman of the Finance and Services Committee (see paragraphs 18.1.1 and 18.1.3). On Wednesdays, questions to the lead department are interrupted at 12 noon for questions to the Prime Minister to be taken (see paragraph 7.5.3). The rota of oral question times, and the timings of the individual slots, are decided by the government, and following their instructions a wall sheet headed *Order of Questions* is distributed towards the end of each parliamentary term, showing which departments are answering oral questions on which days over the course of the next parliamentary term. It also indicates the latest date for tabling of questions to each Minister. An example of a typical monthly cycle is given in Figure 19.

ORDER OF QUESTIONS

Monday 13th October – Thursday 6th November

NOTE

Questions for oral answer may be submitted any time after the previous question time for the that Department up to 12.30pm three days (excluding Fridays, Saturdays and Sundays and Bank Holidays) before the day of answering, except for Questions to the Secretaries of State for Northern Ireland, Scotland and Wales and the Advocate General, where Questions may be submitted up to 12.30pm five days (excluding Fridays, Saturdays and Sundays and Bank Holidays) before the day of answering (Orders of 29th October 2002 and 23rd January 2003). All Questions so submitted will be included in the random shuffle to determine the order of Questions. Members may table no more than two Questions for oral answer on a single day, and only one Question per Department.

Mon. 13 Oct	Tues. 14 Oct	Wed. 15 Oct	Thurs. 16 Oct
Culture, Media and Sport Church Commissioners, Public Accounts Commission and Speaker's Committee on the Electoral Commission[7]	**Foreign and Commonwealth Office**	**International Development Prime Minister[5]**	**Treasury**
Last tabling at 12.30 for			
Treasury	*Work and Pensions*	*Transport Cabinet Office[9]*	*Deputy Prime Minister Prime Minister*

Mon. 20 Oct	Tues. 21 Oct	Wed. 22 Oct	Thurs. 23 Oct
Work and Pensions	**Transport Cabinet Office[8,9]**	**Deputy Prime Minister Prime Minister[5]**	**Environment, Food and Rural Affairs**
Last tabling at 12.30 for			
Environment, Food and Rural Affairs Scotland Advocate General	*Home Office Northern Ireland*	*Constitutional Affairs Leader of the House and House of Commons Commission[4]*	*Prime Minister*

Mon. 27 Oct	Tues. 28 Oct	Wed. 29 Oct	Thurs. 30 Oct
Home Office	**Scotland Advocate General[2] Constitutional Affairs[3] Leader of the House and House of Commons Commission**	**Northern Ireland Prime Minister[5]**	**Education and Skills Solicitor General[6]**
Last tabling at 12.30 for			
Education and Skills Solicitor General[1]	*Defence Wales*	*Health*	*Prime Minister*

Mon. 3 Nov	Tues. 4 Nov	Wed. 5 Nov	Thurs. 6 Nov
Defence	**Health**	**Wales Prime Minister[5]**	**Trade and Industry Minister for Women[8]**
Last tabling at 12.30 for			
Trade and Industry Minister for Women	*Culture, Media and Sport Church Commissioners, Public Accounts Commission and Speaker's Committee on the Electoral Commission*	*Foreign and Commonwealth Office*	*International Development Prime Minister*

[1] **Also answers on behalf of the Attorney General.**
[2] **Starting not later than 11.55 am.**
[3] **Starting not later than 12 noon. Includes questions for the Lord Chancellor and President of the Council.**
[4] **Starting not later than 12.20 pm. Includes questions to the Finance and Services Committee.**
[5] **Starting not later than 12 noon.**
[6] **Starting not later than 12.20 pm. Also answers on behalf of the Attorney General.**
[7] **Starting not later than 3.15 pm.**
[8] **Starting not later than 12.20 pm.**
[9] **Includes questions to the Chancellor of the Duchy of Lancaster.**

FIGURE 19
EXAMPLE OF AN ORAL QUESTIONS ROTA

8.3.3 The earliest day on which notice of an oral question can be given is immediately following the end of the previous question time to that department. The latest time at which notice can be given is fixed, under paragraph (5) of S.O. No. 22, is at the discretion of the Speaker, provided that it allows the notices to be printed and published at least two full days (excluding Fridays, Saturdays, Sundays and Bank Holidays) before the day on which they are to be answered. In the case of questions to the Secretaries of State for Northern Ireland, Scotland and Wales, this minimum period is extended to five days, excluding Fridays, Saturdays, Sundays and Bank Holidays. In practice this means that, other than for the Secretaries of State for Northern Ireland, Scotland and Wales, the latest time has been fixed by the Speaker at 12.30 pm on Monday for Thursday, on Tuesday for Monday, on Wednesday for Tuesday and on Thursday for Wednesday.

8.3.4 Before each holiday adjournment (see paragraph 5.2.10), under the provisions of paragraph (8) of the standing order, the normal periods of notice are superseded and the Speaker sets different periods of notice for tabling questions for oral answer on the first sitting days after the recess. A memorandum announcing these dates is published in the **Order Paper** about a fortnight before the start of the recess.

8.3.5 On the latest day on which notice for oral questions to a Minister or other Member scheduled for question time on a later day may be given, Members must deliver their notice of questions in person to the Table Office (see paragraph 8.13 above) by 12.30 pm at the latest if they wish to have the chance of having a question on the Order Paper. Shortly after 12.30 pm, the names of all those Members who have given notice during the period since the last question time are electronically shuffled by a computer, which prints out the names in the order thus determined. Only the notices of questions from Members whose names appear sufficiently high in this list to have some chance of being reached during question time are printed on the **Notice Paper** (see paragraph 15.1.34) and subsequently the **Order Paper** (see paragraph 15.1.8). The quotas are between eight and twenty-five. Those questions which are drawn too low in the shuffle to be within the quotas do not appear in print and are not answered.

8.3.6 Because questions cannot be tabled in one session for another, the first day of a session will be the latest day for giving notice of questions for oral answer from the fourth sitting day, so no oral questions other than **Urgent Questions** can be answered before the fourth sitting day of a session.

Written questions

8.3.7 Unlike oral PQs, a written question may be addressed to any Department for answer on any sitting day. There are two types of question for written answer: "ordinary" written questions and "questions for written answer on a named day". The distinction is simply that in the latter case the Member giving notice of his or her question can specify a date on which the Minister is required to give an answer. This can be no sooner than three sitting days after the day on which notice was given (ie notice on Monday for answer on Thursday, on

Tuesday for Friday (Monday if the Friday is a non-sitting day), on Wednesday for Monday, on Thursday for Tuesday and on Friday for Wednesday). A Member may table only five questions for answer on a named day on any one day. There is no quota for questions for ordinary written answer, which are notionally put down for answer on the day two sitting days after they are tabled and appear in the **Questions Book** for that day, but the answer may be given on any day after that. By convention the answer to a question for ordinary written answer should normally be given within one working week of its appearance in the Questions Book.

Written Ministerial Statements

8.3.8 It was formerly the practice for Ministers to make relatively uncontroversial announcements in response to so-called "planted questions", which were usually tabled the day before they were to be answered. In response to a feeling, expressed by the **Modernisation Committee** among others, that this procedure was open to abuse, these kind of announcements are nowadays made as "written ministerial statements", a new procedure introduced in the 2002–03 session, and given formal authority under the new S.O. No. 22A. Notices of future written ministerial statements (which may be given up to five sitting days in advance) are included in section E of the future business section and those due to be given on any particular day are listed at the end of the **Order Paper** for that day's sitting.

8.4 PRINTING OF QUESTIONS

8.4.1 All questions for written answer tabled on each sitting day appear on the blue **notice paper** published with the **Vote Bundle** on the following day (see paragraph 15.1.34). Questions for written answer on a named day are distinguished by an **N** in the margin. Questions for oral answer which have been selected in the random shuffle (see paragraph 8.3.5 above) appear the day after the shuffle.

8.4.2 On the day on which the questions are due for answer, they appear on the Order Paper or in the Questions Book. Oral questions are the first item on the Order Paper before the Orders of the Day and Notices of Motions (see paragraphs 15.1.8 and Figure 9). Written questions appear in Part 1 of the Questions Book (see paragraph 15.1.39) rather than on the Order Paper.

Withdrawing and unstarring questions

8.4.3 Up to the point at which an oral question is asked, the Member in whose name it stands may give an instruction for it to be withdrawn. The same may be done with a question for written answer before it has appeared in the Questions Book for answer that day. A notice to that effect appears in the next day's issue of the blue notice paper. A Member who has a question for oral answer outstanding may give an instruction for it to be unstarred, that is converted to a question for written answer. Again, if this happens before it has appeared on the Order Paper, a notice appears in the blue notice paper of the unstarred question. A Minister may, however, insist on giving an answer to any PQ which *has* appeared on the Order Paper (see also paragraph 7.5.4) even if it has been withdrawn.

8.5 ANSWERS

8.5.1 A description of oral question time on the floor of the House is given at paragraph 7.5.1. Questions for oral answer which are not reached during question time on any particular day receive a written answer at around 3.30 pm (or 12.30 pm) in the same manner, and are printed among the written answers in Hansard for that day. The same is done for oral questions not reached at sittings in Westminster Hall (see section 6.3) or a sitting of one of the grand committees (see paragraph 14.2.5).

8.5.2 The written answers to oral questions are delivered to Members, with copies to the Library, the Table Office, the Official Report and the Press Gallery, at the end of Question Time on Mondays to Thursdays. Other written answers should arrive at around 9.30 in the morning. They are printed within a day or two in the supplement to the daily edition of Hansard (see paragraph 15.4.3).

8.6 URGENT QUESTIONS

8.6.1 Urgent questions (formerly known as Private Notice Questions or PNQs) are oral parliamentary questions which, exercising his power under S.O. No. 21(2), the Speaker allows to be asked because of the urgency and importance of the matter they raise, although they have not been tabled within the time limits set out in the standing orders and so have not appeared on the **Order Paper**. S.O. No. 21(2) provides that before giving consent for such a question to be asked, the Speaker must be of the opinion that it is of an urgent character and that it relates to a matter of public importance.

8.6.2 A Member seeking the Speaker's consent to ask such a question must inform the Speaker's Office at the earliest opportunity, before noon on a Monday or 10.30 am on a day on which the House sits at 11.30 am or 10 am on a Friday, of the terms of the proposed question and the grounds for claiming its urgency and importance. Such an application made after these times will be considered only if the issue had arisen after that hour. If the Speaker decides to allow the question, this will be advertised on the annunciator and the Member will be informed. Urgent questions are taken at the end of question time on Mondays to Thursdays or at 11 am on Fridays (see paragraphs 7.5.5 and 7.5.6).

8.6.3 Apart from these special provisions about notice, all the rules relating to PQs apply in principle to urgent questions (except in respect of the **business question**, for which see paragraph 7.5.7).

Chapter 9

DEBATES AND DECISIONS

9.1 Introduction

9.1.1 A debate begins with a Member moving a motion or an order of the day. At the end of his or her speech, the Chair proposes the Question (for example, "That the bill be read a second time", or "That this House has no confidence in Her Majesty's Government"). Debate then takes place on that Question. During debate, amendments may be proposed to the original Question.

9.1.2 If any amendments have been proposed, after they have been disposed of by being withdrawn, made or negatived, the House will come to a decision on the main Question (amended or not as the case may be), unless it is withdrawn, superseded by another Question (a "dilatory motion") or "talked out". The process by which debate is conducted and decisions are made is set out in detail below. The decision of the House is determined by voice or by a division. In almost every case a simple majority of votes is sufficient to decide the Question. If the Question is agreed to, the decision will have effect as either a **resolution** or an **order** of the House.

9.1.3 In **standing committees the** process of debate is broadly the same. In **select committees** the rules governing debate are largely irrelevant.

9.2 Initiating Debate

Moving

9.2.1 Debate is initiated by the Chair calling a Member to move a motion or an order of the day (see paragraph 7.8.2 for the distinction between motions and orders), or an amendment, new clause or new schedule proposed to a bill. The terms of the motion or order will either appear on the **Order Paper** or it will be a motion of a kind which may be moved without **notice**. Notices of amendments, etc. to bills which are being considered in the House appear on a separate paper. Formally, the mover should commence with the phrase "I beg to move [that the bill be now read a second time/that this House . . .]", but this opening formula is sometimes omitted, or, in relation to a motion or amendment, the mover simply says "I beg to move the motion/amendment standing in my name on the Order Paper". No **seconder** is required for a Question to be proposed, except by tradition for the **Loyal Address** in reply to the **Queen's Speech** (see paragraph 5.2.7). At the end of the mover's speech, the Chair proposes the Question to the House, using a phrase such as "The Question is, That the bill be now read a second time", or "The Question is, That this House . . ./the motion on the Order Paper". After the Question has been proposed, debate ensues, and the Question before the House must be disposed of by being withdrawn, negatived or agreed to, unless debate is talked out (see paragraph 6.1.7) or superseded (see paragraph 9.4.1), in which case the debate stands adjourned, and may (in certain circumstances) be renewed for a future day.

Amendments

9.2.2 Once a Question has been *proposed* to the House, amendments may be offered to it. When the proposer of an amendment is called by the Chair to move it they will rise and say "I beg to move the amendment in my name, in line 1 to leave out the words . . . and insert . . ." or "I beg to move the amendment in the name of my honourable friend and myself", or "I beg to move the amendment as on the Order Paper" or some such phrase. (Amendments proposed to bills at committee or report stage are not printed on the Order Paper, and are dealt with slightly differently, see paragraphs 11.10.18 to 11.10.20).

9.2.3 When the mover of the amendment sits down, the Chair will *propose* the amendment to the House. Debate on the amendment in theory then supersedes debate on what now becomes the "main Question". The amendment must in its turn be disposed of by being withdrawn, negatived or made, before a decision can be made on the main Question (as amended or not, as the case may be). In practice, debate on an amendment will usually be permitted to range across the subject matter of both the main Question and the amendment.

9.2.4 Once an amendment has been disposed of, further amendments to the main Question may, if time is available or the standing orders allow for it, be moved and disposed of in their turn.

9.2.5 It is also possible to propose amendments to amendments. This occasionally happens in relation to amendments proposed to *bills*, but is rare in relation to amendments to motions. In the same way as with an amendment to the main Question, the Question on an amendment to an amendment must be disposed of before the amendment can be disposed of.

Selection of amendments

9.2.6 Under S.O. No. 32, the Speaker has the power to select amendments for debate. This power is one of the most significant of those possessed by the Chair, and is fundamental to the Chair's ability to control the course of debate.

9.2.7 Briefly stated, the power of selection means that the Speaker may decline to allow any amendment (whether to a bill or to a motion) to be proposed to the House. By this means the House's attention during a debate can be focused upon the particular amendment or amendments that the Chair has selected, and the House knows that these are the Questions on which a decision will have to be taken in the course of the debate. There is no appeal against the Speaker's decision not to select an amendment for debate, nor is the Speaker required to give reasons. It is out of order to refer in debate (other than in passing) to an amendment which the Speaker has not selected.

9.2.8 The power of selection is devolved by S.O. No. 32(2) to the Chairman of Ways and Means and his deputies when the House is in Committee, and the Chairman of Ways and Means also has power of selection during consideration of Estimates (see section 10.3), though in modern practice this is rarely relevant.

Selection applied to motions

9.2.9 Paragraph (4) of the standing order also extends this power of selection to motions which are contingent upon stages of bills, for example reasoned amendments (see paragraphs 11.6.2 to 11.6.4 and 11.14.4), instructions (see section 11.8) or committal motions (see section 11.7), which are all treated as if they were amendments for the purposes of selection.

Selection of amendments to bills

9.2.10 The power of selection also applies to amendments proposed to bills at their various stages, but the mechanics of how it operates are rather different. This power is delegated to chairmen of standing committees under S.O. No. 89(2)(a). A description of how this power is exercised in relation to bills (which is a rather more complex exercise) is given in paragraph 11.10.10.

Publication or announcement of selection

9.2.11 The Speaker's (or the Chairman of Ways and Means's) selection of amendments to a bill is published in typescript form and made available to Members on the day on which the bill to which it relates is to be taken on the floor of the House (or on Thursday afternoon for a Friday sitting). Where there is a very complex selection relating to some matter other than a bill, it may also be published in this way. Where, however, it is a straightforward selection of one or two amendments to a motion, or of a motion contingent upon a stage of a bill's proceedings, the Chair will simply announce the Speaker's selection of amendments at the outset of the debate.

9.3 GENERAL CONVENTIONS AND RULES OF DEBATE

Entering and leaving

9.3.1 When entering or leaving the Chamber or a committee room, Members bow to the Chair. Members should not cross the sight-line between the Chair and the Member who is speaking.

Choice of Members to speak in debate

9.3.2 Members are called to speak by the Chair. Members rise in their places between speeches in order to indicate that they wish to be called, but only the Member addressing the House or committee should be standing at other times. Certain conventions obtain as to who will be called in debate and in what order, but the freedom of choice of the Chair remains untrammelled in principle. It has been proposed to adopt a speakers' list, as in other assemblies, but this has so far been resisted as a formal practice, though it is well known that the Chair does often have an informal list, and that it is worth indicating to the Speaker's office in advance a wish to participate in a particular debate (perhaps giving reasons). The mover of the motion or order of the day will be called first. Where this is a Minister or opposition **shadow**, his or her opposite number will have the presumptive right to be called next, and the appropriate spokesman or woman of the second largest opposition party may expect to speak early in the debate if he or she seeks to do so. In the general debate which follows the Chair may have regard to Members who have a particular interest, which might be a constituency interest (if such an interest is direct the Member may expect to be called), or it might be that he or she is the chairman of the relevant **departmental select committee**, or an acknowledged expert on the matter at issue or has some other special claim to be heard. However, the Chair gives precedence above such considerations to the balancing of opinion from each side of the House and, unless there are no Members rising to speak from one side, will almost invariably alternate speakers from the government and opposition benches.

9.3.3 At the end of most debates there are usually the "winding-up" speeches, concluding with the Minister replying on behalf of the government. On an opposition motion the official opposition spokesman or woman will open but the order of closing speeches will not be reversed. Where there is a single main motion and amendments to it are moved, the order of speeches will usually remain the same as if there were only a motion before the House, even though debate on the amendment(s) has in theory supervened over debate on the main Question. The decisions on both the amendment and the main Question are usually taken at the conclusion of debate. (For the manner in which amendments to a bill are dealt with at the committee or report stage, which is rather different, see paragraphs 11.10.18 to 11.10.26.)

Rule on speaking twice and right of reply

9.3.4 The mover of a *motion*, or of an *amendment*, has the right of reply at the end of debate on the motion or amendment. Otherwise, in the House and at **sittings in Westminster Hall**, Members may speak only once to a Question, unless they are given the leave of the House to speak a second time. Such leave must be unanimous, and will usually be ascertained by the Chair before the Member is called to speak a second time. The mover of an *order of the day* (see paragraph 7.8.2) does not have the automatic right of reply to the debate, but he or she may reserve the right to speak later in a debate by moving the order formally (that is by saying no more than "I beg to move") at the outset. Under S.O. No. 76, during the report stage of a bill (see section 11.13.12), the rule is relaxed in respect of the Member in charge of the bill (see paragraph 11.2.6) and the movers of any amendment or new clause etc.

Interventions

9.3.5 The Member who "has the floor" may choose to give way to other Members who are indicating a wish to intervene. The choice as to whether to do so is at the discretion of the Member who is speaking. They indicate this by announcing "I give way to the honourable Member/my honourable friend for . . ." and resuming their seat. An intervention should be brief and to the point, and after it has been made, the Member who has the floor resumes their speech. An intervention does not exhaust the right of any Member making it to speak in the debate, nor are any prevented from making an intervention if they have spoken previously in the debate (see also paragraph 9.7.3).

Speaking more than once in committee

9.3.6 In standing committees, or when the House itself is in committee of the whole House, the rule against speaking more than once does not apply. Thus the notion of intervening is of less significance in committee, but the convention that a Member may give way to another while retaining the floor of the committee still obtains.

9.3.7 The only exception to the relaxation of the rule against speaking more than once to a Question in committees is when a second reading debate takes place in a standing committee (see paragraph 11.6.6 to 11.6.16), where it still applies. In all other types of committees Members may speak to the same Question as often as they wish, if called by the Chair.

Place of speaking

9.3.8 In the House, Members speak from their places (they cannot speak from the gangways or wherever), except for the Ministers and **shadow ministers** who speak from the **despatch boxes**. At **sittings in Westminster Hall** and in standing committees, all Members speak from their places.

Forms of address, etc.

9.3.9 Whenever a Member is speaking in the House or in committee or in Westminster Hall, he or she must address the Chair. It is out of order to address another Member directly (for example by referring to "your speech" or saying "you must admit"). Other Members should be referred to in the third person and by reference to their constituencies. Only the Chair may refer to Members by name. Thus, a Member of one's own party is referred to as "my honourable friend for Belsize Park", a Member of another party is referred to as "the honourable Member for Belsize Park". Members who are **privy counsellors** are referred to as "my right honourable friend/the right honourable Member"; Members who are Queen's Counsel are referred to as "my [right] honourable and learned friend/the [right] honourable and learned Member". It is usual to refer to Ministers by their titles, eg "the Secretary of State", "the Minister of State", or "the Parliamentary Secretary". The House of Lords is sometimes referred to as "the other place" but may quite properly be referred to by its name.

Respect for the Chair

9.3.10 The occupant of the Chair in the House should be addressed as Mr Speaker, Mr/Madam Deputy Speaker as appropriate. The same rule applies at sittings in Westminster Hall when chaired by one of the Deputy Speakers (see paragraph 3.2.6). When the House is in committee, the Chair may be addressed as Mr/Madam Chairman or Mr/Mrs Smith, as appropriate; and the same convention applies in standing committees. When the occupant of the Chair stands, all other Members (including the one speaking) should resume their seats. While in general private conversations during debates should be discreet and brief, it is particularly the case that Members should keep silent when the Chair is speaking.

Courtesies to other Members

9.3.11 The House has reaffirmed that Members should be present to listen to the opening speeches of a debate in which they intend to seek to participate and should remain present at least for the two speeches which follow their own. If they do speak in a debate, they should also be present to listen to the reply of the Minister or other Member at the conclusion of that debate, and if they cannot, they should apologise to the House in advance in their speech.

9.3.12 A Member who intends to refer to another Member on the floor of the House should make every reasonable effort to ensure that the Member who is the object of any remarks (especially if personally critical) is aware of this intention. Similarly, a Member who intends to raise matters relating to another Member's constituency should inform that other Member in advance.

Content of speeches

9.3.13 The general rule governing the language of debate is that the principles of courtesy and moderation should be observed at all times. In particular, it is disorderly to impute dishonourable motives to any other Member's words or actions. The most grievous breach of this convention is to accuse another Member of lying to the House or deliberately misleading the House or one of its committees (which would be a contempt of the House and would therefore, if seriously alleged, properly be the subject of a formal complaint under the procedure described in paragraph 4.2.12). If the attention of the Chair is called to such an accusation made in the course of debate, the Member making it will be required immediately to withdraw it. It is also disorderly to call into question the conduct of either House. Points of order may be raised about the proceedings of the Commons, but the proceedings of the Lords should not be questioned or impugned.

9.3.14 Members speaking in debate should stick to the subject of debate. If the relevance of the points they are making is not apparent, the Chair will call them to order. S.O. No. 42 empowers the Chair to order a Member to resume his or her seat and to stop speaking if he or she persists in irrelevance or the tedious repetition of arguments already made either by that Member or by previous contributors to the debate.

9.3.15 The Chair deprecates extensive quotation from documents, particularly those which are not of an official nature and which have not been laid before the House. Members other than those speaking from the **despatch box** (see paragraph 9.3.8) should not read their speeches, though it is quite usual to refer to notes.

9.3.16 The House has imposed a self-denying ordinance upon itself through its *sub judice* resolution against referring in debate to matters which are before the courts. The resolution was re-affirmed, in modified form, on 15 November 2001, in response to a recommendation of the Joint Committee on Parliamentary Privilege of March 1999. It is set out in Figure 20.

The Sub-Judice Resolution

That, subject to the discretion of the Chair, and to the right of the House to legislate on any matter or to discuss any delegated legislation, the House in all its proceedings (including proceedings of committees of the House) shall apply the following rules to matters *sub judice:*

1. Cases in which proceedings are active in the United Kingdom courts shall not be referred to in any motion, debate or question.

(a)(i) Criminal proceedings are active when a charge has been made or a summons to appear has been issued, or, in Scotland, a warrant to cite has been granted.

(ii) Criminal proceedings cease to be active when they are concluded by verdict and sentence or discontinuance, or, in cases dealt with by courts martial, after the conclusion of the mandatory post-trial review.

(b)(i) Civil proceedings are active when arrangements for the hearing, such as setting down the case for trial, have been made, unless the proceedings are ended by judgement or discontinuance.

(ii) Any application made in or for the purposes of any civil proceedings shall be treated as a distinct proceeding.

(c) Appellate proceedings, whether criminal or civil, are active from the time when they are commenced by application for leave to appeal or by notice of appeal until ended by judgement or discontinuance.

But where a ministerial decision is in question, or in the opinion of the Chair a case concerns issues of national importance such as the economy, public order or the essential services, reference to the issues or the case may be made in motions, debates or questions.

2. Specific matters which the House has expressly referred to any judicial body for decision and report shall not be referred to in any motion, debate or question from the time when the resolution of the House is passed until the report is laid before the House.

3. For the purposes of this resolution –

(a) matters before Coroners Courts or Fatal Accident Inquiries shall be treated as matters within paragraph 1(a):
(b) 'Motion' includes a motion for leave to bring in a bill;
(c) 'Question' includes a supplementary question.

FIGURE 20
THE SUB-JUDICE RESOLUTION

9.3.17 The new version of the rule is pretty much self-explanatory. It clarifies two things which were previously undefined. These are: that the rule does not apply to judicial review of ministerial decisions; and that it does apply to proceedings in committees, including, for example, examination of witnesses by a select committee. It also clearly reasserts that its application is, in the end, always a matter for the Chair, and that the rule cannot prevent reference during a debate on either primary or subordinate legislation to a case before the courts if it is clearly relevant to that legislation.

9.3.18 In accordance with the same principle of forbearance from interfering with the independence of the courts, it is out of order to criticise the actions of judges. Judges of the higher courts can only be removed from office by an address of both Houses to the Crown. This emphasises the importance attached to the separation of the courts from Parliament, subject always to Parliament's final sovereignty.

9.3.19 It is out of order to attempt to use the name of Sovereign or the heir to the throne to influence debate. It is also out of order to make personal reflections on the words or actions of members of the royal family, though some latitude is allowed where a public statement has been made by one of them. It has in the past been held to be out of order to criticise the actions of the Queen's representatives (eg governors general and so forth) or the heads of state or governments of Commonwealth countries or other countries with which the United Kingdom has friendly relations, but this convention is nowadays rarely enforced.

9.3.20 It is also out of order to criticise the Chair or the presiding officer of the Lords, or to question decisions of the Chair.

9.3.21 The general exemption to the rules against criticism of these various classes of persons described above in debate is that it is always open to the House to consider and debate a substantive motion critical of any individual or group. It is therefore open to a Member to table an early day motion (see chapter 16) critical of any such person, although it could only be debated if the government (or opposition) made time available to do so.

9.3.22 It is out of order to draw attention directly to the presence of **strangers** in the House or in a committee, such as civil servants advising a Minister from their box, or persons present in the public and other galleries of the House.

Disorderly conduct

9.3.23 It is in general out of order to seek to disrupt the proceedings of the House by actions calculated to do so, for example by persistently interrupting the Member who is speaking by sedentary interruptions or attempts to drown out his or her speech, by refusing to resume one's seat when ordered to do so by the Chair, by remaining in the gangways of the Chamber when directed by the Chair to disperse, or by other deliberate obstruction.

9.3.24 Under S.O. No. 43, the Chair may order any Member, the content of whose speech or whose conduct is grossly disorderly, to withdraw immediately from the House for the remainder of that day's sitting. If the Member refuses to obey such a direction the Chair may direct the Serjeant at Arms to enforce the order, but would normally have immediate resort to its power to name a Member.

9.3.25 Under S.O. No. 44, the Chair has the power to "name" a Member guilty of disorderly conduct. The Chair would normally deploy this power only after every effort had been made to persuade the Member to desist from his or her disorderly conduct. As soon as the Chair pronounces "I name Mr X", a Minister (the **Leader of the House** if available) will immediately move the motion "That [such Member] be suspended from the service of the House", and the

Chair immediately puts the Question on that motion. Out of respect for the authority of the Chair, Members may in general be disinclined to oppose such a motion, but if it is opposed, and tellers for the Noes can be found, it may be forced to a **division**. It would be very unusual for any front benchers to fail to support the Chair in such a division, whatever party the Member named might belong to. There is a particular obligation on members of the Chairmen's Panel (see paragraph 3.2.6) to support the authority of the Chair in such circumstances.

9.3.26 When such a motion has been agreed, the Member is automatically suspended for five sitting days from the service of the House. During this period of suspension he or she may not sit, speak or vote in the House or in any committee, may not table questions or motions and may not have any questions answered. Any questions or motions standing in his or her name are removed from the **Order Paper**, **Notice Paper** and **Order Book** (see section 15.1) for the duration of the suspension.

9.3.27 If a Member is suspended under this standing order for a second time in a session, the suspension is automatically for twenty sitting days. On a third such occasion, the suspension is for the remainder of that session of Parliament.

9.3.28 Once such a motion is passed, the Member named must immediately (in accordance with S.O. No. 45) withdraw from the House, as soon as the Chair so directs. If the Member fails to do so, and the Chair is forced to require the Serjeant at Arms to enforce the direction, the suspension is automatically increased to last for the remainder of that session.

9.3.29 Paragraph (3) of the standing order provides for the Chair to name more than one Member at once if they have acted jointly in disobeying the Chair.

9.3.30 Even if a Member has been named, as S.O. No. 44 picturesquely puts it, nothing in that standing order "shall be taken to deprive the House of the power of proceeding against any Member according to its ancient usages".

9.3.31 Under S.O. No. 45(2), a Member suspended is still obliged to attend any committee on a private bill (see section 11.19) to which he or she may have been nominated, even during a period of suspension.

9.3.32 Under S.O. No 45A, a Member suspended from the House receives no parliamentary salary for the duration of the suspension (this provision includes occasions when they are suspended for reasons other than disorderly conduct pursuant to S.O. No. 44).

9.3.33 S.O. No. 46 gives the Chair power to suspend the sitting for a specified time or even to adjourn the sitting completely in cases of grave disorder.

Disorder in committees

9.3.34 Chairmen of standing committees do not have delegated to them the powers available to the Speaker and his deputies in the House for dealing with defiance of the authority of the Chair. If a Member who is not so entitled attempts to intervene in debate in a standing committee, or sits in one of the places reserved only for Members appointed to that committee, or if a Member of a committee behaves in a disorderly manner, the chairman would direct him or her to desist. If this instruction was ignored, the chairman would normally suspend the committee to give an opportunity for the matter to be resolved. If the Member were to persist in defying the Chair when proceedings were resumed, the government **Whip** on the committee would move a motion to report the Member to the House. When that had been agreed, if the disorder still persisted, a motion to adjourn the committee would be moved. In extreme circumstances the chairman might adjourn the committee without putting the Question.

9.3.35 After a committee had passed a motion to report a Member the chairman would, at the earliest opportunity, make a brief report to the House either orally or in writing. Usually, the **Leader of the House** would subsequently (probably at the next sitting) move a motion to give power to the chairman to act appropriately if the disorder recurred at a subsequent sitting of the committee.

9.3.36 If disorder occurred when the House was sitting as a committee of the whole House, and it was necessary for the Chair to name a Member, the House would come out of committee to enable the necessary suspension motion to be moved.

Disorder in the galleries

9.3.37 If a Member were to attempt to speak from the galleries other than the Members' galleries in the Chamber, or from the public gallery in a committee room, he or she would be subject in principle to the same penalties as if the offence occurred on the floor.

9.3.38 Any member of the public attempting to intervene in the proceedings of the House from the gallery, or otherwise causing disorder, is committing a contempt of the House and will be removed by the Serjeant at Arms and detained (usually for the remainder of the sitting). In cases of grave disorder the House in theory has the freedom to punish an offender as it sees fit, but where a criminal offence had occurred it is likely that the person would be handed over to the police. If the House did choose to pursue an offender, the matter would be referred to the **Committee on Standards and Privileges** (see section 4.1) which, after investigation, could recommend punishment.

9.4 Interrupting or Abandoning Debate

Dilatory motions

9.4.1 Although, in principle, once a Question is before the House (or a committee) it must be disposed of before the House (or committee) can proceed to other business, it is possible to supersede the Question by a "dilatory motion". This is a motion for the adjournment of the debate, or of the House, or of the committee. In debates on bills, it may be a motion that further consideration of the bill be adjourned, or that the chairman do report progress. S.O. No. 34 confines the scope of debate on such a motion to "the matter of such motion". More importantly, S.O. No. 35 gives the Chair power to decline to propose such a motion if it considers that it is an abuse of the rules of the House. This power is delegated to the chairmen of standing committees by S.O. No. 89. It is rare, though far from unprecedented, for the Chair to allow such a motion from a Member other than a member of the government or the Member in charge of a bill (see paragraphs 11.2.6 and 11.2.7) which is under discussion.

Absence of a quorum and motions to sit in private

9.4.2 Although not a dilatory motion under the terms of S.O. Nos. 35 and 36, the motion "That the House sit in private" (formerly "That strangers do now withdraw") is usually called in order to interrupt the business in hand. (If passed, it requires persons who are not Members or officers of either House to withdraw, although the Speaker has power to require this without a motion). A Member wishing to have such a motion put to the House may at any time rise in his or her place and move "That the House sit in private" (they do not need to be called to speak by the Chair). Under S.O. No. 163(1), the Chair is required immediately to put the Question. No debate is possible, and the Chair has no discretion to refuse the motion. The purpose of forcing this motion to be put is most often to test whether a **quorum** of the House is present. Under S.O. No. 41(1), a quorum of the House is forty, and therefore in any division at least thirty-five Members must be recorded as voting (since the four tellers and the occupant of the Chair count towards the quorum). If fewer than this number are recorded as voting when the tellers report the result to the House, the standing order requires that the business then before the House stands over to another sitting, and that the House should proceed to the next item of business. In this way, if a division on a motion to sit in private is inquorate, a debate may be terminated in mid-stream. Paragraph (2) of S.O. No. 41 prevents the question of whether a quorum is present being raised other than in a division. Such a motion can be made only once in a sitting.

9.4.3 At sittings in Westminster Hall, the quorum is three. If fewer Members are present, debate cannot continue.

9.4.4 A fundamental difference between the House and a *standing committee* is that the latter must have a quorum of its members present at all times for proceedings to continue. The quorum is one-third of the total membership, with fractions rounded up. The chairman is not included in the total in calculating the quorum, but counts towards it when the committee is sitting. If no quorum has gathered within twenty minutes of the time appointed for a committee to meet, the chairman will adjourn the committee to its next appointed time of sitting. If Members leave the committee once it has begun so as to reduce the numbers present below a quorum, the chairman must immediately suspend the sitting until a quorum is present. If a quorum does not regather within twenty minutes, the chairman will adjourn the committee until the next time at which it is appointed to sit.

The previous Question

9.4.5 Debate on a Question may also be superseded by moving the **previous Question**. This takes the form "That the Question be not now put." Any Member who has the floor may move this Question at any point in a debate. It is debatable. It may itself be subject to the closure (see paragraph 9.7.4 below).

If agreed to, it has the effect of immediately adjourning the debate on the Question previously before the House and moving the House on to the next item on the **Order Paper**. If it is negatived, the effect is to require the Chair to immediately put the Question previously before the House (rather in the manner of the closure proper). The previous Question is now considered a rather antique procedure and is rarely used.

Withdrawal of a Question

9.4.6 At the conclusion of debate, the mover of the Question may decide, rather than pressing the issue to a decision, to withdraw the motion or amendment. Only the mover of a Question may seek to withdraw it. However, once a Question has been proposed by the Chair it is in the possession of the House or committee and cannot be unilaterally withdrawn. The mover who seeks to withdraw a Question should end his or her reply to the debate with the formula "I beg leave, therefore, to withdraw the motion [or amendment]" or words to that effect. It can then only be withdrawn with the unanimous agreement of the House or the committee. If there is a single call of objection to the request for leave to withdraw, the Question cannot be withdrawn and must be put by the Chair for decision. After the mover has been given leave to withdraw a Question, no further debate can take place. If another Member rises to speak, this in itself signifies objection to the request for leave to withdraw, and means that the Question must eventually be put for decision. Once leave to withdraw a particular Question has been refused it cannot subsequently be sought again.

9.5 CONCLUDING DEBATE

Ending debate

9.5.1 Debate may be brought to a conclusion in a number of ways. At its simplest, when no further Members rise in their place to indicate to the Chair that they wish to speak, the debate will have ended and the Chair will *put* the Question to the House or the committee (see paragraph 9.5.4 below). Usually, as the **moment of interruption** arrives (see paragraph 6.1.7) the House will voluntarily end its debate so that the Question before it may be decided, although on occasions a Member will seek deliberately to talk out a debate by speaking up to the moment of interruption. In these circumstances, the **closure** (see paragraphs 9.7.4 and 9.7.5 below) may be claimed at the moment of interruption.

9.5.2 Alternatively, the Chair may be required to put a Question at a specified time, or at the end of a specified period of time, under the provisions of a standing order, or of a business motion which has previously been passed by the House in relation to the particular item or items of business (see paragraph 7.7.6) or under a programme order (see section 11.18). A programme order will specify that all the Questions necessary to conclude specified stages of a bill must be put successively at this point, that is, all amendments or contingent questions as well as the Question immediately before the House and the main Question, plus all government amendments relating to the parts of the bill for which the time available for debate has expired. In these circumstances the Chair will simply interrupt debate and put the Question or Questions to the House or committee.

9.5.3 S.O. No. 31(2) provides for a special procedure for concluding debates on opposition days (see paragraph 2.2.2). Almost invariably, on such days, the government will table an amendment to leave out all the effective words of the motion proposed by the opposition (that is, everything from the words "That this House") and insert alternative words. The standing order provides that where such an amendment is proposed, instead of the Question on the amendment being put first as would usually happen, the first question to be put is "That the original words stand part of the Question". When this is defeated, the Question that the amendment be made is put forthwith and, if agreed, the Speaker declares the main Question, as amended, to be agreed to. This provision has the effect of enabling the first division on an opposition day to be on the opposition motion rather than on the government's amendment, and generally makes a second division unnecessary.

9.5.4 At **sittings in Westminster Hall**, the time limit on debate is defined by a duration from the start of the sitting, allowing for time taken by divisions in the House (though if debate ended early, the sitting could resolve to adjourn itself). At the end of that time limit, the Chair simply interrupts proceedings and the Question before the sitting lapses. There is no provision for extending time limits. At sittings of delegated legislation standing committees (see paragraphs 12.3.23 to 12.3.29) and European standing committees (see paragraphs 13.2.10 to 13.2.16), a similar rule applies (with varying time limits depending on the type of business). When the time limit expires, the Chair simply interrupts proceedings and puts the Question for decision (including any Question on amendments to the main Question).

Making a decision

9.5.5 In the House, when debate is concluded by whatever means, unless the Question has lapsed, or been withdrawn or superseded, the Chair puts the Question that has previously been *proposed* to the House. It does this in the form "The Question is the motion on the Order Paper/that the House do now adjourn/that the amendment be made" (or whatever). The Chair then immediately "collects the voices" by saying "As many as are of that opinion say Aye", at which point those in favour call "Aye", then "As many as are of the contrary opinion say No", at which point those who disagree with the proposition before the House may call out "No".

9.5.6 If there are either no calls of "Aye" or none of "No", the Question is negatived or agreed to, as the case may be, without further ado. If there are calls from both sides, the Chair, "having regard to the probabilities of the case" (that is normally presuming the government is in the majority) as well as to the volume of the calls from each side will announce "I think the Ayes [or the Noes] have it". If the opinion of the Chair is not challenged at that point, the Question is determined in accordance with that opinion and is agreed to or negatived as the case may be. If, when the Chair announces "I think the Ayes have it", Members continue to call "No" (or vice versa), the House or committee proceeds to a division.

9.6 DIVISIONS

Procedure on divisions

9.6.1 If its opinion is challenged as described above, the Chair is required (except in the case where a division is automatically deferred, for which see below) by S.O. No. 38(1) to announce "Clear the lobby", which is the signal for the **division bells** to be rung throughout the House and its precincts, and elsewhere where they are installed. There are two short bursts of continuous ringing. This is the signal for Members who wish to vote to come to the Chamber and enter the **division lobby** of their choice.

9.6.2 Not more than two minutes after the direction to clear the lobby has been given, the Chair again puts the Question to the House (by now usually half empty as Members have departed for the division lobbies), collects the voices once more and declares its opinion as to whether the Ayes or Noes have it. If its opinion is not challenged at this point, the division is called off, and the Question is determined in accordance with the Chair's opinion. If it is to be challenged, both sides must have given the names of two tellers to the Chair. If either side has failed to nominate two tellers, the opinion of the other side is deemed to have prevailed and the division is called off. The names of the tellers are announced by the Chair, after which they repair to the exits from each lobby (one from each side to each exit).

9.6.3 When the tellers arrive at their places, the doors are opened wide enough to permit one Member to leave at a time. Before leaving the lobby, each Member must pass a desk at which a Clerk records his or her name on a list which is used to publish in the **Official Report** the names of Members voting on each side. As each Member leaves the lobby, one of the tellers counts out loud the total number who have passed, and the opposing side's teller checks that the tally is accurate.

9.6.4 Not less than eight minutes after giving the direction to clear the lobby, the Chair gives an instruction for the doors to be locked. After this, no further Members may enter either division lobby. Any still present in the lobbies make their way out, being counted by the tellers. The last Member out (usually a **Whip**) announces "all out" to the tellers, who then return to the **Table** and report to the Clerks the number of Members who have voted on their side. When both pairs of tellers have made their report, they go down and stand five paces before the Table, facing the Chair. The pair from the side which is in the majority are to the Speaker's left. They bow, advance to the Table, bow again, and one of the tellers for the majority reads out the result from the slip provided. A Clerk then takes that slip to the Chair, who repeats the figures and announces "so the Ayes [or Noes] have it". The Question is then decided.

9.6.5 S.O. No. 39(1) makes clear that a Member does not have to have been present in the Chamber to hear the Question put in order to be able to vote in a division.

9.6.6 S.O. No. 39(2) states that no Member is obliged to vote in a division. This principle is qualified by the practice of the House that vote should follow voice. In other words, it is not permissible for a Member who has called Aye or No when the Chair collected the voices to then record his or her vote in the opposite lobby or to fail to vote in the division at all. If this were to happen and it was raised on a **point of order**, the Chair could direct that the Member's vote should be recorded in the division lists in accordance with their voice.

Abstentions

9.6.7 There is no real provision for Members to record an abstention on a division, other than by ensuring that their name is absent from the division lists. Sometimes a Member will choose ostentatiously to remain in his or her place in the Chamber while a division is in progress to signifiy abstention. Occasionally, however, a Member will vote in both lobbies where he or she has voted the wrong way through inadvertence and wishes to cancel that vote.

Division unnecessarily claimed

9.6.8 Under S.O. No. 40, the Chair may, if of the opinion that a division is unnecessary because one side is so clearly in a minority, curtail the process of a full division. If the Chair were to choose to exercise this power, after the expiry of the two minutes from the direction to clear the lobby, at the point when the Question is put the second time, the Chair would call for the Members in favour and the Members against the Question to rise in turn in their places, and, if it was clear which side was in the majority, declare the Question to be decided accordingly, or allow the division to proceed if the majority was not clear. This power is very rarely exercised.

Quorum on divisions

9.6.9 The quorum of the House is forty, but in contrast to standing committees (see paragraph 9.4.3 above), it is only when the result of a division is announced that the question of whether the House is quorate (see paragraph 9.4.2 above) arises. For a division to be valid, at least thirty-five Members must be recorded as voting (as the four tellers and the Chair count towards the quorum).

Deferred divisions

9.6.10 A temporary standing order was introduced in the 2000–01 session, and renewed for the 2001–02 and again for the 2002–03 sessions, introducing into the proceedings of the House the entirely novel concept of "deferred divisions". Its purpose is to increase the predictability of the times at which Members need to be present in the House. This order provides (with certain exceptions described below) that if on any sitting day the Speaker's opinion on collecting the voices on any Question put *after* the **moment of interruption** is challenged, the division does not then take place, but is automatically deferred. When this happens, the vote on that Question is postponed to the following sitting Wednesday. On that Wednesday, a voting paper is published with the daily **Vote Bundle**. The paper lists all the Questions to which the process of deferral has been applied in the previous week, with boxes against each Question in which Members may mark their votes "Aye" or "No". Between 12.30 pm and 2 pm on that day, Members may deposit their voting papers with the Clerks who are on duty in the No lobby to receive them. (If a division is called in the House during this period, the voting on the deferred divisions is suspended, and the closing time for depositing voting papers is extended to allow for the times taken by any divisions occurring between 12.30 pm and 2 pm.) At the end of this time the votes are counted by the Clerks, and the results are immediately reported to the Chair, who announces them to the House at the earliest convenient moment. The decisions are recorded in the **Votes and Proceedings**, and the lists of Members voting on each side on each Question are published in the following day's **Hansard**.

9.6.11 The temporary standing order disapplies this process of automatic deferral from a number of specified types of Question. All Questions relating to proceedings on bills, or to the timetabling of proceedings on bills (by way of **allocation of time motions** or **programme motions**) are exempt, and are proceeded with in the normal way. Any motion which can be moved without **notice** is similarly exempt (this might for example be a motion **naming** a Member). Any amendment which has been proposed to a motion is again exempt, as is the motion to which the amendment is proposed (because it would be impossible to decide such a Question in a deferred division since it would not be known whether or not the main Question which Members were being invited to decide upon had been amended). Any **ten o'clock motion** (taken at seven o'clock on Tuesdays or Wednesdays or 6 pm on Thursdays or 2.30 pm on Fridays) exempting other business on that day's **Order Paper** from the effect of the **moment of interruption** (see paragraph 7.10.4) is exempt from deferral (for obvious reasons). **Ways and Means motions** providing for a bill to be brought in (usually the Finance Bill) are also exempt, as are the other types of motion which follow the **Budget Statement** or come at the end of the Budget debate (see paragraphs 10.2.19 to 10.2.24). So are **Money Resolutions**, whether under the standing orders they fall to be decided without debate or after forty-five minutes time-limited debate (see paragraphs 10.2.1 to 10.2.5). Motions to approve the **Estimates** taken on Estimates Days, on which the **Consolidated Fund Bills** are founded (see section 10.3), are also exempt from deferral.

9.6.12 As well as the classes of Questions exempted which are described above, the temporary standing order also provides for a Minister to move a motion after the **moment of interruption** to provide that deferral shall not apply to any division forced on any subsequent Questions relating to business standing on the **Order Paper** for that day. Such a motion, obviously, is itself exempt from deferral, and if moved is decided without debate.

Divisions in standing committee

9.6.13 Divisions in standing committee are taken by roll call. If the Chair's opinion as to how the voices on a Question have voted is challenged, he or she will announce a division. Up to two minutes are allowed for Members not present to arrive, after which the Chairman gives the instruction to lock the doors of the committee room. The Clerk then calls out the name of each Member present in turn, and each replies Aye or No (or "No vote") as they wish. The Clerk then tots up the figures, hands the result to the Chairman, who announces it and gives the instruction to unlock the doors.

Casting vote

9.6.14 The Chair (whether in the House or in standing committee) only votes in the event that the numbers voting in a division are equal on both sides. Although the Chair has the right to cast its vote as it thinks fit, in practice the choice is determined by precedent. There are two basic rules. The first is that, whenever possible, the Chair should cast its vote in such a way as to allow the House (or committee) a further opportunity to reach a decision on the matter before it. Therefore, on the Question that a bill be read a second time, the Chair would vote Aye, to enable the House to give further consideration to the bill at its later stages. The second and subordinate governing principle is that a decision should not be made unless there is a majority in its favour. Therefore, on the Question that a bill be read the third time, the Chair would vote No, because there is no further opportunity for consideration by the House, and a majority has not been obtained. At the committee or the report stage of a bill the Chair, in accordance with the second principle, would vote on an amendment or new clause in such a way as to leave the bill in its original state. On procedural motions (such as one for the adjournment) the Chair would generally vote so as to enable the House or committee to make progress with the business in hand.

Divisions in select committees

9.6.15 Divisions in select committees are held by roll call, as with standing committees. Unlike in the House or in standing committee, a Member who was not present to hear the Question put cannot vote in a division on that Question. The results of all divisions and the names of the Members voting on either side are recorded in the *Minutes of Proceedings* of the committee. Where there is an equality of votes in a select committee, the Chair may cast its vote in accordance with personal judgement, rather than precedent.

Irregularities in divisions

9.6.16 Where something disorderly or untoward has happened in a division in the House, the matter should be reported to the Chair as soon as possible, even during the division, on a **point of order**. The Chair has ordered the results of divisions to be altered where a Member was recorded incorrectly as voting in one or the other lobby. Where Members have refused to leave a lobby during a division the Chair has sent the **Serjeant at Arms** to order them to do so.

Westminster Hall

9.6.17 No divisions can be taken at sittings in Westminster Hall. S.O. No. 10 provides a mechanism for referring substantive Questions which are not agreed to unanimously at a sitting in Westminster Hall to the House for decision. So far, no substantive motion or order of the day has been referred to Westminster Hall (see section 6.3).

9.7 CURTAILING DEBATE

Introduction

9.7.1 The usual ways in which debate may be drawn to a conclusion are described in paragraphs 9.5.1 and 9.5.2 above. This may be because no further Members wish to speak, under the provisions of a standing order or under the provisions of a **business motion** or a **programme order** applying to a specific item, or specified items, of business. Where none of these apply, there are other methods of curtailing debate or bringing the House to a decision.

Closure on proposal of a Question

9.7.2 Under S.O. No. 29, during proceedings on a bill in the House or in a committee, if a Member has prolonged his or her speech in moving an amendment or making any motion (such as moving a new clause), so that the Question cannot be proposed, and cannot therefore be closured, a Member may interrupt the speech and claim to move "That the Question be now proposed". Unless the Chair considers this an abuse, it immediately puts that Question to the House or committee and, if it is agreed to, immediately proposes the Question, thus terminating the mover's speech. This standing order is rarely invoked.

Short Speeches

9.7.3 Under S.O. No. 47, the Speaker may announce at the beginning of a debate that he intends, between specified times or during the whole of the debate, to limit the length of back bench speeches to a period of not less than eight minutes (and usually no more than fifteen). This rule does not apply to Ministers, official opposition front bench spokesmen or one nominated Member speaking on behalf of the second largest opposition party. If the Speaker has made such an announcement, at the end of the permitted period the Chair may direct any Member to whom the standing order applies to resume his or her seat. Under paragraph (2) of the standing order, the Chair *is required* to add one minute to this time limit for one intervention (plus the time actually taken by the intervention), and a maximum of two minutes for two or more interventions (plus the time actually taken by the first two interventions). For the meaning of "intervention" see paragraph 9.3.5 above.

Closure

9.7.4 Under S.O. No. 36, during a debate any Member may interrupt whoever is speaking and rise in their place and claim to move "That the Question be now put". This is known as *claiming the closure*. If the Chair is willing to allow the motion (and it has complete discretion in the matter, though certain tacit conventions apply), the Question is immediately put to the House for decision. If a division is forced on the closure, in order for it to be agreed, S.O. No. 37 requires that the Ayes must not only be in the majority but must also have at least 100 Members voting in that lobby. If the closure is agreed, the Chair must immediately proceed to put the Question which has been closured for a decision. If there are subsequent Questions which are contingent on the Question which has been successfully closured, the Member who claimed the closure may also request the Chair immediately to put those Questions (for example, if it was the Question on an amendment that was closured, the main Question is also effectively subject to the closure).

9.7.5 The closure may be claimed at the **moment of interruption** (see paragraphs 6.1.6 and section 7.10), and Questions consequential on a closure successfully claimed may be decided after the moment of interruption.

Closure in standing committee

9.7.6 The closure may be claimed in standing committee, and the Chair has the same discretion whether to accept it as is described in paragraph 9.7.4. The number voting for the closure in a standing committee must at least equal the quorum of the committee (and be the majority) for it to be agreed. The closure on proposal of the Question (see paragraph 9.7.2) can also be claimed in standing committee.

Timetabling of Bills

9.7.7 S.O. No. 83 still provides for a Minister to propose a motion in the House (formally known as an **allocation of time motion**, and colloquially as a "guillotine") which comprises a complex series of provisions requiring all the Questions necessary to dispose of specified stages of bills to be put at specified times. The use of such motions is described more fully in section 11.18. Guillotine motions may only be moved by a Minister, and can only apply to proceedings on bills. The standing order requires the Question on such a motion to be put three hours after the debate on it has commenced. However, in current practice, guillotines have been largely superseded by the routine use of "programming" for government bills.

9.7.8 Following proposals from the **Modernisation Committee** made in 1997 and subsequently elaborated and further endorsed in 2002, the House has experimented in recent sessions with the use of so-called programme orders for certain of government bills. Since the beginning of the 2001 Parliament the use of programme orders has become routine for virtually every government bill. Programme motions are moved immediately after the second reading of a bill. They have the effect of setting a detailed timetable (with the use of supplementary motions) for each and every stage of a bill's progress after second reading. The temporary standing orders make standard provisions relating to these timetables which used to have to be passed separately for each guillotine. They are described more fully in paragraphs 11.1.6 to 11.1.8 and section 11.18.

Time limits and Questions put forthwith

9.7.9 A whole variety of types of business are subject to specified time limits under the provisions of different standing orders. Most of these have been described in paragraphs 7.10.9 to 7.10.16, and they are set out in tabular form in Figure 17. When the specified time has passed, the Chair is required to interrupt debate and put the Question for decision.

9.7.10 Another wide category of Questions is not debated at all under the provisions of various standing orders. Most of these are types of motions relating to matters which have already been considered by, and reported from, standing committees (see paragraphs 11.6.11, 11.6.13, 11.6.17, 11.6.19, 12.3.11 and

13.2.16). There are others which are of a contingent or formal nature. The types of Question which are put **forthwith**, that is, without debate, are set out in Figures 16 and 18.

On the nod

9.7.11 Of course, a wide range of Questions (for example, government amendments to bills, business motions, changes in committee membership and many other motions) are not debated because no Member wishes to debate them. The Question may be proposed formally by a Member (simply by nodding or saying "I beg to move" when called by the Chair) and if no other Member rises to speak, the Chair puts the Question for immediate decision, and it will usually be agreed without division. Such Questions are described as having been taken "on the nod", and many Questions are decided in this way both before and after the **moment of interruption**.

9.8 Avoiding Decisions: Substantive Adjournment Motions

9.8.1 Sometimes it is deemed convenient for the House to have a debate without being required to come to any decision on a specific motion. In these cases it debates the motion "That this House do now adjourn". The proposed subject for debate is shown in a rubric on the **Order Paper** under the terms of the motion. Such debates are almost invariably taken in what is technically government time, although it is frequently used to provide for opportunities for back benchers to choose the subject of debate. For example, this device is currently used for all the debates which take place at sittings in **Westminster Hall** (see section 6.3). In the House, when an adjournment motion is being used for the purposes of the main debate of the day, it is generally either withdrawn or simply talked-out at the **moment of interruption**.

9.8.2 Adjournment motions under S.O. No. 24 to discuss an urgent matter (see paragraph 7.6.6) are a special type of substantive adjournment debate. If the House has given leave for such an urgent motion to be moved, it is usually taken as the first business on the day after leave has been granted. The debate may, under paragraph (2) of the standing order, continue for three hours.

9.8.3 If, for some reason, Members wish to signal their disapproval of the government at the end of a debate on an adjournment motion, they may force a division on the Question. In these circumstances the government will normally vote against its own motion in order to protect the following business. If, however, the motion is agreed to, the House must immediately adjourn, and no further business can be taken at that sitting.

9.8.4 Such substantive motions for the adjournment should be distinguished from dilatory motions (see paragraph 9.4.1 above) or the daily adjournment motion under S.O. No. 9 (see paragraph 7.12.1). To the uninitiated it can seem rather odd that the House may spend the whole day debating whether it should adjourn and that immediately that debate has lapsed at the **moment of interruption** the very same Question is again proposed under S.O. No. 9 and agreed to half an hour later. Of course, it is rather odd.

9.9 REVERSING OR REVISITING DECISIONS

9.9.1 It is a general rule that once the House (or a committee) has made a decision on a particular Question, that same matter cannot be brought before it again in the same session. It would for example be out of order to attempt to reintroduce a clause that had been deleted from a bill by the House by way of another bill, or to reintroduce a bill on which the House had already reached a decision (whatever the decision was). The same rule applies to motions. In many cases, of course, the question of whether a subsequent bill, motion or whatever is identical in substance, if not in exact wording, to an earlier one can be rather difficult to decide.

9.9.2 If the House, or a committee, wishes to reconsider a matter already decided in the same session, it must first rescind the earlier decision, which can be done on an explicit motion to that effect of which **notice** must have been given. This is rare.

9.9.3 On occasions, the House has agreed to declare earlier proceedings null and void where a procedural error has subsequently been discovered. The proceedings in question have generally been stages of legislation.

9.9.4 Decisions of the House about the regulation of its own proceedings are often of continuing effect (see for example paragraph 9.3.16). This is essentially what the standing orders are. The House may return to such resolutions and orders to repeal or amend them from time to time. The House frequently repeals one of its standing orders, usually in order to replace it with an amended version.

Chapter 10

PUBLIC MONEY

10.1 INTRODUCTION

10.1.1 The "control of **supply**" was, historically, the foundation of Parliament's control of the Crown. In modern times this control is exercised over the government. The power of the Commons to refuse to allow taxes to be levied on the people, or to refuse to vote money to be spent by the government, are the ultimate sanctions which Parliament can invoke to prevent the executive disregarding the will of the legislature.

10.1.2 It is held to be a fundamental principle of the British constitution that it is for the Crown (that is the government) to propose expenditure and for Parliament to grant (or refuse) it, and the same principle applies to proposals to raise taxation. S.O. No. 48 expressly states this fundamental principle that proposals for expenditure can only be recommended by the Crown. In the case of proposals to increase or raise new taxes, the same principle applies by virtue of historical practice. The Commons itself, as distinct from Ministers, does not therefore initiate expenditure or taxation.

10.1.3 In general terms taxes ("charges upon the people" as the standing orders call them) are authorised by Ways and Means resolutions and subsequently by legislation. New expenditure consequent upon proposals contained in a bill is authorised by a money resolution. This resolution provides the founding authority for the clauses in a bill which entail such expenditure. Recurring annual expenditure under existing statutory provision (and other, non-statutory, expenditure) is authorised by the House voting the Estimates, and subsequently by the passage of the annual Consolidated Fund and Appropriation Acts. A simplified outline of the system of parliamentary control of taxation and spending is shown in Figure 21 below.

10.1.4 In former times the House considered matters of public finance in committee of the whole House. When considering requests for taxation, the House sat as a Committee of Ways and Means. When considering the Estimates for expenditure (see below), the House sat as the Committee of Supply. The Committee of Supply was replaced by a system of **Supply Days**, which in 1982 were replaced by **Opposition Days** (see paragraphs 2.2.2 and 2.2.3). The House now has three **Estimates Days** (see section 10.3 below) for consideration of the Estimates. The Committee of Ways and Means has been replaced in modern practice by the special arrangements for debate following the **Budget Statement** (see paragraphs 10.2.19 to 10.2.24).

10.1.5 In accordance with its resolutions of 1671 and 1678, and reinforced by subsequent decisions in 1860 and 1910, the Commons asserts to itself the sole right to determine taxes and to authorise public expenditure on the initiative of the government. The Lords have long acknowledged this exclusive right of the Commons, without challenge in effect since 1909. The effects of this principle, known as the Commons' financial privilege, are described below.

10.1.6 The centrality of financial control to parliamentary authority is reflected in the complexity of the House's procedures in relation to public money. The relevant procedures which occur in the House are described in more detail below. However, the actual formal consideration of taxation and supply occupies relatively little of the House's time. That function has, at least in principle, been largely delegated to the departmentally-related select committees (see section 17.2) and the Public Accounts Committee (see section 10.5), and the work of the departmental select committees forms the basis of debate on the Estimates (see section 10.3).

10.2 MONEY IN BILLS

Money resolutions

10.2.1 S.O. No. 49 requires that any charge upon the public revenue shall be authorised by a resolution of the House. This in particular applies to provisions in bills which will involve the future expenditure of public money. These resolutions (nowadays more often than not couched in very broad terms) are tabled by the government shortly after a government bill has been read the first time, and will appear among the **remaining orders**. Such a resolution may only be initiated by the Crown (ie moved by a Minister), and it is for this reason that the words *Queen's recommendation signified* follow the title of each such motion on the **Order Paper**.

10.2.2 Where a bill starts its parliamentary progress in the Commons, certain parts of it may be printed in italics. These indicate provisions which require the authorisation of a money resolution. In the case of a government bill, the money resolution is normally moved immediately after the bill has been given its second reading (when, under S.O. No. 52(1)(a), it is put **forthwith** and may be decided after the **moment of interruption**). In the case of private Members' bills, where they include words in italics, it is for the government to decide whether to propose a money resolution to authorise that expenditure but, generally speaking, if the bill obtains a second reading, a Minister does move the necessary motion. In these cases, the resolutions are usually moved shortly before the committee stage of the bill is expected to begin (see paragraph 10.2.5 below).

10.2.3 After a bill has been committed (see section 11.7), no clause or schedule which includes provisions requiring the authorisation of a money resolution may be agreed in committee to stand part of the bill before the necessary money resolution has been agreed by the House.

10.2.4 A money resolution may be proposed at any stage during a bill's progress if the government wishes to enlarge the scope of admissible amendments to the bill to cover other new areas of expenditure not previously authorised by a resolution. Not infrequently, for example, a supplementary money resolution is proposed before the report stage of a bill (see section 11.13), where the government wishes to introduce new matter by way of amendment which will involve expenditure not already covered by the original resolution.

10.2.5 Where such a motion is moved on a day other than that on which the bill to which it relates had a second reading, S.O. No. 52(1)(b) provides that it may be debated for up to forty-five minutes, regardless of the **moment of interruption**, after which period the Chair must put the Question for decision.

Money in Lords Bills

10.2.6 Where a bill is brought to the Commons having first passed through the Lords, it is (unhelpfully) not printed with italics to indicate the provisions which involve expenditure. Despite this, an authorising resolution is still required in the Commons before the relevant provisions can be agreed after second reading.

10.2.7 Any bill brought from the Lords which involves expenditure which would require a money resolution will include, as the last subsection of its final clause, a disclaimer stating that "nothing in this Act shall impose any charge on the people or on public funds . . .". This is printed in bold, and there is a note on the first page of the bill stating that these words "were inserted by the Lords to avoid questions of privilege". The words themselves are of course a polite fiction representing the recognition by the Lords of the Commons' financial privilege (see paragraphs 10.2.8 to 10.2.11 below). They are invariably the subject of an amendment in the Commons to leave out the words. If this is the only amendment made by the Commons to a Lords bill, the Lords' consent to the amendment is purely formal. Without this so-called "privilege amendment", the bill would fall foul of S.O. No. 80(a), which would prevent it from proceeding in the Commons.

The Commons' financial privilege

10.2.8 It is in recognition of the Commons' assertion of its exclusive right to initiate or change taxes or authorise public expenditure that the Lords insert the privilege disclaimer into bills initiated in their House which involve expenditure (see paragraph 10.2.7). Additionally, where a bill is sent from the Commons to the Lords, the Commons asserts its right to reject without other reason any amendment proposed to it by the Lords which touches upon public expenditure, although the Commons often chooses to waive its privilege in relation to such amendments and to agree them (see paragraph 11.15.12).

10.2.9 Although the Commons' financial privilege is often waived in relation to expenditure, the power to approve taxation is jealously guarded. In most cases proposals either to initiate or vary taxation provisions cannot be amended by the Lords. This is why, for example, **delegated legislation** relating to taxation is required to be approved only by the Commons under the terms of its parent Acts. However, under S.O. No. 79 the House waives its financial privilege generally in respect of bills brought from the Lords where the Lords propose a bill, or an amendment to a bill, which imposes any "pecuniary penalty, forfeiture or fee" either where these are fines for the punishment of offences or are otherwise intended to secure the operation of the Act, or where they are (broadly speaking) of a kind which would not in the Commons require the authorisation of a Ways and Means resolution (see paragraphs 10.1.3 above and 10.2.18 below). The waiver is also applied generally in the case of private bills (see section 11.19).

Bills of aids and supplies

10.2.10 A bill of aids and supplies is a bill whose primary purpose is to levy taxes or to authorise expenditure. The Consolidated Fund Bills and Finance Bills (see below) are the most obvious examples of bills of aids and supplies. The Commons asserts its sole right to initiate and amend such bills under resolutions of 1671 and 1678, the latter of which states "that all aids and supplies, and aids to his Majesty in Parliament, are the sole gift of the Commons, and all [such] bills . . . ought to begin with the Commons . . . which ought not to be changed or altered by the House of Lords" (see Commons Journals 1667-87, page 509). The Lords in modern times have invariably respected this jealously guarded privilege, and make no attempt to amend a Finance Bill, even though it may not be a money bill within the meaning of the Parliament Act 1911 (see paragraphs 10.2.15 and 10.2.16 below).

10.2.11 Bills of aids and supplies have a special enacting formula at the beginning which indicates (to a very expert eye) the subsidiary role of the Lords in approving them. This is the only overt indication of their special status. Bills other than the Finance and Consolidated Fund bills may fall into the category of bills of aids and supplies, but they are rare.

Bills having expenditure as their main purpose

10.2.12 The effect of the rule (set out in S.O. No. 49 and described in paragraph 10.1.1 above) that expenditure can only be authorised by a resolution initiated by the Crown, is to prevent any Member other than a Minister from initiating legislation of which the main effect is to cause an increase in public expenditure. An example of such a bill might be one to increase the level of state pensions or child benefit. However, to fall foul of this rule, it must be the *main* purpose of such a bill to spend money. Thus if, for example, a bill proposed to establish a new public body, although this would almost certainly require public expenditure and the authority of a money resolution, the *main* purpose of the bill would be the establishment of the new body and the expenditure would be incidental to that purpose.

10.2.13 However, S.O. No. 50 explicitly allows such a bill (of which the "main purpose" is to increase public expenditure) to be introduced by a Minister and for the authorising resolution to be passed *after* the bill has had its second reading. Paragraph (2) of the standing order also permits a Minister to "take up" (see paragraph 11.3.11) a bill brought from the Lords which has as its main purpose an increase in expenditure. S.O. No. 80(b) provides that where such a bill is is taken up by a Minister, it may proceed in the Commons without a prior authorising resolution.

10.2.14 The restriction of the application of S.O. No. 50 and S.O. No. 80(b) to bills introduced or taken charge of by Ministers means that no **private Member** may introduce a bill into the Commons, or take charge of a bill brought from the Lords, the main purpose of which is to create a charge on central government expenditure.

Money bills

10.2.15 A bill of which the *sole* purpose is to raise taxation or to authorise expenditure is defined, under the terms of section 1 of the Parliament Act of 1911, as a "money bill". If the Speaker is satisfied that a bill as passed by the Commons is a money bill within the terms of the Act, he certifies the bill as such (see paragraph 15.1.29) and it is endorsed accordingly before being sent to the Lords (at the beginning of each Parliament, two senior Members are appointed by the House to assist the Speaker in making this determination). The most obvious form of money bill is a Consolidated Fund Bill (see paragraphs 10.3.13 to 10.3.15 below). If a bill so certified is sent to the Lords at least one month before the end of a session, and has not been agreed by the Lords within one month, it may be presented for the royal assent (see section 11.16) without the agreement of the Lords. Thus the Lords have no power to prevent the passing of a money bill into law. The Lords could, in theory, propose amendments to such a bill and the Commons could choose to agree them without invoking the provisions of the Parliament Act, but in practice (and certainly if the bill is also a bill of aids and supplies), the Lords will not consider such a bill in committee.

10.2.16 A money bill is not the same as a bill of aids and supplies, over which the Commons asserts its privileges by virtue of its resolutions long preceding the 1911 Act (see paragraph 10.2.10 above). The annual Finance Bill (see paragraphs 10.2.19 to 10.2.24 below), for example, will always be a bill of aids and supplies, but because sometimes it includes provisions falling outside the definition in the Parliament Act 1911, it may not be capable of certification as a money bill.

Ways and Means resolutions

10.2.17 "A charge upon the people", which means mostly a tax, must, before being incorporated in statute, be authorised by a Ways and Means resolution.

10.2.18 The definition of a charge upon the people extends to charges which, while not explicitly taxation, are in the nature of a compulsory levy. An example might be a requirement upon a class of businesses to pay a levy to finance the activities of some regulatory body established by Act, the benefits from which do not accrue solely to the industry concerned. Provisions in bills requiring money to be paid *into* the Consolidated Fund (see paragraph 10.3.13 below) also require to be authorised by a Ways and Means resolution (unless they are purely incidental to the exercise of a function involving expenditure, in which case the authority forms part of the relevant money resolution).

The Budget and the Finance Bill

10.2.19 Although other bills occasionally require certain of their provisions to be authorised by a Ways and Means resolution (see paragraphs 10.2.17 and 10.2.18 above), the main bill founded upon such resolutions is the **Finance Bill,** which gives legislative effect to the government's taxation proposals announced in the Budget. There is usually only one annual Finance Bill following each annual Budget, but on occasions circumstances (such as the timing of a general election or a change of government) may require a second Budget and bill.

10.2.20 The pre-cursor to the regular annual Budget Statement is the Chancellor of the Exchequer's pre-budget statement (or "green budget") which is made in the autumn. In March or early April (or occasionally at other times) he makes his Budget Statement to the House, setting out, among other matters relating to the state of the economy, his taxation and spending proposals for the next financial year. At the end of his Budget statement a resolution is usually moved to give immediate provisional effect to certain of the taxation proposals (for example on tobacco, alcoholic drinks and petrol) under the provisions of section 5 of the Provisional Collection of Taxes Act 1968, so that the new rates of tax may take effect immediately, before the Finance Bill has been enacted. Under S.O. No. 51(2), the Question on such a motion is put forthwith. Because the Provisional Collection of Taxes Act 1968 only allows taxes to be levied without full statutory authority for a specified period, it is essential that the bill receives its **royal assent** before that time limit expires.

10.2.21 The next motion to be formally moved is usually the *Amendment of the Law* resolution which gives general authority for the law relating to fiscal matters to be altered. However, on occasions the government may choose not to table such a general motion, and some other motion will be moved instead. The **leader of the opposition** then makes his response. It is on this motion that the general debate on the Budget takes place, usually stretching over four or five days, the debate on the motion being adjourned at the end of each of day and resumed on the following day. On the second day, the **shadow** Chancellor of the Exchequer makes his response in the opening speech. On subsequent days the debate is opened by a different Secretary of State, and this may colour the subject matter of the debate on each of those days. A string of **budget resolutions** is published at the conclusion of the Chancellor's statement, each relating to a specific taxation proposal intended to be included in the Finance Bill. Debate on the Amendment of the Law motion or any other motion moved in its place also ranges over these other proposed resolutions.

10.2.22 On the last day of the budget debate the House may vote on the Amendment of the Law (or another) motion, to which amendments may be proposed (the admissibility of which is, of course, governed by the rules of financial procedure, already described, relating to the Crown's exclusive right to propose increases in expenditure). S.O. No. 51(3) then requires the Chair to put forthwith the Question on each of the remaining motions (often more than 50). There is no opportunity to vote on amendments to the motions, but any of the motions themselves may be the subject of a **division**. All this may take place after the **moment of interruption**.

10.2.23 These resolutions may be followed by a money resolution (see paragraphs 10.2.1 to 10.2.5 above) relating to the Finance Bill. When that has been disposed of the House (without a formal motion) orders a bill to be brought in "upon the foregoing resolutions" which, by tradition, the Chairman of Ways and Means is ordered to prepare together with Treasury Ministers, though in reality he takes no actual part in its preparation. The Financial Secretary of the Treasury presents the bill which is given its formal first reading and ordered to be printed (see section 11.5). Unusually for a government bill there is normally some delay in the actual publication of the bill.

10.2.24 The bill subsequently proceeds largely in the same manner as any other public bill (see chapter 11) except that it is usual for some clauses to be taken in **committee of the Whole House** (see paragraph 11.7.6). The main distinctions are: first, that the scope of amendments which may be proposed to the bill is much more closely governed by the scope of the founding resolutions to which the House has agreed; and second, that because it is a "bill of aids and supplies" (see paragraph 10.2.10 above) it is considered only formally by the Lords. Also, the bill is exempt, under S.O. No. 15(1)(a), from the operation of the **moment of interruption** on any day (see paragraph 7.10.8).

INCOME	EXPENDITURE
WAYS AND MEANS	**SUPPLY**
*Taxes, duties, levies and other payments into the **Consolidated Fund** are authorised by **Ways and Means Resolutions**.*	*Payments out of the **Consolidated Fund** are authorised by **Supply Resolutions**.*
These are required before a charge on the people can be raised (in other words taxes, duties and certain fees).	*These approve the sums set out in the **Estimates**.*
*The main bills authorised by Ways and Means resolutions are the annual **Finance Bills** but other bills may require Ways and Means resolutions if they impose charges.*	*The main bills authorised by supply resolutions are the three annual **Consolidated Fund Bills**, including the annual **Appropriation Act**.*
*No Ways and Means resolution is required to authorise an increase in **National Insurance Contributions**.*	*Other bills which provide for new additional expenditure may require the authorisation of **Money Resolutions** to cover that expenditure.*
*Bills which authorise the raising of charges or the expenditure of money are **'Bills of aids and supplies'**.*	
BORROWING *by the Government is not subject to parliamentary control*	

FIGURE 21
GETTING AND SPENDING

10.3 ESTIMATES AND CONSOLIDATED FUND BILLS

The Estimates

10.3.1 The House of Commons authorises all government expenditure annually by voting the Estimates. These documents are essentially a breakdown of the total of public spending under various categories. The Estimates are presented as a number of "Requests for Resources" relating to specified areas of each Department's activities. They are published each year alongside Departments' reports on their public expenditure plans, which are published shortly after the Budget. Estimates set out the resource budgets for each Department – that is the total gross expenditure and the appropriations-in-aid (income) for each

Request for Resources – and an overall net cash budget for the Department as a whole. With a few exceptions, no money may be spent by the government unless it has been approved for spending on that purpose by the House of Commons "voting" the relevant Estimates.

10.3.2 Each separate Estimate is the responsibility of an **Accounting Officer** (see paragraph 10.5.6 below). Where there is more than one Request for Resources for a Department, the Accounting Officer for each will often be the Permanent Secretary of the Department, but there may be different accounting officers for different Requests. It is these "Requests for Resources" which the House of Commons specifically approves. The level of spending covered by each Request for Resources varies widely.

10.3.3 The Estimates are generally published three times a year (see Figure 10). The *Main Estimates* for the coming financial year are published in March. Under S.O. No. 55(4), these must be approved by 5 August. They are published alongside each Department's annual public expenditure plans report, and those reports include tables which explain purposes of the Requests for Resources contained in the Estimates.

10.3.4 The *Summer Supplementary Estimates* are published around May. These indicate changes in the financial provision required for some Requests for Resources by the government in the current financial year. There may also be *Revised Estimates* for the current year, where extra sums are not required but there is a request to change the "ambit" (ie the formal description of the purpose of the expenditure) of certain Requests for Resources. These Supplementary and Revised Estimates will normally be wrapped up in a single resolution expressing a global amount of cash and resources, for which approval must also be sought before 5 August.

10.3.5 In November the *Winter Supplementary Estimates* are published. These adjust the cash and resources required for that financial year. At the same time the *Votes on Account* for the forthcoming financial year are published. These appropriate the sums (roughly 45 per cent of the previous year's total) necessary to cover government expenditure in the period between the beginning of the next financial year and the House's approval of the Main Estimates in the following July. In accordance with S.O. No. 55(2), these must be agreed by the House by 6 February.

10.3.6 In February the *Spring Supplementary Estimates*, if there are any, are published, making any further adjustment necessary for the financial year which ends in March. *Excess Votes* may also be published around this time. These provide retrospective authorisation for spending in the previous financial year which exceeded the amount voted by the Commons and for which there was not enough time to obtain authority through a Supplementary Estimate (sometimes because the overspending was not detected till after the end of the financial year). They are subject to a process of special scrutiny involving the National Audit Office and the Public Accounts Committee (see section 10.5 below and S.O. No. 55(3)(c)) before they can be presented to the Commons.

10.3.7 Also in February, the *Ministry of Defence Votes A* are published. In accordance with the provision of the Bill of Rights of 1688/89 that the Crown may not maintain a standing army in peacetime (and a war has not been formally declared since 1939) without the authorisation of Parliament, these specify the maximum number of personnel that may be maintained in the Army, Air Force and Navy in the forthcoming year. The Army and Air Force Reserve Forces numbers are also specified in the Resolution put to the House, but for historical reasons numbers of the RNVR are not required to be separately authorised (although they are indicated in the Vote A paper).

10.3.8 Under S.O. No. 55(3), the House is required to approve the Spring Supplementary Estimates, Excess Votes and Defence Votes A by 18 March.

Estimates Days and voting on the Estimates

10.3.9 Under S.O. No. 54 three days are set aside in each session for consideration of Estimates. These will normally be close to each of the deadlines set out in the above paragraphs, ie 6 February, 18 March and 5 August, but the requirement is that they must all take place before 5 August. They may not be on Fridays, and one of the days may be taken as two half-days (see paragraph 7.9.5 above).

10.3.10 Under S.O. No. 145(2) the **Liaison Committee** (see section 3.5) may recommend to the House that certain Estimates are selected for debate on each of these days. Although in theory any Member may approach the Liaison Committee with a proposed subject for debate, in practice these Estimates are each chosen to relate to a recent report of a departmental select committee, or occasionally one of the other select committees such as Environmental Audit or Public Administration (see Chapter 17), the purpose being to link the work of these committees into the House's system for the control of public expenditure. Once the Liaison Committee has reported its recommendation to the House as to which Estimates should be singled out for debate, a motion must be made to agree with it. The Question on such a motion is put **forthwith** and may be decided after the **moment of interruption**.

10.3.11 Although there are usually two Estimates being debated on each such day (or if it is a half-day, debate may end at 7 pm or 4 pm), under the provisions of paragraphs (4) and (5) of the standing order the decision on any Estimate is deferred till 10 pm (or 7 pm), when the House will be asked to agree both those Votes that have been singled out by the Liaison Committee for debate and, in a separate resolution, all other outstanding Estimates set down for that day. The motions relating to the outstanding Main, Revised or Supplementary Estimates for each financial year, or for Votes on Account or Excess Votes, specify two global sums (one a resource request and one a cash request) covering all the expenditure for which the government is seeking authorisation. If the Liaison Committee has not recommended any Estimates for debate, the outstanding Estimates will be voted on formally, before the relevant deadlines, without debate.

10.3.12 The sums contained in the Estimates may be amended, but because the Commons agrees to expenditure on the initiative of the government, rather than initiating expenditure itself (see paragraph 10.1.2 above), an amendment may only *reduce* a Request for Resources. Often when this is proposed, the reduction is a token one of £1,000 "in respect of" whatever area of expenditure the Member tabling the amendment wishes to draw attention to.

Consolidated Fund Bills and Appropriation Acts

10.3.13 On a day when all the outstanding Estimates resolutions have been agreed, the House formally orders a bill to be brought in "upon the foregoing resolutions". In the winter and spring the bill which is then immediately presented by the Financial Secretary simply specifies the global total of the Requests for Resources and sums to be paid out of the **Consolidated Fund** (the government's general "bank account" at the Bank of England) for the year or years in question. The bill presented in the summer is a much more complex publication, as scheduled to it are tables setting out each Request for Resources, showing the exact amount to be appropriated for those specific purposes and no others, and the appropriations in aid (that is receipts of the department in respect of those activities) to be offset against that expenditure. It also "appropriates" the provision for the total numbers of military personnel in the armed forces agreed in voting Defence Votes A (see paragraph 10.3.7 above).

10.3.14 Consolidated Fund and Appropriation Bills are set down for second reading on a day shortly after the relevant Estimates have been agreed. Under S.O. No. 56 the Question on second reading of such bills is put forthwith and, when that is agreed, the Question for third reading is immediately put forthwith, there being no committee or report stage. The bills are thus passed without debate (any debate having taken place on those few areas of expenditure selected for that purpose by the Liaison Committee). Because these are both money bills (see paragraph 10.2.15 and 10.2.16 above) and "bills of aids and supplies" (see paragraph 10.2.10 above), their consideration by the Lords is also purely *proforma*.

10.3.15 The Winter and Spring Consolidated Fund bills in due course become Consolidated Fund Acts. The Summer Consolidated Fund Bill, with the lengthy schedules of appropriations, on receiving the **royal assent**, becomes the Appropriation Act.

10.4 Other financially-related proceedings

Public Expenditure and the economy

10.4.1 In addition to the proceedings relating to the Budget and the Finance Bill, and those relating to the Estimates and Consolidated Fund bills, the House has other means of considering financially related matters.

10.4.2 Shortly after the Budget Statement (see paragraph 10.2.19 above), the departmental expenditure plans are published, which set out the spending plans of each department for up to the next three financial years programme by programme, and give details of the purposes of the spending and measures of the prospective achievement of these objectives. These reports also review outturn figures for previous years, and that estimated for the current year. The

Main Estimates (in the form of a series of Requests for Resources) for expenditure in the forthcoming financial year are published separately by the Treasury, but they are reconciled with the tables of financial information contained in the individual departmental expenditure reports. The Treasury produces a government-wide synoptic volume relating to these spending plans.

10.4.3 These expenditure reports are generally the subject of annual inquiries by each of the departmental select committees (see section 17.2), though the level of detail of such inquiries varies widely between committees and from year to year. The Treasury Select Committee invariably conducts a separate annual inquiry on the Budget.

10.4.4 The Treasury Committee may report on, and the House may debate, the Chancellor of the Exchequer's "pre-budget statement" in the autumn (see paragraph 10.2.19). The Environmental Audit Committee (see paragraphs 17.3.7 and 17.3.8) has also examined this report.

The Resource Accounts

10.4.5 The Resource Accounts for each Department are laid before Parliament by the **Comptroller & Auditor General** (C&AG). These include a report of his audit of the propriety of the spending by each Department and its regularity – that is that it has been in accordance with the appropriations voted by the Commons in approving the Appropriation Act (see paragraphs 10.3.13 and 10.3.14). These are published around nine months after the end of the financial year to which they relate as part of each Department's autumn report on its performance in the preceding financial year. The departmentally-related select committees may review these account and performance data, but general parliamentary oversight of this audit by the C & AG is performed by the **Public Accounts Committee** (see below).

10.4.6 An outline of the House's financial year is given in Figure 22.

10.5 The Committee of Public Accounts and the National Audit Office

The Committee of Public Accounts

10.5.1 Under S.O. No. 148 there is a select committee appointed called the Committee of Public Accounts, better known as the Public Accounts Committee or PAC. The Committee consists of a maximum of fifteen Members and has a quorum of four. The Chairman is invariably elected from amongst the opposition Members. The Financial Secretary to the Treasury is by tradition appointed to the Committee as a member, but he or she does not take an active part in its proceedings.

Powers

10.5.2 The Committee has most of the usual powers of select committees (see section 17.1). However, it may only sit on days when the House sits, and rarely exercises its power to travel. It does not have the power to appoint specialist advisers (see paragraph 17.2.6).

Month	Budget Cycle	Estimates Cycle	Reporting Cycle
October/ November	Pre-Budget Report (the "Green Budget")	Winter Supplementary Estimates (for current financial year) and Votes on Account (for next financial year) presented[1]	Resource Accounts (for previous financial year) presented
December		Consolidated Fund Bill (Consolidated Fund (No.2) Act) passed	Departmental Performance Reports (for previous financial year) published
February		Spring Supplementary Estimates[2] (for current financial year) and Excess Votes[2] (for earlier years) presented	
March	Budget Statement and debate	Main Estimates (for next financial year) presented[3] Consolidated Fund (No.2) Bill (Consolidated Fund Act) passed[2]	

START OF NEW FINANCIAL YEAR

Month	Budget Cycle	Estimates Cycle	Reporting Cycle
April	Finance Bill published and receives Second Reading[3]		Departmental Spending Plans Reports (for current financial year + 2) published
May	Finance Bill in Committee	Summer Supplementary Estimates and Revised Estimates (for current financial year) presented[3]	
June			
July	Finance Bill Third Reading and pro-forma consideration by Lords (Finance Act)	Consolidated Fund (No.3) Bill (the Appropriation Act) passed[3]	

[1] Must be approved by 6 February

[2] Must be approved by 18 March

[3] Must be approved by 5 August

FIGURE 22
THE FINANCIAL YEAR

Functions

10.5.3 The Committee is charged by the standing order to examine the Resource Accounts (see paragraph 10.4.5 above) and such other accounts as it considers fit. It also has special responsibilities in relation to Excess Votes (see paragraph 10.3.6 above and S.O. No. 55(3)(c)).

10.5.4 Since the passing of the National Audit Act of 1983, an increasing proportion of the Committee's work has involved inquiries based upon the value for money (VFM) reports of the Comptroller & Auditor General which examine selected programmes or areas of public expenditure (or revenue). Even in these inquiries, the Committee does not enter into questions of the merits of policy objectives, but focuses on the efficiency, economy and effectiveness with which those objectives were secured.

The Comptroller & Auditor General

10.5.5 The Committee is assisted in its work by the Comptroller & Auditor General (C&AG). Under the 1983 Act he is appointed by a motion moved jointly in the House by the Prime Minister and the Chairman of the PAC. The C&AG is the head of the National Audit Office (see below). The statutory independence from government of the C&AG is emphasised by his being an officer of the House.

Accounting Officers

10.5.6 For each Estimate or Request for Resources (see paragraph 10.3.1 above) there must be an accounting officer, as provided for under the Exchequer and Audit Department Act 1866 (as amended by the Government Resources and Accounts Act 2000). This is usually the Permanent Secretary of the department responsible for the spending in question, though there may be different accounting officers for different parts of an Estimate, and other persons (such as the **Clerk of the House** or the chief executive of an executive agency) may be the accounting officers for certain voted Requests for Resources. Although the Committee has the general power to send for persons, papers and records, it is usually accounting officers, not Ministers, who are summoned to give evidence to the PAC. It is the accounting officers who are under a personal statutory duty to ensure that Ministers act in accordance with the decisions of Parliament in relation to public expenditure, and use that public money not only with propriety, but also with economy, efficiency and effectiveness.

Reports of the Committee

10.5.7 Like other select committees, the PAC makes regular reports to the House on its findings and may make recommendations. The government responds to these reports by way of Treasury Minutes. A selection of these reports and government replies are subject to an annual day's debate in government time.

The National Audit Office

10.5.8 The National Audit Office (NAO) has about 700 staff under the direction of the C&AG, of whom some 450 hold accounting qualifications.

10.5.9 The C&AG is in turn answerable for the management of the NAO to the **Public Accounts Commission**, established under the National Audit Act 1983. This consists of the Chairman of the PAC, the Leader of the House and seven other Members. One of these other Members is elected chairman and, among other duties, is responsible for answering parliamentary questions on the work of the Commission (see paragraph 8.2.5). The Public Accounts Commission is responsible for the general financial oversight of the NAO and in particular for agreeing the **Estimate** to be presented each year to Parliament for its expenditure.

10.5.10 The NAO works under the direction of the C&AG. In addition to preparing the Resource Accounts (see paragraph 10.4.5 above) and other related audit work, it prepares the C&AG's value for money (VFM) reports (see paragraph 10.5.4 above) on the spending of departments.

10.5.11 The VFM reports are laid before Parliament by the C&AG. Most of them will be followed up by the PAC, which will conduct its own inquiry on the basis of the report, taking evidence from the relevant accounting officer. The Committee will then publish its own report on the subject, making such recommendations as it considers appropriate. The cycle is completed by the publication of the government's response, issued as a Treasury Minute (see paragraph 10.5.7 above). On occasions, these reports may also be used by other select committees to inform their inquiries.

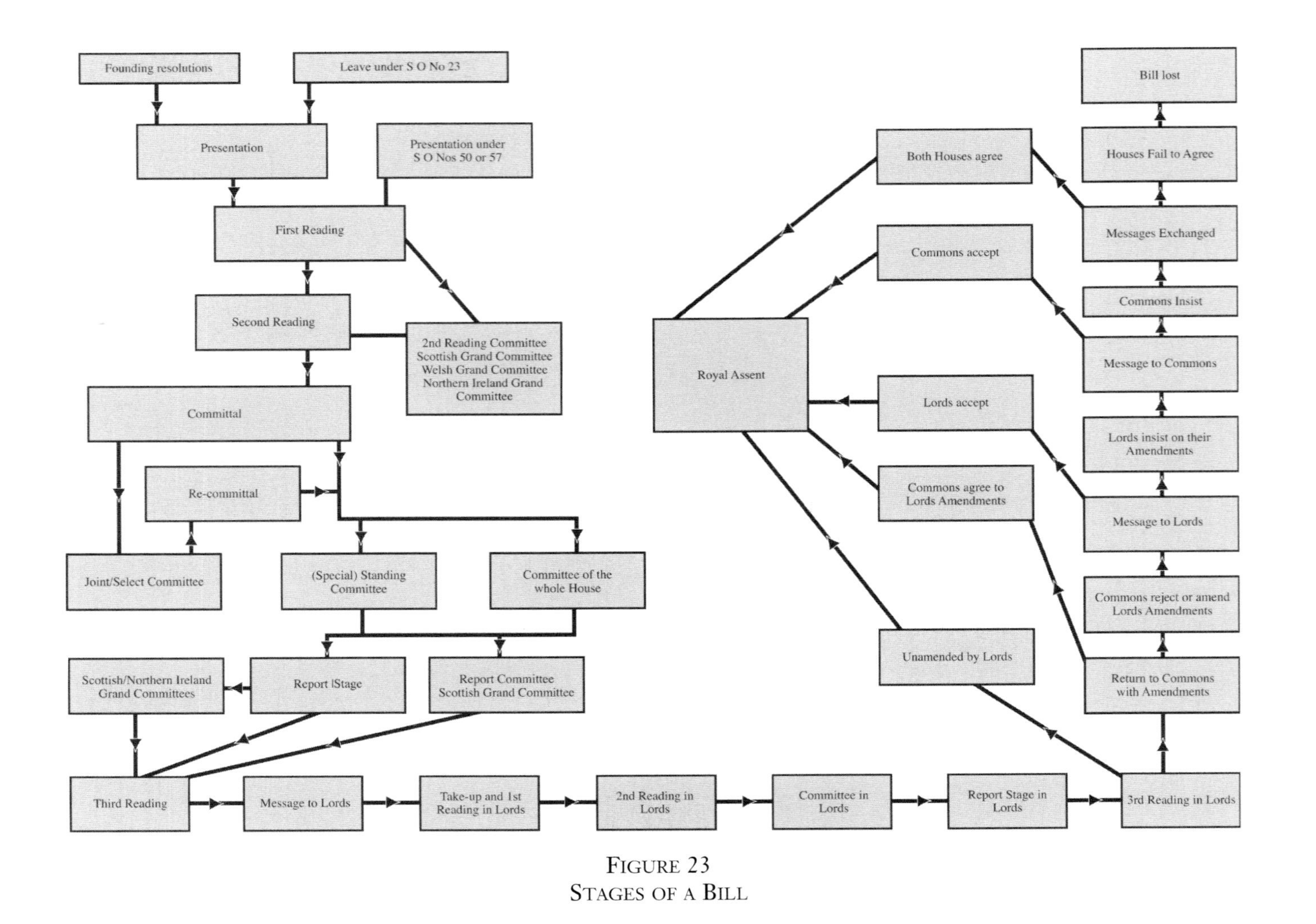

FIGURE 23
STAGES OF A BILL

Chapter 11
BILLS

11.1 INTRODUCTION

Bills

11.1.1 Proposals for legislation are presented to Parliament in the form of bills. Typically, these consist of a number of *clauses* (between two and several hundred) followed by a number of *schedules*. In general terms, schedules contain detailed provisions expanding on some general propositions set out in a clause or clauses, or details of minor amendments required to be made to other Acts of Parliament in consequence of the provisions of the bill. Each schedule is given effect by a specific provision in one of the clauses of the bill, but there is no distinction between the prospective statutory force of a clause or schedule, and the division of types of matter between clauses and schedules is somewhat inconsistent.

Public bills and private bills

11.1.2 There are two basic types of bill. *Public bills*, when enacted, will form part of the general law which applies to all individuals or bodies equally. *Private bills*, which now form a very small part of the House's work, are proposals to give specific powers over and above the general law, usually to corporate bodies such as local authorities or railway undertakers or port authorities. The category of private bills includes *personal bills* which make law in relation to individuals – because it long ago ceased to be necessary to pass a personal bill to obtain a divorce these are very rare. Private bills are subject to complex, but largely invisible, procedures which are not part of the public business of the House (see paragraphs 2.2.5, 7.3.1 and 7.9.2 above). They are not further discussed here except for a very brief synopsis in section 11.19 below, and the remainder of this chapter discusses public bills, in other words proposals to change the general law.

Hybrid bills

11.1.3 There is a type of public bill which has characteristics of a private bill within it. This is generally where it affects some members of a defined class of persons (including corporate "persons") differently in comparison with other members of the same class. These are relatively rare. The most recent significant example of such a "hybrid" bill was the government-sponsored bill for the construction of the Channel Tunnel Rail Link, which self-evidently affected some property owners along the proposed route adversely in comparison with others. Where it appears, on publication after its first reading, that a bill is *prima facie* hybrid in some of its provisions, it is referred, under S.O. No. 61, to the **Examiners of Petitions**. If they report that the private legislation standing orders ought to apply to any provisions of the bill, it is referred after its second reading to a *select committee* appointed for the purpose to examine any petitions from persons or bodies having a *locus standi* (that is, generally speaking, persons adversely affected by those provisions in comparison with other persons of the same kind). The bill then essentially passes through a version of the private legislation procedure, with the full panoply of petitions, hearings with counsel and petitioners, etc. (see section 11.19 below). The committee may amend the bill, and may make a report upon it as well. When the bill has undergone this process, it is usually, after being reported to the House, re-committed to a standing committee, and thereafter progresses as a public bill, as described below. If at any stage of a public bill's progress, it is amended in such a way as to render it *prima facie* hybrid, it might be referred to the Examiners in the same way as above (though by motion rather than automatically as happens before second reading) and be deemed to require to undergo the hybrid procedure.

Acts of Parliament

11.1.4 In order for a bill to pass into law, it must be read three times in each House of Parliament (with intervening stages in most cases) and the two Houses must agree between them a final text of the bill. When they have done so, the bill is recommended to the Queen for her assent. That invariably having been given, and the three parts of Parliament being in agreement, the bill becomes an Act of Parliament and has the force of law (see Figure 17). At this point the "clauses" of the bill become "sections" of the Act, although the schedules retain the same name. The details of a public bill's passage through the House of Commons are set out below.

Draft Bills

11.1.5 In recent years, as part of the reforms to the legislative process initiated by the **Modernisation Committee**, the government has published a number of bills each session in draft form, before they are introduced into Parliament as formal bills. The purpose of this practice is to enable consultation to take place on their form and purpose before the bill is issued in the less readily amendable form of a proper bill. There has not always been formal parliamentary consideration of such draft bills by reference to a committee of either or both Houses, though individual Members are of course able to participate in the consultation process and select committees have sometimes chosen to examine such legislative proposals where they have not been formally referred to a committee. Increasingly, it has become the practice in recent sessions for the House to refer these to a joint committee of the Commons and Lords appointed for the specific purpose of examining and reporting on a named draft bill. On occasions a draft bill may be referred to one of the departmental select committees or a select committee appointed for that specific purpose. These referrals are usually accompanied by an instruction to the committee to report its findings by a specific date.

Timetabling of Bills

11.1.6 In recent sessions, the House has experimented with a new mechanism for timetabling the passage of bills through their various stages, known as "programming". This innovation again arises from the recommendations of the **Modernisation Committee**. In October 2002 the House formally reaffirmed its commitment to the use of programmes as the normal practice for government bills (see paragraph 11.2.1 below). The standing orders applying to these timetables were, however, only renewed on a temporary basis until the end of the 2002–03 session, and the principle of programming, and its detailed application to particular bills, remains controversial.

11.1.7 A "programme motion" is normally agreed immediately after a bill's second reading, and thereafter becomes the "programme order" governing the bill's subsequent progress. These programme orders will be added to and amended by subsequent resolutions which, as each is agreed by the House or by a standing committee, become part of the overall programme order for that bill. The effect of a programme order is, therefore, to make a bill's progress through its various stages much more predictable than heretofore, and to end to a large extent the phenomenon of all night sittings of standing committees and of report stages continuing into the small hours of the morning or running continuously over two days and nights, as has happened in the past. There is much debate about whether programming has reduced the real amount of time available for scrutiny of proposed legislation, or improved or diminished its quality or effectiveness. It certainly renders pointless, for the most part, the use of filibustering as an instrument of opposition, and disinhibits government back benchers from participating in debates on bills which was formerly much discouraged by the **Whips** as tending to, in their view, play into the hands of the opposition.

11.1.8 Programme orders and their application are described in more detail as they apply to the various stages of a bill's progress throughout this chapter, and summarised in section 11.18. When following this chapter, the reader should bear in mind the almost universal use of programming, in current Commons practice, for major government bills. Programme orders cannot, of course, timetable proceedings in the Lords.

11.2 Government Bills and Private Members' Bills

Government bills

11.2.1 Any Member may introduce a bill to the House (see section 11.3 below). A bill introduced by a Minister is known as a government bill. Government bills are generally presented under S.O. Nos. 50 or 57 (see paragraphs 11.3.2 to 11.3.4 below). Government bills are debated in government time (see section 2.1 and section 2.2), and in current practice are usually timetabled (see paragraphs 11.1.6 to 11.1.8 above).

Private Members' bills

11.2.2 A public bill introduced by a Member who is not a Minister is known as a "private Member's bill". If such a bill is to make progress it must be set down for each of its main stages (other than committee) on the floor of the House on one of the Fridays set aside for the purpose (see paragraph 2.2.4). Because of the very limited time available for these stages, only a relatively small proportion of the several dozen private Members' bills presented each session make any progress, and only a fraction of these go on to receive the royal assent.

11.2.3 Because access to this time is so much in demand, a ballot is held at the beginning of each session to choose twenty backbench Members who will have the first claim on the time available for private Members' bills. The ballot is held, under the provisions of S.O. No. 14(6), at 12 noon on the second Thursday of each session. On the two preceding days Members have the opportunity to enter their names in a book kept in the No lobby if they wish to enter the ballot. On the Thursday the Chairman of Ways and Means presides over the ceremonial drawing of the numbers by the Clerk Assistant in Committee Room 10. Twenty numbers are drawn, and the names of the Members who signed against those numbers are announced and immediately published.

11.2.4 The ballot bills are presented on the fifth Wednesday of the session. In the intervening period, the successful Members must give notice of the short and long titles of their proposed bills (see section 11.4 below), which will duly appear (in ballot order) on the **Order Paper**. The bills are presented in turn under S.O. No. 57 (see paragraph 11.3.4 below) and, as each is presented, the **Member in charge** (or his or her nominated proxy) will name one of the seven Fridays set aside under the sessional order for its second reading.

11.2.5 These bills will have the best chance of a second reading debate on one of those Fridays. In particular, the **Member in charge** of the first bill listed on each day may be able to claim the **closure** (see paragraph 9.7.4) on second reading and so avoid the bill being talked out by opponents. This will ensure that the bill is committed to a standing committee, but not that it will make significant further progress. Once this opportunity for a second reading has been taken, balloted bills do not have any particular claim to precedence at subsequent stages of debate. Many other private Members' bills will be presented either under S.O. No. 57 (see paragraph 11.3.4 below) or S.O. No. 23 (see paragraph 11.3.5 below) after the ballot bills. On the subsequent Fridays set aside for private Members' bills, priority is accorded to bills in relation to how far they have progressed towards the conclusion of their parliamentary stages (ie consideration of Lords Amendments, third readings, report stages, committee stages and second readings in that order). This order of priority applies equally to ballot bills and to any other private Members' bills, however originally introduced. However, ballot bills are likely to be furthest ahead.

The Member in charge of a bill

11.2.6 By tradition, the Member who has introduced a bill to the House (who is known as the **Member in charge** of the bill) has certain pre-emptive rights in relation to proceedings on that bill. For a government bill, any Minister (including the **Whips**) can exercise the privileges of the Member in charge. In the case of a private Member's bill, the Chair would be reluctant to allow any other Member to act on behalf of the Member in charge unless it was clear that he or she had the explicit authority of that Member to do so.

11.2.7 The privileges of the Member in charge of a bill include, for example: naming the days for its stages to be taken and subsequently changing these; withdrawing the bill between stages; moving the adjournment of its consideration in a standing committee or at another stage; and proposing any variation in the order in which the clauses and schedules of a bill are considered by a committee or by the House (see paragraph 11.10.17 below).

11.3 Introduction of Bills to the Commons

11.3.1 Bills may be introduced to the Commons in a number of ways.

Bills based upon founding resolutions or presented under S.O. No. 50

11.3.2 In chapter 10 it is described how Finance Bills and Consolidated Fund Bills are ordered to be brought in after the House has agreed to the relevant founding financial resolutions (see paragraphs 10.2.23 and 10.3.13). Historically, other bills of which the main purpose was to authorise public expenditure also required a founding resolution to which the **royal recommendation** had been signified, in order to preserve the right of the Crown to initiate expenditure. In modern practice it is rare for other bills to emerge in this way.

11.3.3 This is because, under S.O. No. 50, a bill the main object of which is the creation of a public charge, (that is one of which the main purpose is to authorise public expenditure of some kind) may be presented by a Minister without the necessity of a preceding financial resolution. The characteristics of a "main-purpose–money" bill are described in paragraphs 10.2.12 to 10.2.14 above. Because proposals for public expenditure may only be initiated by the Crown, no Member who is not a Minister may introduce such a bill. A bill presented under this standing order has a note to that effect at the head of the first page. The manner of presentation, and subsequent proceedings on the bill, have no other special characteristics.

Bills presented under S.O. No. 57

11.3.4 The vast majority of bills, however, are introduced under S.O. No. 57. Any Member may present a bill under this standing order so long as its main purpose is not the creation of a public charge (see preceding paragraph). The manner of giving notice and of presentation are described in paragraphs 7.7.2 to 7.7.4. The particular rules regulating the presentation of private Members' bills and the priority accorded to "ballot" bills are described in paragraphs 11.2.2 to 11.2.5 above. In order to preserve the priority of ballot bills, no private Member may give notice of presentation of a bill before the day after the fifth Wednesday of a session, the day on which the ballot bills are presented.

Ten minute rule bills brought in under S.O. No. 23

11.3.5 On each Tuesday and Wednesday on which the House sits, after the fifth Wednesday of a session, one Member may move a motion for leave to introduce a bill under the provisions of S.O. No. 23. Notice of such a motion must be given to the **Public Bill Office** not earlier than 10 am on the day fifteen sitting days before the day on which it is to be moved. In general, this means exactly three calendar weeks before, but this convenient pattern is frequently disrupted by the effect of recesses intervening between the day for giving notice and the day on which the motion is to be moved.

11.3.6 The opportunity to give notice of such a motion is usually taken on the first day it becomes available. Members will sometimes therefore find themselves in competition for this chance, and certain conventions are tacitly observed about how a queue is established. The basic rule, however, is first come, first served.

Because, under S.O. No.14(7), no notice may be given of such a motion until after the fifth Wednesday of a session (see paragraphs11.2.3 to 11.2.5 above), the available slots for the next three sitting weeks become simultaneously available at 10 am on that day. The **Public Bill Office** can provide details on request of the earliest days for giving notice.

11.3.7 When giving notice of his or her intention to move such a motion, the Member must indicate the short and long titles of the proposed bill (see section 11.4 below). Where they are uncertain of their intentions, or change their mind, it is possible, up to the period of minimum notice of five sitting days specified in the standing order, to withdraw their original notice and immediately give a new one. Members may therefore initially give notice of a holding title (by tradition, the "Statutory Instruments Act 1946 (Amendment) Bill)" which they intend subsequently to replace.

11.3.8 The notice of motion for leave to introduce a ten minute rule bill will appear in the future business section of the **Order Paper** (see paragraph 15.1.20) the day after it has been given, as will notices of withdrawal and new notices.

11.3.9 If, after the motion has been moved, the House refuses leave to a Member to bring in a bill under S.O. No. 23, a bill with the same long title may not subsequently be presented under S.O. No. 57.

11.3.10 The manner of moving a ten minute rule motion is described in paragraphs 7.7.9 to 7.7.11.

Bills brought from the Lords

11.3.11 A bill which has been passed by the Lords is sent by them to the Commons. If it is a government bill, it will be "taken up" (ie taken charge of) by a Minister and set down for second reading. If it is a private Peer's bill, a Member of the Commons may choose to take it up and it will then take its place among the other private Members' bills on any Friday (see paragraph 2.2.4) which that Member names for its second reading. As with bills presented by private Members and ten minute rule bills, in order to preserve the priority of ballot bills (see paragraphs 11.2.3 to 11.2.5 above), a private Member cannot take up a private Peer's bill before the day after the fifth Wednesday of a session.

11.3.12 In order to take up a Lords bill, a Member has only to inform the Clerks at the Table of his or her wish to do so at any point after the bill has arrived from the Lords, and to name a day for its second reading. S.O. No. 57A allows for notice of intention to "take up" a Lords bill to be given in advance, and for the bill to be ordered to be printed when the Commons is not sitting, if it arrived from the Lords when the Commons was adjourned.

11.4 TITLES OF BILLS

Short titles

11.4.1 Bills have two titles: short and long. The short title is that by which the bill is generally known, eg "Housing" or "Criminal Justice". This short title is specified in the citation clause of the bill, which is usually its last. It is printed at the head of the bill.

11.4.2 Bills which start in the Lords have the word [*Lords*] after their short title (or [H.L.] in the Lords) in order to distinguish them from Commons bills, but this suffix is not included in the citation clause.

11.4.3 If a second or subsequent bill of the same short title as one that has already been introduced to either House in a session is introduced in either House in the same session, it is distinguished by having (No. 2) or (No. 3) etc after its short title (eg Housing Bill and Housing (No. 2) Bill [*Lords*]), but this suffix is not included in the citation clause.

11.4.4 The short title of a bill may be changed by an amendment to the citation clause.

Long titles

11.4.5 The long title of a bill is set out at the head of the first page. It should be a reasonably concise description of the content and purposes of the bill, for example "A Bill to amend the law relating to leasehold tenure". A long title may have several clauses (or "legs"), each relating to a different broad purpose of the bill. Though a long title cannot be taken to be a *definition* of the scope of a bill, each proposed long title is examined by the **Clerk of Legislation** to ensure that so far as possible it represents an adequate description of a bill which is available in draft. If, as may be the case with a private Member's bill, the long title is recorded *before* the bill has been drafted, the Clerk of Legislation will satisfy himself before publication that the text of the bill presented by the Member in charge does not go beyond the scope of the long title which has been recorded.

11.4.6 Long titles may be amended during a bill's passage through Parliament, and this is a not infrequent occurrence. Amendments to the long titles are always considered at the end of any stage of a bill's proceedings since they will, in general, only be admissible if they reflect amendments which have been made to the body of the bill (see also paragraphs 11.9.14 and 11.10.16).

11.5 First Reading and Publication

First reading

11.5.1 As soon as a bill is presented (or a Lords bill is taken up) it is deemed, under S.O. No. 57(2), without debate or vote, to have been read a first time. For the process of presentation, see paragraphs 7.7.2 to 7.7.4. If it arrived from the Lords when the Commons was not sitting, and was taken up under the provisions of S.O. No. 57A, its first reading is recorded formally on the next day on which the Commons sits.

Publication

11.5.2 Along with its formal first reading, the House orders any bill which has been presented to be printed, again without debate or vote. (Under S.O. No. 57A this order may be made even if the House is not sitting, in the case of a bill brought from the Lords). Each bill is given a sessional bill number. A government bill (with the exception of the Finance Bill, for which see paragraph 10.2.23) will normally be published immediately on presentation (embargoed copies already having been delivered to the appropriate outlets, including the **Vote Office**), or on the following day. There is sometimes considerable delay between the presentation of a private Member's bill and its publication, since the Member will not always have a text prepared.

	PRE-LEGISLATIVE SCRUTINY	FIRST READING	SECOND READING	COMMITTEE STAGE	CONSIDERATION ON REPORT	THIRD READING	LORDS AMENDMENTS	POST-LEGISLATIVE SCRUTINY
CURRENT OPTIONS	Broad outlines of legislative proposal			Special Standing Committee				
	Green Paper on legislative proposal			Select Committee				
	White paper with worked-up proposals		Second Reading Committee	Divided between Committee of the Whole House and Standing Committee	Recommittal in whole or part			
	Published draft Bill or draft Clauses		Grand Committee	Committee of the Whole House	Report Stage in Standing Committee or Scottish Grand Committee	Scottish, N Ireland Grand Committee		Departmental or ad hoc Select Committee
NORMAL CURRENT ROUTE		Text Published	Detail on Floor of House	Standing Committee	Report Stage on Floor of House	Debated on Floor of House	Consideration on Floor of House	

Standing Committee Style proceedings | Select Committee style proceedings | Other types of proceedings

FIGURE 24
OPTIONS FOR STAGES OF A BILL'S CONSIDERATION IN THE COMMONS

Form of publication before second reading

11.5.3 The printed version of a bill will have a cover page which as well as the short title will have (in the case of a government bill) a statement by the relevant Minister as to whether in his or her view the provisions of the bill are compatible with the rights established under the European Convention on Human Rights, as incorporated into domestic law by the Human Rights Act 1998. This is required under section 19 of that Act. (A bill will, as a matter of practice rather than under any specific standing order, be examined by the Joint Committee on Human Rights (see section 17.5) to see whether the Committee concurs in the opinion of the Minister.) The cover page will usually be followed by the contents page of the bill, which sets out the number and title of each clause and schedule, and may show how the bill is divided into Chapters and/or Parts.

11.5.4 The bill then begins with the "enacting formula", and the clauses follow in numerical order. Each clause has a title as well as a number. Any schedules to the bill follow the clauses. The last page of the bill is the *backsheet* which sets out various details including (for bills starting in the Commons) the name of the Member introducing it together with those of any *supporters*.

Explanatory Notes

11.5.5 When a government bill is ordered by the House to be printed at first reading, it is now the practice for it also to order *Explanatory Notes* to be printed at the same time. These documents, which are prepared by the relevant government department or departments, are given a number in a series running in parallel to the sessional bill numbers (ie "Bill 1" will be accompanied by explanatory notes "Bill 1-EN"). These notes explain the purpose of the bill, may give some background to its provisions, and give a detailed explanation of the intent and effect of the clauses and schedules of the bill in language less technical than that of legislation. They also explain briefly the anticipated effects, if any, that the bill's provisions may have on public sector manpower and their potential implications for costs falling on the public purse. They also give a summary of the "regulatory impact assessment" which broadly analyses the impact of the bill's provisions on the private sector, particularly in terms of any new costs likely to arise as a result of steps needed to be taken to comply with its provisions. They should give the background to a Minister's decision on the "Section 19 Statement" under the Human Rights Act (see paragraph 11.5.3 above). They may explain when the bill's provisions are intended to come into effect, and whether any of them have retrospective effect. On occasions when a bill includes provisions to make significant changes to other existing legislation, they may also include an annex or annexes setting out how that existing legislation would read after such amendments had been made.

Bills not printed not to proceed

11.5.6 A significant proportion of private Members' bills are never published. Particularly in the case of a ten minute rule bill, a Member may feel that the speech seeking leave to bring in the bill is sufficient, since the likelihood of it making further progress is so slight. Under S.O. No. 14(9), if a private

Member's bill has not been published by the day before it is set down for its second reading, the order for its second reading automatically lapses and cannot be revived until the bill has been published.

Reprinting of bills at subsequent stages

11.5.7 A bill amended in committee is, when reported from the committee to the House, again ordered to be printed (see paragraph 11.10.30). The amended bill will have a new bill number in the sessional series. In theory, a bill might be reprinted after each stage, if it had been amended. In practice, since nowadays there is very rarely an interval between the report stage and third reading, bills are rarely reprinted between those stages.

11.6 SECOND READING

Second reading debate

11.6.1 In giving a bill its second reading, the House is giving its assent in principle, rather than in detail, to the proposals which it contains. Debate on the Question for second reading may therefore be fairly general and may cover what the bill *might* have included as well as what it does actually include.

Amendments at second reading

11.6.2 A bill cannot itself be amended at second reading. However, a **reasoned amendment** may be tabled to the motion that the bill be read a second time. Such an amendment generally takes the form "That this House declines to give a second reading to [the such and such bill] which, while doing A and B, fails to do X and Y".

11.6.3 The purpose of a reasoned amendment, as its name suggests, is to give reasons explaining or qualifying the intention to reject a bill, as an alternative to the unqualified rejection of voting against its second reading. However, the effect of agreeing a reasoned amendment would be the same as negativing the Question for second reading: the bill would proceed no further.

11.6.4 Reasoned amendments are subject to selection by the Chair (see paragraphs 9.2.6 and 9.2.9). In deciding whether to select such an amendment for debate, the Chair is likely to have particular regard to whether it is more than simply an expanded rejection of the whole bill or whether (at the opposite extreme) it introduces considerations which are irrelevant to the decision whether to approve or reject the bill, or simply proposes changes that could be achieved by way of amendment.

11.6.5 The scope of debate on a reasoned amendment at second reading is, for all practical purposes, identical to the scope of the second reading debate as a whole. S.O. No. 62(2) provides that when a decision has been made on a reasoned amendment, the main Question "That the bill be read a second time" is put for decision immediately afterwards without further debate.

Second reading committees

11.6.6 Under S.O. No. 90, a bill may be referred to a *Second Reading Committee* for its second reading debate. Such a procedure has historically been reserved for a few very uncontroversial bills. Under S.O. No. 60, *tax law re-write bills* may be automatically referred to a second reading committee (see paragraph 11.6.20 below).

11.6.7 Under paragraph (1) of S.O. No. 90 a Minister may give notice of a motion to refer a bill to a committee for its second reading. The motion cannot be put to the House less than ten days after the notice was given, after which period it may be moved at the commencement of public business (see paragraph 7.7.7) and put **forthwith**. When the motion is made, if twenty or more Members rise in their places to signify their objection, the Question is deemed to be negatived.

11.6.8 Under paragraph (2) of S.O. No. 90, a private Member may move such a motion (provided the required notice has been given) at the commencement of public business on a private Members' bill Friday (see paragraph 2.2.4), but only on one of those Fridays after the days set aside for second readings of balloted bills (usually the first seven, see paragraphs 11.2.2 to 11.2.5 above) have passed. A private Member requires the unanimous leave of the House to move such a motion, so a single call of "object" can prevent it being made.

11.6.9 Under S.O. No. 59, a bill of which the main purpose is to give effect to proposals of a report by one of the **law commissions** is *automatically* referred to a second reading committee after its presentation and first reading. Such bills are usually of a somewhat technical nature, implementing proposals for law reform, and will normally have started in the Lords where they will have been subject to a special select committee style of scrutiny (the "Jellicoe" procedure). Such a bill may be de-referred from a second reading committee by a motion moved by a Minister on a subsequent day at the commencement of public business, or may be referred to the Scottish Grand Committee where appropriate (see paragraphs 11.6.14 to 11.6.17 below).

11.6.10 The debate in a second reading committee follows the same pattern as a second reading in the House and is not time-limited, but, in accordance with S.O. No. 90(4), the motion before the committee is that it recommends "That the bill ought to be read a second time". Though it has never been attempted, it seems likely the committee could also consider a reasoned amendment for recommending that the bill ought not to be read a second time.

11.6.11 After a second reading committee has reported its resolution to the House, when the order for the second reading of the bill is read on a subsequent day, the Question is put **forthwith**.

Second readings in the Welsh Grand Committee

11.6.12 Under S.O. No. 105, a bill may be referred for a second reading debate in the Welsh Grand Committee. The procedures are the same as for referring a bill to a second reading committee (see paragraph 11.6.7 above) except that the right to move the necessary referral motion is reserved exclusively to Ministers.

11.6.13 The procedure on second reading of a bill reported from the Welsh Grand Committee is the same as that for one reported from a second reading committee (see paragraph 11.6.11 above).

Scottish and Northern Ireland Grand Committees: Bills considered in relation to principle

11.6.14 A bill which relates exclusively to Scotland is certified as such by the Speaker. However, such bills are unlikely to appear in Westminster following devolution (for example, the bill which became the Scotland Act 1998 was not such a bill, since its provisions self-evidently affected the whole of the UK). Under S.O. No. 97, if a bill is so certified, a Minister (or in the case of a private Member's bill the **Member in charge** of the bill), may move before its second reading that the bill be referred to the Scottish Grand Committee (see section 14.3). The Question on such a motion is put **forthwith** and may be decided after the **moment of interruption**. A private Member, however, requires unanimous leave to move such a motion, so a single objection would be enough to prevent the motion being made. Under S.O. No. 113, the same procedure may be applied to a bill which relates exclusively to Northern Ireland to refer it before second reading to the Northern Ireland Grand Committee. There is not, however, any provision for the certifying of such bills by the Speaker.

11.6.15 If a motion to refer is agreed, the bill is subsequently considered by the Scottish or Northern Ireland Grand Committee. The debate is essentially a second reading debate, but the motion before the committee is that "the committee has considered the bill in relation to its principle". The debate is limited to two hours, but there is provision for a Minister to move (at the beginning of the debate) a motion to extend the time limit. The Question on such a motion is put **forthwith**.

11.6.16 After the debate the Chairman reports that the Committee has so considered the bill or, if the motion was negatived, that it has come to no resolution in respect of the bill. There is no provision to report reasons for rejecting the bill.

11.6.17 Whatever the Scottish Grand Committee reports, when the order for the second reading of a Scottish bill is read on a subsequent day, a Minister may, under S.O. No. 97(5), immediately move that the bill be committed to a Scottish Standing Committee (see S.O. No. 101 and paragraph 11.10.3) or a Special Standing Committee (see paragraph 11.11.8). The Question on such a motion is put **forthwith** and may be decided after the **moment of interruption**. If it is agreed, the bill is deemed, under paragraph (6) of the standing order, to have been read a second time. In the case of a Northern Ireland bill, after it has been reported from the Northern Ireland Grand Committee, if the question for second reading is subsequently moved in the House, the Question is put **forthwith** and may be decided after the **moment of interruption**, under S.O. No. 113(4).

Consolidation, &c. Bills

11.6.18 Consolidation Bills are, essentially, bills which repeal parts or the whole of existing Acts and re-enact the same provisions so as to draw together all the existing statutory provisions (in relation to, say, water supply or the police) in one convenient statute. They are prepared by the **law commissions**. As part of the consolidation process, the law commissions may also tidy up the statute book with minor repeals of or amendments to existing law. Statute law repeal bills, also prepared by the law commissions, periodically repeal swathes of the statute book which are redundant. Such bills are examined, under the provisions of S.O. No. 140, by a joint committee of the two Houses after they have been presented in the Lords (where they invariably start) to ensure that the measures are strictly consolidating or the repeals are only of redundant legislation or that any amendments made to the existing law are within the strict limits permitted. The Committee reports its conclusions to each House.

11.6.19 Under S.O. No. 58(3), the Question on the second reading of a consolidation or statute law repeal bill is put **forthwith**. Because of this, paragraph (2) of the standing order makes provision for amendments to such bills to be tabled *before* their second reading (though it is by definition very difficult to devise an orderly amendment to a consolidation bill). Under paragraph (4) of the standing order, a motion may, without notice, be moved by a Minister, after the second reading has been agreed, that the bill be not committed. This procedure would appear to be intended, by implication, to be reserved for bills to which no amendments had been tabled (or where the Chairman of Ways and Means had not selected any amendments which had been tabled). The Question on such a motion is put **forthwith**, and if agreed the third reading may immediately be moved and the Question on that is also put **forthwith**, under paragraph (2) of the standing order.

Tax law re-write bills

11.6.20 S.O. No. 60 provides for special procedures to apply to a class of bill known as "tax law re-write bills". This follows the recommendations of the Howe Committee for the undertaking by the Inland Revenue of a systematic programme of simplification of the language of the law relating to direct taxation. These bills, which are prepared by an expert committee in consultation with outside professionals, are broadly intended to recast and simplify the language of the law relating to direct taxation, but not its effects. While the main purpose of these bills is to restate existing law in a more comprehensible form, they may, however, include provisions which effectively alter the law to some degree.

11.6.21 S.O. No. 60(1) and (2) provide for a Minister to move a motion at the commencement of public business, after such a bill has been introduced in the Commons, to provide for it to be proceeded with as a tax law re-write bill. Once such a motion has been agreed, under paragraph (3) of the standing order, the bill stands automatically referred to a second reading committee (see paragraphs 11.6.6 to 11.6.11 above). Under paragraph (4) of the standing order, a bill may be de-referred from a second reading committee on a further motion moved by a Minister at the commencement of public business. Under paragraph (6) of the standing order, once such a bill has been read a second time it stands automatically committed to a special Joint Committee on Tax Law Re-write Bills. Once reported from that Committee, the bill, under paragraph (7) of the standing order, stands automatically re-committed to a committee of the whole House (see paragraphs 11.11.1 to 11.11.6 below) unless the House otherwise orders. Under paragraph (8) of the standing order, a motion may be moved by a Minister at the time of commencing the committee of the whole House stage to discharge the committee from considering the bill and, if it is agreed, the bill is automatically ordered to be read the third time. Such a motion may be made after the **moment of interruption** and is decided **forthwith**.

11.7 COMMITTAL

Programme orders

11.7.1 The still temporary standing orders relating to programming provide that, if before the second reading of a bill a Minister has given notice for the committal of the bill in question, and for it to be subject to a programme, S.O.No. 63 (which provides for committal of bills) is disapplied, and the process of committal takes place through the programme motion. In current practice it is still usual for the vast majority of government bills to be committed by a programme motion to a normal standing committee (or on occasion to be split between a standing committee and a committee of the whole House), although the **Modernisation Committee** in its original proposals envisaged the use of a wider range of types of committee. The types of committal which might be encompassed by a programme motion are generally those described below. If moved immediately after second reading, the Question on such a programme motion is put **forthwith**.

Committal to standing committee

11.7.2 Once a bill has been given its second reading, unless it is a Consolidated Fund or Appropriation Bill (see paragraphs 10.3.13 and 10.3.14) or it is a Consolidation Bill (see paragraph 11.6.18 and paragraph 11.6.19 above) in which the committee stage is omitted, it is immediately committed to some committee of the House. Unless it is to be subject to a separate programme motion, under S.O. No. 63(1), the "default" position is that if no other motion is agreed to by the House the bill automatically stands committed to a standing committee.

Committal motions

11.7.3 However, under paragraph (2) of the standing order, a motion may be moved by any Member, after second reading, to commit the bill to a *committee of the whole House*, a *special standing committee*, a *select committee* or a *joint committee* of both Houses. Such options may also be encompassed in a programme motion.

11.7.4 If a committal motion is made immediately after the second reading vote, it may be moved without notice (that is, it need not appear on the **Order Paper**), and it may be put **forthwith** and decided after the **moment of interruption**. Under S.O. No. 32(4), such motions are subject to the Speaker's power of selection (see paragraphs 9.2.6 to 9.2.9).

11.7.5 A motion of this type may be moved on a later day, discharging a bill from a standing committee to which it was committed by default and committing it instead to some other type of committee. Such a motion *would* require notice. In effect, therefore, such a motion could only be moved by the government. A private Member might put down such a motion on one of the private Members' bills Fridays, but it would not be exempt from the effect of the **moment of interruption** so that for all practical purposes it could not be agreed without the unanimous consent of the House.

Splitting committal motions

11.7.6 Under paragraph (3) of S.O. No. 63, a motion may be moved after the second reading of the bill to divide a bill in a specified way between consideration by a committee of the whole House and a standing committee (see paragraphs 2.3.1 and 2.3.2). Such a motion may only be moved by the **Member in charge** of the bill. He or she may make a brief speech (that is, no more than ten minutes) justifying the proposal, and one other Member may make a brief speech opposing it, after which the Question must be put. If done immediately after the second reading vote, all this may occur after the **moment of interruption** and the motion may be moved without notice (though generally the terms of such a motion *would* appear on the **Order Paper**). If it were moved on a subsequent day, it would be treated as any other motion and the same restrictions as described in paragraph 11.7.4 above would apply. A programme order can similarly divide a bill (in theory between any different types of committee described in S.O. No. 63).

11.7.7 The annual Finance Bill (see paragraphs 10.2.19 to 10.2.24) is frequently split, so that key clauses may be debated in committee of the whole House, with the remainder going to standing committee. Other bills are fairly regularly split in this manner, especially where particular clauses may raise matters of conscience on which the government feels it is appropriate for the whole House to reach a decision (for example capital punishment, the age of consent or hunting). Or again, it may be a matter of reaching decisions upon questions on which the government has an open mind, and on which it wishes the House as a whole to express its opinion.

11.7.8 Where a bill has been divided up in this way, the clauses committed to the whole House will generally be reported first (with or without amendments) and these are ordered to lie upon the Table. When the standing committee has reported its parts of the bill, it is reprinted as a whole, incorporating any amendments made by either committee, and proceeds through its remaining stages (see sections 11.11 to 11.14 and Figure 6 below) as if it had all been reported from a standing committee.

Purpose of committee stage

11.7.9 The committee stage is the key stage in a bill's consideration by the House. The essential purpose is to allow members of the committee to examine, in as much detail as they choose (within the constraints of any programme order), the provisions of each clause and schedule. They may offer alternative propositions by way of amendments, new clauses and new schedules to delete, supplement or replace any part of a bill.

11.8 INSTRUCTIONS

11.8.1 After a bill has received its second reading and been committed, occasionally motions may be moved to give *instructions* to the committee which is to consider the bill. If notice has been given of a proposed instruction, it will be printed on the **Order Paper** immediately below the order of the day for second reading of the bill to which it refers. S.O. No. 32(4) allows the Speaker to select instructions (see paragraphs 9.2.6 to 9.2.9), and he is most unlikely to select one which a Member seeks to move without **notice**.

11.8.2 An instruction is generally framed in the form "That it be an instruction to any committee to which [the such and such] bill may be committed that it have power to make amendments having such and such effect". The purpose of an instruction is usually to enable the committee to make amendments to a bill which would otherwise fall outside the scope of amendments permitted by S.O. No. 65 (see paragraph 11.9.14 below). For example, an instruction is necessary before a committee can extend the geographical scope of a bill to parts of the United Kingdom not originally encompassed by its provisions. But an instruction may also be framed so as to require a committee in effect to do something at the behest of the House (for example, to report a bill by a specified date – though this would nowadays normally be done by a programme motion), and its intention may be to narrow rather than enlarge the freedom of a committee to make amendments. However, such mandatory instructions are, in general, applicable only to select committees on bills or private bill committees, unless they form part of a programme order.

11.8.3 Instructions which go way beyond the scope of the bill to which they apply would, however, be out of order. For example, an instruction to enable a committee to in effect tack an entirely unrelated set of provisions on to the bill before it by way of amendment would be inadmissible.

11.8.4 Instructions may also permit or require committees to do a variety of other things such as split a bill into two bills, join two bills into one, report a portion of a bill separately or reconsider decisions previously taken. They may also make provisions in respect of the procedures a committee may use. Examples of such instructions are rare.

11.8.5 Though instructions are generally moved immediately after second reading, they may be moved at any stage in a bill's progress after its second reading.

11.9 AMENDMENTS IN STANDING COMMITTEE AND COMMITTEE OF THE WHOLE HOUSE

Amendments

11.9.1 Once a bill has been committed to a standing committee or to a committee of the whole House, amendments may be tabled to it. Amendments to bills committed to select or joint committees are dealt with by the committees in private, though they would generally adopt something like standing committee procedure to do this.

Tabling of amendments

11.9.2 Amendments do not, in theory, require written notice to have been given before they can be moved in committee. In practice, the chairman will only in very exceptional circumstances select amendments moved without notice (known as *manuscript amendments*). Nor will a chairman generally select an amendment which was tabled only on the previous sitting day (known as a *starred amendment* because when printed on the Amendment Paper for a committee sitting it is marked by a star in indicate that it has not previously appeared). Thus in practice, in order to be eligible for selection, an amendment must have been tabled at the latest on the sitting day or non-sitting Friday before the sitting day before that on which it is debated.

11.9.3 By practice, amendments tabled on the same day that the bill has received its second reading must be tabled at the **Table** of the House, not in the Public Bill Office. Otherwise, amendments may be tabled in writing in the **Public Bill Office** at any time between 10 am (or the meeting of the House if earlier) and the rising of the House on any sitting day. On non-sitting Fridays (see paragraph 6.1.5), S.O. No. 12(4)(b) provides that they may be tabled between 11 am and 3 pm. S.O. No. 64 provides that when the House is not sitting during one of its holiday breaks (see paragraph 5.2.10), amendments may be tabled up to 4.30 pm on the last day of the holiday (excluding weekends and Bank Holidays), and will be treated as if tabled on a sitting day.

11.9.4 Amendments may not be tabled before a bill has been given its second reading, unless the House has passed a motion specifically authorising this. There is an exception made to this rule under S.O. No. 58 for Consolidation Bills (see paragraphs 11.6.18 and 11.6.19 above).

Printing of amendments

11.9.5 All amendments tabled on a sitting day are printed and published the following day with the Vote Bundle (see paragraphs 15.1.32 and 15.1.37).

11.9.6 Amendments are each given a number by the printers in the order in which they arrive. There are separate numbering sequences for new clauses (NC1, NC2 etc) and for new schedules (NS1, NS2, etc). Each amendment, new clause or new schedule retains this unique identifying number through the remainder of the committee's consideration of that particular bill.

11.9.7 When amendments are first published in the blue pages of the notice papers, they will be printed in the order in which they were tabled, which may be quite random in respect of the order in which they relate to the bill.

Marshalled lists

11.9.8 On the day immediately preceding the first meeting of a committee to consider a bill, a *marshalled blue list* will be published. This list will set out all the amendments so far tabled in the order in which they relate to the bill. Where two amendments are proposed in exactly the same place, priority will be given to one to leave out and insert words over one to leave out words only. Where two amendments have equal claim, priority will be given to any in the name of the **Member in charge** of the bill, or else they will appear in the order in which they were tabled.

SCB 115

House of Commons
Tuesday 29th February 2003
STANDING COMMITTEE B

New Amendments handed in are marked thus ★

KNIVES BILL

NOTE
The Amendments have been arranged in accordance with the Order of the Committee (15 February 2003)

Mr William Wordsworth **3**

Clause **1**, page **1**, line **8**, leave out 'may' and insert 'shall'.

Mr Bob Southey **11**

★ Schedule **1**, page **4**, line **14**, leave out 'with the consent of the Treasury'.

NEW CLAUSES

Definition of "carrying"

Miss Jane Austen **NC 1**

To move the following Clause:–
'. In this Act, "carrying" includes carrying in a bag or other receptacle.'.

FIGURE 25
EXAMPLE OF AN AMENDMENT PAPER

11.9.9 Because each amendment retains its unique identifying number given to it when it was first printed, the sequence of numbering of amendments printed in a marshalled list may appear at first glance completely random. Amendments are *not* considered in numerical order but in the order in which they relate to a bill, and the index number of an amendment is no indication of its place in a bill.

11.9.10 Where a resolution of a programming sub-committee has been reported, or if an order of consideration motion has been tabled by the Member in charge (see paragraph 11.10.17 below), the amendments will be marshalled in accordance with order of consideration proposed in that motion or resolution, and a note to that effect will be printed at the start of the marshalled list.

11.9.11 On each day that a committee is due to sit a marshalled list of amendments on white paper is published with the **Vote bundle** (see paragraph 15.1.32 and Figure 25).

11.9.12 Amendments may continue to be tabled throughout the period when the committee is considering a bill. Amendments may be withdrawn before they are reached in committee. No notice of such withdrawals is printed.

11.9.13 As the committee progresses through a bill, amendments will be duly made or otherwise disposed of. A committee cannot go back in its consideration of a bill, so an amendment to a part of the bill which falls before the point which the committee has reached in its consideration cannot be proposed. On each day that the committee sits, therefore, the marshalled list will begin with the first amendment that falls to be considered after the point in the bill where the last decision of the committee to alter the bill (or to stand a clause part of the bill) was made at the previous sitting, or after the point at which the programme order required proceedings to be concluded at the previous sitting.

Amendments which are out of order

11.9.14 S.O. No. 65 gives power to all committees to which bills are committed to make amendments, but restricts them to making only those amendments that are relevant to the subject matter of the bill. This concept of "relevance" is usually referred to as the "scope of the bill". In deciding whether or not a proposed amendment falls within the scope of the bill, where the case is not obvious one way or the other, the chairman will rely on precedent and his or her own judgement. The long title of a bill indicates but does not define its scope, since under the same standing order, No.65, it may be amended as a consequence of amendments which are made to the bill. If a chairman decides that an amendment is outside the scope of the bill, then it cannot be moved. A bill which has only one purpose (a very rare creature) cannot have any other purposes added to it. But where it has two or more purposes, amendments to enlarge the number of things it does are admissible, as long as they relate to the original purposes of the bill. Being out of order (unless a gross case) is, however, no bar to an amendment being printed.

11.9.15 S.O. No. 49 requires any proposal within a bill to create a charge on the public revenue to be authorised by a separate resolution of the House (see paragraphs 10.2.1 to 10.2.5). This rule applies equally to any amendment proposed to be made to the bill. If the Chairman is of the opinion that an amendment, if made, would entail public expenditure of a kind which is not authorised by a money resolution relating to the bill, the amendment is out of order and cannot be proposed.

11.10 Standing Committee Procedure

Introduction

11.10.1 As described in section 11.7 above, bills may be committed to a committee of the whole House, a select committee or a joint committee as well as to a standing committee or special standing committee. The vast majority of bills, however, are committed to a standing committee, and a small number each year go to a committee of the whole House. Special standing committees on bills have been relatively rare, and select committees and joint committees rarer still. Therefore, for convenience, standing committee procedure is described first in this section. Procedure in committee of the whole House is, in its essentials, the same as procedure in standing committee. The ways in which the procedure in other types of committees differs from it are described in the next section. In current practice, where government bills are almost invariably subject to a programme order, the proceedings in a standing committee will be governed by two important factors: the latest date by which the committee is required by the order to report the bill to the House; and the decisions of the committee's programming sub-committee about the allocation of time to each section of the bill, divided up between specified sittings of the standing committee, with timings for the commencement and conclusion of each sitting and requirements that all proceedings relating to specified parts of the bill must be concluded at specified times.

Membership of committees

11.10.2 Under S.O. No. 86, the **Committee of Selection** (see section 2.4) nominates between sixteen and fifty Members to each standing committee on a bill. The usual number is between sixteen and thirty, though the Finance Bill standing committee is often larger. The total will usually be determined by agreement between the usual channels (see section 2.5). With the exceptions set out in paragraph 11.10.5 below, only those Members nominated to a standing committee on a bill may participate in its proceedings or sit in the body of the committee.

11.10.3 Bills relating exclusively to Wales have been very rare, but this may begin to change as the National Assembly for Wales becomes more established, as primary legislation for Wales can only be made at Westminster, not at Cardiff Bay. S.O. No. 86(2)(ii) requires that a standing committee to consider such a bill should include *all* the Members sitting for Welsh constituencies. The standing orders provide for bills certified by the Speaker as relating exclusively to Scotland (see paragraph 11.6.14) to be committed to a *Scottish Standing Committee*. This provision is pretty much irrelevant following the establishment of the Scottish Parliament. The *First* Scottish Standing Committee would consider government bills while the *Second* Scottish Standing Committee has the same function as Standing Committee C (see paragraph 11.10.8 below) in respect of private Members bills relating exclusively to Scotland. Under S.O. No. 86(2)(i), these committees must include at least sixteen Members representing Scottish constituencies.

11.10.4 Under S.O. No. 87(1), any holder of the office of Attorney General, the Advocate General or the Solicitor General who is a Member of the House may participate in debates in any standing committee on a bill, but they may not move motions or amendments and cannot vote. Under paragraph (2) of the standing order, *any* Minister may participate in the debate of a standing committee on a bill brought in upon a Ways and Means resolution. For all practical purposes, this means a Finance Bill Committee (see paragraphs 10.2.23 and 10.2.24).

11.10.5 When a committee has reported a bill to the House, all the Members nominated to it in respect of that particular bill stand automatically discharged, and new Members must be nominated in respect of another bill.

Allocation of bills to standing committees

11.10.6 Under S.O. No. 84(2), the Speaker allocates each bill to a standing committee. There is no limit to the number of standing committees on bills that may be set up at any one time. Over the course of an average session there will usually be five or six. They are given the title Standing Committee A, B, etc. Once established, they remain in existence for the remainder of the session, and bills may be allocated to each of them successively. There is sometimes a queue of bills in a standing committee awaiting consideration, and the government may, under S.O. No. 84(4), determine the order in which they are considered (except in the case of Standing Committee C, for which see next paragraph). Once a committee has entered on its consideration of a bill it must conclude that consideration (or make some other report to the House if it cannot do so) before it commences consideration of another bill.

11.10.7 Under paragraph (3) of S.O. No. 84, one standing committee is reserved to private Members' bills, and the government has no power to determine the order in which bills are considered by that committee. The Committee of Selection (see section 2.4) invariably designates Standing Committee C for this purpose each session. Except by agreement, or in the case of excessive delay, bills are considered by Standing Committee C in the order in which they are committed to it by the House. The **Member in charge** of a bill allocated to this committee has some influence with the **Committee of Selection** in relation to which Members are nominated to it in respect of his or her own bill.

11.10.8 The Speaker may transfer a bill from one committee to another at the request of the **Member in charge**, if consideration of it has not begun. If this is done, the Members nominated to the first committee in respect of that bill are automatically transferred to the second. Occasionally the **Member in charge** of a private Member's bill may ask for it to be transferred from Standing Committee C to another if it appears that the other committee has no government bills to consider.

Programming sub-committees

11.10.9 Under the temporary standing orders relating to programming of bills, where a programme order applies to a bill committed to a standing committee, the Speaker must appoint the chairman (or one of the chairmen) of that standing committee, and seven other members of that committee to a programming sub-committee (of which the quorum is four). The sub-committee is chaired by the chairman and will include Ministers, front-bench spokespeople and whips. The standing orders provide for the sub-committee, at a meeting lasting no more than two hours, to come up with a resolution setting out the timetable for the bill's consideration by the committee. Its resolution is reported to the standing committee, and on a motion being made in the same terms, there may be a debate on it which may last half an hour, at the end of which period the chair must put the questions necessary to dispose of the motion. The timetable will then be set. The sub-committee may make subsequent proposals to vary this timetable, which must be agreed by the main committee to have effect. The sub-committee may also recommend that the House vary a programme order to extend the deadline by which the bill must be reported back to the House, or make recommendations as to the timetabling of subsequent stages of the bill's consideration by the House. Such motions are either put **forthwith** (generally where the motion is to agree with the recommendations of a sub-committee), or may be debated by the House for forty-five minutes, at the end of which time the necessary questions to dispose of them must be put by the chair. When agreed to, they become part of the overall programme order. All these proceedings are exempt from the effect of the **moment of interruption**.

Selection and grouping of amendments

11.10.10 Under S.O. No. 32 as applied by S.O. No. 89(3)(a), the chairman of a standing committee has the power of selection among those amendments, new clauses or new schedules which are in order (see paragraph 11.9.14 and paragraph 11.9.15 above). In other words, the chairman decides whether or not any amendments can be debated or considered by the committee. Although this power is arbitrary, and there is no appeal beyond the chairman, it is generally exercised with discretion and chairmen are predisposed to give the balance of any doubt to the Member proposing the amendment. Possible reasons for a chairman not to select an amendment might include: that it sought to reopen a question already thoroughly covered; that the amendment was offered in the wrong place in the bill or should more properly be a new clause; that the amendment is itself nonsensical, or that it would make a nonsense of the rest of the bill without the making of consequential amendments which had not been tabled; that it was a wrecking amendment which would destroy the purpose of the bill as agreed to by the House on second reading, or that it would reverse all the effective provisions of a clause; that it was trivial, or vexatious in intention; or that it was otherwise without merit. Under S.O. No. 32(3), as applied by S.O. No. 89, the chairman can request a Member to explain the purpose of a proposed amendment to a committee before making a decision on whether to allow it to be moved. It is out of order to question publicly the chair's decision either to select or not to select a proposed amendment. If an amendment is proposed by the **Member in charge** (ie the Minister in the case of a government bill) and it is in order, the chairman will select it.

11.10.11 The Chair's exercise of the power of selection over amendments and new clauses or schedules facilitates the well-ordered consideration of the provisions of a bill and those alternative or supplementary provisions proposed by way of amendments. To assist the efficiency and clarity of the process, having selected amendments from among those which are proposed and are in order, the chair then proposes *groupings* of amendments to a committee. There is no explicit provision for this in standing orders – but it may be regarded as an extension of the power of selection.The purpose of this exercise is to group together all those amendments relating to a particular theme or point. There are two obvious types of groupings which the chair will propose. The first is where amendments represent alternative and incompatible propositions. If they were

STANDING COMMITTEE E

LICENSING (AMENDMENT) BILL

Chairmen's Provisional Selection of Amendments

Tuesday 29 February 2003 at 9.10 am and 2.30 pm

(Arranged in accordance with the terms of the resolution of the Programming Sub-Committee)

Clause 1
1 + 2 + NC1 + 6
Proceedings to be concluded at 11.20 am on Tuesday 29 February

Clause 2
3 + 4 + 5 + 7

Schedule 1

Clause 3
18 + 9 + 21
Govt 41 + Govt 42 to 46

Clause 4
Proceedings to be concluded at 6.55 pm on Tuesday 29 February

Schedules 2 and 3
Govt 47 + Govt 48 to 52

Clauses 5 to 11

New Clauses
Govt NC2 + 8
NC3 + (a) + (b) + (c) + (d) + 9 + (a)

New Schedules
Govt NS1
Proceedings to be concluded at 6.55 pm on Thursday 31 February

Chairmen
Mr William Wordsworth
Sir Walter Scott

FIGURE 26
EXAMPLE OF SELECTION LIST FOR A STANDING COMMITTEE

debated separately, a decision to agree the first would effectively rule out debate on the second or subsequent proposals, so it is obviously for the convenience of the committee to be able to debate the arguments for and against all the competing proposals before taking a decision. The second obvious type of group is that in which a number of amendments are clearly interdependent, and if one stands or falls the rest must stand or fall with it. Again, it is obviously for the convenience of the committee to consider all the constituent parts of the proposition in one debate. The third general type of group is one which brings together amendments which, while not actually strictly interdependent or mutually incompatible, are all addressed to a similar theme running through the bill. There will always be room for disagreement about which amendments do and do not fall within a definition of some broad theme, but the chairman will be seeking to facilitate debate in the committee and generally his or her groupings will appear convenient to the Members.

Rules of debate in committee

11.10.12 Fundamentally the same rules of debate apply in committee as apply in the House, and these are described in chapter 9. The main distinction is that the rule against speaking more than once to the same Question does not apply in committee. The powers of the chair as applied by S.O. No. 89 are described in paragraphs 3.3.3 to 3.3.7, and the manner of dealing with disorder in paragraphs 9.3.32 to 9.3.36.

Sittings of standing committees

11.10.13 For the usual pattern of standing committee sittings, see paragraphs 6.2.1 to 6.2.7. In current practice, the pattern of sittings will usually be governed by a programme order, as filled-out by a resolution of a programming sub-committee. Occasionally, the Members of a standing committee (usually on a private Member's bill, but possibly on a very uncontroversial government bill) will come to its first meeting in the general expectation that they will be able to dispose of the bill before them in one sitting. In such circumstances the committee will launch into its consideration of the bill without any preliminaries. More often, the first business before the committee will be to consider a resolution of its programming sub-committee or (in the case of a private Member's bill) a sittings motion moved by the **Member in charge** of the bill. The resolution or motion sets out the proposed weekly timetable of sittings of the committee during its consideration of the bill. Programming sub-committee resolutions do this in much more detail than sittings motions.

11.10.14 Motions to agree with the resolution of a programming sub-committee must be disposed of within half an hour. Sittings motions may be moved without **notice**, but usually the Member in charge will have arranged for notice of the proposed motion to appear on the amendment paper. Amendments may, if the chairman selects them, be moved to alter the proposed pattern of sitting. Debate on these sittings motions can be disposed of very quickly or can sometimes range rather widely and be fairly prolonged. Once a programme order or a sittings motions has been agreed, that pattern of sittings continues for the remainder of the bill's consideration, unless the committee decides subsequently to vary its pattern of sittings by agreeing a supplementary programme order or sittings motion, or agrees at the end of a particular sitting to vary the effect of a sittings motion.

11.10.15 A motion for a committee to sit in the afternoon cannot be moved on the day on which it is proposed to do so unless oral notice of that intention has been given on a previous day. The effect of this rule is to prevent a committee from sitting twice on its first day of meeting. It can only do so if the House has previously passed a motion authorising it to do so, which may well have been done as part of a programme order.

Order in which a bill is considered

11.10.16 Unless otherwise provided for, the committee goes through the clauses of and schedules to a bill in the order in which they are printed. Any new clauses which are proposed to the bill are taken after the clauses, and any proposed new schedules after the schedules. Amendments proposed to the long title are taken at the very end.

11.10.17 More often, however, the bill will be subject to a programme order which may vary the order in which the bill's provisions are considered, or the **Member in charge** will propose an *order of consideration* motion at the outset of a bill's consideration, at the first meeting of the standing committee, which specifies a different order in which the clauses and schedules are to be considered, and may also vary the points at which new clauses and new schedules are considered. At their most straightforward, such rearrangements are designed simply to bring consideration of schedules forward to follow the particular clauses to which they relate. Sometimes the proposed rearrangements are highly elaborate.

Manner of considering a bill

11.10.18 A list showing the chairman's provisional selection of amendments and proposed groupings (see paragraphs 11.10.10 and 11.10.11 and Figure 26) is made available before each sitting of a standing committee. This will also indicate the points at which the programme order requires specified proceedings to be brought to a conclusion. Where amendments have been grouped (see paragraph 11.10.11 above), they are listed with the *first* amendment in that group to occur in the bill. Thus if the first amendment is No. 14 (which occurs in clause 1, for the sake of argument) and grouped with it are amendments No. 102 to clause 9, No. 54 to clause 21 (a government amendment), No. 2 to schedule 2 and new clause 1 and new schedule 3 (consequential on amendment No. 54), the grouping will be shown under clause 1 as follows:

14 + 102 + Govt 54 + NC1 + 2 + Govt NS3

The Member in whose name amendment No. 14 stands will move it, and the chairman will indicate when calling him or her the amendments that have been grouped with it. Thus, while the actual Question before the committee only relates to the first amendment in the group, debate in fact ranges over the subject matter of all the amendments in the group.

11.10.19 When the debate is concluded, the Question on that lead amendment in the group must be disposed of by its being withdrawn, negatived or agreed to. Sometimes the fate of the succeeding amendments in the group will be sealed by the fate of this first one. If it is negatived or withdrawn, the Chairman will only call successive amendments on the same subject for a decision if asked to do so, and if there seems good reason to do so. If the lead amendment is agreed to, it may mean that some subsequent ones in the group must logically be called to be formally agreed. Amendments proposed to a government bill in the name of a Minister, (which are distinguished by the prefix "Govt" on the selection list) are almost always called for decision, as are generally those amendments in the name of the **Member in charge** (distinguished by the prefix "p" in the selection list) of a private Member's bill.

11.10.20 Any amendments which have already been debated as part of a group will, if subsequently called by the chairman for decision, be moved formally. In other words the Member moving it will say simply "I beg to move" or give some other indication and the chairman will immediately put the Question for decision. Between the debate on a group of amendments and the decision on one of the later amendments in that group there may be several other debates on amendments or groups of amendments. In the example given in paragraph 11.10.18 above, where the first amendment was to clause 1 and the last was a new schedule, there could in theory be several weeks between the debate on the proposed new schedule and its actually being put for decision. This is because the grouping of amendments, which is done for the convenience of *debate*, does not override the fundamental rule that the committee makes *decisions* on proposed amendments in the order in which they occur in the bill (or in the order determined by a programme order or an order of consideration motion). Under a programme order, when one of the points at which proceedings related to a specified portion of a bill must be concluded is reached, the chairman is required to put a series of specified questions to dispose of all further amendments, etc. As well as those necessary to dispose of the question then under debate, these include the questions on any government amendments still outstanding relating to those parts, and on any other amendments which the chair has selected for separate division. Where Questions relating to government amendments run successively, these must be put *en bloc*. There will almost certainly need to be questions put to "stand part" various clauses and schedules at one of these cut-off points.

Clause or schedule stand part

11.10.21 Each clause of or schedule to the printed bill has to be separately considered by the committee. A committee may leave out clauses or schedules altogether; it may rearrange the order of the printed clauses; it may even decide to negative every effective clause of a bill, perhaps replacing them with a set of entirely new clauses.

11.10.22 When all the amendments proposed to a clause which have been selected for debate have been disposed of, the chairman proposes the Question "That the clause [,as amended,] stand part of the bill". The chairman proposes this Question without any Member moving it because it is a duty placed upon the committee as a whole to consider each clause sent to it by the House.

11.10.23 Under S.O. No. 68, as applied by S.O. No. 89, the chairman of a committee may, if he or she takes the view that the subject matter of a clause has been exhaustively debated in the course of the debate on amendments proposed to the clause, put the Question that the clause stand part of the bill **forthwith**, without further debate.

11.10.24 Debate on clause stand part will be the only question proposed in relation to a clause to which no amendments have been proposed or where none tabled have been selected. Where there are long stretches of successive clauses with no amendment, a chairman may propose the Question on several of them together, but this can only be done with the unanimous consent of the committee. Any Member on the committee may insist on their right to a clause stand part debate, or at least to a separate vote if no debate is possible under a programme order.

11.10.25 Debate on each schedule follows the form for a debate on a clause. Amendments which are selected are debated, and when all have been disposed of the chairman proposes the Question "That the Schedule [,as amended,] be the Xth Schedule to the bill". The provisions of S.O. No. 68 (described in paragraph 11.10.23 above) and of the standing orders relating to programmes apply equally to schedule stand part debates.

Debate on new clauses and new schedules

11.10.26 When a new clause selected for debate by a chairman is reached, one of the Members in whose name it stands is invited to move it. When he or she concludes the speech, the clerk of the committee reads out the title of the clause and, under S.O. No. 69, it is deemed to have been read a first time (the reading of the title being the residue of the reading of the whole clause). The chairman immediately proposes the Question "That the clause be read a second time". Debate takes place on this motion. If there are amendments proposed to the new clause which have been selected, they will usually be grouped for debate with the second reading debate. At the end of the debate, if the Question for second reading is negatived that is the end of the matter. If it is agreed, then any amendments may be moved formally, and after they are disposed of the chairman proposes the Question "That the clause [,as amended,] be added to the bill", which will, in turn, usually be put without debate. Debate on a new schedule follows the same pattern as that on a new clause. Where a new clause is reached after debate has been curtailed by a programme order, the chairman can only put the question for adding a new clause or schedule to the bill, leaving out the second reading question in each such case.

Record of proceedings

11.10.27 On the morning following each day on which a standing committee has sat, the *Proceedings of the Committee* are circulated with the Vote bundle, pursuant to S.O. No. 89(5). This takes the form of a marked up version of the previous day's amendment paper, showing the fate of each amendment, new clause, etc up to the point in the bill the committee had reached when it adjourned.

Reporting a bill

11.10.28 A committee's consideration of a bill may last for anything between a few minutes and a few months. Under a programme order, when the final deadline arrives, and all outstanding questions have been disposed of, the chairman is required to report the bill to the House without putting any final Question. In other circumstances, when a committee has concluded consideration of all the clauses and schedules, and any amendments, new clauses and new schedules selected by the chairman, the final Question proposed by the chairman is that he or she report the bill (with or without amendment, as the case is) to the House. As soon as the report has been made, the committee is adjourned indefinitely and the Members appointed in respect of that bill stand discharged.

11.10.29 The report from the committee appears in the **Votes and Proceedings**. The bill is ordered to be reprinted, if it has been amended, and this amended version will be published within a few days (see paragraph 11.5.7). Any new clauses or schedules which have been added to the bill by the committee are inserted in the places chosen by the **Member in charge**. Some clauses may have been left out, and the order of the clauses printed in the second reading copy of the bill may have been changed.

11.10.30 If it is a government bill it will also be ordered formally to be considered **tomorrow**; this simply means on some future day (see paragraphs 7.7.4 and 15.1.17). If it is a private Member's bill, the **Member in charge** will usually appoint one of the forthcoming Fridays set aside for consideration of private Members' bills for its report stage (see paragraph 2.2.4).

11.11 OTHER COMMITTEES ON BILLS

Committee of the whole House

11.11.1 All Members of the House are of course members of a committee of the whole House. The House sitting as a committee meets in the Chamber.

11.11.2 Procedure in committee of the whole House is essentially the same as in standing committee. Divisions, however, are taken in the same way as in the House (see section 9.6). The House in committee sits at the normal hours of sitting and the cut off of the **moment of interruption** applies. It is rare for a bill (other than a Finance Bill) to have more than two days' consideration in committee of the whole House.

11.11.3 The **Chairman of Ways and Means** (see paragraphs 3.2.1 to 3.2.3) is the chairman of all committees of the whole House, and exercises the functions of selection, grouping, etc described above (see paragraphs 11.10.10 and 11.10.11). When presiding over the House in committee he sits not in the Speaker's chair but in the place at the **Table** usually reserved for the **Clerk of the House**. The **Mace** is also placed on a rest below the Table to signify that the House is in committee.

11.11.4 When the order for a committee stage is read out by the Clerk, under S.O. No. 66 the House simply resolves itself into the committee without any Question being put.

11.11.5 Bills are committed to a committee of the whole House for a variety of reasons: because they are uncontroversial and no amendments are expected; because they need to be passed with great speed; because, with private Members' bills, there is no time for the standing committee stage if they are to have a chance of passing within that session; because they are of major constitutional significance or because they are controversial in ways which transcend normal party political divisions. The last will usually be the reason for committing a portion of a bill to a committee of the whole House (see paragraph 11.7.5 above).

11.11.6 If a bill is not amended in committee of the whole House it does not have a report stage, but goes directly to its third reading. A bill which has been split between committee of the whole House and standing committee must undergo a report stage, whether or not it has been amended. Where a bill is committed, under a programme order, to a committee of the whole House, or to any other kind of committee other than a standing committee, the work undertaken by the programming sub-committee of the standing committee described above, is instead undertaken by a programming committee appointed by the Speaker from among the membership of the whole House.

Special standing committees

11.11.7 Members are appointed to a special standing committee in exactly the same manner as appointments to an ordinary standing committee are made (see paragraphs 2.4.2 and 2.4.3).

11.11.8 Procedure in special standing committees is governed by S.O. No. 91, unless its provisions are superseded by those of a programme order. In essence, this provides for the committee to hold one private deliberative meeting and three public evidence taking sessions (none of more than three hours' duration) during the twenty-eight days following the bill's committal. During these three evidence taking sessions the committee behaves much like a select committee, and paragraph (2) of the standing order provides that a Member who is not a member of the Chairmen's Panel (see paragraph 3.2.6) may be appointed by the Speaker to chair these sittings. It has often been the chairman of the relevant departmental select committee. Once these four sittings are over, the committee proceeds in exactly the same manner as a standing committee. The period of twenty-eight days during which these evidence sessions may occur may be extended by a motion made in the House. If such a motion is moved by a Minister, it may be debated after the **moment of interruption**.

Select committees

11.11.9 If a bill is referred to a select committee, the House will have to pass a separate order establishing the committee, naming its Members, fixing its quorum, and granting it any necessary powers to call for documents and witnesses, to travel, or to sit when the House is not sitting. This might all be done as part of a programme motion. In recent times only a small number of bills, other than hybrid bills (see paragraph 11.1.3), have been committed to select committees. Otherwise, consideration of bills by select committees has been in the form of *draft* bills (see paragraph 11.1.5) though select committees have frequently reported on bills before the House which have not been formally referred to them. In such cases, they cannot, of course, amend the bill directly.

11.11.10 Select committees to which bills are referred take evidence and deliberate like any select committee, and may produce a report. At the conclusion of their inquiry, they may make amendments to the bill in private session. Proposed amendments are not published outside the committee. To some extent the committee can choose its own procedure for doing this, but by and large is likely to adopt something like standing committee procedure. The chairman of a select committee on a bill does not, however, have the power of selection of amendments (see paragraph 11.10.10). At the conclusion of their proceedings they report the bill to the House in the usual way and, if it has been amended, it will be reprinted. Bills considered in select committee are generally re-committed (see section 11.12 below) either to a standing committee or a committee of the whole House.

Joint committees

11.11.11 If the House resolved under S.O. No. 63(2) that it was expedient to commit a bill to a joint committee of Lords and Commons, it would send a message to the Lords informing them of this and inviting their agreement to the proposal. If the Lords concurred, they would return a message to that effect. The Commons would then nominate its Members to the committee and send a further message to the Lords informing them and inviting them to nominate an equal number of Peers, and the Lords would reply in due course with their nominations. It is difficult to see how a programme order could be applied to a joint committee.

11.11.12 A joint committee of the Commons and Lords would be likely to proceed in broadly the same manner as a select committee, as described in the preceding paragraphs, though joint committee procedure has certain differences. The committee would presumably report the bill to whichever House had originally proposed that it be committed to a joint committee. Tax law re-write bills (see paragraphs 11.6.20 to 11.6.22) are automatically committed to a special Joint Committee on Tax Law Re-write Bills. A number of *draft* bills (see paragraph 11.1.5) have recently been committed to joint committees.

11.12 RE-COMMITTAL

11.12.1 The House may order a bill reported from one committee (say a select committee) to be re-committed to another committee (probably a standing committee or a committee of the whole House). This might be provided for as part of a programme order. A tax law re-write bill reported from the special joint committee, under S.O. No. 60(7), automatically stands re-committed to a committee of the whole House (see paragraphs 11.6.20 to 11.6.22 above). Sometimes a bill is re-committed to a committee which has already considered it.

11.12.2 The House may re-commit the whole of a bill or specific parts of a bill in order to correct errors made by the committee or to introduce some urgent new matter or for some other reason. A bill may be re-committed before, during or after its report stage (but it must be done before third reading).

11.12.3 If a motion is made to re-commit a bill as a whole, S.O. No. 74 provides that the Chair shall put the Question on the motion after allowing no more than a brief explanatory statement from the Member moving it and from one opposing it.

11.12.4 An instruction may be given to a committee (see section 11.8) in respect of a re-committed bill. This is likely to occur if the re-committal is in order to correct some error or irregularity.

11.12.5 A re-committed bill or portion of a bill is treated, for procedural purposes, in the same way as a bill normally committed.

11.13 REPORT STAGE

Introduction

11.13.1 Under S.O. No. 73, a bill proceeds to its report stage (more properly known as "consideration on report" or just "consideration") after its committee stage, or possibly after being re-committed and further reported. Under S.O. No. 72, a bill which has its committee stage in **committee of the whole House** and is not amended does not have a report stage; other bills which have no report stage are Consolidated Fund and Appropriation Bills (see paragraphs 10.3.13 to 10.3.15), Consolidation Bills which have had no committee stage (see paragraph 11.6.19) and tax law re-write bills which are discharged, under S.O. No. 60(8), from a committee of the whole House (see paragraphs 11.6.20 to 11.6.22).

11.13.2 However, if no amendments are tabled to a bill at consideration stage, or none of those tabled is selected, the stage is omitted and the bill moves directly to its third reading.

Procedure at report stage

11.13.3 The report stage of a bill is essentially a compressed re-run of the committee stage. As it is taken on the floor of the House, all Members may participate. Amendments, new clauses and new schedules for consideration may be tabled as soon as the bill has been reported from committee. They are printed in much the same way as committee stage amendments (see section 11.9) and marshalled lists are produced in the same way. On the day on which a bill is to be considered on the floor, a marshalled amendment paper is published.

11.13.4 A report stage may be adjourned at one sitting and resumed at another, but report stages rarely last more than two sittings. A government bill will, in current practice, be likely to be subject to a programme order, and the timetable for consideration on report will be determined by agreeing (or disagreeing) to a resolution of a programming sub-committee or programming committee. For a government bill, notice of a ten o'clock/seven o'clock motion to suspend the operation of the **moment of interruption** (see paragraph 7.10.4) is almost invariably given in respect of a report stage to which a programme order (see section 11.18) does not apply. If a programme order does apply, the moment of interruption is irrelevant.

11.13.5 The same rules relating to scope and to the effect of money resolutions apply to amendments at report stage as apply at committee stage (see paragraphs 11.9.14 and 11.9.15). The scope of amendments which may be considered on report may be altered by means of a resolution of the House (required by S.O. No. 75) which is similar in effect to an instruction to a committee (see section 11.8 above). A supplementary money resolution may also be passed to widen the scope of amendments relating to public money (see paragraphs 10.2.1 to 10.2.5) and other types of supplementary financial resolutions may also be passed if necessary (see paragraphs 10.2.17 and 10.2.18).

11.13.6 The Speaker exercises at report stage the same power of selection and grouping of amendments as the chairman of a committee (or the Chairman of Ways and Means in a committee of the whole House) exercises (see paragraphs 11.10.10, 11.10.11 and 11.11.3 above) with the variations described below.

Distinctions between report and committee stages

11.13.7 The Speaker, in making his decision on selection and grouping of amendments at report stage, applies broadly the same principles as described in paragraphs 11.10.10 and 11.10.11. However, because of the pressure of time there is not the same degree of predisposition in favour of selection as in committee. In particular, amendments relating to subjects which have been thoroughly debated in committee will be subject to rigorous scrutiny. Amendments which seek radically to unpick decisions already made by the House are also likely to be considered particularly carefully in relation to their selection. However, the presumption in favour of selecting government amendments or amendments in the name of the **Member in charge** of the bill still obtains. The details of the Speaker's selection are made available before the sitting at which the bill is to be considered in the House.

11.13.8 The conventions about giving notice of amendments and the non-selection of starred amendments described in section 11.9 above generally apply at report. The Speaker is likely to exercise discretion about the selection of **starred amendments** if the report stage is taking place very rapidly after the bill has been reported from committee.

11.13.9 There are two main distinctions between procedure at report stage and committee stage. These are: the order in which new clauses and schedules are taken; and the absence of the clause stand part debate.

11.13.10 The default order of consideration of a bill at report is: new clauses; amendments relating to the clauses; new schedules; amendments relating to the schedules. This order can be altered by a programme order or an order of consideration motion (see paragraph 11.10.17 above), but these are likely to broadly respect the priority accorded at this stage to new clauses and schedules. Because new clauses are considered first, debate on these often takes up the major portion of the time available at report stage. New clauses in the name of the **Member in charge** of the bill are considered first (in such order as that Member chooses) followed by other new clauses in the order in which they were tabled, as affected by any programme order. The same applies to new schedules.

11.13.11 There are no clause (or schedule) stand part debates (see paragraphs 11.10.21 to 11.10.25) at report stage. Only amendments to clauses and schedules, new clauses and new schedules are considered. It may, however, be possible to secure the equivalent of a clause stand part debate by tabling an amendment to leave out a whole clause. Generally speaking, the manner of considering new clauses and amendments on report are the same as in committee (see paragraphs 11.10.18 to 11.10.20 and 11.10.24 to 11.10.26). When a time limit under a programme order expires, the provisions for disposing of outstanding business which is required to be concluded at that point is much the same as for standing committees (see paragraph 11.10.20 above).

11.13.12 Although S.O. No. 76 relaxes the rule against speaking more than once for report stage in relation to the **Member in charge** of the bill and the mover of an amendment or new clause, the chair is unlikely to call anyone more than twice in any debate on an amendment or new clause except in exceptional circumstances.

Conclusion of report stage

11.13.13 After all the new clauses, new schedules and amendments which have been selected have been disposed of, the bill may in principle be set down for third reading on a future day and, in those circumstances, may be reprinted in its further amended form before third reading. In modern practice, however, the third reading is now almost invariably moved immediately after the conclusion of the report stage and taken at the same sitting, and programme orders generally embody this convention. The practice of the House forbids successive stages of a bill brought in upon a Ways and Means resolution (see paragraphs 10.2.17 to 10.2.24) being taken at the same sitting, but nowadays a resolution is nearly always passed by the House before the report stage of the Finance Bill to allow its third reading to take place immediately after the conclusion of the report stage (which could again be done as part of a programme order).

Report stage in standing committee or in the Scottish Grand Committee

11.13.14 S.O. No. 92 provides for a bill which had its second reading debate in either a second reading committee, or the Scottish Grand Committee (see paragraphs 11.6.6 to 11.6.17), to be referred, on a motion made by a Minister, to a standing committee of between twenty and eighty Members, or once again to the Scottish Grand Committee, for its report stage. This provision has been used only once, in 1968. It is a mechanism which could, at least in theory, be adopted as part of a programme order.

11.14 THIRD READING

General

11.14.1 The third reading of a bill is by way of being its final review by the House before it is sent or returned to the Lords or sent for the royal assent. The scope of debate is distinguished from that at second reading in as much as it is supposed to be confined to what the bill now (after any amendments that have been made) includes, and should not stray into what it does not, but might have, included.

11.14.2 The Question "That the bill be read a third time" is moved by a Minister or the **Member in charge**. No Member may speak more than once in a third reading debate except with the unanimous leave of the House.

Amendments at third reading

11.14.3 S.O. No. 77 states that no amendments, not being purely verbal, may be made at third reading. This provision in effect means that no amendment of substance, or having *any* substantive effect, can be made at third reading. The scope of such amendments is effectively confined to such as may be necessary to correct errors without altering the meaning of any phrase. Such amendments are, in any event, very rare.

11.14.4 It is possible, however, to move a *reasoned amendment* at third reading in a similar way to a reasoned amendment at second reading (see paragraphs 11.6.3 to 11.6.5 above). Reasoned amendments on third reading are subject to the Speaker's power of selection. The scope of debate on a reasoned amendment is the same as that on the Question for third reading. S.O. No. 62(2) provides that if a reasoned amendment is negatived, the Question for third reading is put forthwith.

Third reading in the Scottish Grand Committee or Northern Ireland Grand Committee

11.14.5 Under S.O. Nos. 97(7) to (10) and 113(5) to (8), a bill which had its second reading debate in the Scottish Grand Committee or the Northern Ireland Grand Committee (see paragraphs 11.6.13 to 11.6.16 above) may, after its report stage, be referred on a motion made by a Minister to the same Grand Committee to be *further* considered in relation to its principle. The procedure is in almost all respects exactly as for consideration of a bill before its second reading. The debate is limited to an hour and a half, though it may be extended on a motion made in the Committee by a Minister. This procedure, introduced in 1996, has never been used.

Passing a bill

11.14.6 Once a bill has been read a third time, it is said to have been *passed*.

11.14.7 A bill which originated in the Commons, once passed, is sent to the Lords in the form that it was finally agreed by the Commons, with any amendments made in committee and on report incorporated. A message is sent with it inviting the Lords to agree it. Thus the final form of a bill as agreed by the Commons is usually only published when the Lords print their first version of the bill before second reading.

11.14.8 Where a bill originated in the Lords, after it has been passed by the Commons, it is returned to the Lords together with any amendments proposed to it by the Commons and a message inviting the Lords to agree to them.

11.14.9 Where a bill which originated in the Lords is passed by the Commons without amendment, it is returned to the Lords with a message to that effect, and in due course is sent for the **royal assent**. Similarly, where the Lords agree a bill sent to them by the Commons without amendment, the Commons are so informed and the bill proceeds to its royal assent. However, where either House amends a bill sent to them by the other House, the procedures described below apply.

11.15 LORDS AMENDMENTS (AND COMMONS AMENDMENTS)

Introduction

11.15.1 If the Lords make amendments to a bill passed by the Commons, they return the bill to the Commons together with the amendments they propose and a message inviting the Commons to agree them. Before the Commons can consider those amendments, they must be "taken up" (see paragraphs 11.3.11 and 11.3.12), and this is usually done by the **Member in charge** of the bill. When taking them up, that Member will name a date for their consideration by the Commons. In the case of a government bill, when the Lords Amendments will be taken up on the instructions of a Minister, this will as usual be "tomorrow", meaning some future date to be fixed. In the case of a private Member's bill, he or she will name one of the Fridays set aside for private Members' bills (see paragraph 2.2.4).

Printing of Lords Amendments

11.15.2 Once the Lords Amendments to a bill have been taken up, they are ordered, under S.O. No. 78, to be printed. If the message from the Lords arrives when the Commons is not sitting, S.O. No. 57A provides for them to be ordered to be printed if a Member has given notice of his intention to take them up to the Clerks. They are printed in a format not dissimilar to a bill, and are given a bill number in the sessional series (see paragraph 11.5.2). They are set out in the form of amendments proposed to the bill as it was when it left the Commons (that is the version of the bill as first printed by the Lords), and in order to make sense of the Lords Amendments a copy of the Lords first print of the bill is necessary for reference.

Amendments to Lords Amendments

11.15.3 Once the Lords Amendments have been taken up, amendments to them proposed by Members of the Commons may be tabled. These take broadly the same form as an amendment to a bill (eg "Lords Amendment No. 24, leave out lines 13 and 14 and insert . . ."). The scope of any proposed amendment is restricted to the scope of the Lords Amendment which it seeks to amend. It is also open to propose an alternative amendment to a Lords Amendment. This is known as an "amendment in lieu". The same rule of scope applies to an amendment proposed in lieu. It is also possible to propose consequential amendments, which may relate to parts of the bill other than the one directly affected by the Lords Amendment, but the definition of consequential is very narrowly interpreted. Where an amendment in lieu is proposed, it is necessary first to disagree to the original amendment. Otherwise, when it comes to the consideration of Lords Amendments by the House, it is always for the **Member in charge** to move a motion in respect of each Lords Amendment, and he or she will choose whether to move to agree or disagree with it. Where the Member in charge proposes to move to disagree with a Lords Amendment, notice of a motion to this effect is usually given for the convenience of the House, but no notice is *required* of such a motion. Occasionally, a Member other than the Member in charge may table a motion to disagree to a particular Lords Amendment, but he or she will not, as a rule, be called to move it.

11.15.4 Amendments proposed to Lords Amendments are tabled and printed in the same way as amendments proposed to a bill (see paragraphs 11.9.5 to 11.9.8).

Consideration of Lords Amendments

11.15.5 When the House comes to consider Lords Amendments to a Commons bill it may therefore be necessary to make reference to three separate documents in order to make sense of the debate. First, a copy of the bill as first printed by the Lords; second, a copy of the Lords Amendments as printed by the Commons; and third, a copy of the marshalled list of amendments proposed to those Lords Amendments by Members of the Commons.

11.15.6 The Lords Amendments (of which there can be several hundred to a major bill) may be grouped for debate in broad themes in the same way as the Speaker or chairman groups amendments for debate in committee or on report (see paragraph 11.10.11). However, these groupings are determined not by the Speaker but by the **Member in charge**, who informs the **Public Bill Office** of his or her intended groupings.

11.15.7 The Speaker's power of selection applies to any amendments proposed to the Lords Amendments, and decisions on selection will be made in accordance with broadly similar criteria as those applied in making selections in committee (see paragraph 11.10.10) and on report (see paragraph 11.13.7).

11.15.8 The groupings proposed by the Member in charge and the Speaker's selection of any proposed amendments are published in the usual way on the day on which the Lords Amendments are to be considered in the House.

11.15.9 The Lords Amendments are considered in the order in which they are printed, but where several are grouped, the debate on the first amendment in the group will range over all those grouped with it, and motions to agree or disagree with later amendments will be called by the chair to be moved formally (see paragraphs 11.10.18 to 11.10.20 above). It remains the firm rule that *decisions* are taken in the order in which the amendments relate to the bill. The order in which the Lords Amendments are considered, can, however, be altered by an order of consideration motion (see paragraph 11.10.17 above) or a programme order.

11.15.10 When any amendments proposed by the Commons to a Lords Amendment have been disposed of, the Member in charge moves "That this House agrees/disagrees with the Lords Amendment [, as amended]". If no amendments have been proposed to a Lords Amendment, the Chair calls the Member in charge to move his or her choice of motion, and any debate takes place on that motion.

11.15.11 Where an amendment has been proposed in lieu of a Lords Amendment, the Question on the alternative proposed by the Commons is put immediately after the Lords Amendment for which it is a substitute has been disagreed to, wherever that alternative amendment would appear in the bill itself. Similarly, where consequential amendments have been proposed, the decisions on these are made immediately after the Lords Amendment to which they relate has been agreed.

11.15.12 Where the Lords have proposed an Amendment which the Speaker judges has potentially infringed the financial privilege of the Commons (see paragraphs 10.2.8 to 10.2.11) the chair informs the House to this effect before it reaches any decision on each such Amendment so that it is aware that if it agrees to the proposed Amendment it is deliberately choosing to waive its financial privilege.

11.15.13 The House must make a decision on each and every Amendment to a bill which the Lords have proposed, whether to agree or disagree (with or without amendment), and whether to propose amendments in lieu of those disagreed to. Where a programme order applies to a bill, it is likely also to apply to consideration of Lords Amendments and other messages from the Lords relating to that bill, and the temporary standing orders make provision for bringing proceedings on such business to a conclusion when a deadline is reached.

Reasons Committees

11.15.14 If the House resolves to disagree with any of the amendments proposed by the Lords without offering any amendment of its own in lieu, it must give a reason to the Lords for doing so. It does this by appointing a committee to draw up a reason (or reasons). This is done by a motion moved immediately after the House has concluded its consideration of all the Lords Amendments to the bill. The committee is ordered to withdraw immediately. This it does, to a room immediately behind the Speaker's chair. It is a select committee in procedural terms, so its first duty is to elect a chairman (see paragraph 3.4.2) unless the motion of appointment has named him or her already. The Minister (or **Member in charge**) then proposes a reason to be given to the Lords in respect of each Lords Amendment to which the Commons has disagreed. Where such an Amendment is one of those that the Speaker has judged to involve financial privilege, the only reason given to the Lords is a statement to that effect. In the case of other Lords Amendments, the reason given will generally be terse. The deliberations of these committees are usually very brief. Once completed, the chairman reports the reason(s) at the **Table** of the House in writing, and an order is made by **book entry**, without motion or debate, for the reasons to be conveyed to the Lords. The temporary standing orders relating to programming make provision for ensuring that reasons committees cannot be used to delay the progress of a bill.

Messages between Commons and Lords

11.15.15 If the Commons have agreed all the Amendments made by the Lords without amendment, they send a message to inform the Lords to that effect, and the bill may proceed to the royal assent. Otherwise, the bill is returned to the Lords, together with any amendments, disagreements or other alterations proposed by the Commons to the Lords Amendments and any reasons for disagreement. A message accompanies it, explaining what the Commons have done and inviting the Lords to concur with their decisions.

11.15.16 If the Lords concur with all the proposals of the Commons, the Lords inform the Commons to that effect and the bill goes for the royal assent in the form agreed between the two Houses.

11.15.17 However, the Lords may decline to accept the alterations proposed by the Commons, or they may insist on their Amendments to which the Commons have flatly disagreed. (However, if the reason given by the Commons for disagreeing to a Lords Amendment was that it infringed the financial privileges of the Commons, the Lords cannot insist on their Amendment.) The Lords may also offer compromises in the form of amendments to or in lieu of the amendments made by the Commons to their Amendments. A message may be returned to the Commons, together with the bill, explaining the Lords position. If the Commons now concur with the Lords, the bill would be agreed. If not, they would return the bill once more to the Lords with a message insisting on their previous disagreement or disagreeing with the compromise proposals. If the Lords declined at this point to concur with the Commons, a stalemate would in effect have been reached, and the bill would be lost.

11.15.18 In normal circumstances, therefore, each House is given one opportunity to resile from absolute disagreement with the other, either by conceding altogether or by proposing an alternative form of words in the bill. However, the exchange of messages offering alternative compromises can continue indefinitely till the end of a session, at which point the bill would be finally lost.

Commons Amendments to Lords Bills

11.15.19 Where a bill starts in the Lords, the procedures for securing the agreement of both Houses to a single text of the bill are essentially the same as above, with the roles of the two Houses reversed. When a Lords bill has been passed by the Commons with amendments, the bill, along with the amendments, is sent back to the Lords with a message inviting their concurrence. The Lords take up and print any amendments proposed by the Commons. They may subsequently agree them, propose amendments, etc and the process of exchanging messages proceeds until agreement is reached.

11.16 Royal Assent

11.16.1 It is the responsibility of the Lord Chancellor to secure the royal assent to a bill which has been agreed by both Houses. Once it is granted, the Lords immediately inform the Speaker, who announces to the Commons the list of royal assents at the earliest convenient point in the proceedings of the House. Where the royal assent is due to be signified to any bills on the last day of a session, it is usually done by the Lords Commissioners immediately before they read the proclamation of the prorogation of the two Houses (see paragraph 5.2.3).

11.16.2 Once a bill has received the royal assent it becomes an Act of Parliament, and in due course is published by the Statutory Publications Office in the form agreed by the two Houses.

11.17 The Parliament Acts 1911 and 1949

11.17.1 The Parliament Act 1911, as amended by the Parliament Act 1949, provides that where the Lords fail to agree a bill which has been passed by the Commons and sent to them at least one month before the end of a session, the bill may, in a subsequent session be presented for the royal assent by the Commons alone, without the concurrence of the Lords.

11.17.2 To be eligible for this procedure, the bill must be passed by the Commons in the second session in exactly the form that they passed it in the preceding session. The bill must be given its third reading by the Commons at least one year after it received its second reading in the first session and at least one month before the end of the second session.

11.17.3 Once passed this second time, the Speaker certifies that the bill falls within the terms of the Parliament Acts before it is sent up to the Lords. If the Lords having received the bill at least one month before the end of the second session, then fail to agree the bill in the form in which it has been sent to them by the Commons, the Speaker may present the bill for the royal assent without the concurrence of the Lords. (It would not necessarily be an easy matter to determine at what point, before the end of the session, the Lords had halted the progress of such a bill). These procedures have been invoked with considerably greater frequency in recent years than they were in the first fifty years after the Parliament Act 1949 was passed.

11.17.4 The Parliament Acts make provision for the Commons, when sending to the Lords a bill which is certified as complying with the provisions of the Parliament Acts, to send along with it proposed amendments to the bill as passed. This enables a compromise to be offered without vitiating the powers of the Commons to invoke the procedures of the Parliament Acts.

11.17.5 The Parliament Acts procedures do not apply to any bill which proposes to extend the life of a Parliament beyond five years.

11.17.6 The provisions in the Parliament Acts in respect of money bills are described in paragraphs 10.2.15 and 10.2.16.

11.18 Timetabling and Carry-over

Programmes

11.18.1 "Guillotines", the formerly used method of curtailing proceedings on a bill to enable the government to secure its legislation, have now largely been superseded by programme orders, although the standing orders providing for programmes still remain, at least in theory, experimental. Guillotines are still used where it is proposed to timetable *all* proceedings on a bill, including the second reading, usually for bills which are required to pass all their stages in one day. Programme orders, the procedural effects of which have been described throughout earlier sections of this chapter, are similar in effect in many ways to the old guillotines but with some important differences in the circumstances and ways in which they are used.

11.18.2 Overall, the intention of the new procedure is to enable the House to establish at the *outset* of a bill's progress (as opposed to some way through it as was usually the case with guillotines) a timetable for consideration of the bill at all its stages, as well as time limits for debate on all the contingent motions necessary to meet that timetable or to subsequently amend it. The temporary standing orders relating to programmes passed at the beginning of the 2001 Parliament embody in their provisions many of the complex arrangements for curtailing debate and ensuring the necessary Questions are put at each stage of a bill's progress, which previously had to be re-enacted afresh for each guillotine.

11.18.3 The broad provisions of the programme orders are usually expressed in terms of final dates by which bills must be reported out of standing committees and numbers of **allotted days** on the floor of the House for stages taken there. These are then filled-out by resolutions of programming sub-committees or programming committees, depending on whether the bill is committed to a standing committee or otherwise, which set more specific deadlines within these overall limits. The standing orders provide for supplementary resolutions from such committees, varying the provisions of a programme order, to be considered by the House either **forthwith** or for forty-five minutes. They also include provisions to accommodate hypothetical events (such as emergency debates under S.O. No. 24) which could otherwise disrupt these deadlines. They also provide for all proceedings on programme motions and supplementary motions, and all proceedings on bills under programme orders, to be exempt from the time limits on sittings of the House provided for under other standing orders.

Guillotines

11.18.4 The provisions for guillotines remain, although they seem unlikely ever to be used except in cases where the government wishes to timetable all proceedings including second reading. Allocation of time motions (guillotines) may be introduced under S.O. No. 83 at any stage of a bill's progress through the House. They can be debated on the floor of the House (see paragraphs 9.7.7 and 9.7.8) for a maximum of three hours. Like programmes, the purpose of a guillotine motion was to fix deadlines by which each stage of a bill's progress must be completed. Motions could also specify times at which certain stages must be reached on allotted days. They would also make provision for the putting of questions on amendments, clauses stand part, new clauses and schedules etc., and provide for any government amendments to be decided upon. Once an allocation of time motion had been agreed by the House, a Business Committee would, if necessary, be constituted by the Speaker under the provisions of S.O. No.82, chaired by the **Chairman of Ways and Means**. The task of the Business Committee was to draw up a detailed timetable allocating portions of the bill between the allotted days. Where a guillotine applied to a bill which was still in standing committee, S.O. No. 120 provides for the Speaker to appoint seven Members of that committee to comprise a Business Sub-committee, to be chaired by one of the chairmen of the standing committee. Its task was essentially the same as a Business Committee's, but is exercised in relation to proceedings in the standing committee rather than in the House.

Carry-over of bills

11.18.5 As described in paragraph 5.2.4, the effect of prorogation is normally that any bill which has not recived the royal assent "dies", and if it is to be revived, it must start its parliamentary progress completely afresh in the next session. With the consent of all parties and the intention having been made clear in advance, it has always been possible in theory to "carry over" a government bill from one session to the next, and this has happened in one recent case. In October 2002 the House agreed in principle to the use of "carry-over" motions for selected government bills, to enable them to begin their parliamentary progress in one session, and continue it in the next from the point which had been reached at the time of prorogation. The House passed a standing order to give effect to this decision, which is to have effect until the end of the current Parliament.

11.18.6 The temporary standing order provides for a Minister to move a motion to allow a bill which does not complete its progress by the end of a session in which the motion is agreed to resume its progress in the second session at the point that it had reached in the first, thereby evading the normal fate of bills which fail to complete their stages in one session, and allowing a more relaxed timetable of consideration. If the motion is moved immediately after a bill has had its second reading, it is put **forthwith**. At a subsequent stage it is debatable for one and a half hours (and exempt from the effect of the **moment of interruption**). A carry-over motion can relate only to one bill at a time, and cannot be made in relation to a bill which has previously been carried over.

11.18.7 The standing order then provides for any bill to which a carry-over order has been applied to be restarted in the following session at the point which it had reached in the previous session, and if it was in standing committee, for a committee of the same Members to continue their consideration of the bill. Paragraph (10) of the standing order provides that if consideration of a bill has not been completed within twelve months of its first reading in the previous session, it will "die" like a bill which had not been carried over and had reached the end of a session. However, paragraph (11) makes provision for a Minister to move a motion to extend this deadline for a specified period, and for the Question on any such motion to be put at the end of a one and a half hour debate.

11.19 Private Bill Procedure

11.19.1 The procedures of the House relating to private bills are highly elaborate and complex, and are subject to an entirely separate set of standing orders. It is not intended to attempt any exhaustive description of them here, and anyone seeking such detail should turn to **Erskine May**.

11.19.2 In essence, private bills provide for the granting of powers to bodies corporate (or very occasionally individuals) in excess of or in contradiction to those they enjoy under the general law. Most often they provide for the construction of railways, harbours, docks, piers or bridges, or provide local authorities with special powers (for example, to maintain private police forces). They were a very significant feature of parliamentary business in the nineteenth century, particularly during the railways boom, but steadily diminished in number over the course of the twentieth century. Local government powers are now mostly embodied in general law and, in 1992, the Transport and Works Act removed a large category of major construction projects from the ambit of the private legislation procedure and substituted a public inquiry system in its place. The Act did provide for Parliament to consider in principle, but not in detail, proposals deemed by the appropriate Secretary of State to be of national significance.

11.19.3 Private bills are initiated by *promoters*, working through the agency of *parliamentary agents*. If a bill is given a second reading and committed, persons or bodies which can demonstrate a *locus standi* (in other words who are directly affected by the proposals in the bill) have the right to petition against the bill and to seek alterations to it. They plead their case before a committee of four Members. The committee may reject a bill outright, or may amend it in line with the requests of petitioners. The bill as agreed to by the committee must then be approved by the House.

11.19.4 Private bills and hybrid bills (see paragraph 11.1.3) have often been allowed to carry over from one session to the next, if the House agrees to a motion providing for this in each session.

<table>
<tr><th colspan="2">Affirmative Resolution Procedure</th><th colspan="2">Negative Resolution Procedure</th></tr>
<tr><td colspan="2">Draft instrument (or occasionally a made instrument) laid before parliament</td><td colspan="2">Made instrument laid before Parliament</td></tr>
<tr><td colspan="4">(Draft) instrument considered by the Joint Committee on Statutory Instruments</td></tr>
<tr><td colspan="2">Motion to approve the (draft) instrument tabled by a Minister (and appears on the Remaining Orders)</td><td colspan="2">Motion (“Prayer”) to annul the instrument may be tabled by any Member within 40 days (and is published as an EDM)</td></tr>
<tr><td colspan="2">(Draft) instrument automatically stands referred to a standing committee on delegated legislation</td><td>A Minister may table a motion (which is taken without debate on floor of the House) to refer the instrument to a standing committee on delegated legislation</td><td>The Government (or in theory an opposition party on an Opposition Day) may give time for motion to be debated on the floor of the House</td></tr>
<tr><td>(Draft) instrument debated in standing committee for up to 1½ hours</td><td>Motion to “de-refer” (draft) instrument may be tabled by a Minister, and automatically has effect</td><td>Instrument can then be debated in standing committee for up to 1½ hours</td><td rowspan="3">Motion can then be debated on floor of the House until 1½ hours after the moment of interruption</td></tr>
<tr><td>(Draft) instrument reported to the House from the standing committee</td><td rowspan="2">(Draft) instrument will then be debated on the floor of the House for up to 1½ hours at the end of which motion to approve is put</td><td>Instrument reported to the House as having been considered</td></tr>
<tr><td>Motion to approve the (draft) instrument taken without debate on floor of the House</td><td>Motion to annul could then be put forthwith on floor of the House if Government (or in theory an opposition party on an Opposition Day) placed it on the Order Paper</td></tr>
<tr><td colspan="2">If motion is agreed to, instrument comes into (or continues in) effect (after the House of Lords have also agreed to approve it)</td><td colspan="2">The instrument can come into effect on a date determined by the Minister unless a motion to annul the instrument were agreed to, in which case the instrument would cease to have effect (whether or not the House of Lords also agreed to annul it)</td></tr>
</table>

FIGURE 27
DELEGATED LEGISLATION PROCEDURE

Chapter 12
DELEGATED LEGISLATION

12.1 INTRODUCTION

Standing orders

12.1.1 The main standing orders relevant to the treatment by the House of delegated legislation are Nos. 16, 17, 18, 98, 114, 115, 118, 141, 151, 152B, 158 and 159. A summary of delegated legislation procedure is given in Figure 19.

Nature of delegated legislation

12.1.2 Most Acts of Parliament nowadays include provisions giving powers to Ministers to make "delegated legislation" (sometimes also called "subordinate" or "secondary" legislation). The scope of these powers varies widely. Sometimes they will simply provide for the updating of provisions of the Act (say the level of fines or other monetary amounts) over the course of time. Often the powers will be limited to technical provisions. For example, many Acts include commencement powers which allow Ministers to bring different provisions of the Act into effect on future dates when it appears timely to do so, and many give powers to Ministers to make "consequential and transitional" provisions. Often, however, the delegated powers give wide discretion to Ministers to fill-out the broad provisions enacted by Parliament with detailed regulations.

12.1.3 Acts which grant these delegated powers to Ministers are known as "parent Acts" or "primary legislation", and the legislation made by Ministers under those powers is known as delegated or secondary legislation. There is no distinction in statutory force between primary and delegated legislation except in one important respect. A Minister is open to challenge in the courts that delegated legislation that he has made is *ultra vires*, that is that it falls outside the scope of the discretion afforded to him by Parliament in a parent Act.

12.1.4 With the qualified exception of proposals for regulatory reform orders (see section 12.4 below), remedial orders (see section 12.5 below) and orders made under section 85 of the Northern Ireland Act 1998 (see paragraphs 12.2.3 and 12.2.4 below), it is the general rule that Parliament cannot propose amendments to delegated legislation even where it is subject to affirmative resolution procedure. Generally, it can only approve, disapprove or annul such legislation.

Types of delegated legislation

12.1.5 There are many different types of delegated powers. Those which grant power to Ministers to make general legislation almost invariably provide for this to be done by means of statutory instruments. These may be *orders* (which as their title implies usually give effect to a ministerial decision) or *regulations* (which are generally in the nature of detailed provisions about how things may or may not be done); occasionally they are described as rules (which generally apply to a specific area of activity). *Orders in Council* are an of elevated type of order, usually quasi-primary in nature, which require the royal assent made with the consent of the Privy Council. Frequently Acts provide for Ministers to have powers to make codes of practice, arrangements etc. which may (or may not) be given effect as statutory instruments, depending on the precise terms of the enabling Act.

12.1.6 Statutory instruments are subject to different degrees of control. In broadly ascending order of rigour these are:

- those which have only to be made to come into effect;
- those which have to be laid before Parliament after being made;
- those which have to be laid before Parliament after being made and which are subject to the provision in their parent Act that if either House resolves within forty sitting days that the instrument should be annulled they cease to be of effect (the negative resolution procedure);
- those which are required under the terms of their parent Act to be laid before Parliament in draft and to be approved by each House before being made and brought into effect (the affirmative resolution procedure);
- a small category of instruments which are laid before Parliament when made rather than in draft but which cease to be of effect if not approved by each House within a period specified in the parent Act; and
- a relatively new class of so-called "super-affirmative" instruments (currently encompassing regulatory reform orders, remedial orders and certain types of orders made under the Northern Ireland Act 1998) which, except in certain cases of urgency (when they may be made and must be approved within a set time to remain in effect), have to be preceded by "proposals" to make such orders which, during a statutory period, are subject to various forms of consultation and parliamentary procedure which allow for amendments to be proposed by parliamentary committees or others. Ministers may choose to incorporate in the draft order changes which follow from the consultation on the proposal to make such an order.

There are proposals under consideration to establish a joint committee of the Commons and Lords to "sift" negative resolution and affirmative resolution instruments to recommend which of them raise significant questions which need to be debated. The work of such a sifting committee might affect the application of parliametary procedures to different categories of instruments.

Regulatory reform orders

12.1.7 The Regulatory Reform Act 2001, which replaced the Deregulation and Contracting-out Act 1994, replaced "deregulation orders" with a new category of statutory instruments known as regulatory reform orders. The essential characteristic of deregulation orders, which distinguished them from other forms of delegated legislation, was that through them Ministers were able to amend or repeal primary legislation where there was no specific provision in the Act which they affect for any of its provisions to be so altered by means of delegated powers.

12.1.8 The new regulatory reform orders are somewhat wider in scope than deregulation orders. In particular, they can impose "burdens" as well as remove them, as long as those burdens are proportionate to the benefits expected to result, and a fair balance is struck between the public interest and the interests of those on whom these burdens fall. Second, they can repeal and re-enact previous legislation with amendments. This, along with the first point above, enables the reform of whole regulatory regimes, instead of merely the removal or reduction of individual "burdens". Third, they can extend the statutory powers of a person or body (to relieve a burdensome situation caused by the lack of a statutory power to do something). Fourth, they can remove "burdens" from public bodies as well as the private sector. Fifth, they can include power to allow further amendment by way of subordinate legislation – a kind of sub-delegated legislation. They can apply to the provisions of any Act not less than two years old, or which have not been "substantially" amended in the previous two years. These types of order are subject to a parliamentary procedure which is described in section 12.4 below, and are considered in the Commons by the Regulatory Reform Committee.

Remedial orders

12.1.9 The Human Rights Act 1998 (which came into effect on 2 October 2000) makes provision for Ministers to make a form of delegated legislation known as remedial orders. Like deregulation and regulatory reform orders, these allow primary legislation to be amended by subordinate legislation even where there was no provision for this in the Act which is amended. The trigger for the exercise of this power is a declaration made by a court in the UK that some statutory provision is incompatible with the provisions of the Human Rights Act. A Minister may also exercise the power in response to a decision of the European Court of Human Rights in Strasbourg. These remedial orders are also subject to a separate procedure which is described below in section 12.5.

Church of England Measures

12.1.10 Under the Church of England (Assembly) Powers Act 1919, the General Synod of the Church of England has the power to propose legislation on matters relating to the government and organisation of the Church. These items of legislation are known as Measures. When a Measure has been agreed by the Synod it is submitted to the Ecclesiastical Committee established under the 1919 Act, which consists of Members of both Houses of Parliament nominated by the Speaker and the Lord Chancellor. Its status as a statutory body makes it quite distinct from committees established by Parliament, but it adopts the procedures of a joint committee (see section 17.5). Having examined a Measure, the Committee makes a report as to whether it considers that it is "expedient that the Measure be made", a draft of which is communicated to the Legislative Committee of the Synod. With the Synod's agreement, the Measure and the report of the Ecclesiastical Committee are laid before Parliament, in the Commons by the Second Church Estates Commissioner who is invariably a Member of that House. The House will then be invited on a motion (moved in the Commons by the Second Church Estates Commissioner) to agree that the Measure should be presented for the royal assent.

12.2 Devolution and Delegated Legislation

Scotland

12.2.1 The Scottish Parliament has the most extensive legislative powers of the three devolved legislatures in the UK. There are likely therefore to be fewer incidences of problems arising from overlap or interaction between delegated powers exercised by Ministers of the government of the UK and that of Scotland. Schedule 7 to the Scotland Act 1988 also sets out a complex set of provisions relating to Orders in Council made under that Act and the procedures which shall apply to them in each Parliament.

Wales

12.2.2 The National Assembly for Wales presents the most complex problems relating to the exercise of delegated legislative functions, since its own legislative competence is broadly defined by the powers previously granted by Parliament to the Secretary of State for Wales to make delegated legislation, and future Acts of Parliament will delegate further powers to be exercised by the Assembly in this way. By these means the Westminster Parliament is effectively excluded from consideration of such delegated legislation made by the National Assembly.

Northern Ireland

12.2.3 The Northern Ireland Act 1974 suspended the government and parliament of Northern Ireland and introduced direct rule from Westminster. It included provision for legislation applying to Northern Ireland to be made by means of Orders in Council made under the Act. Such Orders in Council made between 1974 and 1999 most often reproduced (with local variations) legislation enacted by Parliament for England and Wales. The Northern Ireland Act 1998 which repealed the 1974 Act also includes provisions for making Orders in Council relating to "excepted" and "reserved" matters, and other matters relating to the competence of the Northern Ireland Assembly and so forth. Proposals for Orders in Council (other than Orders in Council made without Parliamentary approval by reason of urgency) dealing with certain reserved matters must be laid for a period of sixty days to allow for consultation. The reserved matters are set out in paragraphs 9 to 17 of Schedule 3 to the 1998 Act: they include public order, criminal law, criminal injuries compensation, firearms, explosives, police, the civil service, civil defence and emergency powers. Such orders may have retrospective effect, may delegate functions and may amend or repeal Acts of the UK Parliament or Northern Ireland Assembly.

12.2.4 The Act also obliges the government to refer a proposal for an Order in Council under this procedure to the Northern Ireland Assembly. The Assembly may report its views on the proposal, and *must* do so if requested by the Secretary of State. The government has indicated that it will also normally refer such proposals to the Northern Ireland Grand Committee for debate (see section 14.5). The Act specifically provides for the Secretary of State to take into account resolutions of the Assembly and either House of Parliament, and reports or resolutions of any committee of either House or of the Assembly, when considering representations on the proposal.

12.2.5 Following the conclusion of the consultation period, the Secretary of State may lay a draft Order before Parliament for approval by affirmative resolution. The draft must be accompanied by a summary of representations made; a copy of any report made by the Northern Ireland Assembly; and a statement of any changes which have been made to the draft since the proposal stage.

12.2.6 Following affirmative resolution by both Houses, the draft Orders are subsequently made by Her Majesty in Council. Orders in Council may be made under an urgency procedure, but must be approved by both Houses within forty days of making.

12.2.7 If the Assembly is suspended under the provisions of the Northern Ireland Act 2000, then the super-affirmative procedure described above is replaced by the standard affirmative resolution procedure. Under this, draft Orders must be approved by both Houses before being made: orders made under the urgent procedure must be approved by both Houses within forty days.

12.2.8 The time limit for debates on instruments relating exclusively to Northern Ireland in standing committees (see paragraphs 12.3.23 to 12.3.30 below) is extended to two and a half hours.

12.3 PROCEDURE ON DELEGATED LEGISLATION

Laying of instruments

12.3.1 A significant proportion of statutory instruments are required by the provisions of their parent Act only to be made to come into effect. However, where the delegated legislation is of any significance, the parent Act usually requires a statutory instrument or other item of delegated legislation to be laid before Parliament. S.O. No. 159 provides that in the Commons this is effected by the delivery of a certified copy of the instrument to the Votes and Proceedings Office (part of the **Journal Office**). This may be done on any day during the existence of a Parliament (in other words except during a dissolution). Instruments which require approval in draft by Parliament before being made (under the affirmative resolution procedure) must obviously be laid before Parliament in draft form. S.O. No. 159 applies only to *made* statutory instruments; those which are required to be laid in draft can only be laid on a day on which the House is sitting.

12.3.2 Appendix I to the **Votes and Proceedings** for each day on which the House sits (see paragraphs 15.1.23 to 15.1.25) lists, among other types of papers, all statutory instruments etc. laid before Parliament on the previous sitting day (or non-sitting Friday). In the first issue after a holiday or recess, it lists all those laid since the last day on which the House sat. The Appendix divides these into categories of those subject to affirmative resolution procedure, those subject to negative resolution procedure and others. Copies of all these papers should be available from the **Vote Office**.

12.3.3 The government has given an undertaking that, so far as possible, statutory instruments will be laid before Parliament at least twenty-one days before they come into effect. Under S.O. No. 160, a Minister may notify the Speaker that an instrument has come into operation (because of some emergency) before copies of the instrument had been laid before Parliament. When such a communication has been received, the Speaker lays a notice of it before the House at the earliest opportunity and an appropriate entry appears in the Appendix to the Votes and Proceedings.

12.3.4 Every Friday during periods when the House is sitting, (and periodically during recesses), a list is published with the Vote Bundle (see paragraph 15.1.28) listing all statutory instruments laid in the previous week. It also shows all those which have been previously laid and are still awaiting approval and those subject to negative resolution procedure in respect of which the "praying time" (see paragraph 12.3.16 below) has not yet expired.

The Joint Committee on Statutory Instruments

12.3.5 S.O. No. 151 provides for a **select committee** to be appointed to join with a committee of the Lords to consider statutory instruments, known as the Joint Committee on Statutory Instruments (JCSI). It is required to consider not only every instrument laid before the House but also all other general instruments. A general instrument, broadly defined, is one that relates to the general law rather than being of local application. Excluded from their remit are Orders in Council made under the Northern Ireland Act 2000 (see paragraph 12.2.3 above), draft Regulatory Reform Orders (see paragraph 12.1.7 above), and Church of England Measures (see paragraph 12.1.8 above), and remedial orders under the Human Rights Act 1998 (see paragraph 12.1.9 above).

12.3.6 The Committee is required to examine each instrument against criteria set out in the standing order. Broadly, these are: whether it includes provisions incurring public expenditure or taxation (that is of a type covered by the rules relating to financial resolutions described in section 10.2); whether it is protected by the parent Act against legal challenge; whether it is to have retrospective effect; whether it has been laid before Parliament in good time; whether its meaning is unclear or it is defectively drafted; and, most importantly, whether it is *ultra vires*, that is whether it is properly made within the powers conferred by the parent Act. The Committee is specifically excluded under the terms of the standing order from considering the merits of the proposals embodied in an instrument.

12.3.7 The Committee is assisted in its work by the legal service of the Commons and their Lords equivalents. It has the power to require departments to submit explanatory memoranda, and to require witnesses from government departments to give oral evidence about matters within its competence. It may also take evidence from HMSO about the printing and publication of instruments. It cannot receive or hear evidence other than from the government.

12.3.8 Periodically (roughly weekly when the House is sitting) the Committee produces reports listing the instruments it has considered and drawing the special attention of both Houses to any instruments which raise questions within its terms of reference. Where it proposes to draw the special attention of both Houses to an instrument, it is required to give the relevant department an opportunity to give an explanation. Sometimes the department will withdraw an instrument with which the Committee has found fault and re-lay it in an amended form to meet the Committee's objections, or more often it will undertake to take note of the Committee's comments in drafting future instruments of the same type. When the Committee has drawn the special attention of the House to an instrument, a note to this effect is printed beneath any motion relating to that instrument which appears on the **Order Paper**.

12.3.9 Under paragraph (10) of the standing order, the Select Committee on Statutory Instruments (that is, the Commons Members of the JCSI only) considers separately those instruments which are required to be laid only before the Commons. These are generally those relating to taxation or other matters falling within the Commons' financial privileges (see paragraphs 10.2.8 to 10.2.11).

Affirmative resolution procedure

12.3.10 Where the parent Act provides that an instrument must be approved by Parliament before it can be made (or if it is to continue in force), it is described as being subject to the affirmative resolution procedure. Under S.O. No. 118(3), once a Minister has given notice of a motion to approve a draft instrument (or one of those relatively few made instruments which require retrospective approval within a specified period), which is usually done on the day the draft is laid, the instrument automatically stands referred to a standing committee on delegated legislation (see paragraphs 12.3.23 to 12.3.30 below). This automatic referral may be stopped by the Minister giving notice of a further motion that the instrument be not so referred. Curiously, this "de-referral" is effected simply by virtue of a motion to that effect appearing on the **remaining orders** (see paragraph 15.1.17). The motion for de-referral is never considered by the House. Similarly, if a motion is made under S.O. No. 98(1) to refer the instrument to the Scottish Grand Committee (see paragraph 14.3.4), or under S.O. No. 115(1) to refer the instrument to the Northern Ireland Grand Committee (see paragraph 14.5.6), the instrument is automatically de-referred from a delegated legislation standing committee.

12.3.11 Once an instrument has been considered and reported by a delegated legislation standing committee (or by the Scottish or Northern Ireland Grand Committee), as described below at paragraphs 12.3.23 to 12.3.30, the motion to approve it may be moved on the floor of the House and the Chair is required, under S.O. No. 118(6), (or S.O. No. 98(3) or S.O. No. 115(1)), to put the Question on it **forthwith**, without debate. It may be decided after the **moment of interruption**.

12.3.12 If an affirmative instrument *has* been de-referred from a standing committee on delegated legislation, it falls to be considered on the floor of the House. Proceedings are governed by S.O. No. 16. Debate on the motion to approve the instrument is limited to one and a half hours. Such debate can continue, or take place, after the **moment of interruption** (see paragraph 7.10.11). At the end of the period the chair interrupts debate if it is still continuing, and puts the Question.

12.3.13 A motion to approve a statutory instrument is not amendable.

12.3.14 Other forms of what are in effect delegated legislation but which are not statutory instruments may require the approval of the House under the provisions of their parent Acts. These cognate instruments are subject to the same procedures as statutory instruments. They would not be automatically referred to a standing committee under the provisions of S.O. No. 118(2), but might be so referred on a motion made under paragraph (4)(a) of that standing order. Under paragraph (4)(b), Church of England Measures (see paragraph 12.1.10 above) can also be so referred. A motion for such a referral is moved at the commencement of public business (see paragraph 7.7.7) and is decided **forthwith**. When the Question is put, if twenty or more Members rise in their places to signify their objection to the referral, the motion to refer is deemed to have been negatived.

Negative resolution procedure

12.3.15 Where the parent Act provides that an instrument made under its provisions may be annulled in pursuance of a resolution of either House of Parliament, the instrument is described as being subject to the *negative resolution procedure*.

12.3.16 Under the Statutory Instruments Act 1946, the period in which such a resolution can be passed is set at forty days after the day on which the instrument was laid before Parliament. This period is calculated to exclude any period during which either House is adjourned for a continuous period of more than four days. This has the effect of stopping the clock during those periods when Parliament is taking one of its seasonal breaks. Periods of prorogation and dissolution are also excluded. Because the two Houses are frequently out of sync in their holidays, the only authoritative statement of how much of this period has expired is the weekly statutory instruments list (see paragraphs 12.3.4 and 15.1.31). This forty day period is known as the "praying time". This soubriquet derives from the form of motion used to seek to annul an instrument "That an humble Address be presented to Her Majesty, *praying* that [the said instrument] be annulled".

12.3.17 During this period of forty days, any Member may table such a motion (known colloquially as a "prayer"). Notices of such motions appear on the blue notice paper published with the Vote Bundle among the early day motions (see paragraph 15.1.36 and chapter 16). After the praying time has expired, motions in different forms (for example to "revoke" the instrument) may be tabled in respect of an instrument, although such motions, if passed, would have no statutory effect.

12.3.18 Despite the apparent implications of the Statutory Instruments Act 1946, successive governments have not acknowledged any obligation to arrange for "prayers" and equivalent motions to be debated, and often no further parliamentary proceedings take place on the instrument after a prayer has been tabled. Where the government does consent to facilitate debate, two alternative procedures are available. Under S.O. No. 118(4), the instrument may be referred to a standing committee on delegated legislation under the procedure described in paragraph 12.3.14 above. Alternatively, the government may make time available on the floor of the House to debate the prayer. Generally speaking, prayers in the name of the **leader of the opposition** are debated in one of these ways. The majority of other such motions are not debated.

12.3.19 If an instrument which has been prayed against is referred to a standing committee, it is debated in the manner described in paragraphs 12.3.23 to 12.3.30 below. Once the committee has considered and reported the instrument it would, in theory, be possible for the prayer to be moved on the floor of the House when, under S.O. No. 118(6), the Question on it would be put **forthwith** and could be decided after the **moment of interruption**. In practice this does not happen. It would also in theory be open to the opposition to place a prayer on the **Order Paper** on one of their allotted days (see paragraphs 2.2.2 and 2.2.3) either for debate or for decision forthwith after being reported from a standing committee.

12.3.20 If time is made available to debate a prayer on the floor of the House, S.O. No. 17 applies. This provides that proceedings on a prayer (or on a cognate motion) may continue up to one and a half hours after the **moment of interruption** (but may not be commenced more than an hour after that time). This allows for a maximum of ninety minutes debate, but does not protect that time from being eaten into by divisions on previous business, points of order, etc. At the end of that period the chair is required to interrupt debate and put the Question. There is, however, a proviso to the standing order allowing the chair to adjourn the debate if of the opinion that because of the time at which it started, or the importance of the subject matter, there has been insufficient time for debate.

Cognate motions

12.3.21 Other statutory instruments which are not explicitly subject to the negative resolution procedure under the terms of their parent Acts may be treated in a like manner, if a motion to disapprove them or to take note of them or whatever has been tabled and the government wishes to allow an opportunity for debate. However, such motions, if passed, would have no statutory effect. The same procedures may also be applied to other things done under Acts (the making of arrangements, giving of directions, preparation of schemes, formulation of codes of practice or whatever), either because they fall within the terms of S.O. No. 118(4)(a) or on a specific motion to apply these procedures.

12.3.22 Instruments which have been prayed against or are the subject of cognate motions may also be referred to the Scottish Grand Committee (see paragraph 14.3.4) under the provisions of S.O. No. 98(1) or to the Northern Ireland Grand Committee (see paragraph 14.5.6) under the provisions of S.O. No. 115(1).

Standing committees on delegated legislation

12.3.23 S.O. No. 118(1) provides for standing committees to consider delegated legislation. There can be any number of these set up in a session, and they are known as the "First", "Second" and so on. In fact, they have no continuing existence, and these titles are irrelevant. The members of each committee are appointed to the committee in respect of each instrument or group of instruments and cease to be members of the committee as soon as that instrument or those instruments have been considered.

12.3.24 The Members are appointed to a delegated legislation standing committee by the **Committee of Selection** (see section 2.4). The size of such a committee is not fixed and can be any number between sixteen and fifty, but is usually under twenty. However, unlike standing committees on bills, *any* Member of the House is entitled to attend a meeting of a standing committee on delegated legislation and to take part in its debate, although they may not move motions or vote and do not count towards the committee's quorum (see paragraph 9.4.3).

12.3.25 The chairman of each sitting of a delegated legislation standing committee is appointed by the Speaker from the Chairmen's Panel (see paragraph 3.2.6 and paragraph 3.3.1), and they enjoy broadly the same powers (see paragraph 3.3.3) as chairmen of standing committees on bills. The powers to select amendments or to accept motions for closure are, however, largely irrelevant to these committees.

12.3.26 Instruments subject to affirmative resolution procedure are referred automatically to a delegated legislation standing committee (see paragraph 12.3.10 above). Negative instruments and other instruments may be so referred under the procedures described in paragraphs 12.3.14, 12.3.18 and 12.3.21 above. The Speaker then allocates each instrument which stands referred to a standing committee to a particular committee and appoints a chairman. The **Committee of Selection** then nominates Members to that committee in respect of that instrument. Occasionally the Speaker, at the behest of the **usual channels**, will allocate a group of related instruments to the same committee to enable them to be considered together.

12.3.27 Under S.O. No. 118(5), the standing committee considers the instrument on the motion "That the committee has considered [the said] instrument". The committee cannot consider any other form of motion (other than a **dilatory motion**, for which see section 9.4) nor are any amendments admissible. In respect of instruments subject to approval, the motion is moved by a Minister. In the case of instruments subject to some form of negative procedure the motion will be moved by an opposition front bench spokesman, or by another Member who initiated the motion to annul or otherwise disapprove of the instrument.

12.3.28 The standing order requires the chairman to put the Question on the motion one and a half hours after debate has commenced. If the committee is considering several instruments as a group, the chairman first ascertains if the committee is content to debate them together. If no Member objects, the debate may range over all the instruments before the committee. At the end of the ninety minutes the chairman will interrupt the debate if it is still continuing and put the Question on the motion relating to the first instrument, and then successively put **forthwith** the Questions on any remaining instruments if they are moved. If any Member of the committee objects, at the outset, to debating the group of instruments together, they must be debated separately, and the time limit of an hour and a half will apply to each debate on each instrument. The time limit is extended to two and a half hours for an instrument relating exclusively to Northern Ireland (see paragraph 12.2.8).

12.3.29 When the debate is concluded, the committee may vote on the motion that the committee has considered the instrument. The government always vote for the motion, even if it has been moved by the opposition. However, whatever the result of any division, it makes no procedural difference since the chairman is only empowered, under S.O. No. 118(5), simply to report the instrument to the House, even if the motion is negatived. An entry is made in the **Votes and Proceedings** recording this report.

12.3.30 The procedures followed in the House in respect of instruments reported from standing committees are described in paragraphs 12.3.11 and 12.3.19 above.

12.4 REGULATORY REFORM ORDERS

Statutory basis

12.4.1 Section 1 of the Regulatory Reform Act 2001 gives Ministers powers to make a form of delegated legislation known as regulatory reform orders. Their special characteristics are briefly described in paragraph 12.1.7 above.

12.4.2 The Act requires the Minister to undertake certain specified forms of consultation in respect of any proposals to make regulatory reform orders. It also requires him or her to lay a proposal for such an order before Parliament in the form of a draft order, together with details of the consultations undertaken and other specified matters. The Minister is also required, before proceeding to lay the actual draft order before Parliament, to take account of any report published by the appropriate committee of either House on the proposal.

12.4.3 The parliamentary proceedings on these orders are sometimes known as the "super-affirmative" procedure.

12.4.4 A period of sixty days (excluding periods when Parliament is prorogued or dissolved or when either House is adjourned for a continuous period of more than four days) must have elapsed after the *proposal* for a regulatory reform order has been laid before Parliament before the Minister may lay the actual draft order before Parliament for its approval.

The Regulatory Reform Committee

12.4.5 It is during this period of sixty days between the laying of a *proposal* for an order before Parliament and the laying of the *draft regulatory reform order* before Parliament that the Regulatory Reform Committee does its work.

12.4.6 S.O. No. 141 provides for a select committee of eighteen Members, called the Regulatory Reform Committee, to examine each proposal for a regulatory reform order laid before Parliament by a Minister. The Committee has broadly the same powers as other select committees, as described in section 17.1, those being: to require written evidence and examine witnesses, to employ specialist advisers, to appoint a sub-committee (of which the quorum is two), to communicate, and to meet concurrently, with other committees (including Lords committees examining regulatory reform orders), to travel (within the United Kingdom only) and to make reports. It also has the right (shared with the Joint Committee on Statutory Instruments and the European Scrutiny Committee) to use the services of the Speaker's Counsel and their Lords equivalents. It also has the unique power to *invite* other Members of the House to participate in the examination of witnesses.

Regulatory Reform Procedure	
Stage 1	Proposal for a regulatory reform order laid before Parliament
	During the subsequent 60 days[1] the Regulatory Reform Committee considers and reports whether – (a) a draft regulatory reform order in the same terms as the proposal should be laid before the House; or (b) the terms of the proposal should be amended before a draft regulatory reform order is laid before the House;[2] or (c) the proposed use of the order-making powers is in its opinion inappropriate.[2] Other (non-parliamentary) bodies may also comment on the proposal.
Stage 2	Draft regulatory reform order may be laid before the House after the 60 day[1] period has expired
	The Regulatory Reform Committee must report within 15 sitting days whether it recommends that the draft order should be approved[3] or not approved[2]
Stage 3	After the Committee has reported, a motion to approve the draft order may be moved on the floor of the House – (a) and taken without debate if the Committee's recommendation to approve it was unanimous; (b) and debated for 1½ hours if the Committee's recommendation to approve was divided on; or (c) only after a motion to disagree with the Committee's recommendation not to approve has been agreed at the end of a debate which may last up to 3 hours

[1] Exclusive of any period when either House is adjourned for more than four days

[2] In which case the Committee must, before reporting, afford the government department an explanation of its position

[3] Indicating, in the case of a recommendation to approve, whether the recommendation was divided upon in the Committee

FIGURE 28
REGULATORY REFORM PROCEDURE

12.4.7 The Committee considers each proposal laid before Parliament under section 6 of the 2001 Act. It may, if it so chooses, take written or oral evidence on the proposal, and it may report to the House its conclusions on "any matter arising" from its consideration. It is required, by paragraph (6)(A) of the standing order to consider each proposal against specific tests. These include those questions of whether it represents an appropriate use of delegated powers and whether it is *intra vires*, matters of public expenditure and taxation, and questions of retrospective effect and doubtful drafting which the Joint Committee on Statutory Instruments is required to take into account when examining other types of instrument (see paragraph 12.3.6 above). In addition, the Committee is required to consider whether, in accordance with the Act, the proposal is designed to remove a burden and also to continue any necessary protection; whether the proposal is likely to conflict with European law; and whether consultation on the proposals has been properly conducted. Paragraph (6)(B) requires the Committee to apply five further tests. These are whether the proposed order would: prevent anyone exercising a right or freedom that they might reasonably expect to; meet the conditions of proportionality set down in sections 1 and 3 of the Act (see paragraph 12.1.8 above); be desirable in accordance with section 3(2)(b) of the 2001 Act; take into account the costs and benefits of what is proposed; and include only appropriate provision for the making of further subordinate orders.

12.4.8 The Committee reports formally to the House: whether a draft order in the same terms as the proposal should be laid before the House; whether the proposal should be amended before a draft order is laid before the House; or whether the proposal should not be proceeded with. Under paragraph (13) of the standing order, the Committee is required, if it intends to recommend that the proposal be amended or not proceeded with, to give the relevant government department an opportunity to present its defence. The appropriate resolution of the Committee appears in the Votes and Proceedings. The Committee also produces a substantive report on the proposal, covering all the matters it has considered during the allotted sixty-day period (see para 12.4.7 above).

12.4.9 After the end of the period of sixty days referred to in paragraph 12.4.4 above (usually not less than a week after that period has ended), during which time the Committee is likely to have made its report on the proposal, the Minister may lay the draft order before Parliament. The text of the draft order may take account of any criticisms of the proposal made by the Regulatory Reform Committee (or might not). The Act requires the Minister to lay a statement with the draft order giving details of the reports made by the Committee (and its counterpart in the Lords) and any other representations received during those sixty days, and the changes, if any, made to the proposal in the light of these.

12.4.10 Paragraph (14) of S.O. No. 141 requires the Regulatory Reform Committee then to report to the House, within fifteen *sitting* days of a draft order being laid, whether the Committee recommends that the draft order ought, or ought not, to be approved. Under the standing order, the Committee is required to consider how the Minister has responded to its report on the proposal, and what response the Minister has made to any other representations received during the sixty day period. The Committee is again required to afford an opportunity to the department to present a defence if it proposes to report that a draft order should not be approved. As with proposals for orders, a report of the Committee's resolution is printed in the **Votes and Proceedings**, although in the case of draft orders, if the Committee is recommending the approval of the Order, the resolution is accompanied by a note as to whether or not the Committee divided on the recommendation (see next paragraph). The Committee also produces a substantive (if usually brief) report on the draft order.

Proceedings on regulatory reform orders

12.4.11 After the Committee and its Lords counterpart have each made their report, a Minister may move a motion to approve the draft regulatory reform order on the floor of the House. Under S.O. No. 18(1), if the Committee recommended approval of the draft order without a division, the Question on the motion to approve the draft order is put **forthwith**. If the Committee divided on the recommendation to approve the order, debate on the motion to approve the draft order may continue for one and a half hours, after which the Question must be put (see paragraph 7.10.14).

12.4.12 Under S.O. No. 18(2), if the Committee recommended that the draft order ought not to be approved, a motion to approve the draft order cannot be moved before the House has resolved to disagree with the Committee's recommendation. Debate on a motion to disagree with the Committee's recommendation may continue for three hours, at the end of which the Question must be put. If the House does resolve to disagree with the Committee, the Question on the motion to approve the draft order may then be put **forthwith**. The government has yet to defy the Committee in this way.

12.4.13 Under paragraph (3) of S.O. No. 18, proceedings on all such motions relating to draft regulatory reform orders may be taken after the **moment of interruption**.

Regulatory reform orders list

12.4.14 Each Wednesday when the House is sitting, a list of all regulatory reform proposals and draft orders laid before the House, and the state of their progress, is published and circulated with the **Vote Bundle** (see paragraph 15.1.31).

12.5 REMEDIAL ORDERS

Statutory basis

12.5.1 Section 4 of the Human Rights Act 1998 allows a court in the UK to make a "declaration of incompatibility" between the law on which it has based a decision and the Human Rights Act itself (insofar as that Act brings the provisions of the European Convention on Human Rights listed in Schedule 1 of the Act into UK domestic law).

1. UK court makes declaration of incompatibility under s.4 of Human Rights Act 1998
or
European Court of Human Rights judgement appears to indicate incompatibility in UK law

2. When legal process is exhausted or discontinued Minister decides there are compelling reasons to proceed by means of Remedial Order to remedy the incompatibility

URGENT PROCEDURE	NON-URGENT PROCEDURE
3. Remedial Order made and laid before Parliament Representations, including any Report from JCHR, *may* be made within 60 days* of the Order being *made*	3. Proposal for a draft Remedial Order laid before Parliament. Representations, including Report from JCHR, must be made within 60 days* of the Proposal being *laid*. JCHR *must* report within this period.
4. After these 60 days* have expired, if representations have been received the Minister must report these to both Houses, and may choose to make and lay a replacement Order.	4. After these 60 days* have expired, Minister may lay a draft Order before Parliament, together with statement of any representations received on Proposal and any changes made.
5. Original Order or replacement Order must be approved by both Houses within 120 days* of the making of the *original* Order, or it ceases to be of effect. JCHR *required* to report at least once during the statutory period. Once approved by both Houses, Order becomes of permanent effect.	5. During a further period of 60 days* the JCHR *must* report whether the draft should be approved. Motion to approve the draft Order cannot be made until 60 days* have passed from date of laying of draft Order. Once approved by both Houses, Order may be made and brought into effect.

*Exclusive of any period when Parliament is prorogued or dissolved or both Houses are adjourned for more than four days

FIGURE 29
REMEDIAL ORDER PROCEDURE

12.5.2 Section 10 of the Act enables a Minister to make, or propose to make, a remedial order to make the necessary changes in the law to remedy the incompatibility identified by the court. It also provides for this power to be exercised in response to a finding of the European Court of Human Rights. Paragraph (2) of that section requires there to be compelling reasons for remedying any such incompatibility by means of subordinate rather than primary legislation.

12.5.3 Schedule 2 to the Act sets out the parliamentary procedures for making such a remedial order. They closely mirror those for regulatory reform orders described above. The schedule contemplates two kinds of procedure – a normal and an urgent one.

12.5.4 Under the normal procedure, the Minister must lay a proposal for a draft remedial order before Parliament. The proposal must be accompanied by a statement of the circumstances which led to the proposal to make an order and an explanation of what it proposes to do. There then follows a period of sixty days (exclusive of any period when Parliament is prorogued or dissolved or when *both* Houses are adjourned for a period of more than four days) in which representations may be made upon the order. After that period has expired, the Minister may lay a draft remedial order. This must be accompanied by a statement of the nature of any representations received on the proposal and any changes made to the proposal as a result of those representations. There then follows a further period of sixty days (calculated subject to the same exclusions as above), after the end of which a motion may be moved in the House to approve the draft order.

12.5.5 Under the urgent procedure, a Minister may make and lay a remedial order with immediate statutory effect. It ceases to be of effect if both Houses have not passed a resolution approving it within a period of 120 days (subject to the exclusions described above). During the first sixty days, representations may be made about the order. If after considering those representations, the Minister is so minded, he or she may withdraw the original order and make a new one in its place. This must be approved by both Houses within the remaining sixty days or it ceases to have effect.

12.5.6 The two Houses have given the Joint Committee on Human Rights (see section 17.5 below) the duty of considering and reporting on these proposals for remedial orders, draft remedial orders or urgent procedure remedial orders within the various statutory periods described above. The relevant standing order in the Commons is S.O. No. 152B. It requires the Committee, in the case of a proposal for a draft remedial order, to report within the first period of sixty days whether a draft order in the same terms as the proposal should be laid, and in respect of the draft order, to report within the second period of sixty days whether the draft order should be approved. In the case of an urgent procedure remedial order, the Committee is required to report (implicitly, at least if it is going to do anything but recommend approval within the first period of sixty days) whether: (a) the order should be approved in its original form; (b) the order should be replaced by a new one; or (c) the order should not be approved. If it were to choose option (b), the implication is that it would be expected to report again on any replacement order or, if no such replacement were made, whether the order should now be approved.

12.5.7 In making any or all of these reports at various stages, the Committee is empowered to report on incidental matters arising from its considerations. When reporting on draft orders or urgent procedure orders, the Committee is also required to examine them against the tests applied by the Joint Committee on Statutory Instruments under S.O. No. 151 to other statutory instruments (see paragraphs 12.3.5 to 12.3.9 above). Remedial orders are therefore not considered by the JCSI separately.

12.5.8 In contrast to the provisions of S.O. No. 18 relating to regulatory reform orders, (see paragraphs 12.4.11 and 12.4.12 above) no procedural consequences are triggered by either a positive or a negative report of the Joint Committee on Human Rights, and the motion to approve a draft remedial order or urgent procedure order is subject to the same rules as for any other affirmative procedure instrument (see paragraphs 12.3.10 to 12.3.14 above). Such an instrument would stand referred to a standing committee on delegated legislation (see paragraphs 12.3.23 to 12.3.30 above), and would be debated in that forum whatever the Committee recommended, unless it was de-referred on a motion tabled by a Minister (see paragraph 12.3.10 above).

Resolution of 17th November 1998

(1) No Minister of the Crown should give agreement in the Council or in the European Council to any proposal for European Community legislation or for a common strategy, joint action or common position under Title V or a common position, framework decision, decision or convention under Title VI of the Treaty on European Union:

(a) which is still subject to scrutiny (that is, on which the European Scrutiny Committee has not completed its scrutiny) or

(b) which is awaiting consideration by the House (that is, which has been recommended by the European Scrutiny Committee for consideration pursuant to Standing Order No. 119 (European Standing Committees) but in respect of which the House has not come to a Resolution).

(2) In this Resolution, any reference to agreement to a proposal includes:

(a) agreement to a programme, plan or recommendation for European Community legislation;

(b) political agreement;

(c) in the case of a proposal on which the Council acts in accordance with the procedure referred to in Article 251 of the Treaty of Rome (co-decision), agreement to a common position, to an act in the form of a common position incorporating amendments proposed by the European Parliament and a joint text; and

(d) in the case of a proposal on which the Council acts in accordance with the procedure referred to in Article 252 of the Treaty of Rome (co-operation), agreement to a common position.

(3) The Minister concerned may, however, give agreement:

(a) to a proposal which is still subject to scrutiny if he considers that it is confidential, routine or trivial or is substantially the same as a proposal on which scrutiny has been completed;

(b) to a proposal which is awaiting consideration by the House if the European Scrutiny Committee has indicated that agreement need not be withheld pending consideration.

(4) The Minister concerned may also give agreement to a proposal which is still subject to scrutiny or awaiting consideration by the House if he decides that for special reasons agreement should be given; but he should explain his reasons:

(a) in every such case, to the European Scrutiny Committee at the first opportunity after reaching his decision; and

(b) in the case of a proposal awaiting consideration by the House, to the House at the first opportunity after giving agreement.

(5) In relation to any proposal which requires adoption by unanimity, abstention shall, for the purposes of paragraph (4), be treated as giving agreement.

FIGURE 30

THE SCRUTINY RESERVE RESOLUTION

Chapter 13
EUROPEAN SCRUTINY

13.1 INTRODUCTION

The Treaty of Rome, etc

13.1.1 On its accession to the European Economic Community in 1972, and its agreement to the Treaty of Rome, the UK government accepted certain obligations to incorporate into domestic law the elements of Community law which are from time to time agreed by the Council of Ministers, the legislative authority of the Community. These obligations were extended by the treaty known as the Single European Act ratified in 1986, by the Maastricht Treaty, which Parliament ratified in 1992 and by the Amsterdam Treaty of 1997 which came into force on 1 May 1999.

European legislative process

13.1.2 The legislative process of what is now the European Union is highly complex. Briefly described, proposals for legislation are made by the Commission of the European Union (its central administrative body), are scrutinised by the European Parliament and are agreed at the Council of Ministers, the legislative authority of the Union on which the national governments of each of the member states are represented. Decisions of this body are made either by unanimity or under the system of qualified majority voting (QMV), in which the member states have voting powers roughly in proportion to their populations. In certain cases, a process involving the European Parliament known as "co-decision" is used. Whether an item of legislation falls to be agreed by unanimity, by QMV or by co-decision will depend upon under which article of the various treaties it is made.

European Union Documents

13.1.3 European Union legislation is principally effected by means of *regulations* and *directives*. Proposals for legislation are *draft regulations* and *draft directives*. There are several other types of document produced by the Commission and by other institutions of the Union, some of which are not legislative proposals although they may be binding on member states: these may include the equivalent of Green or White Papers (that is, preliminary proposals for possible legislation); draft Council decisions; draft Council resolutions; and reports of various kinds on the activities of institutions of the Union such as the European Central Bank or the Court of Auditors.

13.1.4 Under the provisions of the Maastricht and Amsterdam Treaties, the competence of the Union was extended into the areas of the "Common Foreign and Security Policy" and "Co-operation on Justice and Home Affairs" (known as "Pillars 2 and 3" of the Union). The outcome of Union actions in these areas may be a common strategy, joint action, common position, framework decision, decision or convention agreed by the Council of Ministers or the European Council.

13.1.5 Documents embodying legislative or other proposals or reports, when received from the Commission, the Council of Ministers or another institution by the UK government, are deposited in Parliament. They are available from the European section of the **Vote Office**, and they are also submitted to the European Scrutiny Committee (see below).

The Scrutiny Reserve

13.1.6 Procedures for scrutinising European legislation and other European Community documents in the House have existed since 1974. On 30 October 1980 the House passed a resolution stating that no Minister should give his or her agreement in the Council of Ministers to any proposal for European legislation which had not been scrutinised by its then European Legislation Committee, and if that Committee had recommended that the proposals should be debated by the House, agreement should not be given until the debate had taken place. This is known as the "scrutiny reserve".

13.1.7 On 24 October 1990 the House passed a further resolution elaborating this resolution in the light of developments in the Union and also providing for Ministers to give their agreement to legislative proposals before the completion of their scrutiny by the Commons in certain defined circumstances. On 17 November 1998 the House agreed a new version of the resolution to take account of the wider field of action at European Union level provided for in the Maastricht and Amsterdam Treaties. It is set out in Figure 30.

Incorporation of European legislation

13.1.8 EU Regulations, once agreed by the Council of Ministers, become law in each member state without the need for any further domestic legislation, although it may be necessary to provide in domestic legislation for penalties for breaching the regulations. The direct application of Council Regulations is provided for in section 2(2) of the European Communities Act 1972.

13.1.9 The making of a directive by the Council of Ministers does not in itself make that law part of the law of each member state. Section 2(2) of the European Communities Act 1972 provides for the making of Orders in Council or regulations (see paragraph 12.1.5) to incorporate European law into the law of the United Kingdom. European legislation may also be incorporated by means of primary legislation.

13.2 THE SCRUTINY PROCESS

Deposit of documents

13.2.1 When a European document arrives in the UK (which may be some time after its publication because of the need for translation), the relevant government department has two working days in which to deposit it in Parliament (that is in the European Section of the Vote Office and with the European Scrutiny Committee). The department has a further ten working days in which to prepare and deposit an *Explanatory Memorandum* which may outline the government's position on the proposal and give an expected timetable for its passage through the decision making processes of the EU.

European Scrutiny Committee

13.2.2 Under S.O. No. 143 a select committee of sixteen Members, known as the European Scrutiny Committee, is appointed to consider all European documents. The Committee has the usual powers of a select committee (see section 17.1) including: to require the submission of written evidence and to examine witnesses; to make reports; to obtain specialist advice; to travel; to appoint sub-committees; and to sit on days when the House is not meeting. The Committee also has the right (like the Joint Committee on Statutory Instruments and the Regulatory Reform Committee) to the assistance of **Speaker's Counsel**. In addition to the normal complement of select committee staff, the Committee is also served by Clerk Advisers (usually former civil servants) who assist in the expert scrutiny of the very large volume of paper it is required by the House to consider.

13.2.3 The Committee also has the unique power to seek from any of the **departmental select committees** (or their sub-committees), the **Public Accounts Committee**, the Public Administration Committee or the Environmental Audit Committee an opinion on any document it has received. The Committee may meet concurrently (see paragraphs 17.1.20 to 17.1.24) with the other select committees of.the House which have investigative powers.

13.2.4 With the assistance of its staff, the Committee sifts through the documents received. It is required by S.O. No. 143 to report its opinion on the legal and political importance of each document and to make recommendations as to which should be further considered by the House. Around two-thirds of the documents on average are considered by the Committee to be insignificant in legal and political terms and they take no further action. In respect of the remainder, they may take three courses of action. First, they may report the issues a document raises but recommend no further action. Second, they may refer the document for debate by one of the three European standing committees (see below). Third, they may recommend that the document be debated on the floor of the House. The Committee's conclusions are made public in its regular weekly reports (which do not have specific titles but are called simply the "First Report", the "Second Report", etc). Occasionally, the Committee will publish a separate report on a particular topic. Examples include changes in the legal structure of the EU proposed in treaty amendments or the procedures of the House in relation to European scrutiny.

13.2.5 The reference by the Committee of a document to a European standing committee is binding. Such references are noted by means of a memorandum in the **Votes and Proceedings**. A further recommendation that a document ought to be debated on the floor of the House is advisory. A motion to de-refer the document from one of the standing committees, so making it available for debate on the floor can only, under S.O. No. 119(2), be moved by a Minister. Such a motion is taken at the commencement of public business and the Question on it is put **forthwith** (see paragraph 7.7.7).

European Community Document List

13.2.6 A list of all documents referred for debate in either European standing committee or for debate on the floor of the House is published every Monday when the House is sitting. It indicates the date of referral, the date considered in a committee or appointed for consideration in a committee and the date a resolution was agreed to by the House or appointed for a debate in the House.

Debate on the floor of the House

13.2.7 If a document is de-referred from a European standing committee in accordance with the procedure described in paragraph 13.2.5, the government will in due course table a motion for debate on a day of its choosing. The motion will usually be in the form "That this House takes note [of the said document or documents]", followed by words expressing the government's general attitude to the proposal and perhaps indicating the course of action it proposes to take. Amendments may be proposed to such a motion. These are subject to the Speaker's power of selection (see paragraphs 9.2.6 to 9.2.8).

13.2.8 Debate on such a motion is governed by S.O. No. 16, which limits the debate to an hour and a half, at the end of which the chair must put the Question on the motion. Such debates may continue over or commence after the **moment of interruption**.

13.2.9 Once the debate has been concluded and the motion voted upon, the scrutiny process has been completed, and Ministers may then properly exercise their vote in relation to the document in the Council of Ministers or another forum of the Union.

European standing committees

13.2.10 There are three European standing committees established under S.O. No. 119(1) to consider such documents as are referred to them by the European Scrutiny Committee (see paragraphs 13.2.2 to 13.2.4 above). They are called A, B and C. Paragraph (6) of the standing order allocates to European Standing Committee A consideration of documents falling within the responsibilities of the Departments of Environment, Food and Rural Affairs, Transport, and the local government and regional responsibilities of the Office of the Deputy Prime Minister, and matters relating to forestry as well as the analagous responsibilities of the Northern Ireland, Scotland and Wales Offices in relation to these matters. European Standing Committee B deals with matters falling within the responsibilities of the Treasury, the Department of Work and Pensions, the Foreign and Commonwealth Office, the Department for International Development, the Home Office, and the Department for Constitutional Affairs and any other matters not otherwise allocated. European Standing Committee C deals with matters falling within the responsibilities of the Departments of Trade and Industry, Education and Skills, Culture, Media and Sport, and Health.

13.2.11 Each committee has thirteen Members appointed by the **Committee of Selection** (see section 2.4). Uniquely amongst standing committees, these Members are appointed for a whole Parliament rather than *ad hoc*. The quorum of the committees is specified as three by paragraph (4) of S.O. No. 119, which also specifically excludes the chairman from counting towards this. The chairman for each sitting is appointed *ad hoc* by the Speaker from amongst the Chairmen's Panel (see paragraphs 3.3.1 and 3.3.2). As with delegated legislation committees, any Member of the House may attend a sitting of a European standing committee and participate in its proceedings (including the moving of amendments), but cannot vote and does not count towards the quorum.

13.2.12 The government decides when documents referred by the European Scrutiny Committee to each standing committee will be considered. Any proposed meetings of a committee and the documents which it is to consider are announced in the Business Question/Statement (see paragraphs 7.5.7 and 7.6.1). On that Thursday (usually) the government will table a motion for the committee to consider in the form "That the committee takes note [of the document]", and expressing some view upon the proposal it contains. These notices of motion appear among the blue notice paper pages of the **Vote Bundle** the following day (see paragraph 15.1.38), and are reprinted on white paper on the day on which the committee is to consider the motion (see paragraph 15.1.32). Amendments may be tabled to these motions by any Member, whether or not appointed to the committee.

13.2.13 The sitting of the committee to consider the motion begins with a brief opening statement by the Minister in whose name the motion stands, lasting up to about ten minutes. This is intended to be largely explanatory. At the conclusion of the statement, Members (whether or not appointed to the committee) may question the Minister. No notice is given of the questions. Members are called by the chairman, and may be called more than once. The period of questioning may continue for up to an hour after the *commencement* of the Minister's statement.

13.2.14 At the conclusion of question time (or when no further Members rise to ask questions) the chairman will announce his or her selection of any amendments that have been proposed to the motion before the committee and will invite the Minister to move the motion on the Notice Paper. More often than not, Ministers choose to do this formally by simply saying "I beg to move" or whatever, and reserve their opportunity to speak to the end of the debate. Only a Minister may move a motion. The chairman usually then calls the opposition **shadow** to speak, and he or she may move an amendment to the motion. However, any Member may move an amendment, if it is selected. Debate then follows, and may continue for the period up to the end of two and a half hours from the beginning of the committee's sitting (that is one and a half hours after the end of questions, if those occupied the full hour available).

13.2.15 At the conclusion of debate, or when the two and a half hours have passed, the chairman puts the Question on any amendment that has been moved and when that is disposed of, on the motion (as amended or not as the case may be). Under paragraph (8) of the standing order the chairman then reports the resolution as agreed by the committee to the House. If the motion is negatived, the chairman reports that the committee has come to no resolution. These reports (including the text of any resolution agreed) appear in the **Votes and Proceedings** for that day.

13.2.16 Paragraph (9) of S.O. No. 119 provides that, once the chairman has reported the conclusions of a European standing committee on any documents, a motion relating to those documents may be moved in the House and the Question on it be put **forthwith**, without further debate. These motions will appear on the **Order Paper** on a day of the government's choosing. On occasions they have been placed on the Order Paper on the same day that a committee is to consider the documents referred to on the presumption that the committee will complete its consideration. The standing order requires only that such a motion should *relate* to the same documents that a committee has considered, *not* that the motion must be in the same terms as any resolution reported from the committee. Generally it is in the same terms as the committee's resolution, but occasionally it is not. The standing order also provides for an amendment to such a motion to be moved, if selected, and for the Question on any such amendment to be put **forthwith** before the Question on the motion (amended or not) is put **forthwith**, and these Questions may be decided after the **moment of interruption**.

13.2.17 Once the House has voted on a motion on documents considered by one of the standing committees, the scrutiny process is complete, and Ministers are free to cast their votes on the relevant proposals in the Council of Ministers or elsewhere.

Grouping of documents

13.2.18 The European Scrutiny Committee often proposes that specified documents should be debated together, or occasionally the government may itself group together related documents. This may be done for debates on the floor of the House or in standing committee. Where this is done, a single motion taking note of all the documents is moved, and the time limits described in paragraphs 13.2.7 and 13.2.14 above apply to the motion, not to each document. It is not possible for Members to object procedurally to documents being debated together in this way.

13.2.19 Occasionally, both on the floor of the House and in the European standing committees, other documents are "tagged" to a motion. A tag is an italicised note after the motion stating that "Such and such a document/documents are also relevant". Documents so tagged are considered to have completed the scrutiny process once the motion to which they are tagged has been considered.

13.2.20 A simplified diagram of the procedures described above is at Figure 31.

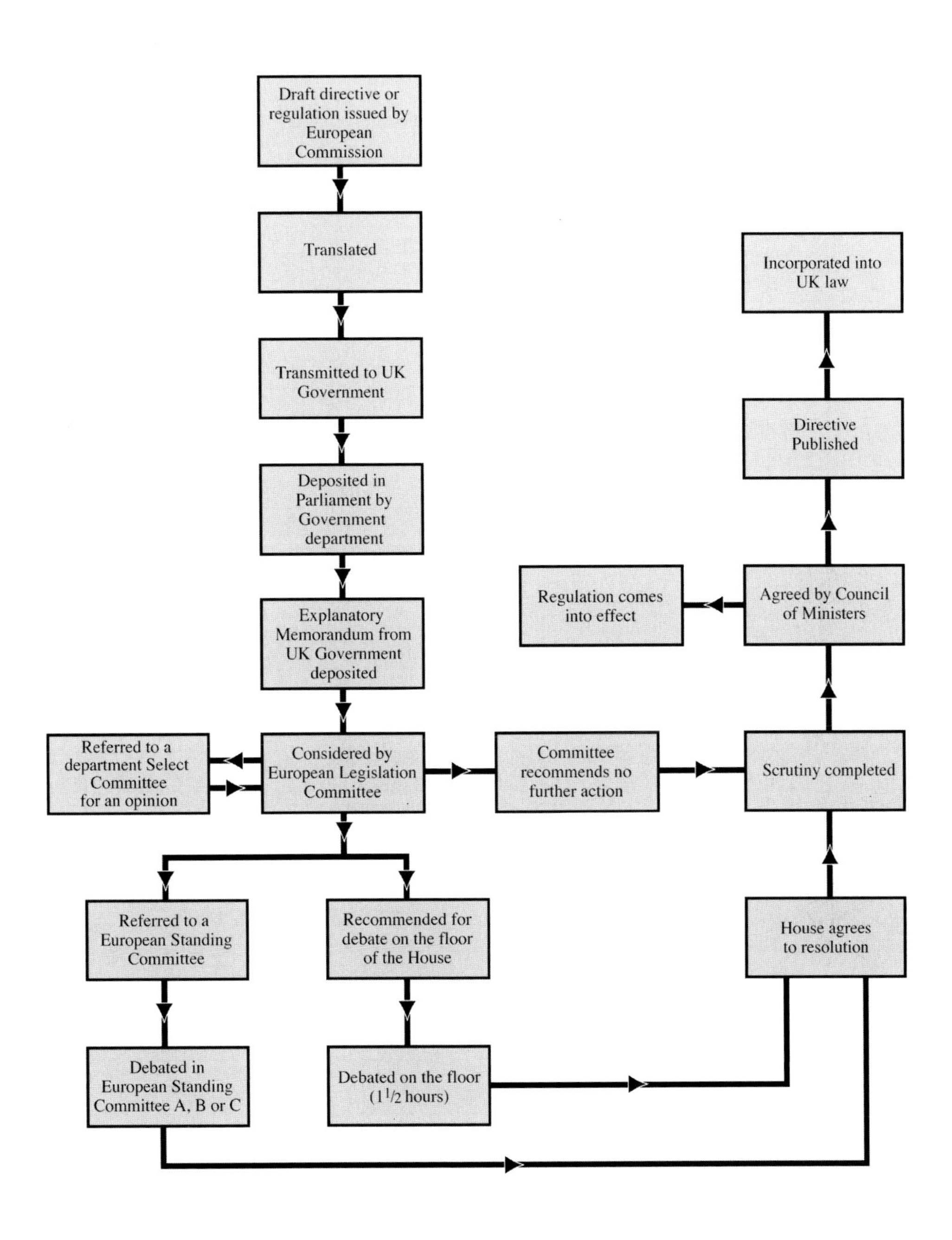

FIGURE 31
UK STAGES OF EUROPEAN LEGISLATION

Chapter 14

THE GRAND COMMITTEES AND THE REGIONAL AFFAIRS COMMITTEE

14.1 INTRODUCTION

The Grand Committees

14.1.1 There are currently three standing committees of the House which have the title of grand committee. The oldest is the Scottish Grand Committee (S.O. Nos. 93 to 101) which has been in existence for over a century. The Welsh Grand Committee (S.O. Nos. 102 to 108) has existed since 1960. The Northern Ireland Grand Committee (S.O. Nos. 109 to 116) was established in 1994.

14.1.2 These three committees all share the characteristic that all Members sitting for constituencies in the relevant countries are automatically Members of the appropriate grand committee. In the case of the Welsh and Northern Ireland committees there is provision for the **Committee of Selection** to appoint additional Members from constituencies outside the borders of those countries.

14.1.3 Prior to devolution, in the period from 1992 to 1997, the procedures of the three grand committees were substantially revised, allowing them to hear statements, take oral questions, debate bills and delegated legislation and hold adjournment debates, among other things. These procedures are described below. However, since the establishment of the Scottish Parliament, the National Assembly for Wales and the Northern Ireland Assembly, the role and parliamentary significance of the grand committees has much diminished. They now meet relatively infrequently, and the scope for legislative work is much more circumscribed.

The Standing Committee on Regional Affairs

14.1.4 S.O. No. 117 provides for a Standing Committee on Regional Affairs. It has thirteen members, all of whom must sit sit for constituencies in England. Any Member of the House representing an English constituency may participate in its debates. It is therefore somewhat analogous to an English Grand Committee.

14.2 COMMON FEATURES OF THE PROCEDURES OF THE COMMITTEES

14.2.1 The rules of debate in the three grand committees and the Regional Affairs Committee are largely the same as for the House, and the chairmen have the same powers as those enjoyed by chairmen of other standing committees (see section 3.3).

14.2.2 The chairmen of the committees are appointed for each of their sittings from among the members of the **Chairmen's Panel** in the same way as the chairmen of other standing committees (see paragraph 3.3.1).

14.2.3 Unlike other standing committees, each of these committees may meet away from Westminster, at locations chosen by the House in their respective countries. This is currently a much less common feature of their activities than it was in the 1992–97 Parliament. Again unlike other standing committees, each of these committees may meet only on days and at places determined by a resolution of the House (S.O. Nos. 100, 108 and 116), so that they do not have power to determine their own pattern of sittings.

14.2.4 Each of the committees has the power to hear ministerial statements (S.O. Nos. 96, 105 and 112), though the details of the provisions differ slightly for each one. The rules allow Ministers who are not members of the committees to participate in their proceedings (S.O. Nos. 93(3), 102(4) and 109(4)), though they cannot vote and do not count towards the quorum (unless of course they are members of a grand committee by virtue of the constituency they represent). In the case of the grand committees (but not the Regional Affairs Committee) Ministers who are members of the House of Lords may make such statements and reply to questions after them, but not from the body of the committee (S.O. Nos. 96(1) and (4), 105(1) and (4) and 112(1) and (4)).

14.2.5 The three grand committees (but not the Regional Affairs Committee) have provision for oral question times at the start of meetings (S.O. Nos. 94, 103 and 110 - forty-five minutes in length for the Scottish Grand, thirty minutes for the other two). The arrangements for giving notice of such questions, and the rules governing their content, are much the same as those for oral questions in the House (see paragraph 7.5.1 and chapter 8). Only members of each committee may table such questions, and they can only be addressed to the relevant Secretary of State for each committee. The written answers to any such questions which are not reached in the time available are published as a supplement to the Hansard report of that sitting (see paragraph 15.4.7).

14.2.6 Each of the three grand committees (but again not the Regional Affairs Committee) also have a provision for a period for taking "short debates" (S.O. Nos. 95, 104 and 111). There may be a half-hour period of short debates at the commencement of a sitting, or immediately after oral questions, if any. Members of the Committee may give notice of the subject they wish to raise ten sitting days in advance. The order of debates is decided by ballot. The Member introducing the debate may speak for five minutes, as may the Minister replying. Other Members who are called may speak for a maximum of three minutes. No Member may give notice of more than one subject and it must relate to the responsibilities of the appropriate Secretary of State. This procedure has not been much used by any of the committees.

14.3 The Scottish Grand Committee

Constitution of the Committee

14.3.1 The Scottish Grand Committee consists of all Members sitting for constituencies in Scotland (seventy-two in the 2001 Parliament) and no others. The quorum of the Committee is ten, except during the half-hour adjournment debates (see paragraph 14.3.2 below) when it is three. Other Members of the House may not take part in the Committee's proceedings.

Meetings of the Committee

14.3.2 Under S.O. No. 100, a motion may be moved in the House by a Minister specifying the days on which and the places where the Scottish Grand Committee is to meet. The motion determining the day, place and time of the sittings may also specify the type of business to be taken at each such sitting. The motions may also specify the time at which meetings held away from Westminster are to conclude. Paragraphs (4) to (6) of the standing order describe this as the moment of interruption and provide that the business under discussion at the moment of interruption shall stand adjourned or shall lapse. Paragraph (6) provides for a half hour adjournment debate to take place after the moment of interruption, and this is organised along the same lines as the daily adjournment in the House (see section 7.12). During this period, the quorum of the Committee is three.

Substantive adjournment motions

14.3.3 S.O. No. 99 provides, uniquely for the Scottish Grand, for the Committee at certain of its meetings to debate a substantive adjournment motion (see paragraph 9.8.1). This is the most regular item of business at its sittings. The subject for debate during these sittings is (for the duration of the current Parliament) chosen by the government and by the other opposition parties under a formula which tends to vary from Parliament to Parliament. A proviso to paragraph (3) of the standing order allows in certain circumstances for one meeting of the Committee to count as two "days" for the purposes of this calculation.

Bills and delegated legislation

14.3.4 The procedure for consideration of bills in relation to their principle before either their second or third reading in the House under S.O. No. 97 is described in paragraphs 11.6.14 to 11.6.17 and 11.14.5. The procedure for referring bills to the Committee for their **report stage** under S.O. No. 92 is described in paragraph 11.13.14. (The effect of these provisions taken together is that, in theory, a Scottish bill might have its second reading, report stage and third reading all in the Scottish Grand Committee – though in practice this has never occurred.) The procedure for referring an item of delegated legislation to the Scottish Grand Committee is described in paragraphs 12.3.10 and 12.3.22. The procedure for debating a statutory instrument in the Scottish Grand Committee is in all respects the same as that for standing committees on delegated legislation (see paragraphs 12.3.23 to 12.3.30) except that other Members of the House may not participate.

14.4 THE WELSH GRAND COMMITTEE

Constitution of the Committee

14.4.1 Under S.O. No. 102, the Welsh Grand Committee consists of all Members sitting for constituencies in Wales (forty) plus up to five other Members nominated by the **Committee of Selection.** These additional Members continue to be Members for a session unless discharged or replaced. The quorum of the Committee is seven, except during the half-hour adjournment debates (see paragraph 14.3.4 below), when it is three. Other Members of the House may not take part in the Committee's proceedings.

Business of the Committee

14.4.2 Under S.O. No. 102, the Welsh Grand Committee has power to take oral questions; to hear ministerial statements; to consider bills prior to their second reading; and to hold short debates. There is no provision for the reference to the Committee of delegated legislation; or for the consideration of bills prior to their third reading; or for substantive motions for the adjournment. There is, however, provision for the Committee to have referred to it for consideration matters relating exclusively to Wales (see paragraph 14.4.6 below).

Meetings of the Committee

14.4.3 Under S.O. No. 108, a motion may be moved in the House by a Minister to establish a future programme of sittings for the Committee, specifying the place, day and time of the sittings and the types of business to be conducted at each of those sittings. The Question on such a motion is put **forthwith**, without debate, and may be decided after the **moment of interruption**. The same procedure applies to any subsequent motion to supplement or vary the provisions of a previous motion.

14.4.4 Paragraphs (3) to (5) of S.O. No. 108 provide for any proceedings of the Committee under way to stand adjourned at the moment of interruption specified in the resolution of the House fixing the days and times of sittings. After the moment of interruption, a half hour adjournment debate may take place, and these debates are organised along the same lines as the **daily adjournment** debate in the House (see section 7.12). During this period, the quorum of the Committee is three.

Use of the Welsh Language

14.4.5 Under certain conditions, the Welsh language may be used in proceedings of the Welsh Grand Committee when it is meeting in Wales, subject to the overall discretion of the Chairmen. Simultaneous interpretation facilities are provided at given sittings. Speeches appear in **Hansard** in translation (see paragraph 15.4.7)

Matters relating exclusively to Wales

14.4.6 Under S.O. No. 107, a Minister may move a motion at the commencement of public business to refer to the Welsh Grand Committee for its consideration a specific matter or matters relating exclusively to Wales. Such matters might be for example Education in Wales, Housing in Wales or the implications of the Budget for Wales, or whatever. After the Committee has considered the matter, the motion agreed is that the chairman reports to the House that the Committee has considered the matter. Such debates are therefore somewhat similar in nature to the substantive adjournment debates of the Scottish Grand Committee, but without formal provision for subjects to be chosen by the opposition parties.

Bills

14.4.7 Under S.O. No. 106, a bill may be referred to the Welsh Grand Committee for its consideration before second reading. The procedure is described in paragraphs 11.6.12 and 11.6.13.

14.5 THE NORTHERN IRELAND GRAND COMMITTEE

Constitution of the Committee

14.5.1 Under S.O. No. 109, the Northern Ireland Grand Committee consists of all Members sitting for constituencies in Northern Ireland (eighteen) plus up to twenty-five other Members nominated by the **Committee of Selection**. These additional Members continue to be Members for a session unless discharged or replaced. The quorum of the Committee is ten, except during the half-hour adjournment debates (see paragraph 14.5.4 below), when it is three. Other Members of the House may not take part in the Committee's proceedings.

Business of the Committee

14.5.2 Under S.O. No. 109, the Northern Ireland Grand Committee has power to take oral questions to Northern Ireland Office Ministers; to hold short debates; to hear ministerial statements; to consider bills prior to their second and third readings; to consider legislative proposals and "matters" relating exclusively to Northern Ireland, and to consider delegated legislation relating to Northern Ireland.

Meetings of the Committee

14.5.3 Under S.O. No. 116, a motion may be moved in the House by a Minister to establish a future programme of sittings for the Committee, specifying the place, day and time of the sittings and the types of business to be conducted at each of those sittings. The Committee may meet on two days in each session in Northern Ireland; other meetings may be held at Westminster. In practice, the Committee has not met away from Westminster. The Question on such a motion is put **forthwith**, without debate, and may be decided after the **moment of interruption**. The same procedure applies to any subsequent motion to supplement or vary the provisions of a previous motion.

14.5.4 Paragraphs (3) to (5) of S.O. No. 116 provide for any proceedings of the Committee under way to stand adjourned at the moment of interruption specified in the resolution of the House fixing the days and times of sittings (or at 1 pm or 11.30 am if no time is specified). After the moment of interruption, a half hour adjournment debate may take place, if provided for in the motion agreed to by the House, and these debates are organised along the same lines as the **daily adjournment** debate in the House (see section 7.12). During this period, the quorum of the Committee is three.

Legislative proposals and matters relating exclusively to Northern Ireland

14.5.5 Under S.O. No. 114, a Minister may move a motion at the commencement of public business to refer to the Northern Ireland Grand Committee for its consideration a legislative proposal or a specific matter or matters relating exclusively to Northern Ireland. Such matters might be, for example, "Public Spending Plans for Northern Ireland", "Housing in Northern Ireland" or the **Estimates** of the Northern Ireland Office or whatever. A "legislative proposal" means a proposal for a draft Order in Council relating to Northern Ireland (see paragraphs 12.2.3 and 12.2.4). Debate takes place on the motion "That the Committee has considered the proposal/matter".

Bills and statutory instruments

14.5.6 The procedure under S.O. No. 113 for consideration by the Northern Ireland Grand Committee of bills in relation to their principle before either their second or third reading in the House is described in paragraphs 11.6.14 to 11.6.17 and 11.14.5. The procedure for referring an item of delegated legislation to the Northern Ireland Grand Committee under S.O. No. 115 is described in paragraphs 12.3.10 and 12.3.22. The procedure for debating a statutory instrument in the Northern Ireland Grand Committee is in all respects the same as that for standing committees on delegated legislation (see paragraphs 12.3.23 to 12.3.30) except that other Members of the House may not participate. The time limit for a debate on a statutory instrument is two and a half hours, which may be extended to three hours by a motion moved by a Minister at the outset of a debate.

14.6 The Standing Committee on Regional Affairs

14.6.1 Under S.O. No. 117, there is a Standing Committee on Regional Affairs which may consider any matter relating to regional affairs in England which may be referred to it by the House.

14.6.2 The Committee consists of thirteen members, who must have seats in England. They are appointed by the **Committee of Selection**. They continue to be members until the Committee of Selection discharges them. The quorum of the Committee is three. Any Member who sits for an English constituency may take part in the Committee's debates, but may not move motions or amendments or vote, and does not count towards the quorum. Any Minister who is a Member of the House of Commons, whether representing an English constituency or not, may likewise participate in its proceedings, and may initiate debate by moving motions to consider matters referred to the Committee. Unlike in the grand committees, Ministers who are members of the House of Lords may not participate in the Committee's proceedings.

14.6.3 Again in contrast to the grand committees, the Regional Affairs Committee has very limited procedures, which are borrowed in part from those for European standing committees (see paragraphs 13.2.10 to 13.2.15). It may only consider a "matter" referred to it by the House, which it does on a motion "That the committee has considered the matter". In effect, this is similar to a substantive adjournment debate (see paragraph 9.8.1), but with the subject chosen by the House. More than one "matter" may be referred for consideration at a single sitting.

14.6.4 The first part of the sitting at which a matter is being considered may be taken up by a statement from a Minister, followed by questions from the floor of the Committee, much along the lines of a ministerial statement in the House (see paragraphs 7.6.3 and 7.6.4) or those made at the commencement of a sitting of a European standing committee (see paragraph 13.2.13). The statement must relate to the matter or matters which are being considered at that sitting. The period of questioning following the statement must conclude no later than one hour after the *commencement* of the Minister's statement.

14.6.5 After the conclusion of the statement and subsequent questioning (which may be before the end of the hour maximum allowed), the Minister moves the motion on which the Committee debates the "matter". At the conclusion of a period of three hours (unless varied by an order of the House as described in the next paragraph) from the commencement of proceedings (including any statement) the Chair must put the Question on the motion, and whatever the result of any division, reports to the House simply that the matter has been considered by the Committee.

14.6.6 Under paragraph (6) of the standing order, a Minister may move a motion in the House to: specify the matter (or matters) which the Committee is to consider at any sitting; specify the period to be allotted to each matter; specify when and where in England the Committee is to meet (so, like the grand committees, it is a standing committee which may meet away from Westminster); specify the start and finishing times of a sitting; and specify on which days it may sit at Westminster. Such a motion may be moved at any time, including after the **moment of interruption**, and is decided **forthwith**, without debate.

Chapter 15

PUBLICATIONS AND PAPERS

15.1 THE VOTE BUNDLE

Introduction

15.1.1 The Vote Bundle (or just "the Vote") is the collection of papers issued each sitting day to guide Members and other readers through past and forthcoming events relating to the proceedings of the House. In its full form it is a document of sometimes more than 200 pages.

15.1.2 The Bundle is divided into two basic parts, one coloured white, the other blue. Each of these parts may be sub-divided into a number of sections. Broadly, the white pages deal with current and past business and the blue pages with future business.

15.1.3 The white pages in a bundle published on a sitting day include:

- the summary agenda
- the Order Paper (including Future Business)
- the Votes and Proceedings
- amendment papers relating to bills to be considered on that day either in standing committee or on the floor of the House
- motions to be considered that day in European standing committees
- memoranda of various kinds

With very rare exceptions, the first four items will appear in every issue of the Bundle. Amendment papers, etc. will appear only on certain days. On non-sitting Fridays (see paragraph 6.1.5), the first two items relating to the next sitting day are published in blue. Outstanding questions for written answer are printed in a separate daily document known as the "Questions Book".

15.1.4 The blue pages on a sitting day include:

- notices of questions given on the previous day
- notices of motions and otheı business for fixed days
- notices of private business to be considered on that day and on future days
- notices of motions for which no days have been fixed (ie, early day motions)
- notices of amendments relating to bills to be considered on a future day
- notices of motions for European standing committees

Notices of questions and of early day motions will almost invariably appear in each issue of the Bundle. The other items will appear less regularly.

15.1.5 There is a separate Order Paper for sittings in Westminster Hall (see section 6.3). Business set down for future sittings in Westminster Hall is listed in section B of the future business pages of the Order Paper (see below).

The Order Paper

15.1.6 The Order Paper is fronted by a summary agenda of the House's business for the day, which gives approximate indications of timings for each of the main items of business. The Order Paper proper sets out in full the business for the day's sitting in the House, and must be finalised before the rising of the House on the previous sitting day.

No. 13 **333**

House of Commons

Tuesday 29th February 2003

Order of Business

At 2.30 p.m. Prayers

Afterwards

Private Business

Note: Private Business is not debated at this time, and may not be proceeded with if opposed.

CONSIDERATION OF LORDS AMENDMENTS

BILL WITH AMENDMENTS

Land at the Globe Theatre, Southwark (Acquisition of Freehold)

[*Copies of the Amendments may obtained by Members from the Vote Office or inspected in the Private Bill Office.*]

Afterwards

Oral Questions to the Secretary of State for Culture, Media and Sport

1 **Mr William Shakespeare** (Stratford upon Avon): What plans she has to celebrate the 23rd April as a national holiday; and if she will make a statement. [R]

2 **Mr William Wordsworth** (Cumbria): If she will increase the stipend of the poet laureate. [R]

3 **Mr Tom Eliot** (East Coker): What plans she has to improve the approach to the City via London Bridge by means of commissioning works of art. [R]

Notes: [R] *indicates that the Member has declared a relevant interest.*

Questions for oral answer not reached receive a written answer.
Supplementary questions will also be asked. Other Ministers may also answer.

FIGURE 32
EXAMPLE OF AN ORDER PAPER

15.1.7 On Mondays to Thursdays, the first item of business shown on the Order Paper is notices of motions, etc. relating to private business, if any have been set down for that day (see paragraph 7.3.1).

15.1.8 The next item on Mondays to Thursdays is the notices of questions for oral answer (see paragraphs 7.5.1 to 7.5.3, chapter 8 and Figure 23). At the end of questions a heading "At 12.30 pm" (or 3.30 pm on Mondays) indicates that urgent questions and statements *may* then be taken (see paragraphs 7.5.5, 7.5.7 and 7.6.3).

15.1.9 Notices of oral questions may be followed by a heading indicating notices of business to be taken under the terms of various standing orders "*at the commencement of public business*", called "Preliminary Business" in the Order Paper (see section 7.7 and Figure 32). These will be in the order: notices of presentation of bills; business motions relating to business to be taken later that day; various kinds of motions to be put forthwith (see paragraph 7.7.7 and Figure 16); and notices of motions for leave to bring in a bill under the ten minute rule (see paragraphs 7.7.8 to 7.7.13, 11.3.5 to 11.3.10 and Figure 33). It would be very rare for all these categories of business to appear on any one day, and on some days (especially Fridays) there will be no business in this category. If there is a motion on the Paper to suspend the **moment of interruption**, a note drawing attention to this will be placed here.

15.1.10 The next section is headed "Main Business" and contains the *orders of the day and notices of motions* as the standing orders call them (see section 7.8 and Figure 33). Under this are listed the main items of business to be taken at that day's sitting. Government business is distinguished by a dagger mark next to its title. Under titles of notices of motions there will be the names of the Members proposing that motion.

15.1.11 Among the main business there may appear an item headed "At 10 pm", or "At 7pm" on Tuesdays and Wednesdays, or "At 6 pm" on Thursdays or, very rarely, "At 2.30 pm" on Fridays. This is the notice of a motion to be moved at the **moment of interruption** (see paragraphs 6.1.6 and 6.1.7 and Figure 33). Such motions exempt specified items of business set down for that day's sitting from the operation of the moment of interruption (see paragraph 7.10.4). These are positioned after the items of business to which they actually relate. A note after preliminary business draws attention to their existence. There may be italicised rubrics under some of the items of business indicating that the Question on them is to be decided without debate, or indicating time limits on debate or exemptions from time limits under specified standing orders or under business motions decided by the House on an earlier day (or which will be effective if the motion to suspend the **moment of interruption** is agreed to).

15.1.12 At the end of all the items of main business for that day is an item headed "At the end of the sitting", giving the name of the Member chosen to speak in the daily adjournment debate and the nature of the subject to be raised (see section 7.12 and Figure 33).

At 12.30 p.m. Urgent Questions (if any)
Ministerial Statements (if any)

Preliminary Business

Notice of Presentation of Bill

† 1 *OUTLAWRIES* ***[No debate]***

Mr Secretary Canning

Bill to provide for the more effective prevention of clandestine outlawries; and for connected purposes.

Formal first reading: no debate or decision.

† 2 *DELEGATED LEGISLATION* ***[No debate]***

Mr William Wordsworth

That the Stratford on Avon (transfer of Sites of National Interest) Order 2002 (S.I., 2002, No 23) be referenced to a Standing Committee on Delegated Legislation.

To be decided without debate (Standing Order No. 118(4)).

Ten minute rule Motion

† 3 *BANK HOLIDAY (23RD APRIL)* ***[Up to 20 minutes]***

Mr William Shakespeare

That leave be given to bring in a Bill to establish a national holiday in England on the Monday nearest to 23rd April.

The Member moving and a Member opposing this Motion may each speak for up to ten minutes (Standing Order No. 23).

Note: Provision has been made for a Business Motion to be moved at 7 p.m. (Standing Order No 15).

Main Business

† 4 LOCAL GOVERNMENT BILL: Second Reading ***[Until any hour]***

Debate may continue to any hour if the 10 p.m. Business Motion is agreed to.

† BUSINESS OF THE HOUSE ***[No debate]***

The Prime Minister

That at this day's sitting, the Local Government Bill may be proceeded with, though opposed, until any hour.

To be decided without debate (Standing Order No. 15).

At the end of the sitting

5 ADJOURNMENT

Proposed subject: ***Future of the Globe Theatre, Southwark*** *(Mr Richard Burbage)*

Debate may continue until 7.30 p.m. or for half an hour, whichever is later (Standing order No. 9).

---

† *Indicates Government business.*
Timings are indicative only.

FIGURE 33

EXAMPLE OF AN ORDER PAPER FOR BUSINESS TAKEN AFTER QUESTIONS

Committee notices

15.1.13 Following the main business, there is a list of the standing, select and joint committees meeting that day, if any. These may be followed by a section headed "Standing Committee Notices", giving details of standing committees which are to meet in the following week. This generally appears on a Thursday, but may appear at other times.

Written statements

15.1.14 At the end of the items covering the day's agenda in the Chamber and in committees, there may be a section listing the written statements to be made by Ministers on that day. Written statements, introduced in 2003, replace the former practice of making such announcements by way of "planted" PQs.

Future Business

15.1.15 Following these comes a section headed "Future Business" (see Figure 34). It is divided into five sections (A, B, C, D and E). The first of these is a list of the business which the **Leader of the House** has announced in the previous **Business Statement** is to take place on subsequent days of the week and the week following (where this is known) set out day by day. Some of these items may re-appear in the Remaining Orders.

15.1.16 The second section, B, is a list of the business to be taken at sittings in Westminster Hall (see section 6.3) over the next two sitting weeks. Where these are timed adjournment debates, the timed slots with the name of the Member who is leading the debate and the subject matter are listed.

15.1.17 The third section of future business, C, is headed *Remaining Orders and Notices*. Strictly speaking, the remaining orders are part of the day's Orders and Notices. In fact, the items on the remaining orders are in practice a waiting list of government business which will, on some future day, be put on the effective orders. These may include items which are listed in the section A. For example, government bills which are set down for "tomorrow" appear on the remaining orders. There they may sit, re-appearing each "tomorrow", for many days or weeks, until the government chooses to put them on the effective orders. Another large category of items which appear on the remaining orders are motions to approve various statutory instruments subject to the affirmative resolution procedure (see paragraphs 12.3.10 to 12.3.14). The remaining orders are a useful source of information on upcoming government business, but they continue to have notional status as part of the orders of the day.

15.1.18 Occasionally, private Members will place notices of motions on the remaining orders rather than among the early day motions (see chapter 16), or a private Member's bill which has for some reason not been set down for a private Member's Friday but instead for "tomorrow" will appear among them. Some of these items will appear in due course on the effective orders: for example, motions in the name of the Second Church Estates Commissioner relating to Church of England Measures (see paragraph 12.1.10) or motions in the names of the trustees relating to Members' pensions.

15.1.19 Because the remaining orders are part of the orders of the day, it would in theory be possible to proceed through them as unopposed business (see paragraphs 7.10.2 and 7.10.3) at the end of the day's effective orders (and indeed this has been done). In practice, however, this does not happen, except in extremely abnormal circumstances.

15.1.20 After the Remaining Orders, the fourth section of future business, D, is a list of other business set down for specific future days, sometimes well into the future, listed chronologically. These will mainly be private Members' bills and notices of presentation or for leave to bring in such bills (see section 11.3).

15.1.21 The final section of the future business part, E, lists notices of written ministerial statements (see paragraph 8.3.9) to be made on future days. Notice of these may be given up to five days in advance, but in practice, these are more often announced on the main Order Paper (see paragraph 15.1.14 above) only on the day they are to be made.

15.1.22 On Tuesdays, Wednesdays and Thursdays, future business will be followed by the Order Paper for the day's sitting in Westminster Hall. (On a day following a sitting in Westminster Hall (see section 6.3), a minute of that sitting appears, see below.) At the end of all these, there is a list of the various constituent sections of the Vote Bundle which are published on that day (effectively a table of contents for the remainder of the bundle).

The Votes and Proceedings

15.1.23 The next most important section of the Bundle is the *Votes and Proceedings* (the "Vote"), after which the whole is named (see Figure 35). This is essentially a minute of the previous day's sitting of the House. It records the fate of the various items of business taken at the sitting, and also records the various matters reported to the House from different sources. It is not a minute in the sense generally recognised in the world at large: it contains no summary of views expressed or speeches delivered but is a record only of decisions and reports, that is of matters of fact in the narrowest sense.

15.1.24 The Vote includes appendices (see Figure 36), of which there may be as many as three. They are: the list of papers laid before the House (Accounts and Papers); the lists of Members nominated to standing committees by the **Committee of Selection** (see section 2.4); and the list of matters reported from select committees. The first of these appears almost invariably in each issue, the other two more irregularly.

15.1.25 The appendices to the Vote show written reports and papers deposited in the **Journal Office**, rather than things done in the House. There are other entries describing actions which do not in fact take place on the floor of the House but which nonetheless appear in the body of the Vote. These include reports from standing committees on bills (see paragraph 11.10.29), from standing committees on delegated legislation (see paragraphs 12.3.29, 12.4.8 and 12.4.10) and from European standing committees (see paragraph 13.2.15). An entry such as this is known as a "book entry", that is an entry in the Vote which records a proceeding which occurs without any visible proceedings on the floor of the House. For example, the Member in charge of a bill may defer a date for any of its stages or withdraw the bill by means of a book entry (see paragraph 11.2.7).

100 **1127**

House of Commons

Wednesday 29th February 2002

Future Business

A. **Business for the period ending on Monday 3rd March**
This section includes the business announced by the Leader of the House (which may be changed up to the rising of the House on the day before it is to be taken and is therefore provisional).

B. **Business to be taken at sittings in Westminster Hall**

C. **Remaining Orders and Notices**
This section consists of items of business set down *formally* for today but not expected to be taken today. (These may include items included in the business statement and therefore listed in part A.).

D. **Other future business**
This section consists of items of business set down for specific days after Thursday 30th February.

E. **Notices of Written Ministerial Statements**
This section consists of notices of Ministerial Statements to be made in writing on the days indicated.

A
Business for the period ending on Monday 3rd March

Includes the business announced by the leader of the house (which may be changed up to the rising of the House on the day before it is to be taken and is therefore provisional).

Thursday 30th February

- ◆ Questions to the Chancellor of the Exchequer.
- ◆ Second Reading of the Knives Bill.
- ◆ At the end of the sitting: Adjournment: Support for the theatre from public funds (Mr John Osborne).

B
Business to be taken in Westminster Hall

Wednesday 24th April

Subjects proposed to be raised on the Motion for the Adjournment:

9.30 a.m. - 11.00 a.m. Rev Colly Cibber Alcohol abuse.

11.00 a.m. - 11.30 p.m. Richard Burbage Funding and management of London Theatres

The sitting will be suspended from 11.30 a.m to 2.00 p.m.

2.00 p.m. - 3.30 p.m. Mr Bellingham Security arrangements in the House of Commons

3.30 p.m. - 4.00 p.m. Aphra Benn Disclosure of previous sexual history in rape trials

4.00 p.m. - 4.30 p.m. Mr George Chapman Case of Mr John Keats

Thursday 25th April

- ◆ Debate on the Second Report from the Culture, Media and Sport Committee on the National Theatre, Session 2001–02, HC 555

C
Remaining Orders and Notices

Consists of business set down formally *for today but not expected to be taken today. (These may include items included in the business statement and therefore listed in part A above.).*

4 KNIVES BILL: Second Reading

5 KNIVES BILL *[MONEY]: Queen's Recommendation signified*
Mr Kit Marlow
That, for the purposes of any Act resulting from the Knives Bill, it is expedient to authorise any increase in the sums payable into the Consolidated Fund resulting from the imposition of charges for licences for the carrying of knives.

D
Any future business

The following list consists of items of business set down for specific days after Thursday 30th February.

Monday 3rd March

- ◆ At the end of the sitting: Adjournment: Melancholia (Mr Robert Burton).

FIGURE 34
EXAMPLE OF FUTURE BUSINESS

No. 87 **666**

House of Commons
Wednesday 29th February 2002
Votes and Proceedings

The House met a half-past Eleven o'clock.

PRAYERS.

1 Land at the Globe Theatre, Southwark (Acquisition of Freehold) Bill, – The Order of the day being read, for further consideration of the Land at the Globe Theatre, Southwark (Acquisition of Freehold) Bill, as amended by the Chairman of Ways and Means;

Ordered, That the Bill be further considered on Monday 15th April at Seven o'clock.

2 First Standing Committee on Delegated Legislation, – Miss Aphra Benn reported from the First Standing Committee on Delegated Legislation the draft Actors' Support (Miscellaneous Amendments) Regulations 2002.

Minutes of Proceedings of the Committee to lie upon the Table.

3 Housing (Retired Thespians) Bill, – Mr Richard Burbage reported from Standing Committee C, That is had gone through the Housnig (Retired Thespians Bill) and made amendments thereunto.

Bill, as amended in the Standing Committee, to be considered on Friday 31st April; and to printed [Bill 444].

Minutes of Proceedings of the Committee to lie upon the Table, and to be printed [888].

4 Child Actors (Safeguards for Unaccompanied Travel), – *Ordered*, That leave be given to bring in a Bill to make provision to safeguard the welfare of child actors travelling to the United Kingdom without their parents: And that Mr William Shakespeare, Mr Ben Jonson, Mr Kit Marlowe and Dame Merry Windsor do prepare and bring it in.

5 Child Actors (Safeguards for Unaccompanied Travel) Bill, – Mr William Shakespeare accordingly presented a Bill to make provision to safeguard the welfare of child actors travelling to the United Kingdom without their parents: And the same was read the first time; and ordered to be read a second time on Friday 19th July and to be printed [Bill 117].

6 National Theatre Bill, – The National Theatre Bill was, according to Order, read a second time.

7 Public Petitions, – A Public Petition from women of the United Kingdom for the outlawing of the playing of women characters by male actors in theatrical performances was presented and read; and ordered to lie upon the Table and to be printed.

8 Adjournment, – A Motion was made, and the Question being proposed, That this House do now adjourn – (*Angela Smith*);

And the Motion having been made after Seven o'clock, and the Debate having continued for half an hour, the Speaker adjourned the House without Question put, pursuant to the Standing Order, it being then twelve minutes to Eight, till to-morrow.

[Adjourned at 7.48 p.m.]

FIGURE 35
EXAMPLE OF VOTES AND PROCEEDINGS

15.1.26 Appendix I (see Figure 36) records all the papers laid before or presented to the House on the previous day. Statutory instruments, categorised under affirmative or negative resolution (see paragraph 12.1.6) appear first, followed by other papers. These include other statutory instruments (not subject to either affirmative or negative procedure) as well as Act Papers or Command Papers, which are described in paragraphs 15.3.1 to 15.3.3 below.

APPENDIX I

Papers presented or laid upon the Table:

Papers subject to Affirmative Resolution:

1 National Heritage,—Draft Places of Historic Interest (Designation Procedures) Regulations 2003 [by Act] [Mr Secretary Cromwell].

Papers subject to Negative Resolution:

2 Licensing,—Licensing Magistrates (Composition of Appeal Boards) Order 2003 (S.I., 2003, No. 333), dated 31st January 2003 [by Act] [Secretary Sir Thomas More].

Other Papers:

3 Senior Salaries,—Twentieth Report of the Review Body on Senior Salaries [by Command] [Cm. 6060] [The Prime Minister].

APPENDIX II

Standing Committees

1 Knives Bill

(1) The Speaker has allocated the Bill to Standing Committee C and appointed Mr Charles James Fox and Mr William Pitt Chairmen; and

(2) The Committee of Selection has appointed sixteen Members to serve on Standing Committee C in respect of the Knives Bill, viz.: Miss Jane Austen, Ms Charlotte Bronte, Mr Robert Browning, Fanny Burney, Mr S. T. Coleridge, Mr Wilkie Collins, Mr Charles Dickens, Mr George Eliot, Mrs Elizabeth Gaskell, Mr James Hogg, The Reverend Charles Kingsley, Mr Charles Lamb, Sir Walter Scott, Mr Bob Southey, Mr Robert L. Stevenson and Mr William Wordsworth.

APPENDIX III

Reports from Select Committees

1 Culture, Media and Sport,—First Report from the Culture, Media and Sport Committee [Designation of Places of Historic Interest], together with Appendices to the Minutes of Evidence taken before the Committee, to be printed, with the Minutes of Proceedings of the Committee relating to the Report [No. 33-I and II] [Mr William Shakespeare].

FIGURE 36
EXAMPLE OF APPENDICES TO VOTES AND PROCEEDINGS

15.1.27 If there is a report from the **Committee of Selection** (see section 2.4) or other matters relating to **standing committees**, they will appear as Appendix II (see Figure 27). This will generally consist of details of the Speaker's allocation of bills to committees and the appointment of chairmen and lists of the Members appointed to standing committees on bills or on delegated legislation. There may also be additional Members appointed to the Welsh and Northern Ireland Grand Committees (see sections 14.4 and 14.5). Occasionally, changes to previously notified appointments will appear. Since the Committee of Selection meets regularly on Wednesdays, this Appendix appears most often in the Vote published on a Thursday.

15.1.28 Appendix III (or sometimes II) lists matters reported on the day in question from select committees. These will be either minutes of evidence or reports (see paragraph 17.1.13 to 17.1.19 and Figure 36).

15.1.29 At the end of the Votes and Proceedings, there may be memoranda relating to the decisions of the Speaker (for example to certify a bill as a money bill, see paragraph 10.2.15, or as relating exclusively to Scotland, see paragraph 11.6.14). The minute of proceedings in Westminster Hall (see section 6.3) will also be published as an Appendix to the Votes and Proceedings.

Petitions, etc

15.1.30 Public petitions, and observations upon them by Ministers, are printed as supplements to the Votes and Proceedings (see chapter 19).

Lists

15.1.31 In the Bundle issued on a Saturday but generally seen on a Monday (or the day after the House rises for one of its breaks) the Public Bill List and the European Community Document List (see paragraph 13.2.6) are included. On Wednesdays, the Bundle includes the list of regulatory reform proposals and draft orders (see paragraph 12.4.14). The Statutory Instrument List (see paragraph 12.3.4) is published on Saturdays but, although technically part of the Bundle, it is made available separately.

Amendment papers and standing committee proceedings

15.1.32 The remaining white pages in the Bundle (if any) will consist of marshalled amendment papers for bills being considered in the House or in standing committee on the day in question (see paragraphs 11.9.8 to 11.9.11 and Figure 25), or of the record of proceedings on bills which were considered in standing committees on the previous day (see paragraph 11.10.27). Notices of motions to be considered by one or more of the European standing committees on the day in question are also included (see paragraph 13.2.12).

Grand Committee order papers

15.1.33 The Order Papers for meetings of the Scottish, Welsh and Northern Ireland Grand Committees and the Standing committee on Regional Affairs are printed in separate series, and are included in the Bundle on days on which one or other of the committees are meeting (see chapter 14).

No. 13 **345**

House of Commons
Notices of Questions given on
Wednesday 29th February 2003

MONDAY 4th MARCH

1 **Mr William Shakespeare** (Stratford upon Avon): To ask the Secretary of State for Transport,
N what steps he is taking to discourage the use of private cars. *[Transferred]*

2 **Mr William Wordsworth** (Cumberland): To ask the Secretary of State for Transport, what representations he has received concerning the Ribble Viaduct.

WEDNESDAY 14th MARCH

NOTE

★ *Indicates a Question for Oral Answer*
† *Indicates a Question which was included in the random selection process. The number shows where the Question appeared in the selection.*

Questions to the Prime Minister will start at 12 noon

★3 **Mr Bob Southey** (Camden North): To ask the Secretary of State for Social Security what was the pensioners' Christmas bonus in each of the last ten years.

****

★1 **Mrs Elizabeth Gaskell** (North and South): To ask the Prime Minister, if he will list his official engagements for Wednesday 14th March.

NOTE: Questions marked thus ★ are for oral answer. Questions marked **N** *are for written answer on a named day under S.O. No. 22(4). Questions marked thus* **[R]** *indicate that a relevant registered interest has been declared.*

FIGURE 37
EXAMPLE OF NOTICES OF QUESTIONS

Notices of questions

15.1.34 The first section of the blue pages is the notices of questions for written or oral answer given on the previous day. These are arranged by date for answer, and within each day in roughly alphabetical order of department to which they are addressed (see paragraphs 8.21 and 8.22 and Figure 37).

House of Commons

Wednesday 30th February 2003

Notices of Motions for which no days have been fixed ('Early Day Motions')

NOTICES OF MOTIONS FOR WHICH NO DAYS HAVE BEEN FIXED ('EARLY DAY MOTIONS')

★The figure following this symbol is the total number of Members' names submitted in support of the Motion, including names printed for the first time in this paper.

After the initial printing, Motions are reprinted only when names are added or amendments are submitted; only the first six names and any names added since the last printing are listed. After the week in which a Motion is submitted and the following week, added names and amendments appear only in the paper distributed on the next Thursday. In the meantime they are available for inspection by Members in the Table Office and the Library.

2 *SUPPORT FOR DRAMA* **16:1:03**

Mr William Shakespeare
Mr Beaumont Fletcher
Mr John Webster
Mr Kit Marlow
Mr Benedict Jonson
Mrs Aphra Benn **★52**
Mr John Osborne

That this House believes that the policy of Her Majesty's Government towards support for the theatre from public funds should be reviewed.

3 *LICENSING (S.I., 2003, No. 333)* **30:2:03**

Mr William Wordsworth
Sir Walter Scott **★2**

That an humble Address be presented to Her Majesty, praying that the Licensing Magistrates (Composition of Appeal Boards) Order 2003 (S.I., 2003, No. 333), dated 31st January 2003, a copy of which was laid before this House on 28th February 2003, be annulled.

FIGURE 38
EXAMPLE OF EARLY DAY MOTIONS

Private business

15.1.35 There is a separate series of notice papers relating to **private business** (see section 11.19). This includes notices of motions which are to appear on the Order Paper on future days.

Early Day Motions

15.1.36 The blue notices of early day motions, which come next in the Bundle, are described in chapter 16 (see also Figure 38). For the particular distinction between the Notice Paper published on Thursdays and those published on other days of the week, see paragraph 16.3.6.

Notices of amendments, etc

15.1.37 The Bundle also includes in the blue pages *notices of amendments* tabled on the previous day to bills which are being considered in the House or in standing committee on a future day. For a fuller description, see paragraphs 11.9.2 to 11.9.7.

15.1.38 Notices of motions to be moved in one or other of the European standing committees (see paragraph 13.2.12) in the following week are also published in the blue pages.

The Questions Book

15.1.39 Each sitting day a Question Book is published in two parts. Part 1 lists the questions set down for written answer on that day and Part 2 lists all outstanding notices of questions for future days, arranged day by day.

15.1.40 The Scottish, Welsh and Northern Ireland Grand Committees have separate order books setting out their future business (see chapter 14), which are updated as the need arises. These are available from the **Vote Office** on request.

15.2 THE JOURNAL

15.2.1 The Journal of the House of Commons is the permanent record of its decisions. In its modern form it is essentially a consolidated and corrected version of the Votes and Proceedings, published for each session in a bound form. The Journal is also indexed. The Index is divided into two parts, the first recording all the papers laid before the House in the Session, the second part being a mixture of a procedural and subject matter index. This second part is consolidated into a decennial index for each decade, published some two or three years after the last session of the decade.

15.2.2 The earliest Journal dates from 1547. With a few gaps (particularly 1584 to 1601) and some uncertainties in the seventeenth century, the series is continuous to the present day.

15.3 OTHER PAPERS

Act Papers

15.3.1 Many Acts of Parliament require papers to be laid before Parliament. These include statutory instruments (see chapter 12) as well as annual reports and accounts of various bodies and other documents. All papers required to be laid before Parliament by Act have their delivery recorded in the Appendix to the Votes and Proceedings (see paragraph 15.1.25 above and Figure 25). Some of them will be ordered to be printed in the House of Commons series (see paragraphs 15.3.2 to 15.3.4 below).

House of Commons Papers

15.3.2 Any paper (other than a bill, for which see below) which is ordered to be printed by the House will receive a number in a sessional series. These House of Commons papers are known by this HC number, eg "HC 17". They include papers laid under various Acts (see preceding paragraph): the minutes of evidence and reports of select committees (see chapter 17); the **Resource Estimates** (see section 10.3); the **Resource Accounts** (see paragraph 10.4.5); and the *minutes of proceedings* of various of the House's committees.

Command Papers

15.3.3 Where there is no explicit statutory provision for a Minister to lay a certain type of document before the House, but he wishes to do so, he presents the paper by Command of Her Majesty. This is, in effect, a minor example of the exercise of the royal prerogative. Such papers include "White Papers" (proposals for legislation), certain "Green Papers" (discussion and consultation documents) and the texts of new treaties and international agreements, as well as miscellaneous other documents. These papers are known as Command Papers. They are numbered in consecutive series, each indicated by a prefix which is an abbreviation of the word Command (Cmd, Cmnd, etc), each series running from 1 to 9999. The current series is Cm. All papers presented in this manner are recorded in the Appendix to the Vote (see paragraph 15.1.25 above and Figure 27). Under S.O. No. 158, such papers may be presented to Parliament even on days when neither House is sitting.

Bills

15.3.4 When the House orders a bill to be printed (see paragraphs 11.5.2 to 11.5.7), it is given a number in a sessional bill series, running from "[Bill 1]". Explanatory Notes to Bills (see paragraph 11.5.5) are published in a parallel series (EN 1 etc.). When a bill is reported from a committee with amendments, the House orders it to be reprinted as amended, and the new version of the bill is given a new Bill number (see paragraphs 11.5.7 and Figure 35). Lords Amendments to Commons bills are also printed in the bill series.

Other papers

15.3.5 If a paper is not a bill, and there is no statutory authority for it to be laid before the House, it cannot officially be brought before the House except as a command paper (see paragraph 15.3.3 above), unless it is as a return to an order (see section 7.4). However, Ministers make numerous other documents available to the House, either by placing them in the Library or making them available in the **Vote Office**. Such documents might include pamphlets made available to the general public, consultation documents, draft bills or whatever. Such documents may only be made available to Members in this way by Ministers; there is no provision for private Members to do so. Such documents do not have an official parliamentary status and are not protected by parliamentary privilege (see paragraph 4.2.5)

15.4 HANSARD

Introduction

15.4.1 Hansard, more formally known as the Official Report, has been on an official footing for a century. Its production is the responsibility of a separate department of the House presided over by the **Editor**.

15.4.2 In essence, the official report is an edited verbatim record of what is said in debate or other proceedings of the House (including Westminster Hall) or its standing committees. It includes procedural material, though the official and conclusive record of the decisions of the House is the Journal (see section 15.2 above).

Daily parts

15.4.3 On the day after each day on which the House has sat, a daily edition of Hansard is published. This contains, generally, the full record of the previous day's proceedings from Prayers to the adjournment of the House. When the House has sat exceptionally late, the last parts of the proceedings may have to be held over to the next daily part. The report of proceedings in **Westminster Hall** is also published in the daily part, numbered in a separate pagination series (WH 1 etc.) After the record of what was said in the House and in Westminster Hall there follows the separately numbered columns of written statements (see paragraph 11.1.13) and written answers (see paragraphs 8.23 and 8.24) to PQs which were made on the previous day, set out by department. These answers have more frequently, due to pressure of time or space, to be held over to a subsequent daily part.

Weekly edition

15.4.4 Each week's set of daily parts are subsequently reissued as weekly volumes. These simply contain the daily parts bound together, without correction or rearrangement.

Bound volumes

15.4.5 Some considerable time after the issue of the weekly volumes, the hard-bound volumes are issued. These may incorporate corrections made by the Editor to the daily parts. These corrections may be made at the instigation of Members or departments, but the Editor's decision whether to incorporate them is final. In the bound volumes the record of the House's proceedings and proceedings in Westminster Hall are separated out from the columns of written statements and written answers, which are bound after the debates. Each bound volume generally covers about a fortnight's business.

Division lists

15.4.6 The lists of Members voting in either lobby in divisions are printed in Hansard (and may be corrected in the bound volumes). Consolidated, bound and corrected versions of these lists are also kept as a separate series in the Library.

Standing committees

15.4.7 An Official Report is also produced of the proceedings of all standing committees. The daily parts of these are generally published the day following each sitting of the committee. These are not formally reprinted in the way that the Official Report of the House's proceedings are, but bound sets of the parts for all the sittings relating to each Bill are published separately, and sets are of course kept in the **Library**. In the case of the grand committees (see chapter 14), the Official Reports of sittings at which oral questions were taken include written answers to those questions which were not reached in the time available. For the record of public proceedings of select committees, see paragraphs 17.1.15 to 17.1.19.

15.5 Parliament on the Web

15.5.1 Nowadays, almost all the publications referred to above can be found on the House of Commons section on Parliament's website at www.parliament.uk. The publications include the main contents of the Vote Bundle, including the Order Paper and Questions Books, Votes and Proceedings, Early Day Motions and the various lists referred to above. The Hansard reports of debates and answers to both written and oral questions in the House, and debates in Westminster Hall and all standing committees are also available. These are searchable.

15.5.2 All reports published by the House's select committees are on the website on the day of publication. Transcripts of oral evidence sessions with Ministers held by select committees are often published a day or two later in uncorrected form, and transcripts of evidence taken from other witnesses are published in corrected or uncorrected form on the web.

15.5.3 The website also contains links to Her Majesty's Stationery Office's (HMSO) website (www.hmso.gov.uk), on which the full texts of Acts and statutory instruments can be found. The Stationery Office (TSO) website (www.thestationeryoffice.com/) will also give access to other official publications such as command papers and can lead to the texts of many government publications on departmental websites.

15.6 THE VOTE OFFICE, ETC

The Vote Office

15.6.1 The core function of the Vote Office is, as its name implies, the distribution of the Vote Bundle, supervised by the Deliverer of the Vote and his deputies. However, it is also responsible for the distribution of all the parliamentary papers described in the preceding sections, and all the European Community Documents described in chapter 13.

15.6.2 The main Vote Office is located at basement level, below the Members' Lobby. In the Lobby itself there is an outlet for the use of Members and Officers of the House. It also has outlets in the outbuildings of the House. The European Section of the Vote Office is situated in the Norman Shaw North Building.

The Library

15.6.3 Copies of all papers laid before or presented to the House are also placed in the Library, where they are available for inspection. The Library holds series of Command Papers, House of Commons Papers and most Act Papers from time immemorial (which for present purposes is probably the mid-nineteenth century). The Library will also have copies of those papers informally presented to the House by Ministers (see paragraph 15.3.5 above).

The Parliamentary Bookshop

15.6.4 Under the aegis of the Vote Office, there is a parliamentary bookshop serving the general public, and others who wish to purchase copies of parliamentary papers, situated on the corner of Parliament Street and Bridge Street, just across from the main entrance to the Commons. Copies of all current parliamentary and government papers can be purchased from it, as well as many other publications relevant to Parliament, including this book.

Chapter 16
EARLY DAY MOTIONS

16.1 INTRODUCTION

16.1.1 There is no opportunity provided under the standing orders for private Members to have motions in their names appear on the **Order Paper** and be debated by the House (except in the very unusual circumstances of the government choosing to give time for such a motion to be debated). The exceptions to this general rule are motions in the names of leaders of opposition parties on **opposition days** (see paragraphs 2.2.2 and 2.2.3) and "prayers" against statutory instruments (see paragraphs 12.3.16 to 12.3.18). Every Member, however, has the right to give notice of motions on subjects on which they wish to express an opinion.

16.1.2 The way in which this is done is to table a notice of motion for which no day has been fixed for debate. By these means Members may give publicity to issues which concern them or express an opinion for which they seek the public support of their colleagues. These motions, which are printed each day in a separate section of the **Notice Paper**, are known as *Early Day Motions* (EDMs) (see Figure 38). In an average session over a thousand such motions are tabled.

16.2 RULES FOR THE CONTENT OF EDMS

16.2.1 A motion must be expressed in the form of a resolution. This means that it must begin with the word "That" and be in the form of a single sentence. The Speaker has ruled that an EDM may be no more than 250 words long.

16.2.2 A motion must conform with the House's rules of order (see paragraphs 9.3.13 to 9.3.20). It must be couched in parliamentary language, may not attack the House's actions or reflect on decisions of the Commons or Lords, or call into question the motives of honourable Members in an unparliamentary way (but see paragraph 9.3.21).

16.2.3 The sub-judice rule applies to motions (see paragraph 9.3.16 and Figure 20).

16.2.4 Motions should not consist of an undue proportion of direct quotation from other documents, or be designed merely to write into the proceedings of the House the content of speeches made outside it or the contents of unofficial publications such as newspaper articles.

16.2.5 Paragraphs 9.3.18 to 9.3.20 detail a number of matters which may only be raised by way of substantive motion. Such matters cannot be raised as an incidental part of a wider motion or by way of amendments proposed to other motions.

16.2.6 It is not in order to table a motion on a subject that is not a suitable matter for debate, or the purpose of which is merely to irritate, or which is tendered in a spirit of mockery or irony. The Speaker has deprecated attempts to conduct a campaign by the tabling of multiple motions on the same subject or versions of essentially the same motion multiplied with slight variations, and has on occasion ordered their removal from the notice paper.

16.3 NOTICES OF EDMS

16.3.1 Notice of an EDM must be given to the **Table Office** (see paragraph 1.3.2). It must be in writing, and must bear the signature of at least one Member. If a Member gives instructions to add the names of other Members to a motion when printed, he or she should have their express authority to do so. A Member who has a registrable interest in relation to a motion (see paragraph 4.3.7) must give an indication of this.

16.3.2 Each motion should have a title which is strictly descriptive and which is not argumentative or in the form of a slogan.

16.3.3 Amendments may be tabled to any EDM. These must conform to the rules set out above relating to the contents of motions, including that on word length.

Adding of names

16.3.4 Members may indicate their support for an EDM by adding their names to it. This is done by sending (or delivering) a signed copy of the motion or a signed note indicating the number or numbers of motions to which a name is to be added to the **Table Office**. The names of supporters of a motion are published as described below.

16.3.5 A Member cannot add his or her name in support of both the main motion and an amendment proposed to it. If after signing the main motion a Member adds his or her name in support of an amendment to that motion, the Table Office will automatically withdraw the name from the main motion and a notice to this effect will be printed in the notice paper.

Printing of motions

16.3.6 On the day after the text of an EDM has been tabled, it is published in the blue notice paper, together with a list of the names of Members who have added their names in support of it (see Figure 36). Against the name of any Member who has declared an interest in relation to an EDM (see paragraph 4.3.7) an "[R]" is printed. During the week in which it was tabled and that following, the motion will be reprinted in the blue notice paper on any day following one on which a further Member or Members have added their names in support of it. After that, the motion will be reprinted on a Thursday if any names have been added during the previous week. After its first appearance, only the names of the first six Members to put their names to the motion plus those of any who have added their names since its previous appearance are printed in the notice paper. Printed in the margin beside the motion is the figure for the total number of Members who have added their names in support of it. A full list of all Members who have added their names to any particular motion is available on a computer printout from the **Library**, the **Table Office** or the House of Commons **Information Office**, or through the parliamentary website.

16.3.7 The EDMs are numbered in order of tabling in a sequence running throughout the session. Each motion may continue to be reprinted on any Thursday up to the end of the session if any names have been added in support of it since its last printing.

16.3.8 If an amendment is tabled to an EDM it will be printed (together with the main motion) on the following day.

16.3.9 A Member may at any time give instructions for his or her name to be withdrawn from a notice of an EDM or an amendment proposed to an EDM, and a note to this effect will be published in the notice paper. The Member in charge of an EDM, that is the one whose name appears first in the list of supporters, may at any time withdraw the motion, with or without the consent of the other signatories. A notice of withdrawal is printed in the **notice paper**.

Chapter 17

SELECT COMMITTEES AND JOINT COMMITTEES

17.1 GENERAL

Introduction

17.1.1 A general outline of the select committee system is given in paragraphs 2.3.4 to 2.3.10. The method of election and role of chairmen of select committees is described in section 3.4.

17.1.2 Certain select committees are dealt with elsewhere than in this section. The *Liaison Committee* is described in section 3.5. The *Committee on Standards and Privileges* is described in section 4.1. The *Public Accounts Committee* is described in section 10.5. Select committees on public bills are described in paragraphs 11.1.3, 11.1.5, 11.11.10 and 11.11.11. The *Regulatory Reform Committee* is described in section 12.4. The *European Scrutiny Committee* is described in paragraphs 13.2.2 to 13.2.5. The committees concerned in the running of the House are described in chapter 18.

17.1.3 This section begins by describing the general powers and functions of select committees. The particular characteristics of the departmentally-related select committees are described in section 17.2. The *Committee on Public Administration* and the *Environmental Audit Committee* are described in section 17.3, the *Procedure Committee* (and *Modernisation Committee*) in section 17.4. Joint Committees are described in general terms in section 17.5 below, which refers to where some of these are discussed in more detail. The *Joint Committee on Human Rights* is described in some detail in that section.

Meetings

17.1.4 The general arrangements for meetings of select committees are described in paragraphs 6.2.8 to 6.2.10. Under paragraph (3) of S.O. No. 124, a select committee cannot proceed unless a quorum of its members is present. Under paragraph (1) of that standing order the quorum of a select committee is defined as three or a quarter of its members (with fractions rounded up), whichever is the greater, unless its order of appointment specifies some other figure.

17.1.5 Select committees have essentially three functions: to take evidence from witnesses; to "deliberate" (that is to discuss matters in private and make decisions about what they wish to do); and to agree reports. They do not debate, and other than the verbatim record of their formal cross-examination of witnesses and the relatively uninformative minutes of the formal decisions which they take, their activities are conducted in private and should remain private. Under S.O. No. 125, select committees may choose to admit the public to their meetings during the examination of witnesses. In practice they all do this as a matter of course, and generally pass a resolution to this effect at the beginning of each session. They may occasionally resolve to take evidence in private, usually because confidential matters such as official secrets or commercially confidential information is being discussed. They have no power, however, to admit the public to their meetings at other times than when they are taking evidence.

17.1.6 Any Member of the House may, in theory, attend the private deliberative meetings of a select committee. In practice, this would be considered most unusual unless done at the invitation of the committee. S.O. No. 126 gives select committees power to direct any Member who is not a member of the committee to withdraw from its private meetings, and empowers the Serjeant at Arms, if requested by a committee to do so, to enforce such a direction.

Powers to compel evidence

17.1.7 The House has delegated to most select committees under standing orders or their order of appointment the power to send for persons, papers and records. In effect this grants them the power to request any person or body to attend a meeting of the committee to give evidence orally, to invite any person or body to submit evidence in writing or to require any person or body to submit specified documents to a committee. (S.O. No. 127 forbids the altering or withdrawal of any document received by a committee without its knowledge; however, a document cannot be assumed to have been received by a committee just because it has been sent to it.) Committees do not, however, have the power to compel Members of either House to give oral or written evidence, except in the case of the Committee on Standards and Privileges (see paragraph 4.1.3).

17.1.8 Those requested to give oral or written evidence or to submit documents to a committee will generally do so without demur. If a person were to refuse a request from a committee, it would in the first instance be for the committee to determine how far to press the issue. If the obstruction continued after the committee had agreed a resolution, which had been communicated to the relevant person, requesting attendance or evidence, the committee could seek to move a motion on the floor of the House in support of its demand. If that motion was agreed to by the House, continued obstruction would be a contempt of the House (see section 4.2)

17.1.9 Where a committee requests the attendance of witnesses from a government department, it is for the Minister in charge of the department to decide whether to attend in person or to send another Minister, or which officials to send to represent the department. The question of whether a committee can demand the attendance of named civil servants is something of a grey area.

17.1.10 Evidence given to a committee of the House is privileged, that is to say, in most circumstances those giving it are protected from action for defamation or other civil action in respect of their evidence. This protection is rather more clear cut for oral evidence than it is for written evidence. It is a contempt of the House (see section 4.2) to attempt to intimidate, suborn or otherwise improperly influence a witness before a committee of the House. It is also a contempt of the House to deliberately mislead or lie to one of its committees. Under S.O. No. 132, witnesses may be required to take an oath or make an affirmation before giving evidence. This is a very rare procedure among most select committees, though the Committee on Standards and Privileges has required witnesses before it to take the oath. Were a witness before a committee to refuse to answer any questions addressed to them, it would again be for the committee to decide how far to press the matter. For the style of public cross-examination of witnesses by select committees, see paragraphs 2.3.9 and 2.3.10. Most of the select committees described in this chapter (particularly the departmentally-related committees) take public evidence at the majority of their meetings.

Making reports

17.1.11 S.O. No. 133 gives powers to committees to report their opinions and observations on any matter within their terms of reference. All committees make frequent use of this power – it could indeed be said to be their *raison d'être*. Where a committee wishes to draw the attention of the House to a specific matter rather than make a general report (see, for example, paragraph 17.1.14 below) or some procedural matter has arisen in the course of their work which they need to draw to the attention of the House, they may make a special report to the House on the subject. A special report is also the vehicle regularly used to publish a government reply to a committee's report (see paragraph 17.2.9 below).

17.1.12 The process for agreeing a report is typically as follows. A committee may first discuss the general lines of the proposed report and its broad conclusions. The chairman will subsequently produce (with the assistance of the committee's staff) a preliminary draft report for the committee's consideration. This may be informally considered at one or more meetings, and the chairman may agree informally to amend it in line with the perceived consensus on the committee. Subsequently the chairman will present formally his or her draft report, and the committee agrees formally to consider it paragraph by paragraph. The procedure is broadly parallel to the clause by clause consideration of a bill in standing committee (see paragraphs 11.10.18 to 11.10.22): amendments may be proposed to a paragraph, debated, agreed, withdrawn or negatived and the paragraph (amended or not) agreed to as a whole. No notice is required of amendments and the chairman has no formal power of selection (see paragraph 11.10.10). At the conclusion of the paragraph by paragraph consideration the committee will decide whether to agree the report as a whole, and if it is agreed, the chairman will be directed to report it to the House, together with associated documents, if any. In practice, the "formal" consideration of a Chairman's draft report, which is always conducted in private, can be fairly informal in style when compared to consideration of a bill in standing committee.

17.1.13 When a report has been agreed, the committee orders the chairman to report it to the House and this is done by means of a **book entry** in the **Votes and Proceedings** (see paragraphs 15.1.24 and 15.1.27 and Figure 36). The House is then automatically deemed to have ordered it to be printed. There is usually a gap of some days between a report being recorded as laid before the House in the Votes and Proceedings and its being published. On occasions, a committee will delay making a report to the House until it is actually ready to be published. This is usually done to ensure that the unpublished report is not "leaked", and retains the full protection of parliamentary privilege until the last minute (see paragraph 17.1.14 below).

17.1.14 It is *prima facie* a contempt of the House to publish the contents of a committee's report before it has been reported to the House: to publish them between the date of their being reported to the House and their publication by the committee is a gross discourtesy. It is for a committee to decide what action to take in the event of such a breach of confidence. If the committee believes a contempt has been committed which has caused substantial interference in its work, it may cause the matter to be referred to the **Committee on Standards and Privileges** (see section 4.1 and paragraph 4.2.13) by making a *special report* to the House (see paragraphs 3.5.6 and 17.1.11) setting out the circumstances of the disclosure and the steps it has taken to investigate them. If it intends to do this, it is expected to consult the **Liaison Committee** (see section 3.5) first. A similar course might be taken if a committee believed that a witness had committed some contempt.

Publishing reports and evidence

17.1.15 The report of a committee will be published together with the formal minutes of its proceedings relating to the report, which will indicate where amendments were proposed to the draft report (if any) and by whom, and record any divisions the committee may have had at any stage during the process of considering and agreeing the draft report. S.O. No.134 permits the Clerk of a committee to arrange for embargoed copies of a committee's report to be supplied to government departments, witnesses and the press up to forty-eight hours in advance of the official publication time. All select committee reports and their associated evidence are published on the House of Commons website at www.parliament.uk, usually on the day of publication.

17.1.16 Under S.O. No. 135(1), each select committee has power to publish the oral and written evidence it has taken or received. The committees invariably exercise this power. Oral evidence may be published in daily parts relating to an inquiry. Each "daily part" will include the transcript of the oral examination of witnesses at one sitting, together with their written evidence (and perhaps other relevant written evidence). These daily parts are usually published some time after the evidence was taken. In the case of oral evidence taken from Ministers, and sometimes other witnesses, the transcript will be published on the individual committee's section of the parliamentary website (www.parliament.uk) within a day or two of the hearing. Each daily part will be reported in the Votes and Proceedings where it will be given an House of Commons (HC) number (see paragraph 15.3.2) for the publications relating to a particular inquiry, followed by a suffix to indicate each volume: eg HC 100-i, HC 100-ii and so on. Some committees choose not to publish these daily parts individually but to publish a collected volume of evidence along with their eventual report. Increasingly, committees are relying on the web publication of daily parts, with hard copies only available internally to the House. However, the current practice is that all such evidence, along with most of the written evidence, is published alongside any eventual report. On occasions, committees will take oral evidence and publish it as a freestanding daily part, without intending to publish a report arising from that evidence.

17.1.17 Items of written evidence submitted to a committee's inquiry are known as *Memoranda*, and these may be published with reports. Committees may also publish freestanding volumes of written evidence during the course of an inquiry, or may reserve the publication of memoranda to an evidence volume published together with the relevant report. A committee may choose not to publish all the memoranda submitted in the course of an inquiry but in some cases only to report them to the House. These unpublished items should be listed in the report, and then should be made available for inspection, in the **Library** by Members, and in the Public Record Office of the Lords by the general public.

17.1.18 Under S.O. No. 137, a committee may on its own account, when the House is not sitting (but not during prorogations or dissolutions), direct that any report or minutes of oral or written evidence should be published. Such evidence or reports are deemed to have been ordered to be printed by the House. Under S.O. No. 135(2), the Speaker may authorise the publication of evidence taken by a committee which no longer exists.

17.1.19 At the end of each session, each select committee publishes a volume of its formal minutes, which record the formal decisions made by the committee in its private meetings.

Committees working together

17.1.20 Under S.O. No. 137A, any committee which enjoys the power to send for persons, papers and records (which in practice means almost every select committee), and any sub-committee of such a committee, has certain powers which are designed to facilitate joint working with other committees or sub-committees, including those of the House of Lords and those of the devolved bodies.

17.1.21 Under paragraph 1(a) of the standing order, any such committee can exchange its evidence with any other Commons committee with those powers or any committee or sub-committee of the House of Lords, or the Scottish Parliament, National Assembly for Wales or the Northern Ireland Assembly, or any committee of those bodies. There is a proviso, mainly relevant to the **Public Accounts Committee** (see section 10.5), that if such evidence originates from the **National Audit Office** (see paragraphs 10.5.8 to 10.5.11), it must have been agreed with the relevant government department.

17.1.22 Under paragraph 1(b) of the standing order, any such committee or sub-committee can hold concurrent meetings with one or more other Commons committees or sub-committees, and any committees of the House of Lords. At such joint meetings the main committees may examine witnesses in public, or deliberate or (amongst Commons committees only) consider *draft* reports in private. Sub-committees may not consider draft reports at joint meetings. Such meetings are technically, in strict procedural terms, concurrent (that is simultaneous and co-located but separate) meetings of two or more committees, not joint meetings. This means that the committees are prevented from jointly making any formal decisions at such meetings (apart from the preparation of *draft* reports), because one committee cannot vote on the same matter as another (though they may separately reach identical decisions). In practice, such joint meetings usually proceed as if the members present were all members of one committee, but all joint decisions (except, under paragraph (1)(d) of the standing order, on the question of who is going to chair such a meeting) must be reached by consensus and in unanimity. Because of this, the committees may not *jointly* agree a report as such, but paragraph (2) of the standing order allows them to agree that identical but (technically) separate reports may be published as a "joint report".

17.1.23 Under paragraph (2) of S.O. No. 124, where three or more committees or sub-committees are meeting together for the purpose of deliberating or taking evidence (but not for considering draft reports) the quorum of each is two. Where only two committees are meeting together, or where any number of committees are considering draft reports, the quorum for each reverts to the standard (that is, one quarter of the total membership or three, whichever is the greater). If, during a joint meeting, the number of members present from any participating committee falls below the quorum, the remaining member or members of that committee cannot participate in the proceedings.

17.1.24 Concurrent (or joint) meetings and reports of committees have not in the past been a regular feature of the House's select committees' activities. S.O. No. 137A was introduced in 2001 to facilitate and encourage them. However, during the 1997-2001 Parliament, the Defence, Foreign Affairs, International Development and Trade and Industry committees co-operated on a continuing basis to examine and report on the government's new series of annual reports on strategic export controls. They also examined a draft bill and draft subordinate legislation on the same subject. This arrangement came to be known as the "Quadripartite Committee", and has continued in the current Parliament.

Debates on reports

17.1.25 Reports from select committees may be recommended for debate either on an **Estimates Day** (see paragraphs 10.3.9 and 10.3.10) or at certain sittings in **Westminster Hall** (see section 6.3). The recommendations are made by the **Liaison Committee** (see section 3.5).

17.1.26 Select committee reports may also be "tagged" to a motion or order taken on the floor of the House. This means that the government (usually), at the request of a committee, includes an italicised note on the **Order Paper** under a particular item of business stating that certain reports of select committees are relevant to the debate. Such debates may be on bills, White Papers or similar matters, or substantive adjournment debates on some specified topic to which the reports are relevant (for example the regular debates on aspects of defence policy usually have reports of the Defence Committee tagged to them).

17.1.27 Occasionally, the government will make time to debate a select committee report either on an adjournment motion or a substantive motion, but this rarely happens in cases other than reports from the **Committee on Standards and Privileges** recommending action against named Members found to have breached the requirements of the **Code of Conduct** (see section 4.1), Procedure Committee reports or reports from the **Modernisation Committee** recommending changes to the House's procedures (see section

17.4 below), and reports from the domestic committees (see chapter 18) on which a decision is required. It would be open to the opposition parties to move a motion relating to a select committee report on an opposition day (see paragraphs 2.2.2 and 2.2.3) or to tag a report on a motion they put down, but this never happens.

17.1.28 Taking Estimates Days, Westminster Hall debates and tagged debates together, roughly a quarter to a third of the reports of the departmental select committees are debated on the floor of the House.

17.2 DEPARTMENTAL SELECT COMMITTEES

General

17.2.1 When referring loosely to the "select committees" of the House, commentators more often than not mean the departmentally-related select committees. Each of the departmentally-related select committees appointed under S.O. No. 152 is required by the standing order to consider the "expenditure, administration and policy" of a government department or departments or offices and their "associated public bodies". The titles of the committees and the departments with which they were concerned are set out in Figure 39. The term "associated public bodies" covers a wide range of organisations from the NHS to Forest Enterprise and includes the offices of the various regulators of the national utilities. The Home Affairs Committee covers the Attorney General's Office, the Treasury Solicitor's Department, the Crown Prosecution Service and the Serious Fraud Office, as well as the Home Office. The Scottish Affairs Committee and the Northern Ireland Affairs Committee have analogous responsibilities for legal and criminal justice matters which have not been devolved. The Scottish Affairs Committee and the Welsh Affairs Committee have specific responsibility for relations with the devolved legislatures as well as for matters relating to the responsibilities of the Scotland and Wales Offices within the Department of Constitutional Affairs, but not for the work of the Scottish Executive or for devolved matters which are the responsibility of the Executive of the National Assembly for Wales. Similarly, the Northern Ireland Affairs Committee is principally concerned with the Northern Ireland Office rather than the work of the Executive of the Northern Ireland Assembly or the Northern Ireland Civil Service Departments. The Science and Technology Committee monitors the Office of Science and Technology for which ministerial responsibility has tended to wander around government but for which the Secretary of State for Trade and Industry is currently responsible.

Sub-Committees

17.2.2 Under paragraph (3) of S.O. No. 152, each departmental select committee has power to appoint a sub-committee (the size of which is unspecified but which have a specified quorum of three). The Environment, Food and Rural Affairs Committee has power to appoint two sub-committees. Sub-committees enjoy independently all the powers of the main committees except that to make reports. These must all be agreed by the main committee. The power is permissive, and not all the committees exercise it. Those that do use it in different ways.

Committee	Principal government departments covered	Maximum membership
Constitutional Affairs†	Department of Constitutional Affairs (including the work of staff provided for the administrative work of courts and tribunals, but excluding consideration of individual cases and appointments)	11
Culture, Media and Sport	Department for Culture, Media and Sport	11
Defence	Ministry of Defence	11
Education and Skills	Department for Education and Skills	11
Environment, Food and Rural Affairs*	Department of Environment, Food and Rural Affairs	17
Foreign Affairs	Foreign and Commonwealth Office	11
Health	Department of Health	11
Home Affairs	Home Office; administrations and expenditure of the Attorney General's Office,the Treasury Solicitor's Department, the Crown Prosecution Service and the Serious Fraud Office (but excluding individual cases and appointments and advice given within government by Law Officers)	11
International Development	Department for International Development	11
Northern Ireland Affairs	Northern Ireland Office; administration and expenditure of the Crown Solicitor's Office (but excluding individual cases and advice given by the Crown Solicitor); and other matters within the responsibilities of the Secretary of State for Northern Ireland (but excluding the expenditure, administration and policy of the Office of the Director of Public Prosecutions, Northern Ireland and the drafting of legislation by the Office of the Legislative Counsel)	13
Office of the Deputy Prime Minister: Housing, Planning, Local Government and the Regions	Responsibilities of the Office of the Deputy Prime Minister	11
Science and Technology	Office of Science and Technology	11
Scottish Affairs	Scotland Office (including (i) relations with the Scottish Parliament and (ii) administration and expenditure of the offices of the Advocate General for Scotland (but excluding individual cases and advice given within government by the Advocate General))	11
Trade and Industry	Department for Trade and Industry (but excluding the Office of Science and Technology)	11
Transport	Department for Transport	11
Treasury	Treasury, Board of Inland Revenue, Board of Customs & Excise	11
Welsh Affairs	Wales Office (including relations with the National Assembly for Wales)	11
Work and Pensions	Department for Work and Pensions	11

*Has power to appoint two sub-committees (all others have power to appoint a sub-committee)
†Still called, in July 2003, the Lord Chancellor's Department Committee

FIGURE 39
DEPARTMENTALLY-RELATED SELECT COMMITTEES

Membership, etc

17.2.3 Most of the committees have a membership of eleven, with the exceptions of the Environment, Food and Rural Affairs Committee which has a membership of seventeen, and the Northern Ireland Affairs Committee which has a membership of thirteen.

17.2.4 The members of these committees are appointed by the House on a motion instigated by the **Committee of Selection** (see section 2.4). The proportions of Members from the different parties in the House are reflected in the proportions of Members from those parties on the select committees.

Staff

17.2.5 Each departmental select committee is assisted by a clerk, and usually an assistant clerk. In addition there may be one or more full-time committee specialists appointed to assist the committee. Each committee will also usually be assisted by a committee assistant and a secretary.

17.2.6 Under S.O. No. 152(4)(b), the committees each have the power to appoint expert specialist advisers to assist them in their work. These are often academics, but may be drawn from other walks of life (though they are never government employees). They are retained on an ad hoc basis and paid for each day worked for the committee. In terms of access to the committee's papers and meetings, though not employees of the House, they are treated equally with the permanent staff of the committees and bound by the same duties of confidentiality and impartiality in relation to the inquiries on which they are employed. The different committees make widely different use of this power.

Inquiries and reports

17.2.7 The committees set their own agenda within the very broad limits of the terms of the standing order, though on 14 May 2002 the House passed a resolution setting out "illustrative" or "core" tasks for them to undertake (see Figure 40). The extent to which each concentrates on expenditure or administration or policy varies widely from committee to committee. Most, however, make it their business to give at least some consideration each year to the relevant department's spending plans and resource budgets (see paragraphs 10.4.1 to 10.4.3).

17.2.8 The committees produce reports of greatly varying lengths at widely different rates: some will produce a dozen or more in a session; others only one or two. Some will be only a few paragraphs long, others will run to more than a hundred pages. In recent sessions it has been the practice of each committee to publish an annual report setting out the work they have done and relating it to the core tasks which the House has enjoined them to have regard to in their work.

17.2.9 The reports from departmental select committees typically analyse and assess the evidence received in the course of an inquiry and will generally include a number of recommendations. Where there are recommendations addressed to the government, the government has undertaken to respond to the report within two months of the date of publication. These responses will usually be made either in the form of a Command Paper (see paragraph 15.3.3) or in a memorandum to the committee which may be published by the committee under cover of a special report (see paragraph 17.1.11 above). Occasionally it may be made orally by a Minister on the floor of the House or in standing committee, or by a letter to the chairman of a committee.

Illustrative Tasks for Departmental Select Committees

(Resolution of the House of 14 May 2002)

To consider major policy initiatives

To consider the Government's response to major emerging issues

To propose changes where evidence persuades the Committee that present policy requires amendment

To conduct pre-legislative scrutiny of draft bills

To examine and report on main Estimates, annual expenditure plans and annual resource accounts

To monitor performance against targets in the public service agreements

To take evidence from each Minister at least annually

To take evidence from independent regulators and inspectorates

To consider the reports of Executive Agencies

To consider, and if appropriate report on, major appointments by a Secretary of State or other senior ministers

To examine treaties within their subject areas

FIGURE 40
DEPARTMENTAL SELECT COMMITTEES' CORE TASKS

Travel

17.2.10 The departmental committees tend to take the most advantage, among those select committees which are given by the House the power to travel, of this opportunity. There is no restriction on travel within the United Kingdom provided it is undertaken by a quorum of the committee. Committees can, and do, take formal evidence at meetings away from Westminster. The sums made available by the **House of Commons Commission** (see paragraph 18.1.1) for overseas travel by select committees is fixed for each financial year. The job of distributing this sum between the committees is delegated by the Commission to the **Liaison Committee** (see section 3.5).

17.3 PUBLIC ADMINISTRATION AND ENVIRONMENTAL AUDIT COMMITTEES

Characteristics of the committees

17.3.1 In addition to the departmental select committees described above, and the other types of select committee described elsewhere, there are two further select committees established under the standing orders of the House which do not fit easily into any category – the *Select Committee on Public Administration* and the *Environmental Audit Committee*. In character these are much like the departmental committees, but like the **Committee of Public Accounts** each has a remit which cuts across departmental boundaries and covers aspects of the work of almost all government departments.

The Ombudsmen

17.3.2 Under the Parliamentary Commissioner Act 1967, a Parliamentary Commissioner for Administration (colloquially known as the Ombudsman) is appointed with extensive powers to enquire into complaints of allegations of government maladministration which has led to injustice. The Commissioner can investigate complaints against government departments and other public bodies listed in Schedule 2 to the Act, and may recommend remedies, including compensation. The Commissioner is an officer of the House and makes reports of his findings to Parliament.

17.3.3 Under Acts of 1972 and 1973, similar Commissioners were created to investigate complaints of maladministration by NHS bodies. There are separate Health Service Commissioners for England, Scotland and Wales. An Ombudsman with similar powers and duties is appointed for Northern Ireland.

Public Administration Committee

17.3.4 Under S.O. No. 146, a select committee of eleven Members is appointed to oversee the work of the Commissioners. It is known as the Select Committee on Public Administration. The Committee also has the power to "consider matters relating to the quality and standards of administration provided by civil service departments, and other matters relating to the civil service". The Committee has the usual powers of select committees, including the power to appoint a sub-committee.

17.3.5 In relation to its duty to oversee the work of the ombudsmen, the Committee's usual mode of proceeding has been to select from the Commissioners' reports examples of cases which they believe should be pursued. They may examine relevant witnesses and take written evidence, and make reports and recommendations. They have given particular attention to the annual reports and special reports of the Commissioners. They also, on occasion, have investigated general issues which have emerged from a number of the Commissioners' reports. The Committee has also periodically undertaken wider-ranging inquiries into the general powers and functioning of the Parliamentary Commissioners and its own role, and made reports including recommendations for change.

17.3.6 Since acquiring its wider responsibilities for public administration, the Committee has devoted an increasing portion of its time and energy to examining such matters. It has, in effect, taken on the role of a departmental select committee for the Cabinet Office and the other offices of the centre of government (such as the Government Information Service), mostly those which report directly to the Prime Minister or Deputy Prime Minister. It has inquired into the code of ministerial conduct, the case for a civil service Act, and the role of special advisers to Ministers. It has also considered draft legislation on freedom of information and the work of the Information Commissioner. It has even inquired into the government's proposals for reform of the House of Lords.

Environmental Audit Committee

17.3.7 The Environmental Audit Committee is established under S.O. No. 152A. It has a maximum membership of sixteen, and has power to appoint a sub-committee. It has certain characteristics in common with the Public Accounts Committee (see section10.5). For example, it has a Minister on it (though, as with the PAC, he does not take an active part in its proceedings) and it has a Chairman who comes from the opposition benches. Its remit is "to consider to what extent the policies and programmes of government departments and non-departmental public bodies contribute to environmental protection and sustainable development; and to audit their performance against such targets as may be set for them by Her Majesty's Ministers". The Committee has examined successive **Budgets** and the wider arrangements for the control of public expenditure for their environmental implications. It has reviewed annually the arrangements within and across departments (and selected non-departmental public bodies, otherwise known as Quangos) to appraise the environmental impact of their policies and operations. It has also considered a number of substantive policy areas – both among those directly concerned with environmental protection and those not – for their contributions to environmental protection and sustainable development.

17.3.8 The Committee has all the usual powers of a departmental select committee to require evidence, to travel, meet when the House is not sitting and to sit away from Westminster, and to appoint specialist advisers.

17.4 THE PROCEDURE AND MODERNISATION COMMITTEES

17.4.1 There are two Committees currently appointed to examine the procedures and other aspects of the business of the House. The Procedure Committee is appointed under S.O. No. 147 and has a maximum of seventeen members. It has the usual powers of a select committee (see section 17.1), but no power to appoint a sub-committee. It conducts inquiries (often taking evidence from other Members or officers of the House) and has made recommendations on a wide variety of issues, from financial procedure or the impact of devolution to the use of the Welsh language in proceedings of the Welsh Grand Committee (see paragraph 14.4.5). Its remit overlaps considerably with that of the **Modernisation Committee** (see paragraph 17.4.2).

Committee	Remit	Maximum membership
Accommodation and Works	Domestic matters (S.O. No. 142) (see Chapter 18)	9
Administration	Domestic matters (S.O. No. 142) (see Chapter 18)	9
Broadcasting	Domestic matters (S.O. No. 142) (see Chapter 18)	11
Catering	Domestic matters (S.O. No. 142) (see Chapter 18)	9
Regulatory Reform	Examination of proposals for and draft regulatory reform orders made under the Regulatory Reform Act 2000 (S.O. No. 141) (see Chapter 12)	18
Environmental Audit	To consider to what extent the policies and programmes of government departments and non-departmental public bodies contribute to environmental protection and sustainable development and to audit performance against targets set by Ministers (S.O. No. 152A)	16
European Scrutiny	To examine European Union documents and to report its opinion on the legal and political importance of each document and on any matters of principle, policy or law; to make recommendations for the further consideration of any document by the European standing committees; and to consider any issue arising (S.O. No. 143) (see Chapter 13)	16
Finance and Services	To consider expenditure on and the administration of services for the House and, to prepare the Estimates for the House; to monitor the financial performance of the Departments of the House; and to report to the Commission or the Speaker on the financial and administrative implications of recommendations made by other committees (S.O. No. 144) (see Chapter 18)	11
Information	Domestic matters (S.O. No. 142) (see Chapter 18)	9
Liaison	To consider general matters relating to the work of select committees, to give advice relating to their work to the Commission, to recommend committee reports to be debated on Estimates Days and in Westminster Hall, and to take evidence from the Prime Minister (S.O. No. 145) (see Chapter 3)	Unspecified
Modernisation	To consider how the practices and procedures of the House should be modernised (Order of 16 July 2001)	Unspecified
Procedure	To consider the practices and procedures of the House (S.O. No. 147)	17
Public Accounts	To examine public expenditure (S.O. No. 148) (see Chapter 10)	16
Public Administration	To examine the reports of the Parliamentary Commissioner for Administration and the Health Service Commissioner and related matters, and to consider the quality and standards of administration provided by civil service departments, and other matters relating to the civil service (S.O. No. 146)	11
Selection	To appoint members to standing committees and to nominate members to certain select committees (Private Business S.O. 109, S.O. No. 86, etc.) (see Chapter 2)	9
Standards and Privileges	To consider matters relating to parliamentary privileges referred to it by the House; to oversee the work of the Parliamentary Commissioner for Standards; to oversee arrangements for compiling the Register of Members' Interests and to consider any specific complaints made in relation to the registering or declaring of interests referred to it by the Commissioner; to consider matters relating to the conduct of Members, including complaints of alleged breaches of the code of conduct; and to review the code (S.O. No. 149) (see Chapter 4)	11

FIGURE 41
OTHER SELECT COMMITTEES

17.4.2 The Select Committee on the Modernisation of the House of Commons (usually known as "the Modernisation Committee") was first appointed on 4 June 1997 and was reappointed for this present Parliament on 16 July 2001, but is not embodied in the permanent standing orders of the House. The order of appointment specified no maximum number of members. It has the usual powers of a select committee, except that to appoint a sub-committee. It is unusual in that it has been chaired in both Parliaments by a Minister (the **Leader of the House**) and in having representatives of the opposition **front bench** on it (as well as back benchers). The Chairman of the Procedure Committee (see paragraph 17.4.1) has also been a member in both Parliaments. Its *modus operandi* has been rather different from that of most select committees – it has not tended to take much public evidence and on occasions its recommendations have been effected by administrative action rather than by debate and resolution in the House following a government response to its recommendations. It has made wide ranging proposals for the modernisation of the House's procedures on subjects ranging from reform of the legislative process, alterations to the sitting hours of the House and its pattern of recesses, changes to the explanatory material associated with bills (see paragraph 11.5.5), alterations to the format of the **Order Paper** (see paragraphs 15.1.6 to 15.1.19), the creation of the parallel Chamber in Westminster Hall (see section 6.3), the introduction of deferred divisions (see paragraphs 9.6.10 to 9.6.12) and the drawing-up of illustrative tasks for select committees (see paragraph 17.2.7).

17.5 Joint Committees

General

17.5.1 On occasions, the Commons and Lords, which mainly operate entirely independently of each other, find it expedient to work together through committees. When it has been decided to do this, they establish a joint committee of the two Houses. Joint committees are select committees for procedural purposes, and generally are given some or all of the usual powers of those committees.

17.5.2 Some of these committees are established *ad hoc*, and others are embodied in the standing or sessional orders of the two Houses. The initial stage is for one of the Houses (usually the Lords) to pass the necessary resolution establishing a committee to join with a committee of the other House, and then send a message to that other House informing it of what has been done. The other House will then pass its mirroring resolution and send a message back. Where the committee is established under a permanent order, the two Houses need only inform each other that they have appointed members to it. In theory, a joint committee consists of two separate committees from each House sitting together. In practice, they operate in exactly the same manner as if they were a single committee, and are given the power to appoint a single chairman. However, a quorum of members from each House is required to be present for a joint committee to proceed.

Committee	Remit	Number of Commons members and (quorum)
Consolidation, &c. Bills	To consider *(a)* consolidation bills; *(b)* Statute Law Revision Bills; *(c)* bills prepared pursuant to the Consolidation of Enactments (Procedure) Act 1949; *(d)* bills to consolidate any enactments with amendments to give effect to recommendations made by one or both of the Law Commissions; *(e)* bills prepared by one or both of the Law Commissions to promote the reform of the statute law by the repeal of certain enactments which (except in so far as their effect is preserved) are no longer of practical utility, whether or not they make other provision in connection with the repeal of those enactments (S.O. No. 140)	7 (2)
Human Rights	To consider *(a)* matters relating to human rights in the United Kingdom (but excluding consideration of individual cases); and *(b)* proposals for remedial orders, draft remedial orders and remedial orders made under Section 10 of the Human Rights Act 1998 including whether the special attention of the House should be drawn to them on any of the grounds normally considered by the Joint Committee on Statutory Instruments (S.O. No. 152B)	6 (3)
Statutory Instruments	To consider every general (but not local) statutory instrument whether or not in draft and whether or not laid before Parliament – but excluding regulatory reform orders, remedial orders and instruments made by Ministers of the devolved executives or the National Assembly for Wales, unless subject to procedures at Westminster – with a view to determining whether the special attention of the House should be drawn to it on any of the following grounds: (i) that it imposes a charge on the public revenues or contains provisions requiring payments to be made; (ii) that it is made in pursuance of any enactment containing specific provisions excluding it from challenge in the courts; (iii) that it purports to have retrospective effect where the parent statute confers no express authority to do so; (iv) that there appears to have been unjustifiable delay in the publication or in the laying of it before Parliament; (v) that there appears to have been unjustifiable delay in sending a notification that an instrument has come into operation before it has been laid before Parliament; (vi) that there appears to be a doubt whether is is *intra vires* or that it appears to make some unusual or expected use of the powers under which it is made; (vii) that for any special reason its form or purport calls for elucidation; (viii) that its drafting appears to be defective; or on any other ground which does not relate to its merits or to the policy behind it (S.O. No. 151)	Unspecified (2)
Tax Law Re-write Bills	To consider Tax Law Re-write Bills (S.O. No. 152C)	Unspecified (2)

FIGURE 42
JOINT COMMITTEES

17.5.3 The chairmanship of a joint committee has traditionally been considered a prerogative of the Lords, but this has changed. The procedure of joint committees has also traditionally been that of the Lords, where this differs from the Commons. However, there is so little formal procedure in the work of select committees that this is a largely irrelevant consideration. Where the chair is held by the Commons, the outward and visible signs of the committee's operations (such as the format of its reports and other publications) tends to follow that of the Commons. The main administrative support for a joint committee also tends to be provided by the staff of the House to which the chairman belongs.

17.5.4 *Ad hoc* joint committees have been established more frequently in recent years than has previously been the case, and have usually been set up with the specific job of examining a draft bill. When they have completed the task referred to them and made their report, they cease to exist. The standing orders of the Commons now provides for four permanent joint committees. They are as follows.

17.5.5 The *Joint Committee on Consolidation, &c. Bills* is established under S.O. No. 140. It consists of twelve members of each House, and the Commons quorum is two. Its work (which is of a very technical nature) is described in paragraphs 11.6.18 and 11.6.19.

17.5.6 The *Joint Committee on Statutory Instruments* (the "JCSI") is established under S.O. No. 151. No maximum number of Commons members is specified, but a Commons quorum of two is. It is chaired by a Commons member. The work of the Committee is described in some detail in paragraphs 12.3.5 to 12.3.9.

17.5.7 The *Joint Committee on Human Rights* (the "JCHR") is the newest and most unusual of joint committees. It is established under S.O. No. 152B. It has six members from each House and a quorum of three from each House (though this is reduced to two from each House when it is taking evidence). The work of the Committee is described below (see paragraphs 17.510 to 17.5.17).

17.5.8 The *Joint Committee on Tax Law Re-write Bills* is established under S.O. No. 152C. It comprises seven members from each House, and the Commons quorum is two. It is a most unusual committee, which has a task not dissimilar to that of the Joint Committee on Consolidation, &c. Bills, exercised in relation to a new type of legislation which simplifies the language of tax law according to certain principles, but cannot change that law in its effect. The Committee has a Commons chairman, and because it considers and can amend bills, uniquely the chairman is given the power of selection of amendments (see paragraphs 11.10.10 and 11.11.11) which is otherwise available only to standing committee chairmen.

17.5.9 S.O. No. 137A permits most of the select committees of the House to meet concurrently with a committee of the House of Lords for the purposes of deliberating or taking evidence, but not for considering draft reports (see paragraphs 17.1.20 to 17.1.22 above). Joint Committees, in contrast, can and do agree and publish reports under their joint title.

The Joint Committee on Human Rights

17.5.10 The Joint Committee on Human Rights requires separate description. It is the first permanent joint committee to be established with terms of reference as wide as a typical departmental select committee, that is to say it can largely determine its own agenda. The other permanent joint committees described above have very narrowly delimited powers.

17.5.11 The Committee was first established in January 2001, following the coming into effect of the Human Rights Act 1998 on 2 October 2000. Its terms of reference can be divided into two distinct parts.

17.5.12 The first is a duty imposed upon it by each House to examine "remedial orders" made under the Human Rights Act. These, and the parliamentary procedure they undergo, are described in detail in paragraph 12.1.9 and section 12.5, as are the duties imposed on the JCHR in relation to them.

17.5.13 The other leg of the Committee's remit is to "consider matters relating to human rights in the United Kingdom (but excluding consideration of individual cases)". This pretty much allows the Committee to determine its own agenda, and means that, like the PAC, the Public Administration Committee and the Environmental Audit Committee, its work cuts across the activities of all government departments.

17.5.14 The Committee operates much like any other select committee, choosing topics for inquiry, taking evidence on them and publishing reports. It has, however, taken a distinctive approach to one particular self-imposed task. It examines (with the assistance of its full-time legal adviser who is, uniquely, an officer of both Houses) every bill introduced into Parliament, with special attention to whether the provisions of any bill engage the "Convention rights" as defined in the Human Rights Act (see paragraphs 11.5.3 and 11.5.5) or the rights embodied in other international human rights instruments to which the UK is a signatory (of which there are many). Where it finds that there are questions about whether provisions of a bill comply with those rights, it engages in a dialogue (usually in writing) with the responsible Minister about whether changes might be made to ensure compliance. In its regular scrutiny progress reports it draws the attention of each House to those provisions in bills about which it has questions and doubts. It has declared its intention to examine all bills, not only government bills but also private Members' bills and private bills, for compliance with human rights. In addition to its regular scrutiny progress reports, which list those bills which it considers do not raise any human rights questions as well as reportings its concerns about those which it considers might, it occasionally publishes reports on specific bills.

17.5.15 In choosing to do this work, the JCHR has taken on in part a character somewhat akin to the so-called "scrutiny committees" such as the Joint Committee on Statutory Instruments, the Regulatory Reform Committee and the European Scrutiny Committee, even though its terms of reference are very wide and permissive, rather than closely prescribed as is the case with those other committees.

17.5.16 The Committee also undertakes investigative inquiries more typical of select committees and publishes reports which are more wide-ranging.

17.5.17 The Committee has the usual powers of a select committee to travel and meet away from Westminster, to appoint special advisers and to meet on days when neither House is sitting.

17.6 STATUTORY COMMITTEES

17.6.1 There are, in addition to select committees and joint committees, committees of parliamentarians established under statute. These are:

- the *Ecclesiastical Committee* (see paragraph 12.1.10) established under the Church of England (Assembly) Powers Act 1919, comprising fifteen Members of the House of Commons appointed by the Speaker and fifteen members the House of Lords appointed by the Lord Chancellor;
- the *Intelligence and Security Committee*, established under the Intelligence Services Act 1994, comprising nine members of the two Houses appointed by the Prime Minister; and
- the *Speaker's Committee on the Electoral Commission*, established under the Political Parties, Elections and Referendums Act 2000, comprising eight Members of the House of Commons, four ex officio (the Speaker, the Home Secretary, the Chairman of the Home Affairs Committee and the Minister for local government) and five appointed by the Speaker.

These committees are not, however, select committees or committees of Parliament – they are committees of parliamentarians, which are required by law to be made up of Members of the two Houses.

Chapter 18
HOUSEKEEPING

18.1 ADMINISTRATIVE ORGANISATION

The House of Commons Commission

18.1.1 The House is responsible for the management of its own estate, the employment of its own staff, the provision of services to the House and its committees, the broadcasting of its own proceedings, and the administration of the payment of Members' salaries and expenses and the payment and terms of employment of Members' personal staff. Unlike the House of Lords, it enjoys complete financial independence from the government. The funding of the costs of all these services (except Members' salaries and expenses and their office costs allowances (OCA) including the payment of their personal staff, which are carried on the Cabinet Office Votes) are authorised by an annual **Estimate or Request for Resources**. The corporate body with overall responsibility for submitting this Request for Resources to the House, and for the general oversight of the running of the House, is the House of Commons Commission. This was established under the House of Commons (Administration) Act 1978. It is chaired by the Speaker. The other members are the **Leader of the House**, a member nominated by the **shadow** leader of the House (usually himself or herself) and three back bench Members appointed by the House itself (one of whom is by tradition a Member from the third largest party in the House). The Commission is assisted in its work by its Secretary, who is a senior member of the Department of the Clerk of the House.

18.1.2 The Commission is also the statutory employer of the permanent staff of the House. The administrative discharge of this function is delegated to the **Board of Management** (see paragraph 18.2.10 below).

The Finance and Services Committee

18.1.3 In its role as the corporate executive of the House, the Commission is advised by a select committee, appointed under S.O. No. 144, called the *Finance and Services Committee*. This Committee of eleven Members has the task of considering expenditure on the various services of the House. In effect it considers claims for new areas of expenditure and monitors the expenditure on the running costs of the House, and prepares the **Estimates** for submission to the Commission.

18.1.4 The Committee is advised by the four domestic committees appointed under S.O. No. 142 (see below). The chairman of each of the domestic committees is also invariably (though not *ex officio*) a member of the Finance and Services Committee. The Chairman of the Finance and Services Committee is always a member of the House of Commons Commission. There is also an *Audit Committee* of the Commission itself, which is chaired by the shadow leader of the House and includes two external members. It advises the Commission on internal audit procedures and reviews.

18.1.5 The Commission publishes an annual report, which descibes its work and sets out financial information relating to the costs of running the House of Commons.

The Domestic Committees

18.1.6 Under S.O. No. 142, there are four select committees known as the **domestic committees**. These are:

- Accommodation and Works
- Administration
- Catering
- Information.

Each domestic committee has nine members, and invariably these include representatives of the **usual channels**. They have the common powers of select committees (see section 17.1) including the power to hold concurrent meetings with any other committees in either House.

18.1.7 The role of the domestic committees is to enable the views of Members in general to be heard in the planning and provision of the House's services. They are advisory, not executive, except in the few cases where executive powers have been explicitly delegated to them by the Commission. Their areas of interest are broadly divided along the following lines. *Accommodation and Works* advises on the management of the parliamentary estate. *Information* advises on the provision of information technology services and related matters. *Catering* is self-explanatory. Other matters which do not fall within the areas of interest of the other three committees are generally considered by the *Administration Committee*.

18.1.8 Under paragraph (7) of the standing order, the committees have the power to give directions and make rules about matters within their competence, but only with the concurrence of the Speaker and the Commission. Generally, the committees work closely with the heads of the departments of the House to develop existing and new services.

The Broadcasting Committee

18.1.9 Under S.O. No. 139 there is a select committee of eleven members known as the *Broadcasting Committee*. It is responsible for general oversight of the arrangements for the recording and broadcasting of the House's proceedings (see section 6.4), and its terms of reference are similar to those of the domestic committees. The Committee also supervises arrangements for the provision of a continuous live audio-visual feed of the proceedings in the Chamber, including the letting of contracts for the provision of these services. The House also maintains archives of audio and audio-visual recordings of its proceedings. The Committee proposes and interprets guidelines on the broadcasting of the House's proceedings, but day to day control is the responsibility of the **Director of Broadcasting Services**, who works closely with the Committee.

18.2 PERMANENT OFFICERS OF THE HOUSE

Clerk of the House

18.2.1 The House is assisted in its work by appointed permanent officers. The **Clerk of the House**, who is assisted by the **Clerk Assistant**, is the principal authority on the law, practices, privileges and procedure of Parliament, and is the Speaker's principal adviser. (He is also the Chief Executive of the House of Commons, for which see paragraph 18.2.12 below.) The Department of the Clerk of the House, which supports the work of the House and its committees, is divided into five offices each headed by a Principal Clerk. These are: the **Table Office** (Principal Clerk of the Table Office); the **Legislation Service**, divided into the Public Bill Office, Private Bill Office and the Delegated Legislation Office (Clerk of Legislation); the **Journal Office** (Clerk of the Journals); the Committee Office (Clerk of Committees); and the Overseas Office (Clerk of the Overseas Office). The **Vote Office** (see paragraphs 15.6.1 and 15.6.2), headed by the Deliverer of the Vote, is also part of the Clerk's Department.

Serjeant at Arms

18.2.2 The **Serjeant at Arms**, assisted by his Deputies, is responsible for the security of the House, the preservation of good order in its precincts (see S.O. No. 161), and the provision of housekeeping functions. He has overall responsibility for the work of the Parliamentary Works Services Directorate, the Parliamentary Estates Directorate and the Parliamentary Communications Directorate, which between them provide and maintain the physical and electronic infrastructures of the House.

Librarian

18.2.3 The **Librarian** is responsible for the work of the House of Commons Library which includes, as well as traditional library functions, the maintenance of deposited papers, the provision of extensive research facilities for Members and the maintenance of the POLIS (Parliamentary on-line information services) database. The Library also includes the House of Commons **Information Office** and its education section.

Other Principal Officers of the House

18.2.4 The **Editor** of the Official Report is responsible for all aspects of the production of **Hansard** (see section 15.4).

18.2.5 The *Director of Finance and Administration* is the head of the Department of Finance and Administration, which essentially provides the administrative infrastructure of the House through the Fees Office (which deals with Members' pay and allowances and those of their staff, including the office costs allowances), the Finance Office (which deals with the running costs of the House including staff pay) and the Establishments Office, which deals with human resources.

18.2.6 The *Director of Catering Services* is in charge of the Refreshment Department which provides the catering services of the House.

18.2.7 The legal advisers to the House and its committees are the **Speaker's Counsel** and his deputies and assistants, who together form the Legal Services Office, which is part of the Clerk's Department.

18.2.8 The **Director of Broadcasting Services** oversees the arrangements for the broadcasting of the proceedings of the House and its committees (see section 6.4 and paragraph 18.1.9 above).

18.2.9 The **Comptroller & Auditor General** (see paragraph 10.5.5), the **Parliamentary Commissioner for Administration** (see paragraphs 17.3.2 and 17.3.3) the **Parliamentary Commissioner for Standards** (see paragraphs 4.1.2, 4.3.8 and 4.3.9), and the Speaker's Secretary (who heads the Office of the Speaker) are also officers of the House (although only the latter two come within the direct financial responsibility of the Commission).

The Board of Management

18.2.10 The vast majority of the permanent staff of the House are employed within one of its six main departments listed above (the Clerk's Department, the Serjeant's Department, the Library, the Official Report, the Refreshment Department and the Department of Finance and Administration). The six heads of these departments (the Clerk of the House, the Serjeant-at-Arms, the Librarian, the Editor, the Director of Catering Services and the Director of Finance and Administration) make up the **Board of Management**, which is the executive body for the administration of the House. It reports to the **House of Commons Commission**.

18.2.11 The Board of Management is supported by various committees of permanent officials on which the different departments are represented. These include the Business Planning Group, the Human Resources Group, the Group on Information for the Public and the Information Systems Group.

18.2.12 The **Clerk of the House** is the chairman of the Board of Management and Chief Executive of the House of Commons Service. In these functions (as opposed to those he exercises as head of the Department of the Clerk of the House) he is supported by an Office of the Clerk, which is independent of the other six departments. He is also the **Accounting Officer** (see paragraph 10.5.6) with overall statutory responsibility to Parliament for the proper expenditure of money voted by the House for its own running, and the "corporate officer" of the House for certain legal purposes. The day-to-day financial control of the House's expenditure is the responsibility of the Director of Finance and Administration. Because of the Clerk's role as Chief Executive and Chairman, his Department is separately represented on the Board of Management by his deputy.

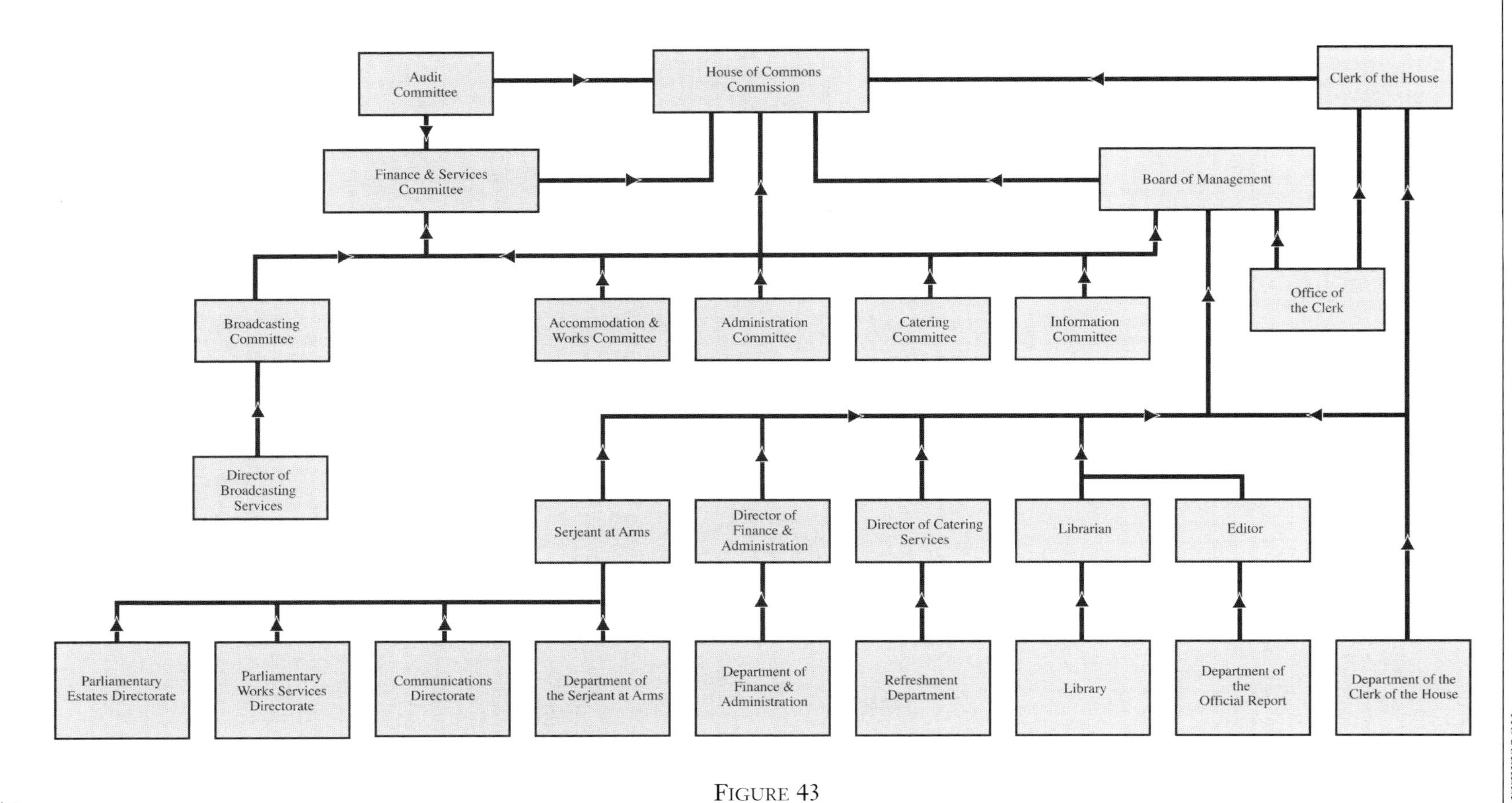

FIGURE 43
ADMINISTRATIVE STRUCTURE OF THE HOUSE

Chapter 19

PUBLIC PETITIONS

19.1 INTRODUCTION

19.1.1 The right to petition Parliament for the redress of grievances is one of the most ancient rights of the subject. Only a Member of Parliament may present a Public Petition to the House. Although it is customary for Members to present a Petition when requested to do so by a constituent, regardless of their view as to its subject matter, the presentation of a Petition to the House is entirely at the discretion of the Member concerned. Members who are Ministers, or the Speaker and his deputies, will generally ask a colleague to present any Petition on behalf of their constituents, although it is not unknown for junior Ministers to present petitions informally.

19.1.2 In most circumstances, those who wish to promote or object to private legislation (see section 11.19) also communicate with Parliament by way of petitioning. The rules on petitions relating to private bills and other forms of private legislation procedure are complex and no attempt is made to describe them here. The remainder of this chapter is concerned only with Public Petitions.

19.2 FORM OF PETITIONS

19.2.1 The essential requirements of Petitions are that they are addressed to Parliament, must clearly state from whom they come, should be couched in respectful language, and should make a request for relief which the House is competent to grant. Formerly there were strict rules as to the wording that had to be used for the introduction and the concluding parts of a Petition, but these rules have now been relaxed. The traditional wording and the recommended wording are shown in Figure 42.

19.2.2 The first sheet of the Petition must be handwritten, and must bear the name, address and signature of at least one petitioner. There must be no erasures, crossings-out or interlineations. The text of the prayer of the Petition (that is the concluding part, specifying the relief which is sought) must be printed at the head of any accompanying sheets, above any supporting signatures.

19.3 SUBJECT OF PETITIONS

19.3.1 A Petition is supposed to seek relief of a kind that the Commons can grant. This provision is now so very widely interpreted as to be almost entirely unrestrictive. S.O. No. 48 forbids the House from receiving a Petition for money to be paid out of the public revenues. This is interpreted to exclude only direct requests for personal payment rather than more general requests which would entail increased public expenditure. S.O. No. 157 explicitly permits the receipt of Petitions against taxes or duties.

19.3.2 Before presenting a Public Petition either formally or informally (see below), the Member must sign the handwritten first sheet of the Petition at the top of the page.

19.4 PRESENTATION OF PETITIONS

Informal presentation

19.4.1 A Member who does not wish to present a Petition on the floor of the House may present it informally by placing it in the large green bag provided for the purpose which hangs behind the Speaker's Chair. This may be done at any time when the House is sitting. If the Clerk of Public Petitions finds that a petition presented in this way is not in order, it is returned to the presenting Member.

Formal presentation

19.4.2 A Member wishing to present a Petition formally, that is to say on the floor of the House, must first have the handwritten first sheet endorsed as being in order by the Clerk of Public Petitions in the **Journal Office**. The Member must then inform the **Table Office** in advance of his or her intention to present the petition. This must be done at the latest by noon on the day chosen for presentation if that is a day on which the House is to sit at 2.30 pm, or 10.30 am on a day on which the House is to meet at 11.30 am, or by the rising of the House on Thursday for a Friday.

19.4.3 The time and manner of presenting Petitions is described in paragraphs 7.11.1 and 7.11.2. S.O. No. 153 confines a Member presenting a Petition to a brief statement of the parties from whom it comes and their number, a brief description of its contents, and the reading of the prayer of the Petition. These proceedings may be conducted after the **moment of interruption**. If a Member does not wish to read out the petition, the Clerk at the Table may be asked to read it to the House.

19.4.4 S.O. No. 154(3) rules out any debate upon a Petition. This is qualified by S.O. No. 155 which allows debate on a Petition complaining of some present personal grievance for which there may be an urgent necessity for providing an immediate remedy. Debate on a motion arising from such a petition may be carried on after the **moment of interruption**. Such proceedings are extremely rare.

Recording and printing of Petitions

19.4.5 Each orderly Petition presented, whether formally or informally, is recorded in the **Votes and Proceedings**. On the next sitting Thursday, a copy of the text of the Petition is printed and circulated as a supplement to the Votes and Proceedings under S.O. No. 156 (see paragraph 15.1.30).

19.5 OBSERVATIONS ON PETITIONS

19.5.1 The Clerk of Public Petitions transmits a copy of the Petition, after it is printed, to the appropriate government department to which its subject matter relates. Departments are under no obligation to comment on Petitions; but if a Department decides to make a formal response, a Minister of that department will in due course send a copy of his or her *Observations* on the Petition to the **Journal Office**, and this copy will be laid before the House under the authority of the **Clerk of the House** and recorded in the Appendix to the **Votes and Proceedings** (see paragraph 15.1.25). On the next sitting Thursday, the text of these ministerial observations will be printed and published under the provisions of S.O. No. 156 as a supplement to the Votes and Proceedings (see paragraph 15.1.30). There, so far as parliamentary procedures are concerned, the matter rests.

Old Style

To the Honourable the Commons of the United Kingdom of Great Britain and Northern Ireland in Parliament assembled.

The Humble Petition of residents of Dunwich in the County of Suffolk.

Sheweth

That our Town is under constant threat of destruction by means of the erosion of the coast by the sea.

That if this continues we will all be rendered homeless and destitute.

That we cannot afford the great cost of erecting sea defences.

Wherefore your Petitioners pray that your honourable House will pass legislation to provide for the securing of the coastline near the Town of Dunwich against further erosion.

And your Petitioners, as in duty bound, will ever pray, &c.

New Style

To the House of Commons.

The Petition of former residents of Dunwich.

Declares that we have been driven from our homes and jobs by the effect of the erosion of the coast by the sea.

The Petitioners therefore request that the House of Commons take steps to provide for the construction of a Dunwich New Town, together with roads and a harbour and adequate sea defences.

And the Petitioners remain, etc.

FIGURE 44

EXAMPLES OF PUBLIC PETITIONS

GLOSSARY of KEY WORDS AND TERMS

¶ = paragraph § = section

accounting officer: the person (usually the permanent secretary of a government department) responsible for accounting to Parliament, in respect of each of the **Estimates** (or part of such Estimate), for the resources voted by Parliament for the public service (see ¶10.5.6).

adjournment motion: although technically a motion moved for the purpose of bringing to a conclusion a sitting of the House or a committee, when it is rarely debated, such a motion is often used as a procedural device for enabling a debate to take place without having to come to a conclusion in terms (see §9.8).

adjournment debate: a debate on **an adjournment motion** (see also **daily adjournment**, and §9.8).

affirmation: see **oath.**

allocation of time motion: see **guillotine**.

allotted days: the days allotted to debate a **bill** under a **programme order** or a **guillotine** (see §11.18), also the 20 days allotted each session as **opposition** days (see ¶2.2.2 and ¶2.2.3).

ambit: the description of the scope of expenditure covered by a **Request for Resource** (see also **appropriation** and **Estimates**).

amendment: a proposal to change the terms of a **motion** or to alter a **bill**, see §9.2, §9.4 and §11.9.

annunciator: the television screens situated around the House and its precincts on which details of the current proceedings and future business of the House are shown.

appropriation: the allocation of money by Parliament to specified purposes. The Resource Accounts are the **Comptroller & Auditor General**'s audited accounts showing that money has been spent in accordance with Parliament's instructions embodied in the Appropriation Act (see also **Consolidated Fund**, **Estimates** and ¶10.4.5).

back bench: the back benches (see Figure 2) are the places where Members who are not government Ministers or official opposition **shadows** sit in the Chamber, hence **back bencher**, the term used to describe a Member who holds no official position in government or in his or her party and who is therefore not bound by the convention of collective responsibility: such a Member may more formally be referred to as a **private Member**, though strictly speaking, this term applies to any Member not in receipt of a ministerial salary.

ballot: the term is used in the House to refer to the draw for **private Members' bills** (see ¶11.2.2 to ¶11.2.5). There is also provision for secret ballots in the House's proceedings relating to the election of its Speaker (see ¶3.1.7 to 3.1.16).

Bar of the House: the line across the floor of the Chamber (see Figure 1) which marks its formal threshold: the Bar is also marked by a rail (now invariably retracted) to which, in former times, **strangers** might be summoned to address the House or to be arraigned before it.

bill: a proposal for legislation formally presented to either House of Parliament (see §11.1).

Black Rod: the Gentleman Usher of the Black Rod, a member of the royal household, the broad equivalent in the Lords of the **Serjeant at Arms**, sent to summon the Commons to the Lords at the opening and closing of **sessions**.

board of management: the executive body of the permanent service of the House (see §18.2).

book entry: an entry in the **Votes and Proceedings** which records as a procedural event something which occurred without any actual proceedings taking place on the floor of the House (see ¶15.1.24).

breach of privilege: an abuse of one of the privileges of the House or an attempt to impede or frustrate the House or one of its Members in the exercise of one of its privileges (see §4.2).

budget resolutions: the series of financial resolutions, passed by the House at the conclusion of the debate on the **budget statement**, on which the **Finance Bill** is founded (see ¶10.2.21 to ¶10.2.26).

budget statement: the annual statement made by the Chancellor of the Exchequer (usually in March) setting out the government's tax and spending plans and proposals for their reconciliation for the forthcoming financial year: at the end of the debate on the budget, the **budget resolutions** are passed and the **Finance Bill** is introduced (see ¶10.2.19 to ¶10.2.24).

business motion: a motion proposing to regulate the time available to the House for consideration of a specified item of business at a specified sitting (see ¶7.7.6, ¶7.10.16 and **ten o'clock motions**).

business question: the question addressed each Thursday to the **Leader of the House** under the **urgent question** procedure in reply to which the main items of business to be taken on each sitting day for the next week or so are announced (see ¶7.5.7 and ¶7.6.1).

by-election: an election in a single constituency to fill a vacancy caused by the death or **disqualification**, etc. of a Member (see ¶7.2.2 to 7.2.4).

C&AG: see **Comptroller & Auditor General**.

Cabinet: the inner circle of the government to which the Minister in charge of each government department belongs (and certain other Ministers), presided over by the **Prime Minister**.

casting vote: where any **division** (either in the House or in **standing committee**) results in a tie, it is decided on the vote of the occupant of the Chair, which is given in accordance with precedent (see ¶9.6.14 and ¶9.6.15).

Central Lobby: the main public area of the Palace of Westminster, equidistant from the two Houses of Parliament, where members of the public are received by Members (see Figure 1 and ¶1.1.12).

Chairman of Ways and Means: the first deputy Speaker, with particular responsibilities for **private business**, **committees of the whole House** and **sittings in Westminster Hall** (see ¶3.2.1 to ¶3.2.3).

Chairmen's Panel: the body of Members appointed by the **Speaker** from amongst whom he chooses the chairmen of each **standing committee** (see ¶3.2.6 and §3.3).

Chief Whip: the senior **Whip** in each party (see §2.5): the government chief whip attends meetings of the Cabinet.

Chiltern Hundreds: the steward or bailiff of the three Chiltern Hundreds is the mythical "office of profit under the Crown" to which Members are appointed when wishing to resign their seats by disqualifying themselves from membership of the House (see **disqualification**): the Stewardship of the Manor of Northstead is also used (in alternation) for this purpose.

Clandestine Outlawries Bill: the bill presented **proforma** on the first day of each session (see ¶5.2.6).

Clerk Assistant: the second **Clerk at the Table**, and first deputy to the **Clerk of the House**.

Clerks at the Table: the senior clerks in the Clerk of the House's Department who sit at the **Table** of the House.

Clerk of Bills: the Principal Clerk with particular responsibility for public and private bills (see §11.1).

Clerk of Legislation: the Principal Clerk in charge of the **Legislation Service** of the House.

Clerk of the House: the principal permanent officer of the House (see ¶3.1.1) and also the **accounting officer** for the House of Commons **Votes** and Chief Executive of the House's permanent service (see ¶18.2.1 and ¶18.2.12).

closure: a procedural device for bringing a debate to a conclusion (see ¶9.7.4 to ¶9.7.6).

code of conduct: the code adopted by the House to guide Members on questions relating to the interpretation of its resolutions in respect of the declarations in the **Register of Members' Interests**, the rule against paid advocacy, the deposit of copies of contracts of employment and other matters relating to financial relationships with outside persons and bodies (see §4.3).

command paper: a government publication (often a **White Paper**) presented to Parliament by "command of Her Majesty" (see ¶15.3.3).

Commissioner for Standards: the officer of the House appointed to supervise the **Register of Members' Interests**, to advise Members on the interpretation of the **code of conduct** and to assist the **Committee on Standards and Privileges** in its work (see ¶4.1.2, ¶4.3.8 and ¶4.3.9).

committal: the act of sending a **bill** to a committee of one kind or another after it has received a **second reading** (see §11.7).

committee: see **committee of the whole House**, **joint committee**, **select committee**, **standing committee**.

Committee of Selection: the committee which appoints Members to **standing committees** and proposes Members to the **departmental select committees** and the **domestic committees** (see §2.4).

Committee on Standards and Privileges: the select committee which investigates allegations of **breaches of privilege**, **contempts** and, with the assistance of the **Commissioner for Standards**, matters relating to the **code of conduct**, in particular complaints about Members in relation to outside financial interests and related matters (see §4.1 and §4.3).

committee of the whole House: the House forms itself into a committee of all its Members when it decides to take the committee stage of a **bill** in the whole House (see ¶2.3.1, §11.7 and ¶11.11.1 to ¶11.11.6 and also ¶10.1.4).

Comptroller & Auditor General: the officer of the House responsible for the running of the National Audit Office and for assisting the **Public Accounts Committee** in their scrutiny of public expenditure (see §10.5).

consideration: the more formal title for the **report stage** of a bill.

Consolidated Fund: the general fund into which almost all government receipts (in the form of taxes, duties, etc.) are paid (under section 10 of the Exchequer and Audit Act 1866) and out of which almost all government expenditure is met: Parliament passes the regular **Consolidated Fund Bills** which appropriate to the government service out of the Fund the total sums voted for particular purposes by way of the **Estimates** (see §10.3).

consolidation bill: a **bill** which consolidates much of the existing law on a particular subject into one convenient statute: because such bills do not (except within strict and very narrow limits) change the law, they are subject to special procedures distinct from the general procedures applying to **public bills** (see ¶11.6.18).

contempt: disobedience to, or defiance of, an order of the House, or some other insult to the House or its dignity or a **breach of privilege** (see §4.2).

crown prerogative: essentially, prerogative actions are those which the executive may take without the sanction of Parliament: they include **prorogation** and **dissolution** of Parliament, the grant of honours, the declaration of war and, in most circumstances, the making of treaties with foreign governments.

CWH: see **committee of the whole House**.

daily adjournment: the half-hour debate at the end of each day's sitting in the House at which a **back bench** Member has the opportunity to raise a matter with a Minister (see §7.12 and §9.8).

delegated legislation: legislation made by Ministers under powers granted to them in Acts of Parliament, usually by means of **statutory instrument** (see §12.1).

departmental select committees: the select committees established under S.O. No. 152 to oversee the work of government departments (see §17.2).

Deputy Chairmen: the First and Second Deputy Chairmen of Ways and Means, who with the **Chairman of Ways and Means** share with the **Speaker** the duties of presiding over the House (see ¶3.2.4 and ¶3.2.5).

despatch box: the two despatch boxes are situated at either side of the **Table**, at the far end from the Speaker's Chair, and serve as lecterns for those leading debate (or answering questions) from the government and official opposition **front benches** (see Figure 2 and ¶9.3.8).

dilatory motion: a motion for the adjournment of debate or for the adjournment of the House or a standing committee moved for the purpose of superseding the business in hand (see ¶1.1.4 and ¶9.4.1).

Director of Broadcasting Services: the officer of the House responsible for day to day oversight of the broadcasting of its proceedings (see §6.4).

disqualification: the House of Commons (Disqualification) Act 1975 sets out in its schedules a large number of offices the holding of which disqualify a person from sitting as a Member of the House of Commons. Broadly speaking, these fall within the general disqualifying category of "offices of profit under the Crown", though the holders of ministerial office (up to a maximum of 95) are exempt from disqualification on those grounds (see also **Chiltern Hundreds**). There is also a general disqualification for civil servants, police officers, members of the armed forces, judges (though not all persons commonly described as judges fall within this disqualification) and members of non-Commonwealth overseas legislatures. So too, in general terms, are persons ineligible to vote in a general election, for example Peers entitled to sit in the House of Lords, aliens, minors (though for this purpose the age of majority remains 21 not 18), sentenced prisoners and persons detained under the Mental Health Act 1983. So too are bankrupts, under the Insolvency Act 1986. Members may also be disqualified after an election if their candidature or conduct of an election is found to have been in breach of electoral law.

dissolution: on the advice of the Prime Minister, the Queen may at any time dissolve Parliament, thereby initiating a general election (see §5.1).

division: the means by which the House or one of its committees ascertains the number of Members for and against a proposition before it (see §9.6) when the Chair's opinion as to which side is in the majority on a **Question** is challenged.

division bell area: the area from within which it is deemed possible to reach the **division lobbies** within the period from the ringing of the **division bells** to the closing of the lobby doors during a **division**.

division bells: the bells, situated in the House and its precincts and outbuildings, and elsewhere (such as government offices, pubs and restaurants and the private homes of Members) within the **division bell area**, which are rung to summon Members to vote in a **division** (see §9.6). Their function has been largely superseded off the premises by pagers, activated by the **Whips** offices.

division lobbies: the lobbies running down either side of the Chamber through which Members must pass to register their votes in a **division** (see Figure 2 and ¶1.1.8 and ¶9.6.1).

domestic committees: the **select committees** concerned with the running of the House (see ¶18.1.6 to ¶18.1.8).

draft bill: a bill presented to Parliament, and published more generally, in draft form (usually as a **command paper**), to enable consultation on its form and contents to take place before a bill is formally introduced into one or other House; their use has been urged by the **Modernisation Committee** and endorsed by the House; and the number published has significantly increased in recent years; they are now regularly referred to a **joint committee** or a **select committee** for consideration and report (see ¶11.1.5)

dropped order: when, for instance, the **Member in charge** of a bill does not name a new day for it to be set down for one of its stages after a stage has been completed or adjourned on any day, the order for that stage becomes a dropped order and the bill enters a sort of procedural limbo where it remains unless the Member in charge revives it (which he or she can do by means of a **book entry**).

dummy bill: when a **bill** is presented to the House by a Member (see §11.3) he or she hands to the **Clerk at the Table** a folded card on which the short and long titles of the bill and the names of any supporters (up to a maximum of 12, including the **Member in charge**) are written, together with other details. These dummy bills are prepared by the **Public Bill Office**. Usually the bill is properly printed and published shortly afterwards, but in the case of **private Members' bills**, they sometimes never have an existence beyond this dummy form.

early day motions: expressions of opinion by Members on almost any subject which are published in the form of motions printed in the **Notice Paper** part of the **Vote Bundle**, to which other Members may add their names to indicate support (see chapter 16).

Ecclesiastical Committee: the statutory committee of Members of both Houses which considers Church of England **Measures** (see ¶12.1.8 and §17.6).

Editor: the officer of the House in charge of the publication of the **Official Report** (aka **Hansard**) of debates in the Chamber and in standing committees (see §15.4).

EDM: see **early day motions**.

effective orders: that part of the **Order Paper** which includes the items of business actually to be taken at a sitting, so called to distinguish it from the **remaining orders**.

Erskine May: Erskine May's **Treatise on the Law, Privileges, Proceedings and Usage of Parliament**, first published by the then **Clerk of the House**, Thomas Erskine May in 1844, and revised by his successors ever since: it is acknowledged as the authoritative text book on the law and practice of both Houses of Parliament: the latest edition is the 22nd, edited by Limon and McKay (Butterworths, London, 1997).

Estimates: the form in which the government presents, for approval by the Commons, its requests for the resources needed to cover recurring public expenditure (see §10.3).

Estimates days: the three days in each session set aside for consideration of the Estimates, in practice used for debate on one or more select committee reports chosen by the **Liaison Committee** (see ¶10.3.9 to ¶10.3.12).

Examiner of Petitions: the officer of the House with responsibility for examining certain matters relating to private bills (see §11.19) and hybrid bills (see ¶11.1.3) for compliance with the standing orders relating to **private business**; there is an equivalent officer in the House of Lords who joins in this examination.

exempted business: business which, under standing orders or under a specific order of the House, may be carried on after the **moment of interruption** (see §7.10).

Father of the House: see **Senior Member**.

Finance Bill: the annual bill, founded upon the **budget resolutions**, which embodies the government's statutory power to levy most taxes and duties, and which may include other provisions relating to taxes management (see ¶10.2.19 to ¶10.2.24).

financial privilege: the right to approve proposals for taxation or for government expenditure which the Commons asserts as its exclusive privilege, not shared with the Lords (see ¶10.2.8 to ¶10.2.11).

financial resolutions: the collective term for **money resolutions**, **ways and means resolutions**, and **supply resolutions**.

first reading: the formal first stage of a **bill**'s progress, which occurs without debate or vote after it has been introduced to the House (see §11.5).

forthwith: where, under standing orders, a Question is to be decided forthwith, that is usually indicated by an italicised rubric on the **Order Paper**. It means that there can be no debate on the Question, and that as soon as it is moved the Chair must immediately put it to the House or committee for decision: although there can be no debate on such a Question, there may be a **division**. Many Questions which are put forthwith are also **exempted business** (see ¶7.7.7 and ¶7.10.15).

front bench: the front benches (see Figure 2) are where Ministers and their official opposition **shadows** sit in the Chamber, hence **front bencher** or **front bench spokesman** (the government front bench is also known as the **Treasury Bench**).

future business: the section of the **Order Paper** (sub-divided into sections A to E) in which business to be taken in the House or at **sittings in Westminster Hall** on future dates is listed (with the exception of **oral questions** but with the inclusion of **written statements**) (see ¶15.1.15 to ¶15.1.21).

grand committee: see §14.1 (the term has a different meaning in the Lords).

guillotine: an order of the House which allocates the time available to debate any stage or stages of a bill; now largely superseded by **programme orders** (see §11.18).

Hansard: the colloquial name for the **Official Report**, the publications containing the accurate and full (though not strictly verbatim as often claimed) reports of what is said and done in the debates of the House and its **standing committees** (see §15.4).

health service commissioners: the officer of the House who acts as the ombudsman for the NHS who also holds the office of **PCA** and who reports to the Public Administration Committee: there are separate commissioners for England, Wales and Scotland (see §17.3).

House of Commons Commission: the executive body of Members responsible for the running of the House (see §18.1).

human rights: see **section 19 statement** and **Joint Committee on Human Rights**.

Information Office: the office (part of the **Library**) which is set up to answer enquiries from the public about the work of the House; its telephone number is 020 7219 4272.

instruction: after **committal** of a bill, the House may give an instruction to any committee to which it is committed to do certain things that the committee might not otherwise be empowered to do (see §11.8).

JCHR: see **Joint Committee on Human Rights**.

Joint Committee on Human Rights: a **joint committee** charged with examining **remedial orders** and other matters relating to human rights in the UK (see ¶17.5.10 to ¶17.5.17)

joint committees: committees which include Members of both Houses (see ¶2.3.11, ¶11.1.5, ¶11.6.18 to ¶11.6.22, ¶11.11.11 and ¶11.11.12, ¶12.3.5 to ¶12.3.9, ¶12.5.6 to ¶12.5.8, ¶17.1.3 and §17.5)

Journal Office: the office of the Clerk's Department responsible, among other duties, for the preparation of the **Votes and Proceedings**, the oversight of **Public Petitions**, and the preparation of the **Journals** of the House. It is also the office where papers are formally laid before the House by Ministers and others (see ¶1.3.1, ¶15.1.23 to ¶15.1.29 and §15.2).

Journals: the **Votes and Proceedings** are consolidated into the Journals on a sessional basis and these form the authoritative record of the decisions of the House (see §15.2).

law commissions: the law commissions for England and Wales and for Scotland prepare proposals for reform of the law and also for its rationalisation by means of **consolidation bills** and statute law repeal bills (see ¶11.6.9 and ¶11.6.18).

Leader of the House: the Cabinet Minister with this title is charged with special responsibility for the management of the House and its business, but is distinct from the **usual channels**. He is a member, **ex officio**, of the **House of Commons Commission** (see §18.1). He also has responsibility for the cabinet committees dealing with the management of the government's legislative programme. His name will frequently appear on motions relating to the business of the House, and he will initiate government proposals for the reform of its procedures. His most public role is the period of questioning which, each Thursday, follows the **business question** (see ¶7.5.7 and ¶7.6.1). In recent sessions, he or she has also chaired the **Modernisation Committee**.

leader of the opposition: the person elected leader of the second largest party in the House is the leader of the official opposition. He or she receives official recognition in this role in the receipt of a ministerial salary and appointment to the Privy Council. The leader of the opposition has certain well-entrenched conventional rights to initiate certain kinds of business, in particular to demand, and to expect in most circumstances to receive, an opportunity to move a motion of no confidence in the government. He also has certain rights under standing orders (see **official opposition**).

leave: there are a number of types of proceeding which may only be done *by leave of the House* (or a committee). These include to speak more than once to a Question other than in committee (see ¶9.3.4), to withdraw a motion before the House or a committee (see ¶9.4.6) and to move certain types of motion. Generally leave must be unanimous, that is, any single objection from any Member in the House or in a committee means that leave is thereby denied.

Legislation Service: the section of the Department of the **Clerk of the House** comprising the **Public Bill Office**, the Private Bill Office and the delegated legislation office.

Liaison Committee: the select committee consisting mainly of chairmen of other select committees, which under standing orders has certain powers and duties in relation to the proceedings of the House, as well as a more informal role exercising oversight of the work, and as an advocate of the interests, of select committees in general. It also has a power to examine the Prime Minister on matters of public policy (see §3.5).

Librarian: the officer of the House in charge of its **Library** (see ¶18.2.3).

Library: the Library of the House (see ¶18.2.3).

lobby correspondents: certain representatives of the various news media who have the authority of the **Serjeant at Arms** to enter the **Members' Lobby** when the House is sitting and who enjoy certain other privileges of access to areas of the Palace otherwise closed to persons apart from Members and permanent staff. They also subscribe to a code of conduct relating to the disclosure of the sources of their information (hence the expression "on lobby terms").

Lords Amendments: the amendments proposed by the Lords to a **bill** which has been passed by the Commons (see §11.15).

Lords Commissioners: the Peers appointed by the Queen to deliver her **proclamation** proroguing Parliament and her **royal assent** to Acts agreed just before **prorogation** (see ¶5.2.1 to ¶5.2.4).

Loyal Address: the motion moved in reply to the **Queen's Speech** on which the debate on the Queen's Speech takes place (see ¶5.2.7 to ¶5.2.9).

Mace: the symbol of the Crown's authority in Parliament, which is displayed on the **Table** whenever the House is in session (see ¶1.1.4).

maiden speech: the first speech delivered by a Member after he or she is first elected to the House. By convention it includes a tribute to his or her predecessor, an encomium to his or her constituency, and avoids controversy (though this latter tradition shows signs of dying out). Also, by tradition, it is heard without interruption from other Members.

main committee corridor: the corridor on the first floor of the Palace, accessed **via** the upper and lower waiting halls, off which the standing committee rooms and the majority of select committee rooms are situated (see Figure 1).

manuscript amendment: an amendment of which no **notice** has been given, which is presented to the Chair during debate in manuscript or typescript form, and only selected in very rare circumstances (see ¶11.9.2).

Measure: a legislative proposal of the General Synod of the Church of England (see ¶12.1.10).

Member in charge: the Member in charge of a bill is the one who introduces it to the House, and he or she has certain prerogatives in relation to that bill. In the case of a government bill, any Minister (including a **Whip**) may exercise the rights of the Member in charge (see ¶11.2.6).

Members' lobby: the area immediately outside the Chamber (see Figure 1) generally reserved to Members and **lobby correspondents** and staff of the House when the House is sitting (see ¶1.1.9 to ¶1.1.11).

Minister: a member of the government, entitled to receive a ministerial salary (though there have occasionally been "Ministers" appointed who do not receive any such official salary) and bound by the convention of collective responsibility for decisions of government: for procedural purposes, all members of the government (including **Whips**) are regarded as being able to act on behalf of any other Minister.

Modernisation Committee: the Select Committee on the Modernisation of the House of Commons, chaired by the Leader of the House, appointed in June 1997 and re-appointed in July 2001 for the remainder of the Parliament to bring forward proposals for the modernisation of the procedures and practices of the House (see §17.4).

moment of interruption: the time set by standing orders at which the main business of a day's sitting normally ends after which business may only be taken if it is **exempted business** or unopposed business (see ¶6.1.6 to ¶6.1.9 and §7.10).

money bill: a bill which is concerned exclusively with raising or spending public money and which, under the terms of the **Parliament Acts**, cannot be amended by the Lords (see ¶10.2.15 and ¶10.2.16).

money resolution: a **resolution** of the House, agreed on a motion which may only be moved by a **Minister**, authorising the provisions of a **bill** which entail novel forms of public expenditure (see ¶10.2.1 to ¶10.2.5).

naming: a Member who persistently defies the authority of the Chair in the House may be **named** by the Chair, which immediately causes a motion to be moved to suspend the Member from the service of the House (see ¶9.3.23 to ¶9.3.33).

National Audit Office: the office under the direction of the **Comptroller & Auditor General** which audits the expenditure of government departments (see §10.5).

Northstead, Manor of: see **Chiltern Hundreds**.

notice: where it is a requirement of standing orders or the rules of the House that a motion requires notice, it means that such a motion cannot be moved unless it appears on the **Order Paper**. In most circumstances, the latest time for giving notice of a motion to appear on a Paper for the next sitting day is the rising of the House on the previous sitting day. Standing orders in certain circumstances have more stringent requirements of notice: for example, a motion to refer a bill to a second reading committee (see ¶11.6.6 to ¶11.6.10) requires at least ten days' notice; a motion in the name of the **Committee of Selection** to nominate Members to certain select committees must appear at least once on the **remaining orders** before it can be put on the **effective orders** (see ¶2.4.4). While there is no formal requirement for notice of amendments to bills in committee or on report, the Chair will generally not select **manuscript amendments** or **starred amendments** for debate (see ¶11.9.2). Written notice is required of oral and written **PQ**s (see ¶8.13 and ¶8.20) except **urgent questions**. Notice is required of presentation of bills (see ¶11.3.4) and there are rather complicated rules relating to notice of a motion for leave to bring in a **ten minute rule bill** (see ¶11.3.5). Notices generally appear on one or other of the **Notice Papers**, or otherwise on the **remaining orders**.

Notice Paper: the blue pages of the **Vote Bundle** include the Notice Papers for notices of questions, notices of motions for future days, notices of **early day motions** and notices of amendments to bills (see §11.9 and ¶15.1.32 to ¶15.1.38).

oath: on their election at a general election or a **by-election**, each Member is required to take the parliamentary oath or to make the required affirmation before taking his or her seat (see ¶5.1.5 and ¶7.6.5). Witnesses before a committee of the House may also be required to take an oath or affirm before giving evidence, though this requirement is generally only imposed on witnesses before a private bill committee.

office costs allowance: the element of expenses to which Members are entitled to cover the costs of maintaining and staffing their personal offices (see §18.1).

official opposition: the party with the second largest number of Members in the House is the official opposition, a status which gains it certain privileges by long standing convention (such as the right of its official spokesmen and spokeswomen to sit on the **front bench** and to address the House from the **despatch box**) as well as certain rights under the standing orders (to initiate debate on the majority of **opposition days**) and by statute (such as for certain of its officers to receive ministerial salaries).

Official Report: see **Hansard**.

ombudsman: see **Parliamentary Commissioner for Administration**.

opposition days: the 20 days each session set aside under standing orders on which the opposition parties have the right to choose the business for debate (see ¶2.2.2 and ¶2.2.3).

oral question: see **PQ**.

order: when the House agrees a motion that something should happen (such as a bill being set down for a second reading or for consideration) it becomes an order of the House (see ¶7.8.1 and ¶7.8.2). Other examples of orders might be the outcome of a **programme** motion, **business motion** or **allocation of time motion** (see also **resolution**). The word is also commonly used in a parliamentary context to connote procedural regularity (as in the expression "in order") or to correct parliamentary behaviour (as in the Chair's call of "Order, order", which is also used as a form of oral procedural "punctuation").

Order Paper: the paper, published each sitting day (except the first day of a **session**), which lists the business of the House and for any **sitting in Westminster Hall** for that day, as well as **PQ**s for oral or written answer to be asked that day, **PQ**s for written answer that day which have not previously appeared in print, and certain other items such as notices of **written statements**, committee notices, **remaining orders** and lists of future business (see ¶15.1.6 to ¶15.1.21).

other business: business of the House which is neither **private business** nor **public business**, when there is no **Question** before the House for decision, principally covering question time and ministerial statements (see §2.2).

Outlawries Bill: see **Clandestine Outlawries Bill**.

PAC: see **Public Accounts Committee**.

Parliament Acts: the Parliament Act 1911 as amended and supplemented by the Parliament Act 1949 restrict the powers of the Lords to amend **money bills** or delay other **bills** agreed by the Commons (see §11.17).

Parliamentary Commissioner for Administration: an officer of the House appointed under statute to investigate complaints of maladministration in the public service, commonly known as the ombudsman. Her work is overseen by the Public Administration Committee (see §17.3 and also **health service commissioners**).

Parliamentary Commissioner for Standards: see **Commissioner for Standards.**

parliamentary question: a question (see chapter 8) addressed (generally) to a Minister for answer orally on the floor of the House at question time (see §7.5), or in a **grand committee** (see ¶14.2.5) or at a **sitting in Westminster Hall** (see ¶6.3.5) or in writing in **Hansard** (see ¶15.4.3).

periodic adjournment: the formal name for one of the House's recesses (see ¶5.2.10).

PCA: see **Parliamentary Commissioner for Administration.**

PNQ: see **urgent question.**

PQ: see **parliamentary question.**

point of order: properly, a request by a Member to the Chair for elucidation of, or a ruling on, a question of procedure, but not infrequently misused by Members who do not have the floor of the House or of a committee to interrupt proceedings for other purposes.

prayers: each sitting of the House begins with prayers, conducted by the **Speaker's Chaplain** (see ¶7.2.1). The term is also used colloquially to describe a motion to annul a **statutory instrument** subject to negative resolution procedure (see ¶12.3.16 and ¶12.3.17) and to designate the final paragraph of a **public petition** (see ¶19.4).

prerogative: see **Crown prerogative.**

press gallery: the gallery of the Chamber above and behind the Speaker's Chair reserved to accredited representatives of the various news media (see Figure 4), also used more generally to describe the large area outside and behind this gallery given over to the use of journalists etc. and also to describe collectively the accredited members of the press gallery (see also **lobby correspondents**).

previous question: a procedural device for superseding debate, now generally disregarded in favour of the **closure** (see ¶9.4.5).

Prime Minister: the First Lord of the Treasury and the head of the government; the person who is elected the leader of the party which can sustain a majority in the Commons (see ¶3.4.6).

Prince of Wales's consent: see **Queen's consent.**

private bill: a bill to confer upon individuals, or more commonly corporate bodies of one kind or another, powers in excess of or contradiction to the general law (see ¶11.1.2 and §11.19).

private business: the business of the House for the most part relating directly or indirectly to **private bills** (see ¶2.2.5, §7.3 and ¶7.9.2).

private Member's bill: a **bill** introduced to the House by a Member who is not a **Minister** (see ¶11.2.2 to ¶11.2.5).

private notice question: the formerly used name for what is now called an **urgent question** (see §8.6).

privilege: a privilege enjoyed by the House collectively or its Members individually in excess of or contradiction to the general law which enables it or them to fulfil the functions and duties of their office or of the House (see §4.2).

Privy Counsellor: a Member of the Queen's Privy Council, the body of senior royal advisers which in former times was something equivalent to the **Cabinet**, membership of which is now conferred automatically upon Cabinet Ministers and also upon certain senior judges; it is also by convention granted to the leaders of parties of any size in the Commons and is occasionally conferred as a mark of honour upon junior Ministers or senior back benchers. The Council retains certain judicial functions and residual executive functions. Membership, once conferred, is for life, unless withdrawn.

Procedure Committee: a **select committee** of the House appointed to consider proposals for the reform of its procedures under S.O. No. 147 (see §17.4).

proclamation: the Queen issues proclamations for the **prorogation**, **dissolution** and summoning Parliament, on the advice of the **Prime Minister**.

programme: an order made by the House after a **bill**'s **second reading** to **timetable** the subsequent proceedings on that bill (see ¶11.1.6 to ¶11.1.8 and §11.18)

prorogation: the end of a **session** (see ¶5.2.1 to ¶5.2.4).

Public Accounts Commission: the board of the **National Audit Office** (see ¶10.5.9 and ¶8.12).

Public Accounts Committee: the **select committee** of the House charged with particular responsibility for inquiring into propriety, efficiency, economy and effectiveness in the spending of public money (see §10.5).

Public Bill Office: the office within the **Legislation Service** of the **Clerk of the House**'s department with particular responsibility for the management of legislation and for clerking the **standing committees** of the House.

public gallery: the gallery of the Chamber in which **strangers** may sit to observe its proceedings; there is also an area designated for the same purpose in each committee room and at **sittings in Westminster Hall** (see Figures 4, 5, 6 and 13).

public petition: a petition to the House for redress of a grievance or other relief (see chapter 19).

Queen's consent: where the legislation proposed in a **bill** touches upon the prerogatives or private interests of the Crown, her consent is required for the bill to proceed: this may be required to be given either before the **second reading** or **third reading** (or, conceivably, before **first reading**), depending on the nature of the interest and the extent to which it is fundamental to the bill's purposes. Consent must be obtained from the Queen by a Minister and must be signified at the appropriate time by a **Privy Counsellor**. The Prince of Wales's consent may also be required, as the heir to the throne, before certain bills may be debated at certain stages.

Queen's recommendation: only the government can propose increases in public expenditure and the recommendation of the "Crown" is therefore required for a motion which proposes to increase or widen the scope of public expenditure: such a motion can therefore be moved only by a Minister (see ¶10.2.1 to ¶10.2.5); where a motion of this nature is to be moved in the House the words "Queen's recommendation signified" appear by its title on the **Order Paper**.

Queen's Speech: the speech read by the Queen from her throne on the first day of each session setting out, among other matters, details of the government's proposed legislative programme (see §5.2).

question: see **parliamentary question**.

Question: in procedural jargon, the matter before the House or a committee awaiting decision at any time is "the Question" (see ¶2.1.1 and ¶9.1.1).

question time: the period set aside for **PQ**s to be asked and answered orally on the floor of the House (see §7.5).

Questions Book: a daily publication divided into two parts: Part 1 lists all questions for written answer on that day, Part 2 lists all outstanding PQs for oral or written answer on future days, and other motions and notices for future days (see ¶15.1.39 and 15.1.40).

quorum: the quorum of the House is 40 but only for divisions (see ¶9.4.2); the quorum of a **standing committee** (except a European standing committee) is one-third of its members, with fractions rounded up (see ¶9.4.3 and ¶9.4.4); the quorum of an European standing committee is three of its appointed members, not including the chairman (see ¶13.2.10); the quorum of a **select committee** is a quarter of its membership or three, whichever is the greater, unless otherwise set out in the standing orders or its order of appointment (see eg ¶17.1.4).

reasoned amendment: an amendment proposed to the motion to give a **bill** a **second reading** or **third reading** (see ¶11.6.2 and ¶11.6.4, ¶11.14.3 and ¶11.14.4).

recess: strictly speaking, the period when the House is prorogued (see ¶5.2.1 to ¶5.2.4); now used to refer to the House's holiday adjournments (see ¶5.2.10 and ¶5.2.11).

Register of Members' Interests: the register, published annually, in which Members record their outside financial interests and the receipt of gifts, free travel, etc.; it is updated regularly and made available to the public in updated form on application to the **Registrar of Members' Interests** (see ¶4.1.2 and §4.3).

Registrar of Members' Interests: the officer of the House responsible for the maintenance of the **Register of Members' Interests** (see ¶4.3.8) and for giving advice (along with the **Commissioner for Standards**) about declarations made in it.

remaining orders: the list of forthcoming government business published with the **Order Paper** each day (see ¶15.1.17 to ¶15.1.19).

remedial order: a form of delegated legislation which remedies an incompatibility between UK law and the European Convention on Human Rights (see §12.5).

report stage: the stage of a **bill**'s progress between its being reported from committee and its **third reading**, at which further detailed amendments may be made (see §11.13).

resolution: when a motion is agreed by the House, it becomes a resolution (unless it is an **order**).

resource accounts: the audited accounts of **voted expenditure** authorised by the **Estimates** (see ¶10.4.5).

return: an answer or response to an address from the House (see ¶7.4.1)

royal assent: the Queen's assent to a **bill** agreed to by both Houses of Parliament is the final act which makes that bill an Act of Parliament (see §11.16) .

royal recommendation: see **Queen's recommendation**.

seconder: no seconder is required for a motion to be proposed to the House or a committee, but by tradition the motion for the **Loyal Address** is seconded (see ¶5.2.7).

second reading: the first stage at which a **bill** is debated and voted upon (see §11.6).

select committees: committees established by the House to inquire into particular matters or subject areas and to report back their findings and recommendations (see §17.1).

Senior Member: the Member of the House who has the longest **continuous** period of service in the House, also known (if male) as the **Father of the House** (see ¶3.1.8); on a **select committee** the senior Member on that committee (in which case seniority is calculated by longest cumulative service in the House, regardless of interruptions) has the duty to name the time of its first meeting (see ¶3.4.3).

Serjeant at Arms: the officer of the House responsible for security, housekeeping functions and the maintenance and repair of the physical infrastructure and other services of the buildings (see §18.2).

session: the period between the state opening of Parliament and its prorogation or dissolution, generally a year running from November to November, but often altered by the timing of general elections (see §5.1 and §5.2).

sessional orders: the traditional orders passed on the first day of a **session** (see ¶5.2.6), also any **order** made by the House which is explicitly framed to have effect for a session (for example, those specifying the dates during a session for private Members' bill Fridays and non-sitting Fridays).

shadow: broadly speaking, the official opposition appoints or elects Members of its party to "shadow" each government Minister, that is, to take particular responsibility for presenting in and out of Parliament the policies of the opposition for the areas which are that **Minister**'s responsibility, hence "Shadow Home Secretary" etc (also called **front bench spokesmen or spokeswomen**).

shuffle: the process by which the **PQ**s for oral answer are randomly sorted to determine which Members' questions will be printed on the **Order Paper** on any given day, and in what order (see ¶8.3.5).

sitting: a single meeting of the House or one of its committees (see chapter 6).

sittings in Westminster Hall: the "parallel chamber" of the House of Commons which is to meet in the Grand Committee Room off Westminster Hall (see §6.3).

Speaker: the impartial presiding officer of the House (see §3.1).

Speaker's Chaplain: the personal chaplain to the Speaker, whose main public duty is the leading of **prayers** at the beginning of each **sitting** of the House, but who may also choose to offer a more general pastoral service to Members and staff of the House.

Speaker's Counsel: officers of the House who head its legal services office, including those lawyers providing legal advice to the Speaker and to certain of the committees of the House.

standing committee: a committee to which the House delegates the task of debating certain matters such as **bills, delegated legislation**, proposals for European legislation, etc. (see §2.3).

standing orders: the rules formulated by the House to regulate its own proceedings.

starred amendment: an amendment to a bill which has not appeared on a notice paper on a day before the sitting at which it is to be considered; as a rule, the Chair will not select such an amendment for debate (see also **notice** and ¶11.9.2).

statement: statements on matters of policy or government actions may be made by a **Minister**, or occasionally a **back bench** Member or resigning **Cabinet** Minister may make a personal statement; they occur at the end of **question time** (see ¶7.6.1 to ¶7.6.3); Ministers may also make **written statements**.

state opening: the occasion on the first day of each **session** on which the Queen usually attends in the House of Lords to deliver the **Queen's Speech** (see ¶5.2.5).

statutory instrument: the form in which most **delegated legislation** is made (see §12.1).

strangers: the traditional appellation for anyone who is not a Member, officer or official of the House, hence **Strangers' Gallery** etc. (see also ¶9.4.2 and S.O. No. 163).

Strangers' Gallery: the more traditional name for the **public gallery** (see Figure 3).

supplementary question: an oral question asked as a separate but supplementary question to one which has appeared on the **Order Paper** and has been asked during **question time**; it should be within the scope of that main question to be in order; the Member asking the main question has the prerogative right in general to ask the first supplementary; the **Speaker** then chooses other Members to ask further supplementaries (see ¶7.5.1 to ¶7.5.3).

supply days: the old name for what now are called **opposition days** (see ¶2.2.2 and ¶2.2.3).

supply resolution: one of the **resolutions** upon which the **Consolidated Fund** bills are founded.

Table: the Table of the House, situated between the government and opposition **front benches**, in front of the Speaker's Chair (see Figure 3); in former times this was the place where motions, questions, reports etc. were delivered into the possession of the House **via** the Clerks, hence "tabled" or "laid upon the Table"; nowadays most such things are done in the **Table Office, Journal Office** or **Public Bill Office**.

Table Office: the office, situated outside the Chamber behind the Speaker's Chair, in which **PQ**s and **EDM**s are tabled; it also deals with all matters relating to the business on the floor of the House other than legislation: it may also be regarded as the first port of call for any Member seeking procedural advice. The office on the principal floor is the **Lower** Table Office, there is also an **Upper** Table Office on the third floor above the Chamber.

ten minute rule bill: a **bill** introduced under S.O. No. 23 where the Member seeking the **leave** of the House to introduce the bill, and a Member who opposes granting it, may each make a short speech before the House comes to a decision on whether to allow the bill to proceed (see ¶11.3.5 to ¶11.3.10).

ten o'clock motion: a motion, moved by a Minister, to suspend the operation of the **moment of interruption** which now occurs at ten o'clock only on a Monday (see ¶7.10.4).

Test Roll: the Test Roll must be signed by each Member after he or she has taken the oath or affirmed after being elected to the House (see ¶5.1.5 and ¶7.6.5).

third reading: the final stage of a whole **bill**'s passage through the House (see §11.13), though Lords Amendments to the bill may subsequently be considered.

timetable: In essence, a timetable for a bill fixes the points at which various stages of its consideration will be completed: at present the House generally uses **programme** orders to timetable a proceedings on government bills at the outset of their progress, varying and supplementing their terms at later stages; formerly this was done by **guillotine** motions which were introduced at a later stage.

tomorrow: the day usually named by the government for a bill to be put down for its next stage: in fact this means only that it will be placed on the **remaining orders** and will wait there until the government decides that it is to go on the **effective orders** for a particular day.

upper committee corridor: the corridor above the **main committee corridor** on which select committee rooms 17 to 21 are situated.

Upper Waiting Hall: the lobby area off the **main committee corridor** (see Figure 1).

urgent question: an oral parliamentary question asked without published **notice** relating to an urgent and important matter (see §8.6 and also **business question**).

usual channels: the colloquial name for the discussions which take place between the **Whips**.

voted expenditure: the House's agreement to an **Estimate** represents the detailed **appropriation** of public money to the public service by Parliament (see §10.3).

Votes and Proceedings: the daily minute of the House's proceedings (see ¶15.1.22 to ¶15.1.29).

Vote Bundle: the papers published each day on which the House sits, including among other things the **Order Paper**, the **remaining orders**, the **Votes and Proceedings**, and the **notice papers** (see §15.1).

Vote Office: the distribution centre for all parliamentary papers (see §15.6).

ways and means resolution: a **resolution** authorising a charge upon the people, that is, for the most part, taxes and duties: the **Finance Bill** is founded upon ways and means resolutions (see ¶10.2.17 to ¶10.2.24).

Westminster Hall: the oldest remaining part of the Palace of Westminster (see Figure 1), now used solely as a public area and for occasional ceremonial purposes (see also **sittings in Westminster Hall**.)

Whips: the officers of each party in the House with particular responsibilities for for party management and organisation of the business of the House and its committees (see §2.5).

White Paper: a **command paper** embodying some statement of government policy, often including proposals for legislation (see ¶15.3.3).

writ: the issue of a writ is the formal process for initiating a by-election (see ¶7.2.2 and ¶7.2.3).

written statement: a vehicle which may be used by a **Minister** to inform the House on various types of matter relating to his or her responsibilities; they are announced on the **Order Paper** and published in **Hansard** (see ¶7.6.4 and ¶8.3.9).

INDEX OF REFERENCES TO THE STANDING ORDERS

S.O. No	*Paragraph number*
77	11.14.3
78	11.15.2
79	10.2.9
80	10.2.7, 10.2.14, 10.2.16
82	11.18.3, 11.18.4
83	9.7.7, 11.18.1
84	11.10.7, 11.10.8
85	3.3.1
86	2.4.3, 11.10.2, 11.10.3, 11.10.4
87	11.10.5
88	5.2.13, 6.2.1, 6.2.3, 6.2.4, 6.2.5
89	3.3.3, 3.3.5, 3.3.6, 9.2.10, 9.4.1, 11.10.10, 11.10.12, 11.10.23, 11.10.27
90	11.6.6, 11.6.7, 11.6.8, 11.6.10
91	11.11.8
92	11.13.14, 14.3.4
93	14.2.4
94	14.2.5
95	14.2.6
96	14.2.4
97	3.1.5, 11.6.14, 11.6.17, 11.14.5, 14.3.4
98	12.3.10, 12.3.11, 12.3.22
99	14.3.3
100	14.3.2
101	11.6.17
102	14.2.4, 14.4.1, 14.4.2
103	14.2.5
104	14.2.6
105	11.6.12, 14.2.4
106	14.4.7
107	14.4.6
108	14.2.3, 14.4.3, 14.4.4
109	14.2.4, 14.5.1, 14.5.2
110	14.2.5
111	14.2.6
112	14.2.4
113	11.6.14, 11.6.17, 14.4.5, 14.5.6
114	14.4.5
115	12.3.10, 12.3.11, 12.3.22
116	14.5.3, 14.5.4
117	14.1.4, 14.6.1
118	12.3.10, 12.3.11, 12.3.14, 12.3.18, 12.3.19, 12.3.21, 12.3.23, 12.3.27, 12.3.29

S.O. No	*Paragraph number*
119	13.2.5, 13.2.10, 13.2.11, 13.2.16
120	11.18.5
121	2.3.7, 2.4.4, 7.10.9, 17.2.4
122A	3.4.5
123	6.2.1, 6.2.8
124	17.1.4
125	17.1.5
126	17.1.6
127	17.1.7
132	17.1.10
133	17.1.11
134	17.1.15
135	17.1.16, 17.1.18
137	17.1.18
137A	17.1.20 to 17.1.22, 17.1.24, 17.5.9
139	2.3.5, 17.2, 18.1.9
140	11.6.18, 17.5.5
141	12.4.5, 12.4.10
142	2.3.5, 2.4.4, 18.1.4, 18.1.6
143	13.2.2, 13.2.4
144	2.3.5, 18.1.3
145	3.5.1, 3.5.4, 10.3.10
146	17.3.4
147	2.3.5, 17.4.1
148	10.5.1
149	4.1.2, 4.1.3
150	4.3.8 to 4.3.10
151	12.3.5, 17.5.6
152	2.3.5, 2.4.4, 17.2.1, 17.2.2, 17.2.6
152A	17.3.7
152B	12.5.6, 17.5.7
152C	17.5.8
153	19.4.3
154	7.11.1, 7.11.2, 19.4.4
155	19.4.4
156	19.4.5, 19.5.1
157	19.3.1
158	15.3.3
159	12.3.1
160	12.3.3
161	18.2.2
163	9.4.2

GENERAL INDEX

¶ indicates reference to a paragraph number, § to a section number. There are also references in this index to the separate alphabetical glossary of parliamentary words and phrases (see pages 237 to 252) and to figures in the text (see list of Figures). There is a separate index of references to the standing orders of the House (see pages 253 and 254).

Data processing and typesetting by Vacher Dod Publishing
Printed in Great Britain by The Cromwell Press, Trowbridge, Wiltshire